Dublin's Merchant-Quaker

Dublin's Merchant-Quaker

ANTHONY SHARP AND THE
COMMUNITY OF FRIENDS,
1643-1707

Richard L. Greaves

Stanford University Press
Stanford, California
1998

Stanford University Press
Stanford, California
© 1998 by the Board of Trustees of the
Leland Stanford Junior University
Printed in the United States of America
CIP data appear at the end of the book

Published with the assistance of
the Florida State University

To Bradford, Sandy, and Robert

Preface

The path that led to this book has been a pleasant and invigorating experience. I first undertook substantial research into Irish history for my trilogy on British radicals and nonconformists. There, perhaps, my expedition into Irish history might have ended had not Alan Ford, James McGuire, and Kenneth Milne graciously invited me to address a conference at University College, Dublin, in 1993 on the history of the Church of Ireland. The theme of that address was the relationship between Protestant nonconformists and the established church from the restoration in 1660 to the revolution nearly three decades later. Substantial additional research on this subject resulted in the publication of *God's Other Children: Protestant Nonconformists and the Emergence of Denominational Churches in Ireland, 1660–1700* (Stanford University Press, 1997).

As I explored the world of Irish Quakers, it quickly became apparent that one of its principal shapers was Anthony Sharp, a Dublin merchant of substantial influence, some of whose records happily survive thanks to his brother-in-law, John Crabb. However, apart from a single manuscript book concerning his wife and son Jonathan, Sharp's material exists only as copies made by Crabb. The originals, including epistles Sharp had received from nearly a hundred Friends in Europe and America, amounted to "severall Thousand of papers," according to Crabb. He intended to write a journal of Sharp's "life, Labours and works, from his own writeings now in my hands—from the year 1670 to the year 1705," subject to the Dublin meeting's approval, and to preserve copies of his papers. Such documents, he reflected, "ought not to be layd by as wast papers and lost as Water Spilt on the Ground" (Sharp MSS, S15, fol. 1; S16, fol. 1). By the summer of 1721 Crabb had received compensation from the Dublin meeting for some of the material, but he was unhappy with the remuneration and the group's perceived scornfulness toward him. As he explained to two Dublin Friends, he had laid out his own money to purchase paper and employ an amanuensis. Although he still intended to publish something on Sharp, he failed to do so. Nor did he make copies of all the papers, some of which received only token mention in a skimpy calendar. Of Sharp's treatises he copied only those, in whole or in part, which interested him. The fate of the extraordinary body of original material is unknown; conceivably the manuscripts may survive in an uncatalogued private collection, though the possibility is remote.

In addition to the missing originals of most of Sharp's papers, numerous other documents have been lost or destroyed. This is especially true of guild records and state papers, many of which were destroyed in the catastrophic fire at the Public Record Office in Dublin during the civil war in 1922. Fortunately, the records for the weavers' guild, though incomplete, were housed elsewhere and thus survive, still in the chest where they were deposited at the end of Sharp's life. The Dublin corporation's book of accounts has no entries for the period from 27 September 1687 to Michaelmas 1691; if records were kept for this period, as seems virtually certain, they are not extant; Mary Clark speculates that the Williamites may have destroyed them. Moreover, a number of printed tracts relevant to Sharp seem not to have survived.

Notwithstanding Sharp's historical significance, from a biographer's standpoint his life does not provide the spiritual turmoil characteristic of the youthful John Bunyan, John Locke's murky affiliations with fellow radicals, the riveting political drama in which John Pym was engaged, or the enigmatic personality of Oliver Cromwell. Unlike his fellow Quaker Samuel Clarridge, Sharp was never involved in a sexual scandal, though he was embroiled in several monetary disputes. His marriages—especially his second, to Ann Crabb—were happy, notwithstanding the pain inflicted by the early deaths of many of his children or the foibles of a rebellious son. Sharp manifested neither the egotism of George Fox nor the charisma of James Nayler, and he lacked the literary skills of William Penn, John Bunyan, and Andrew Marvell. Nor did he evince a flair for the dramatic, as did Nayler and Solomon Eccles. Nevertheless, in the early history of Irish Quakerism he is second in importance only to William Edmundson, and among Dublin Friends he had no peer. Moreover, whereas Edmundson is representative of the first generation of rustic Quaker leaders, Sharp, like William Penn, typifies the second generation, many of whose members were successful merchants or colonizers. Through Sharp we have a splendid window into the Quaker community in Dublin, and this book is therefore not only a biography of the man but also an analysis of that community's relations with the wider world (Chapters 3, 4, and 6) as well as its inner life (Chapters 7, 8, and 9). In addition, Sharp's extensive involvement in the weavers' guild has provided an opportunity to explore its affairs in the half-century beginning around 1660 (chapter 5).

Dates are given in the old style, which was ten days behind the new mode used on the Continent; however, I have taken the year to commence on 1 January rather than 25 March, and I have used the traditional names of months and days, though the Friends, of course, did not. Quotations retain the original spelling and capitalization, and the punctuation has been altered only when necessary to facilitate understanding. Abbreviations have been spelled out, and I have not reproduced the often erratic italicization of the original materials. Where folio numbering in the Sharp manuscripts is sometimes erroneous, I have silently corrected it. As a guide for the spelling of place names I have used *Census of Ireland: General Alphabetical Index to the Townlands and Towns, Parishes, and Baronies of Ireland* (Dublin: Alexander Thom, 1861).

For access to manuscripts and other rare materials I am indebted to the fine staffs at the following libraries and archives: Historical Library of the Society of Friends in Ireland, Dublin (Mary Shackleton, Betty Pearson); Dublin City Archives (Mary Clark); Royal Society of Antiquaries of Ireland, Dublin (Orna Somerville, Nicole Arnould); Gilbert Library, Dublin (Dr. Máire Kennedy); Trinity College, Dublin; National Library of Ireland, Dublin; National Archives, Dublin (Gregory O'Connor); Registry of Deeds, Dublin; Public Record Office of Northern Ireland, Belfast (D. M. Neill); Religious Society of Friends, Ulster Quarterly Meeting, Lisburn (George Stephenson); Library of the Society of Friends, London (Malcolm Thomas, Josef Keith, Rosamund Cummings); Bodleian Library, Oxford; Public Record Office, London; Haverford College Library (Elisabeth Potts Brown); Henry E. Huntington Library, San Marino, California (Dr. Mary L. Robertson); and the Interlibrary Loan Department, Strozier Library, Florida State University. The Irish Georgian Society and the Irish Architectural Archive provided assistance as well.

Three esteemed colleagues read a draft of this work and offered invaluable criticism: Kenneth Carroll, whose knowledge of the Friends' history in seventeenth-century Ireland is unrivaled; Larry Ingle, whose biography of George Fox is a major achievement of Quaker historiography; and Ted L. Underwood, who has immersed himself in the history of seventeenth-century religious radicals for more than four decades. Joe Ward graciously answered a number of questions about guilds and Joyce Sampson checked assorted references for me. It is also a special pleasure to acknowledge my indebtedness to the following people: the late William F. Bewley, Mary Clark, Alan Ford, Ian Green, James McGuire, and Geoffrey F. Nuttall. Nearly thirty-five years after completing my doctoral studies under Dr. Nuttall's direction, I remain deeply appreciative of his influence on and contributions to my career. Norris Pope and John Feneron have been splendid editors. Once again, my wife Judith has been a marvelous research assistant, a perceptive critic, and a wonderful companion. Of Judith I can say what Anthony Sharp related of his "tender-hearted Ann": She is "a good & Carefull wife & one that [has] a good understanding." My daughters, Sherry Elizabeth and Stephany Lynn, my son-in-law Michael Zaic, and my mother continue to be sources of welcome encouragement. This book is dedicated to my infant grandson Bradford William Greaves in the hope that his life will be as productive as Anthony Sharp's; my sister-in-law Sandy Duffy-Greaves, who justifiably cherishes her Irish heritage; and her husband Robert, whose friendship and counsel over the years have meant more than he can know.

R.L.G.

Contents

Dublin's Merchant-Quaker

1

"Turned Sion Ward"

From Tetbury to Dublin, the Early Years

THE MOST CALAMITOUS civil war in England's history was less than six months old when Elizabeth Sharp, wife of the woolen manufacturer Thomas Sharp of Tetbury, Gloucestershire, gave birth to Anthony in January 1643. Situated some nine miles southwest of Cirencester on the Bristol-Burford-Oxford road, Tetbury, an old market town founded around 1200, sat astride the road that ran from Malmesbury to Stroud. Travelers approaching the town on either of these routes would have first glimpsed the spire of St. Mary's; much of this church dated from the fourteenth century. They would have gone on to find lodgings in one of more than a dozen taverns, the chief of which was the White Hart.[1]

At the time Anthony was born, some 500 families lived in Tetbury. The 1640s and 1650s were a period of growth for the town, and young Anthony undoubtedly watched the construction of the Three Cups tavern (by 1654) and a new town hall in 1655, which became the focal point of community life. During the seventeenth and eighteenth centuries the townsfolk rebuilt most of the old medieval houses, possibly Elizabeth and Thomas Sharp's among them. As a boy Anthony would have explored the surrounding countryside where more and more land was being enclosed. The town itself was a market for wool and agricultural produce as well as the center of a cloth-making industry. In 1622 the Tetbury market had collected more than £120 in tolls, making it one of the more important ones in England. The town's strategic location on two principal roads contributed to its prosperity, but geographical factors impeded the growth of manufacturing to some degree, for Tetbury, though bounded on the east by the River Avon, often had insufficient supplies of water during the summer to drive fulling-mills. Early in the century the town was home to thirty-four weavers, nine clothiers, thirteen tailors, six glovers, and 116 tradesmen.[2]

Of Anthony's education we know almost nothing. His brother-in-law, John Crabb, whose pen inclined toward hagiography, noted only that Anthony's schooling was "his delight," that he studied those subjects that would qualify him to be "a man of trade," and that he found commerce attractive. Anthony probably attended the grammar school founded by Sir William Romney (d. 1611). Sharp's parents were members of the Church of England and raised him according to its precepts; Thomas Sharp, opined Crabb, was "of a bold and undaunted Spirit in a just cause." The dean and chapter of Oxford Cathedral had granted the rectory of St. Mary's to Lord Berkeley in 1561, but the townspeople purchased the advowson in 1633, giving their agents or feofees the right to select the vicar. In the latter years of Anthony's youth that position was held by Daniel Norris, who became the vicar in 1658, conformed at the Restoration, and served the parish until his death in 1687.[3]

About a year before Norris' arrival in Tetbury, Anthony's parents apprenticed their son, who reputedly had "the pen of a ready writer," to an attorney in Marlborough, Wiltshire. The latter not only taught him law but took Anthony with him on a trip to Ireland, his introduction to the land that would later become his home. Anthony became disenchanted with the prospect of a legal career, perhaps, as Crabb suggests, because of the law's "Suttle designs and contrivances of the Various turns and changes, on all occasions for profits Sake." Whether these sentiments more accurately reflect the views of Sharp or Crabb is impossible to know. In any event, Anthony returned to England and found employment with his father as a journeyman combing worsted. The hands-on experience would prove to be beneficial when Anthony launched his own business career, the initial financing of which came from the £20 he saved during his year as a journeyman by living with his parents.[4]

On 27 March 1663, at the age of twenty-one, Sharp married Esther (or Hester), daughter of the woolen-draper Thomas Curtis of Tetbury. Recurring tragedy marked their marriage, all four of their children dying in infancy: Esther, born on 27 April 1664, perished the following year; Anthony, born in January 1666, died that year or in 1667; a second Anthony lived from 26 January 1668 to 6 January 1671; and their last child, also Esther, lived from 13 October 1669 to 18 August 1671.[5]

Following a year of employment with his father, Sharp entered the worsted trade. Now, or perhaps somewhat later, his parents gave him several hundred pounds to develop his business. Among Sharp's employees was Roger Gillet, a member of the Quaker community that had been present in Tetbury since the mid-1650s under the leadership of Nathaniel Cripps, a justice of the peace who lived in neighboring Upton and at whose house they worshiped. George Fox visited the Tetbury faithful several times. For their testimony, Cripps and others went to jail in 1660. The group influenced Sharp, for he agreed to accompany Gillet and other Friends to visit imprisoned Quakers in Warwick, among them William Dewsbury, John Roberts, Alexander Hayward, and Thomas Townsend. This trip would have occurred sometime between late 1663, when magistrates jailed Dewsbury at Worcester, and the summer or early fall of 1669, when Sharp emigrated to Dublin. While at Warwick, Dewsbury's preaching persuaded Sharp to become a Quaker. "Convinced, much broaken and tendered," Sharp "turned Sion Ward." He felt indebted to Gillet: "i had a love to Roger on that account which i hope none will call foolish." Sharp and Gillet were fortunate not to have been incarcerated at Warwick, for the Quaker Henry Jackson was confined in the same jail when he visited a Friend there in 1663.[6]

Crabb offers some insight into Sharp's spiritual state and personality in these years, though his portrait is admittedly uncritical. As a young man, Sharp was reputedly "of an humble, meek and quiet Spirit," preferring to suffer wrong than offend anyone and manifesting such a respect for life that he refused to step on a worm. "A man of an undaunted Spirit, Whether in Spirituall or temporall concerns," he determined to vindicate just causes, ignoring the criticism of enemies and the plaudits of companions to avoid bias. Attracted to the Friends' practice of silently waiting on God to ascertain the divine will, Sharp joined a Quaker meeting, presumably at Tetbury. Of his convincement he later recalled: "It was the Lord by his good Spirit In me and by his servants and ministers Instrumentally that reached and convinced my understanding of the Blessed way of Truth."[7] The sparse account of his conversion parallels John Calvin's and contrasts trenchantly with those of Martin Luther and John Bunyan. Sharp's convincement was also more sudden than that of George Fox or Bunyan, both of whom experienced a protracted search for religious peace. In Sharp's case, no evidence points to possible neuroses or a psychologically unsettled state either before or after his conversion.[8]

In the late summer or early fall of 1669, Sharp moved to Dublin with his wife and infant son, Anthony, to engage in the woolen trade. The relocation probably occurred around September, when Esther was nearing the end of her third pregnancy, for her last baby daughter was born

on 13 October. When they reached Dublin, Sharp reported their safe arrival to Nathaniel Cripps, who replied on the 29th, expressing joy that
they had reached their "desired Heaven." The voyage across the Irish
Sea had been difficult owing to stormy weather, and Esther had been
frightened and filled with dismay.[9] A sense of what the Sharps experienced may be gleaned from Oliver Sansom's account of a similar passage in 1687:

> They set sail [from Dublin Bay] with a fresh gale of southerly wind and
> about sun sett we were fair by holy head but the wind encreaseing as night
> come on, tost the Ship very much that sometimes in the Storm she seemed to
> Be plunged quite under water. . . . I suppose at least sixty passengers [were
> aboard], among many of whom there was a great cry being in such danger;
> they made a great charm with their prayers for two hours . . . ; towards
> Break of Day it pleased the Lord to abate the wind but the sea was very
> Rough for a time.[10]

Most crossings lasted two or three days.

If the Sharps were fortunate, their ship navigated up the River Liffey
and docked at Wood Quay or Merchants' Quay, either of which provided ready access to the heart of Dublin. But the Liffey was silting up,
the quays were partially clogged with wrecks as well as local cargo and
fishing vessels, and sandbanks and rocks made access difficult. More
likely, the ship that brought the Sharp family to Ireland stopped a mile
below Ringsend, anchored, and then waited for the tide to recede, leaving it to settle on the hard sand. From there, Sharp would have hired a
horse-drawn wooden cart to transport his family across the muddy and
sandy terrain at low tide. The ship might have moored further south, at
Dalkey.[11] The Sharps probably went first to the home of the wealthy
merchant Samuel Clarridge (or Claridge), who had come to Ireland with
Oliver Cromwell's army in 1651 and was now an influential figure in
the Dublin Quaker community. Clarridge lived near the old church of
St. Nicholas, where the Independents Samuel Winter and Samuel
Mather had ministered in the 1650s; the decaying structure, roughly
midway between Christ Church and St. Patrick's Cathedral, would be
rebuilt in 1707, the year of Sharp's death.[12]

The Sharps' relocation to Dublin came at a time when the city's
population was burgeoning, increasing from 5,000 in 1600 to perhaps
15,000 in the late 1650s, and to 45,000 in 1681. William Petty estimated that 2,175 houses were built between 1671 and 1681. Population
growth slowed dramatically during the troubled years of the late 1680s

and early 1690s and then resumed as economic conditions improved. By the time Sharp died in 1707, the city was home to some 62,000 people. The hearth tax returns for 1705 record 7,369 houses, 1,336 of them north of the Liffey. The demographic expansion provided opportunities not only for economic development but also for the Friends' growth. In 1732 approximately half of Dublin's residents were Protestants (up from approximately a third in the 1680s), but the number dropped sharply outside the city, to 23 percent in county Dublin and 21 percent in the province of Leinster. The Quakers were never more than a tiny minority, numbering only 3,000 to 5,000 in the entire country by the mid-eighteenth century.[13]

The Sharps settled in a house at the northern end of New Row, where it adjoined Ormond's (originally Gormond's) Gate. Their house was in the parish of St. Catherine's, but not far away stood St. Audoen's. Several notable residents lived in fashionable Bridge Street, just beyond Ormond's Gate, among them Randall MacDonnell, marquess of Antrim; Sir Winston Churchill, father of the future duke of Marlborough; the merchants John Desmenieres and Walter Motley, who served as lord mayor in 1666 and 1689 respectively; and Sir George Gilbert, coroner. Here too was the home of Sir Michael Creagh, who would represent Dublin in the Jacobite Parliament and serve as James II's paymaster-general in the time of troubles. Sharp probably died just before construction of a Dominican convent in Bridge Street commenced, but he would have known about and probably visited the Brazen Head Inn, where the United Irishmen would meet in the late eighteenth century. In the early years of the eighteenth century the Brazen Head was also the home of a warehouse that sold, at wholesale and retail, a wide selection of cloth, some of which Sharp's own workers might have manufactured.[14]

Ormond's Gate (which the city demolished in 1699) provided access to the old city within the walls, an area one-ninth of a square mile, or a sixth the size of walled London. The older houses were constructed of timber and plaster, unlike the newer brick homes, such as those in Essex Street, some of which featured overhanging summer houses on the river bank that enabled residents to watch the boats. At the southeastern corner of the city stood the castle, with its terraced walls, rows of lime trees, and gardens. In the heart of the old city the Tholsel was the center of municipal government. Rebuilt in 1683, the two-story building housed the recorder's court, the public exchange where merchants gathered to conduct business, a large hall for the Trinity Guild of Merchants, and another capacious room where municipal banquets were held. The weavers' guild, to which Sharp belonged, contributed £7 toward the wainscoting. From the Tholsel's tower one could gaze beyond Dublin harbor to the sea or watch the coaches and carts thread their way through the crowded, narrow streets below. So congested were the streets (at least some of which were paved, though in almost constant need of repair) that in 1683 the aldermen prohibited the sale of woolen cloth, linen, and various other commodities from stalls in the principal streets or in any other manner that blocked traffic. Vendors could hawk only what they could carry in their arms. The intent was not only to facilitate the free passage of people, animals, carts, and coaches but also to encourage petty traders to relocate to the Oxmantown public market. Earlier, in 1670–71, the city had built a market house in St. Werburgh's Street, not far from the Sharps' home, where they may have done some of their shopping. With other Dubliners Sharp undoubtedly benefited when the city installed an organized system of public lighting using lanterns and candles in late 1687; intended for winter operation only, the lights burned from 5:00 to 10:00 p.m. to prevent "mischiefs and inconveniences." The Four Courts relocated in 1698 to new buildings in Christ Church Lane, near the Sharps' house. During his last years Sharp could have watched workers finish building a linen hall in Capel Street in 1702 or start work on Archbishop Narcissus Marsh's library adjacent to St. Patrick's the previous year. Construction of the graceful tailors' hall, which still stands, began in Back Lane, also near Sharp's house, shortly before his death.[15]

Beyond the walls to the east the Sharps might have strolled on St. Stephen's Green, an ancient common the city leveled and drained before adding walls, walks, and trees. To raise money the city assembly apportioned eighty-nine plots around the green to merchants, gentry, and artisans, and buildings began to rise on the north and west sides. Municipal authorities raised additional funds by selling herbage from the green. The Sharps also could have walked up Bridge Street and crossed the old bridge, with its four arches, to Oxmantown, site of the Hospital and Free School of King Charles the Second, popularly known as the Blew Coat School. Chartered in 1671, its mission included the provision of relief for the elderly and the indigent. "This House," attested a public report two years later, "is not intended to be an Hive for Drones, but a profitable Nursery for the Common-Wealth, to breed up youth in vertue and knowledg till they shall be of sufficient growth to be transplanted." Intended to accommodate up to 300 people, it was paid for by subscribers who pledged £3,178 11s. 8d.; among them was Sharp's friend, Samuel Clarridge, who contributed £5. About the time of Sharp's death in 1707, the city constructed a brewery at the hospital. Nearby was the ancient church of St. Michan's, founded in 1095, its simple tower a landmark north of the Liffey. Sharp undoubtedly knew of the construction of a royal hospital for elderly and infirm veterans in Kilmainham beginning in 1680. Built on the site of the priory of the Knights Hospitallers and inspired by Les Invalides in Paris, it is a graceful two-story structure with a great hall and chapel.[16]

When Dubliners were not at work, they could spend their leisure time in numerous ways, some of which the Sharps would have found objectionable. The city reputedly had 1,180 alehouses and ninety-one breweries; some Quakers, as we shall see, succumbed to excessive drinking. St. John's Lane had a racquet court, and bowlers could pursue their sport at alleys near Wood Quay in the old city, on College Green, and in Oxmantown, which had a "bowling house." Horse racing, cock fighting, hurling, foot races, soccer, and gambling were popular pastimes. Playgoers amused themselves at the theater in Smock Alley (now Lower Exchange Street), which opened in the early 1660s. Its galleries collapsed twice during Sharp's lifetime, in 1671 and 1701, killing several members of the audience on each occasion. Dubliners could follow the news, though with some irregularity. The *Mercurius Hibernicus or the Irish Intelligencer* (1663) was only a memory by the time Sharp arrived, and the single-sheet *Dublin News-Letter* did not appear until 1685. The government began publishing the *Dublin Gazette* in 1689, but William III subsequently suppressed it and Anne permitted resumption only in 1705. In the meantime, *The Flying Post, or the Postmaster* had been launched in 1699, the Dublin *Courant* in 1702, and *Pue's Occurrences* in 1703. *The Dublin Intelligence* was available in the same period, as was *The London Post*, which was reprinted in Dublin. Conforming Protestants would have celebrated the major holy days—Christmas, Easter, and Whitsun—as well as the traditional festive seasons of Shrovetide and Maytide, and the patriotic celebrations on 30 January (Charles I's execution), 23 April (Charles II's coronation), 29 May (his restoration), and 5 November (the Gunpowder Plot). The coming of James II to the throne in 1685 added 6 February, the date of his accession; (like his brother he was crowned on 23 April, St. George's day). The municipal government celebrated the coronation and restoration days with substantial wine-drinking (six hogsheads, or 315 imperial gallons in 1669, for example), and it staged displays of fireworks for

special occasions, as when Essex became the lord lieutenant, when Ormond resumed that office, and when James ascended the throne.[17] Sharp
and his fellow Friends rejected both the holy days and the festive seasons, but nothing provoked more hostility, as we shall see, than their refusal to observe Christmas. Presumably they would not have objected to
the city's occasional efforts to encourage sabbath observance. In December 1670 the lord mayor and aldermen prohibited the unlicensed use
of hackney coaches, labor, unlawful exercise, and the frequenting of
taverns, alehouses, and coffeehouses on Sundays. Again, in October
1693 they called for the enforcement of the laws on sabbath observance
and the arrest of those who opened taverns and "Tipleing houses" while
services were underway in the Church of Ireland.[18]

Sharp joined the Quaker movement in Ireland during a time of significant growth. By 1701 the Friends had fifty-three meetings in Ireland,
an increase of 23 (77 percent) since 1660. Most of the meetings were
concentrated in four areas: the principal port towns—Dublin, Cork,
Waterford, and Limerick; Ulster; central Leinster, including Mountmellick, Edenderry, Moate, Newgarden, Athy, and Mullingar; and the small
southeastern towns of Wicklow, Carlow, and New Ross. In Ulster most
Friends engaged in commerce and manufacturing and were relatively
prosperous, whereas elsewhere most Quakers were involved in agricul-
ture and, to a lesser degree, in trade and the linen industry.[19]

The basic structure of the Quaker movement in Ireland was barely in
place when the Sharps settled in Dublin. Indeed, monthly meetings had
commenced by August 1660, but the provincial meeting dated only
from 1668 and the first national or half-yearly meeting convened in
August 1669 in conjunction with Fox's visit. By that time the women
had launched their own assemblies. Fox may have been instrumental in
founding the half-yearly meeting, but otherwise his role was primarily
that of providing encouragement for the nascent meetings. In the carefully worded phraseology of William Edmundson, Fox "settled Men
and Women's Meetings among Friends throughout the Nation." This
pleased Edmundson, who had experienced "a great Concern in those
Things . . . for several Years."[20]

The year of the Sharps' emigration to Ireland was eventful in several
respects. The highlight was clearly the tour of Fox, who had debarked
at Dublin on 10 May with Thomas Briggs of Cheshire, the mariner
James Lancaster, the Yorkshire butcher Robert Lodge, the ex-
Cromwellian soldier John Stubbs, and an unidentified young Quaker
who lived in Ireland. For three months Fox traversed the island, often in

secrecy to elude magistrates intent on his apprehension. Interestingly, Dublin seems to have been the safest place, for after he landed he spent hours asking where he could find Friends, and during his sojourn he attended the first half-yearly meeting as well as men's and women's meetings in the capital. Moreover, in his later testimony to Lodge he recalled that their band had held "many large and pretious Meetings of the Lord's People," and when he was ready to return to England nearly a hundred Quakers escorted him to his ship. After his Irish journey he told Cripps about the "precious meetings" and "Solid and substantiall Freinds" he had met; Cripps reported Fox's reaction to Sharp in Dublin.[21]

Other Friends visited Ireland the same year, among them John Burnyeat, John Wilkinson, John Banks, Thomas Janny, and John Abraham. Katherine Cooper, Hester Lund, and two women from Virginia were among the Quakers who had come to minister. In early September, around the time of the Sharps' arrival in Dublin, one visitor, the music teacher Solomon Eccles, stripped to the waist, placed a pan of smoldering coals on his head, and preached repentance in Galway, first to a Catholic congregation outside the town and then to the city's residents. For such behavior Eccles and his three companions went to prison; magistrates incarcerated 137 other Quakers in Ireland the same year for religious offenses. Among them were a number of Dublin Friends whom authorities arrested at their meetinghouse in Bride Street, imprisoned five weeks, and indicted for illegal assembly. After a grand jury returned a bill of *ignoramus* they were released, probably before the Sharp family reached Dublin.[22]

Sharp himself played a modest role in the visit of William Penn, who traveled extensively in southern and central Ireland between September 1669 and August 1670. Although Penn's base of operations was county Cork, where he owned 12,000 acres of farm land, he spent some time in Dublin. On 7 November 1669 the Friends in the capital gathered at the Bride Street meetinghouse, where Penn heard Sharp and Edmundson speak, and where Edmundson and Philip Dymond, a constable from Cork, prayed. On the 30th of that month Sharp accompanied Penn, Clarridge, an unnamed Quaker, and John Gay, chief marshal of the Four Courts, and his family to Rathcoole in county Dublin. The following day the party journeyed another two miles before Sharp, Clarridge, and their unidentified companion returned to Dublin.[23] Already Sharp was establishing close relations with leading Quakers.

After Penn's departure the Dublin Friends deemed it necessary to testify against Joan Pildren and Alice Sanderson, the first of whom, as Kenneth Carroll has suggested, might have been one of Thomas Loe's converts. Loe had worked with Pildren and believed their relationship was such that he could summon her to explain her behavior. When she refused to appear, Loe sent Pildren a letter castigating her for having grieved the Spirit with "wicked Imaginations" which she had brought "forth in the strength of darkness and blackness in Contempt of the Truth, And to the great dishonour of God, in the Assemblies of his people." He further chastised Pildren because she had indiscreetly worn an "outward and Beastlike Cover" of white frieze in Quaker meetings. Adjudging this "a figure to thy owne Blackness and darkness that is over thy head, and by which thou art wholly Swallowed up," Loe warned Pildren to desist from her "Imaginations and deceit" before God left her "no way to Escape." Concluding with a reminder that he had patiently awaited her reform, he condemned her persistence in "Rebellion and Stiffe neckedness." Following Loe's lead, on 9 December 1669 the Dublin meeting issued a testimony, signed by Sharp and eleven others, against Pildren and Sanderson, her companion.[24]

The Sharp manuscripts provide no clues concerning the Pildren-Sanderson case, but Sharp surely would have followed the discussion with interest and perhaps contributed to it himself. The two women seem to have viewed themselves, as did early female Friends generally, in prophetic or charismatic terms. This was a natural outgrowth of the emphasis the Quakers accorded to Joel 2:28 and its reiteration in the account of the Pentecost in Acts 2:16–21. Pildren clearly attached symbolic significance to the white frieze cloth with which she draped herself, perhaps as a "sign" or "figure" of a prophetic vision.[25] The biblical passage that inspired this incident appears to have been Revelation 3:1–6, which contains an apocalyptic message to the church at Sardis, most of whose members were reputedly near spiritual death owing to their deeds' unacceptableness in God's sight. Only a few people at Sardis had not "soiled their garments" and would therefore walk with God garbed in white. "He who conquers shall be clad thus in white garments, and I will not blot his name out of the book of life." By donning white headgear in Quaker meetings Pildren seems to have signaled to other worshipers that they were impure and would be denied eternal life. In so doing, she rendered herself subject to the Dublin meeting's condemnation of her "leanings."[26]

Controversy of a different sort demanded Sharp's attention in the summer of 1672. When his sister-in-law, Sarah Hodges, embraced the Friends, the vicar of Tetbury, Daniel Norris, wrote to her expressing concern: "I was much troubled for your Brother in law and Hester and in afliction of Spirit have prayed for them; but you as better Known to me have put me to more Greife." Professing that her defection wounded his soul, Norris called her a "Backsliding Daughter" and exhorted her to remember the fate of Lot's wife. Sarah forwarded the letter to Sharp, who professed on 10 August to be "stired up in my Spirit in a holy Zeal and love to the Lord and his blessed truth to answer." Chiding Norris for being misinformed about the Lord's work, Sharp patronizingly told him it was neither strange nor impossible for those with traditional learning to be ignorant of spiritual matters. Catholics, he contended, believed they "had the right way of Serveing God and think so still," yet despite their long historical tradition they remained "fighters against God" and the work of reformation. Sharp considered their apostasy from the divine authority in the primitive church to be a falling from "the life and power of the Pure spirit of God." Turning to the Church of England, he accused its clergy of hypocritically denying their own apostasy and falsely claiming to embrace God's "pure power and Spirit." Reflecting on the relative ease with which most clergy had embraced the revival of episcopacy at the restoration, Sharp pointedly observed: "Witness most of the national teachers goeing from that of prisbyter to Episcopal which I leave to all to adjudge whether that was the Way to goe on with the Lord in this great day of his power."[27] This letter marked Sharp's first known entry into the field of polemics. That he should have attacked the parson who challenged his sister-in-law is hardly remarkable, but the attention he accorded Catholics in this missive suggests that their pervasiveness in Dublin troubled him.

Several months later, Esther's health dramatically declined. For at least a year she had been ill with tuberculosis. A recent visit to England had sapped her strength, leaving her in "a weakening, Coughing, Wasting condition." Around the beginning of October 1672 she confined herself to her chamber and seemed to be "as poor as death in the body." On 19 October she made her will, leaving "Severall Legecies" to friends and relatives with Anthony's consent; he witnessed her will. To the Quakers who visited her she confided that she was "well comforted and Refreshed in her Spirit" and was "sattisfied to depart." On the 21st she wrote to her sister Sarah, telling her she expected to die shortly, exhorting her to be faithful, and sending greetings to their parents and relatives. The following day she was too weak to cough up the phlegm that was now choking her, and at midmorning on the 24th she died "Sweetly and quietly" in the presence of her husband, Clarridge, and another Friend. About 3:00 p.m. the following day the Friends interred her body in their burial ground by St. Stephen's Green. Later that day Anthony poignantly wrote to her parents, praising her as his "beloved yoke fellow," "a right fellow traveller of mine toward eternal rest," and as "dear companion as ever man had." Although letters of bereavement are rarely objective, we can surmise that Anthony and Esther's relationship had been close: "The true love knot was neavour untied, Since the Lords good providence ordered our joyning together; and my Spirit [will] have Fellowship with her integrity for ever." She had, he reflected, been "very tender" with him as she lay dying and had prayed that God would keep him "out of all ill conveniencies." As he contemplated a future that he bleakly depicted as a "journey of troubles," he likened himself to a dove that had lost its mate.[28]

In the month preceding Esther's death Sharp, Clarridge, the linen draper Robert Turner, and William Maine (or Mayne) petitioned the Dublin assembly to grant them freedom of the city—the right to trade on the same terms as other freemen and to vote in municipal elections, dispensing with the usual oath in return for paying an entry fine of £3 each. Moreover, each man agreed to pay 5s. *per annum* until he was willing to swear the oath, and the assembly thereupon granted their petition on 16 September. Five and a half years later, however, there were signs of regret that such action had been taken, apparently because at least some aldermen had expected the Quakers in time to take the required oaths. The aldermen's minutes for 22 February 1678 contain the following terse report:

> Wheras there was a pretended act of assembly made the Sixteenth day of September in the yeare one thousand Six hundred Seaventy two for the admitting of Samuell Claridge, Anthony Sharp, Robert Turner and William Maine to have the frie libertie of tradeing in this Citty as other Freemen have now, it is hereby declared that the Said persons not having taken theire respective oathes as freemen of this Cittie are to pay theire Customes at the Gates and three penny Customes as other foreigners pay notwithstanding the aforesaid act of assembly.

Nevertheless, the four men did not lose their status as freemen.[29]

Sharp had come to Ireland three years earlier to take advantage of improved conditions for the trade of manufactured goods made possible by the English government to counteract the negative impact of the Cattle Act of 1663. That statute imposed a high duty on cattle and sheep exported from Ireland between 1 July and 20 December, and a subsequent law of January 1667 prohibited the import of Irish cattle, sheep, beef, or pork into England. Following a trade slump in the early 1660s, woolen exports rose dramatically in the middle years of the decade. Frieze, the most valuable export because rural workers could readily supply it and because English manufacturers preferred to produce a more expensive and finer cloth, increased nearly 70 percent between 1665 and 1683, and another 50 percent in the ensuing four years. The export of the new draperies—the lighter cloth such as bays—increased 226-fold between 1665 and 1683, and then doubled by 1687. The woolen industry was a significant force in the Irish economy, employing an estimated 30,000 workers according to William Petty. Moreover, England could not produce enough linen to satisfy its domestic needs, and this demand spurred Irish production, particularly in Ulster, where many Scots and northern English had settled. As lord lieutenant, the duke of Ormond encouraged the linen industry, establishing manufactories at Chapelizod west of Dublin and at Carrick-on-Suir in county Tipperary. The export of linen rose eightfold in the two decades beginning in 1665. By the time the Sharps settled in Dublin, its share of the country's trade as measured by the customs had risen from 21 percent in 1616–17 to approximately 47 percent.[30] Emigrating to Ireland at an opportune time for a cloth merchant, Sharp would manifest substantial business acumen in amassing a personal fortune.

Sharp acquired land and houses in the area around the Coombe, to the west of St. Patrick's and beyond the city walls. Here he established a woolen manufactory where by 1680 he employed approximately 500 workers, some of whom were Catholics. At one time or another he owned some twenty-nine houses in Dublin—in Meath Street, Coles Alley (later Meath Place), Elbow Lane, Marrowbone Lane, and Pimlico Street. Here many of his workers would have lived and toiled as spinners, weavers, fullers, dyers, and shearmen. Because wages in Ireland were approximately half those in England, Sharp could afford to hire some laborers for charitable reasons. His reputation for honesty reputedly enhanced his business dealings. From Dublin he exported wool to Chester, London, Gloucestershire, and Bristol, perhaps in the last-named city to Quakers such as Richard Gotley, a merchant involved in the Irish trade late in the century.[31]

The Irish economy experienced a downturn in the early 1670s, primarily because of the Second Dutch War, but the wool trade with England remained reasonably strong notwithstanding the depredations of privateers. Sharp sustained substantial losses at sea, as in the spring of 1674 when a sudden shift in the wind off Wicklow resulted in the loss of a shipload of wool and other goods valued at £655. "The Will of the Lord be done," he wrote to a colleague, "i desire and sense it may be well that wee see the uncertainty of things below." Crabb estimated that Sharp sustained maritime losses worth approximately £2,000 in 1674–75.[32]

Although the time and effort to establish a business strong enough to survive losses of this magnitude in its first six years must have been considerable, Sharp was active in the community of Friends. In 1671 he composed a pithy warning exhorting Dubliners to heed divine mercy and repent of their evil ways. Since his arrival in the city, he attested, he had been troubled by "the true Sence of thy deplorable Estate and condition ... because of the Sin and wickedness that reigneth within Buildings and by the Sence thereof few have." Echoing the Hebrew prophets, he asked Dubliners if they thought the Lord would endlessly seek their repentance, answering this in the negative. The Quaker gospel of the inner light was clearly encountering some contempt, for he admonished the city not to "Stumble ... at the light for it hath been much despised by the Wisdom of this World, but to their shame, for they that hate the light cannot love the apearance of God." Their blood, he warned, would be on their own heads, for God punished heathen nations by sword and plague, by hail and fire. With an eye to the Church of Ireland Sharp recalled the punishment of Nadab and Abihu for offering strange fire that God had not commanded (Numbers 26:61), an allusion to conformist ritual. Sharp went on to ask why men claiming to be gospel ministers persecuted people who followed their consciences. Biblical warnings, he concluded, are "for our learning and For example ... and Especially [for] such that pretend to Worship God, [that they] doe not commit Idolitre."[33]

For unexplained reasons Sharp decided not to make his warnings public in 1671, perhaps out of concern that he not unduly provoke the magistrates. He returned to the manuscript on at least two occasions, the first near the end of the famine of 1673–74, when he added a postscript describing the hundreds who were begging in the city's streets and the many who had perished. He would not have noticed the initial effects of dietary deprivation, such as the depletion of fat deposits, the degeneration of abdominal and thoracic organs, and falling blood pressure, but in time he would have observed the distended bellies caused by the retention of fluids, the gaunt eyes, the grayish skin tones, and, in some victims, the brown blotches on the skin. Diarrhea and cardiovascular collapse marked the final stage of suffering. This famine, which modern scholars have generally overlooked, had its roots in the transformation of the Irish economy owing to demographic expansion. As the population grew, so did arable farming, thereby increasing the dependency on grain in the diet. Moreover, in the aftermath of the Cattle Acts of 1663 and 1667, livestock farming declined. As the supply of dairy products decreased, the people of Ireland became increasingly dependent on grain and potatoes (primarily from August to May). Bad weather in the winter and spring of 1670–71 was particularly hard on livestock, and the outbreak of the Second Dutch War in 1672 further compounded the economic crisis as Dutch privateers disrupted trade, especially with the continent. Economic dislocation, crop failures, and livestock decline owing to inclement weather and the spread of disease caused the famine.[34] As Sharp observed the misery, he was especially struck by those who "Little considered it, nor layd it to heart so that more afflictions must be expected." The extent of the suffering not only moved him but prompted him to consider the famine a divine warning.[35]

He kept the manuscript at hand, turning to it again on 22 July 1677 against a backdrop of the war between France and the Netherlands (and for a while England) that had dragged on since 1672. George Fox the Younger, he recalled, had prophesied of such "great Warrs, confution & destruction." Sharp saw the conflict as the onset of "the great and notable day off God broak & breaking forth." Citing the imagery of the book of Revelation, he envisioned this moment in apocalyptic terms, "the Six[th] Trumpet sounded and sounding, the Six[th] Vial poured & poureing forth and the Six[th] Seal opened and opening, Babylon Fallen and Falling, the great whore com and coming into remembrance, the Kings of the earth destroyed and Destroying her and her Flesh & Will not give their power much Longer to her but rether take it from her, that follows to make her Wicked & lay open her shame."[36] This was a very free rendition of Revelation, reordering its symbolic sequence and honing in on the sixth trumpet, the sixth vial, and the sixth seal. Because the number 666 was commonly associated with Satan, the beast of Revelation, Sharp must have been particularly sensitive to evil's pervasiveness in the summer of 1677. When he wrote this second postscript, he was presumably working from memory, recalling the apocalyptic imagery that had made the greatest impression on him. No less clearly, he was now certain he was living in the last times, and this conviction reinforced his determination to serve God through the Quaker movement to the fullest extent possible.

2

"My Very Tender Affectionals"

Family Life

THE YEARS THAT followed Sharp's decision in 1671 not to publish his prophetic warning to Dubliners were among the most eventful of his life. At the outset of this period he returned to married life, resumed the challenge of raising a family, and accepted his brother-in-law
as an apprentice. Sharp made his decision to remarry in late 1673 or
very early 1674, though well before this he craved intimate female com-
panionship. His conscience, however, persuaded him to wait a decent
interval before seeking another spouse. Many years later he recalled: "I
did Aply my Self to the Lord in prayer to Suply me with a good & fitt
helpmeet, for my Faith was that by my owne wisdom or power I was
not able to find out one that was a fitt wif for me." In fact, he now had
in mind any daughter of Sarah and Thomas Crabb, a substantial wool-
stapler of Marlborough, Wiltshire, and a devout Quaker who had donated land to the Friends for a cemetery. On 2 February Sharp wrote to
Thomas Crabb, explaining his desire to wed one of his children. The letter is worth quoting in full because of its insights into Sharp's emotions
and values at this time:

> i have had in my thoughts a mind to See a daughter of thine and that it still
> remains with me, yet expecting thou may have one fit for a wife for me, but
> modesty as to the time Since the departure of my late wife, and I . . . [have]
> shut up these thoughts until now, and the occation of my discloseing to thee
> is, I considering whether it com to any thing or not, thou being the Father
> and a man I adjudg Fearing God, I could disclose my thoughts to none Fit-
> ter, so free without the discloseing of which it apeared unlikely of being re-
> solved, now this being the first in this of such a matter, Since my late wife,
> that i ever proposed, tho the like hath been offered to me, i desire thy Seri-
> ous Thoughts and Answer to it Whither thou have such an one undisposed

and whither thou beleive such a thing suitable for thy child and me &
whither there may be a clearnes in it from any other, [so that] if wee like
each other, and that above all she love the truth, if thee See it meet I may the
Lord permit com over at Spring or 2d Month [April] next and See her, and
that nothing is intended by me to prejudice to thee or thine, thou shalt have
sattisfaction, i hope in any thing thou desire but that my real Kindness occa-
tions my telling thee my thoughts which i hope thou wilt be as kind in Con-
cealing; if not like to be asserted, in the intrim, thy Answer is desired to him
that is thy truly Lo[ving] freind, Antho: Sharp.[1]

This would be no arranged marriage, though the Friends expected
young people such as Crabb's daughters to obtain parental blessing. The
marriage would take place only after Sharp had met the prospective
bride and the couple found one another attractive.

After weighing the matter for several weeks, Crabb responded positively. Ann, he wrote on 2 March, had not pledged herself to anyone
else, and was moreover a woman of "a grave Modest Carridge" and a
devout Friend. "I shall leave her to her own Freedom in her choyce so
Far as may be convenient," he informed Sharp, "for she is a lass . . . i
have a Great reguard For." Crabb invited Sharp to Marlborough so he
could meet Ann. If Anthony and Ann liked each other, Crabb promised
to "divulge more of [his] mind" at that time.[2]

Sharp found Crabb's answer satisfactory, but he delayed his trip to
Wiltshire to take advantage of the improved commercial opportunities
made possible by the termination of hostilities between England and the
Netherlands. He had purchased a large quantity of wool he wanted to
ship before he traveled to England, which he now expected to do in
June. The anticipation of meeting Ann prompted him to expedite the
shipping arrangements, for he informed Crabb less than two weeks
later, on 1 April, that he hoped to go to England in early May.[3]

No details of Anthony and Ann's initial meeting have survived, but
for Sharp it must have been the proverbial love at first sight, at least as
understood by Friends, who believed that such affection was originally
grounded in their love of God. When, for instance, Robert Barclay proposed to Christian Molleson in 1669, he claimed he had "received a
charge from [God] to love thee." Similarly, a love letter from Daniel
Abraham to Rachel Fell (Margaret's daughter) in 1681 acknowledged
that no love could "be so firm and constant as that which originally is
excited by, and derived from something which in itself is of an immuta-
ble being." Sharp would have seen his love for Ann as an outgrowth of

their mutual love of God. By 15 June he had concluded his visit to Marlborough and traveled to Bristol, from where he wrote a touching love letter to Ann: "My very tender affectionals and unfeigned love is truly yearning unto thee, insomuch that thou art nearly bound up in mine heart in the bonds of Love and Sincerity the which i desire may be continued and renewed dayly." These were strong, perhaps heady emotions for a relationship no more than six or seven weeks old. Couching much of his love in spiritual language, he deemed it a manifestation of divine bounty to them and asked her to join hands in giving themselves to God. His language's double thrust was deliberate: "Dear Ann, the consideration and Sattisfaction I have, beleive and hope concerning thee tenders my very heart on a doble account, both outward and inward." As with the love letters associated with the Fells of Swarthmore, in Sharp's epistles "the leadings of the Light and of the libido were welded together into one tender, spiritualized expression of holy marital union." But Sharp was also a man of commerce, accustomed to making decisions and undertaking his affairs with prudent dispatch. A hint of this found its way into the letter as he concluded with an expression of his longing to see Ann and his concomitant desire to "accomplish [his] buisness."[4]

Indeed, the decision to marry had already been made, for the following day the Friends at Tetbury issued a certificate indicating their approval. Among the signatories was Anthony's brother William. By 23 June Sharp had returned to Marlborough, from where he wrote to the men's and women's meetings in Dublin, announcing his intention to marry "a very honnest Freind" and telling them to expect a letter from the Marlborough meeting requesting certification of his "clearness" to marry. "I cannot expect to com for Ireland," he added, "untill this thing is over." Three days later the Marlborough Quakers issued their own certificate and arranged for the monthly meeting to obtain a similar statement from Friends in Dublin. Among the signatories were Ann's parents.[5] While he waited for the necessary approval, Sharp traveled to London via Reading on business. He tarried a month, expecting to meet someone from Chester. During this period he wrote at least four love letters to "Tender hearted Ann," the last of them from Bristol on 25 July. Each contained deep expressions of his love, framed always in the context of their relationship to God. "I hope in the Lords due time wee shall see and enjoy each other," he wrote on 7 July, "and in the mean time let us submit to providence not onely in this but all other courses and transactions in this life." He not only professed his undying love to Ann but also shared his spiritual experiences with her, underscoring the extent to which human and divine love were conjoined in his mind.[6] Ann's letter to Anthony of 5 July was no less concerned with spiritual experience, though very reserved in expressing her feelings toward him. Finding one of his letters "very acceptable," she indicated a willingness to see him "as soon as stands with Thy conveniency," but her reply is barren of real emotion.[7]

The respective meetings at Tetbury, Marlborough, and Dublin having stipulated the couple's "clearness" to marry and their relatives "being sattisfied," Anthony and Ann wed at William Hitchcocks' home at Marlborough on 17 August 1674. Because the Quakers had no ordained clergy, the simple ceremony was evocative of a traditional handfasting. The couple "did Mutually promise to live together in Love and Faithfullness according to the ordinance of God Testyfied in the holy scriptures untill by death they should be seperated." Besides Ann and Anthony, thirty-four others signed the marriage certificate, including Ann's parents, grandfather, brothers Thomas and John, and sister Sarah Pocock; so too did Sharp's mother and father-in-law William Wilsteed, his brother William and the latter's wife Elizabeth, and Sarah Hodges, sister of Anthony's first wife.[8]

Following the marriage the Sharps visited with friends and relatives before setting out for Ireland accompanied by many of them. Although most of the entourage went only as far as Worcester, Ann's brother John and one of his in-laws escorted Ann and Anthony to Holyhead, where the four boarded a vessel. When it arrived in Dublin the following day, Sharp's family and friends provided a warm welcome.[9]

For physical and personal reasons, Ann had difficulty adjusting to life in Ireland. Although she found the country itself attractive, her health began to decline. More problematic was the separation from her parents, with whom she had enjoyed close relations. Yet she seems to have adapted to married life with little difficulty, and Anthony expressed his hope to her parents in February 1675 that in time she would "be Setled pretty Well; . . . as It is She is not Discontented." Two weeks later she wrote again to her parents, confessing that her love for them "overcoms my heart." She doubted she could visit them that summer "because of my supposed condition [i.e., her first pregnancy] and our much buisness," though she expected her brother John to travel to England.[10]

Ann was in fact pregnant with the first of the couple's sixteen children, seven of whom were daughters. By contemporary standards this was extraordinary: The fertility rate among Irish Quakers in the second half of the seventeenth century was 9.27 compared to 7.43 for other Friends in the British Isles and 7.27 for wives in thirteen English parishes. Unlike most other Irish Quakers the Sharps apparently did not attempt to provide significant intervals between the births of their children or to terminate Ann's reproductive career prematurely. The birth dates of the children cover a period of twenty-one years and eight months, indicating that Ann gave birth every 16.25 months. For Quaker women in Ireland who wed under age twenty-five, as did Ann (who was approximately twenty-two when she married), the interval between the first and second births was 23.5 months, and 24.3 months between the second and third births. The comparable figures for Ann were 11 and 12 respectively. As Richard Vann and David Eversley have demonstrated, the pace of childbearing was higher among Friends in Ireland than elsewhere (until after 1750), making Ann's record even more unusual. Tragically, in one respect the Sharps were typical: Among their fellow Quakers in Ireland the number of children surviving to age fifteen was 5.4, or slightly more than half; five of Ann's sixteen children survived infancy, but of these, one (Jonathan) died at age fourteen.[11]

Ann's firstborn was Sarah, whose brief life extended only from 16 August 1675 to 25 February 1677. During that period Esther (Hester) was either stillborn or died within three days of her birth on 23 July 1676. A third child, Thomas, lived only a fortnight (15–29 or 30 July 1677), and a fourth, Ann, did not reach her second birthday (27 August 1678–10 April 1680), but the sixth and seventh children, Isaac (born 13 January 1681) and Joseph (born 2 May 1682; died before 1731), lived to adulthood. The lives of the next three children—Sarah (11 August 1683–May 1684), Benjamin (21 September–28 December 1684), and John (22 February–March 1686)—were tragically brief. Jonathan did not reach his fifteenth birthday (21 August 1687–8 April 1702), but the ensuing two children fared better: Daniel, who lived from 22 December 1689 to 13 March 1731, and Rachel (born 7 May 1691). The last three offspring—Hannah (23 October 1692–19 March 1702), Benjamin (22 March–6 April 1695), and Martha (17 March 1697–10 June 1701)—died young. Ann was still giving birth in the late 1690s, when she was in her mid-forties. Female Friends who visited the Sharps must have met Ann's "little babes," for they mentioned them when they subsequently reflected on their time in Dublin.[12]

Little information survives about the Sharps' family life, but we can reconstruct its basic outline if we assume that as a leader of the Dublin

Friends Sharp followed their precepts. When Ann gave birth there would have been no feast of celebration common in most families of means nor would the infant have been christened. Quakers were supposed to enjoin midwives and nurses from dressing babies in fancy or superfluous clothing. In May 1696 Ann was one of the thirty-three women who signed a letter from the national women's meeting to the local groups urging mothers to nurse their children if possible, and if not to find wet nurses who were honest, orderly, and compatible with the children and servants; this may have reflected her own practice.[13]

Apart from participation in religious meetings and related activities, as a Quaker wife Ann was normally expected to stay at home and shun unnecessary visiting. Indeed, when she and Mary Barlow went to England in 1701 "in a publick way, by way of publick Testymony," they first had to obtain a certificate from the Dublin men's meeting indicating their husbands approved of the proposed journey. Beginning in the late 1680s Ann and Anthony would have concerned themselves as parents with the Quaker admonitions to have their children dress and speak plainly, eschew idleness, and engage in "honist and proffitable Employments such as may be beneficiall and serviceable to their families, and may tend rather to enrich then Impoverish them." Because some Quaker parents failed to meet these standards, the meetings had to admonish them to fulfil their responsibilities; perhaps the worst case involved Joseph Gunson, another Dublin Friend, whom the men's meeting publicly condemned for "ill governing & keeping a Loose Family."[14]

Like other committed Friends, the Sharps would have taken their children with them to meetings on Sundays and weekdays. After the meetings they were supposed to examine both their children and their servants to ascertain what spiritual benefits they had received and "what they have felt of the tendering power & love of God." The intent was to encourage young people to become witnesses to the life of the inner Spirit. In 1701, however, both the Leinster provincial meeting and the half-yearly national meeting instructed Quakers not to bring their children to national, provincial, or monthly meetings if they were unqualified. These gatherings, of course, were in part devoted to business affairs, and the Friends were concerned that children would be "Exposed to the hazard of more losse in time" and that their behavior might not be circumspect.[15]

Quaker parents were expected to provide their children with education or training suited to their abilities and instruction in appropriate behavior. In part this was done in the home, where heads of families were to read (or have someone else read) the Bible and books written by Friends. The Sharps sent two of their sons, Jonathan and Daniel, to Penketh, near Warrington, Lancashire, to study with Gilbert Thompson, possibly because the Quaker school in Dublin experienced difficulty finding and keeping qualified, stable masters. Jonathan was the first to go, and Ann found lodgings for him at widow Ellen Haydock's home when he was nearly eleven. In a letter to Jonathan dated 17 January 1701 Sharp complimented his son on his improved handwriting, expressed hope that he was making progress in arithmetic and Latin, and outlined his view of a proper education:

> Our care is to have thee well educated, and education that is good, is first to Educate a Child in the fear of God, and in that holy Spirit of Christ that coms from God and is the fountain of all Good and the first principles of all our good desires & actions. 2dly to be educated in the Knowledge of the holy Scriptures, For the prophets, Christ and the apostles is the Foundation of the true church and so in Fellowship and Unity with his people. Next and 3dly after good Leterature, Orthography, Arithmetick, &c.

The practical was not sacrificed to the spiritual, for Sharp made it clear that he expected Jonathan to learn a trade and that his schooling at Penketh was a means to this end. He and Ann thought he might learn the wool trade "or som other."[16]

In March 1701 the Sharps were considering whether to send Daniel, now eleven, to join his brother at Penketh, but they were initially reluctant because Daniel had trouble controlling his bladder during the daytime. Although the problem continued, three months later Ann left for England to take him to the Penketh school, which, according to an early report from Jonathan, he liked "prety Well." In December Sharp reiterated his views on education, this time to both boys. In keeping with other learned second-generation Friends, he wanted his sons to acquire as much Latin as they could, and he purchased a Latin Bible for Jonathan. The study of grammar, he opined, could teach them orthography, etymology, syntax, and prosody. As Jonathan, now fourteen, neared the completion of his studies, Sharp urged him to "Improve" his time.[17] Neither Jonathan nor his father allowed these pedagogical concerns to overshadow their spiritual life. Hoping that God would bless Jonathan as he had Abraham, Isaac, Jacob, and Joseph, Sharp advised his son to "keep down little and low and out of every thing that Defiles and polutes, for the enemy envys the best and then tempts them most to Destroy them." The root of true education, he told both Jonathan and

Daniel, was to know the truth, by which he meant the inner light. "Fly every apearance of evill," Sharp exhorted them. No letters from Daniel survive, but Jonathan's correspondence reveals his sensitivity to spiritual matters. Using Pauline imagery he wrote to his father in July 1701: "I desire that i may not onely run [the Christian race] well For a time, but that i may run Well to the End that i may obtain a Crown of Glory."[18]

Gilbert Thompson's tutelage intensified Jonathan's spiritual experience. Around the time he went to Penketh, Jonathan displayed an ability to defend Quaker principles, and at age twelve he expressed a desire to become a preacher. At first this concerned his parents: "Altho we were glad & thankfull to the Lord that A child of ours was found worthy of such a sarvis for the Lord & his People, yet these Joyes of ours were mixed with a holy care, fear & concerne, that we have a subtile Adversary to make Warr against, for where he cannot prevaile to draw into gross Polutions he will Tempt into Spirituall pride & conseitedness—or into the depths of distrust & Dispayer." Plans to apprentice Jonathan to someone in Bristol or London were laid aside when Anthony and Ann decided that his spiritual calling must have precedence. When Ann took Daniel to Penketh in the summer of 1701, Jonathan joined his mother and her traveling companion, Mary Barlow, on a preaching tour through Cheshire, Shropshire, Worcestershire, Gloucestershire, Wiltshire, and Berkshire. Though not quite fourteen, "his worke of Faith & Labour of Love & Concerne in publike Testimony, prayer & prayses to the Lord was verry acceptable," his mother later recalled. He also accompanied Barlow on a similar trip to Leeds and other meetings in Yorkshire.[19]

Anthony and Ann had thought about terminating Jonathan's studies in the summer of 1701 and having him return to Dublin, but they acceded to his request to stay at Penketh one more year. In April 1702 they asked him to come home to learn his father's business. He reached Dublin on the 23rd, but became gravely ill with a fever that night. His father was in the Wicklow area to attend a funeral, following which local Friends wanted him to remain two days longer to participate in the Wicklow monthly meeting. But "haveing Som Straytness in his mind," as he later recalled, he returned to Dublin, where Jonathan by now was having trouble breathing. He faced death stoically: "I am but young & many Temptations & Exersises attends youth, & if It pleas God to take me now I shall be set free from all those daingers." He died on the 29th. Nearly four weeks later his parents acknowledged their spiritual duty to relinquish Jonathan to God, but they understandably grieved for "the good & holy child, an Innocent, holy, diligent, manlike, free, Kinde, mercifull Child."[20] In fact, Jonathan seems to have been an unusually devout young man judging from his correspondence with his parents.[21] The testimonies about Jonathan issued by his friends after his death reinforce this picture of a spiritually sensitive young person, though the evidentiary value of such statements is minimal owing to their almost hagiographical nature. Yet Thompson and Haydock were probably making a factual observation when they noted "how well freinds were Satisfied with his Service."[22]

Sharp's older surviving sons, Isaac and Joseph, disappointed him by their lack of interest in education. "Your Brother[s] Isaac and Joseph," he told Jonathan and Daniel in 1701, "I Could not perswade to learn So much Lattin as to understand true Spelling," but he blamed himself for this, giving Isaac credit for having "a good mother Wit and I hope the fear of God and love to the truth." In fact he was proud of Isaac's accomplishments. Isaac left for America in November 1700 after spending some time away from Dublin. In October 1702 Sharp told Isaac he had provided him with an estate worth £5,400 comprising houses and land in Ireland, England, and America. Crabb subsequently valued Isaac's inheritance, part of which came after Sharp's death, at £10,000 or more.[23]

Joseph caused his parents considerable grief and embarrassment. He had been an apprentice, but just after he turned eighteen he found himself without employment when his master retired or stopped plying his trade. Having saved nothing during his apprenticeship, Joseph moved back to his parents' home. As Anthony and Ann told Jonathan in July 1700, with a hint of sarcasm, Joseph was again living with them, "having little more but love to thee." Joseph's lifestyle, particularly his relations with women, exacerbated the increasingly tense relations with his father. Although Joseph apologized for his conduct, he insisted his father had been misinformed and that his relationship with his female companions was grounded in love. Unpersuaded, a pained Anthony warned Joseph that he had often displeased him and must now reform or "it will tend to thy own loss." As proof he cited reports of Joseph's conduct: "Thou hast more eyes on thee on my account then thou art aware of, thy Conversation is nought."[24]

By this point (31 January 1701), Joseph had left home, not as the result of a decision to become self-supporting but as an act of defiance against his father. Reflecting both anger and parental anguish, Sharp condemned his actions and implored him to reform:

As for thy laying thy unfortunate actions on love It is thy erroneous mind and that thou art censured for, but thy companying with the women Shews thy polluted mind which is Unstable as well as unchaste; if thou desires to be my Dutifull Son thou must do what I have from time to time advised thee and Resolve to go out at none of their calls.

Inviting Joseph to return home, Anthony promised him the best advice he could give as well as forgiveness for what had previously happened. He signed the letter "Thy abused father." Joseph declined the olive branch, prompting his parents to explain to Jonathan that this act would result in Joseph's "own hurt and our trouble."[25]

The Sharps considered Joseph's behavior sufficiently offensive to place the matter before the Dublin men's meeting. For its members the principal problem was Joseph's refusal to obey his parents and his scandalous act of "absenting" himself from his father. The meeting thereupon appointed the merchant Abel Strettell (or Strettle), the weaver Joseph Inman, and the glover Thomas Ashton to treat with Joseph, explaining the dangerous consequences of his behavior, including public denunciation by Friends. By 1 April the meeting noted that he remained disobedient and that the committee of three had been unable to confer with him because of his absence. When the same conditions prevailed at the next meeting a fortnight later, Sharp publicly testified against Joseph's "wicked, rebellious doeings," and the meeting drafted a formal testimony against his "loose, scandalous behaviour & great disobedience to his parents." In keeping with their mandate to discuss this document with Joseph, the committee met with him in the ensuing week and found him receptive to its concerns. Although Joseph made no attempt to justify his previous actions, he asked to be judged in the future by his behavior rather than have to make promises concerning it. An uneasy truce seems to have been effected, for by December his parents informed Jonathan and Daniel that he was thinking of emigrating to America. "His undutifullness and wildness," they added, "hath been no Smal trouble to us and will be his greatest trouble In the end."[26]

Of the three daughters who survived infancy—Rachel, Hannah, and Martha—the Sharps had little to say in their extant letters to Jonathan and Daniel. Hannah suffered from poor health, which her parents attributed to distemper. Following Hannah's death in March 1702, her parents informed Jonathan that "her Distemper took her In her eyes of which She was Long afflicted and then It came Into her head In great pain, and that remained till her senses Was Lost about a week and then Revived again A little and Departed." She bore her suffering patiently and ultimately "laid Down her head In peace," much as Jonathan himself would shortly do.[27] Much has been written about the emotional distancing between parents and children supposedly common in the sixteenth and early seventeenth centuries, but nothing in Sharp's letters suggests this was true of his family. In fact, the Sharps' relationship with their children reflects the change in "affective relations" that Lawrence Stone charted between 1660 and 1800.[28]

With a single exception the Sharp family was nuclear. The exception involved Ann's brother John, whom she and Anthony offered to accept as an apprentice in the spring of 1675. Irish Friends took apprenticeship seriously, though most of the regulations governing it postdated the Sharps' arrangement with Thomas Crabb. The standard apprenticeship was for seven years, but the Quakers accepted a trial period of up to a year in which a prospective master could ascertain an apprentice's compatibility. In May 1680 the half-yearly meeting approved a regulation requiring Quaker parents to obtain a local meeting's approval before apprenticing their children to non-Quakers, and asking Friends to consult with their meeting before accepting non-Quakers as apprentices. During Sharp's lifetime the Irish Friends accorded the local meetings substantial responsibility for supervising master-apprentice relations, including the provision of financial assistance for masters and oversight to ensure the fulfilment of apprenticeship agreements.[29]

When the Sharps offered an apprenticeship to John Crabb, it was thus a family and a religious matter as well as an economic one. If John and his parents accepted the offer, the Sharps wanted him to come to Dublin in the summer of 1675, for Anthony's most senior apprentice would complete his term the following January. Prior to that time Sharp wanted Crabb to receive further instruction in writing as well as the woolen trade. The Sharps wanted him to operate the business during their expected trip to England in 1676. Suggesting that Crabb take ship in Bristol or Chester, they urged him to "play the man to hasten over." He did, and by the time he was nineteen he was capable of supervising some 500 employees, buying and selling wool, and posting the books.[30]

Crabb subsequently recorded an incident that occurred approximately six months after his arrival in Dublin; it reflects the concern Sharp had for Crabb's religious and moral well-being. In July 1675 one of Sharp's female servants offended the young man by her "light Carridge." Crabb reported this to Sharp, who severely rebuked her. Ostensibly overcome by a sense of sin, she confessed her faults, but Sharp, doubting her sincerity, terminated her employment, offering only "Seasonable councels and Good advise Suitable to her Condition." In Crabb's presence, she responded: "Master, I am Senceible of my Great Sinn against God and have transgressed his Righteous law; . . . is there any hopes to attain Mercy from God For my poor Soul?" Concern over her spiritual welfare seems to have continued for five months, for on 5 December Sharp wrote to her, offering spiritual counsel and urging repentance: "Since the Devil who by name is a destroyer, hath Led thee near the . . . Brink of utter destruction of soul and body, and thou hath been sensible of it . . . I must tell thee it is in my heart from the Lord that if thou hate and fly from the Lords judgment in thy own conscience and would hide thy Sinnes and heal the wound Slightly, like as thou hast taken counsell from the Enimie and hath rejected the Lords counsell, . . . For which evill, wrath and Mischeife hath overtaken thee, even so will the same enimie pursue and hurry you to utter destruction, if thou harden thy heart." With this chilling warning Sharp deemed himself blameless for whatever fate awaited her.[31] This was an extraordinary response to a maid's frivolous behavior which a devout young apprentice found offensive. The incident is significant because it reveals Sharp's keen sense of paternal and spiritual responsibility for his family and his employees.

The relationships between Ann and Anthony, and between them and their children, confirm Sean Connolly's contention that intrafamilial relations in seventeenth-century Ireland had become more affectionate and less authoritarian and formal.[32] The Sharps enjoyed a companionate marriage and close involvement with their children. Indeed, their troubled relations with Joseph were painful precisely because of their love for him, and Jonathan's early death was especially difficult for them, not least because of his devout faith and the fact that he had reached his teens. Notwithstanding Anthony's numerous commitments to the Friends and his business, he found time to correspond with Jonathan and Daniel, and to express clear ideas about what their education should entail. There is, however, no evidence that he was equally concerned with the education of his daughters. In any event, he manifested a pronounced sense of spiritual and paternal responsibility for his family, his brother-in-law, and his employees.

3

"A Lover of Mercy and Truth"

Sharp and the Quaker Community, 1671-1685

IN THE YEARS following his move to Dublin, Sharp played an increasingly active role in the Quaker movement, defending its principles, seeking relief for incarcerated coreligionists, and accepting the responsibilities of a public Friend. His undertakings ranged from admonitions to and dealings with magistrates on the one hand to involvement in the movement's internal affairs, including contentious matters, on the other. During this period he made his first preaching forays to Quaker meetings in other areas of Ireland, but his interests extended much further afield as manifested by his financial investment in America. The extent of his activity, the depth of his commitment, his indefatigable energy, and, as will be seen in later chapters, his monetary support of the Quaker community were responsible for his growing stature among Friends and ultimately his *de facto* leadership of the Dublin Quakers. In this capacity he made a substantial contribution to the movement's survival, growth, and increasing centralization.

From at least 1671, Sharp worked to relieve Friends who were victims of persecution. The extent of such oppression in the 1660s is difficult to gauge; although Quakers in Ireland had begun keeping accounts of their sufferings as early as 1653, not until May 1672 did the six-months meeting provide for the orderly preservation of such information by appointing three men from each province to record the names and circumstances of imprisoned Friends. The same year the Dutch-born linen-weaver Abraham Fuller, a member of the Moate meeting in county Meath, and Thomas Holme, who had received land in county Wexford in payment for his service in the Cromwellian army, published the available data in *A Brief Relation of Some Part of the Sufferings of the True Christians, the People of God (in Scorn Called Quakers) in*

Ireland. A principal source of their information was the data now contained in the unpublished Great Book of Sufferings, but it records only the more dramatic cases of Quaker tribulation, especially in the 1660s. In subsequent decades the Friends placed greater emphasis on registering their sufferings. According to Holme and Fuller at least 533 Quakers went to prison in the period 1660–70, but they also note that others were jailed; a figure of 600 is therefore a reasonable estimate. Persecution was severest in Munster; of the 533 known victims, 60 percent were from that province compared to 32 percent in Leinster and 8 percent in Ulster. The worst periods were 1660–62, when 314 (59 percent) were jailed, and 1669, when 139 (26 percent) went to prison.[1]

Sharp's arrival in Ireland coincided with a peak period of persecution, though we have no evidence that he participated in relief efforts until the fall of 1671. Two factors spurred him to act, the first of which was a letter from John Redman in Limerick dated 14 August 1671. Finding himself a virtual prisoner in his own home, Redman hoped to visit Sharp the following week unless the magistrates formally arrested him. Notwithstanding receipt of the chancellor's order to liberate Redman and an incarcerated companion, the bishop of Limerick, Francis Marsh, refused to implement the directive unless the two men signed a document promising not to take legal action against Marsh if he distrained their goods. This they refused to do.[2]

The more significant factor in triggering Sharp's decision to assist Friends in distress probably grew out of John Banks' work in Ireland. A glover, the Cumberland native had traveled to Ulster and Dublin in 1669 at the invitation of John Tiffin of Pardshaw (who visited Ireland nine times), on which occasion Sharp undoubtedly met Banks in Dublin. In May 1671 Banks returned to Ireland, attended the six-months meeting in Dublin, and remarked favorably on Irish Friends' resolve to travel around the island seeking converts and organizing Quaker meetings. As Banks reported to his wife, he felt called by the Spirit to visit southern Ireland: "As I was waiting upon the Lord, a Weight with an Exercise came upon me, that I was to go to a Place Southward to have a Meeting next First Day." William Edmundson directed him to Wicklow, which had no meeting and few "Friendly People." Responding to a local minister's complaint, troops disrupted the tiny band worshiping with Banks. When he asked the sergeant by what warrant his soldiers acted, the officer brandished his halberd, arrested Banks, and conveyed him to Governor Mannery Hammond's house. Although the local Anglican minister demanded that Banks be punished, Hammond was "pretty Moderate." Banks not only denounced the priest as Antichrist's minister but also addressed the onlookers, whereupon the priest's wife insisted that Banks be jailed. When Hammond accused him of holding an illegal assembly, Banks refuted the charge on the grounds that he and his companions had not preached, read, formally prayed, or engaged in any liturgical act but merely gathered in silence to worship God. Unpersuaded, Hammond incarcerated Banks and two other Friends, but the jailor permitted them to entertain visitors, some of whom embraced Quaker tenets after listening to Banks preach. Three days later the governor released Banks notwithstanding his refusal to promise to appear (or have a surety present) at the next assize or quarter session, or to cease holding meetings in Wicklow. Banks returned to Dublin, where Sharp would presumably have been among those to whom he recounted his experiences.[3]

Banks subsequently traveled to Ulster, but upon his return to Dublin he received an invitation from Quakers in Wicklow asking him to visit them again. This time so many people flocked to his meeting that the house in which they gathered could not accommodate them. "It was," he reflected, "a Blessed Heavenly peaceable Meeting." Shortly thereafter the local cleric began to prosecute Quakers and have them incarcerated for refusing to pay tithes "and such like things."[4] Among them was the glover Thomas Trafford of Garrymore and later Wicklow, who was excommunicated and incarcerated for two years because he would not pay tithes.[5]

Sharp traveled to Wicklow in the late summer or early fall of 1671 to employ some of the town's poor, probably as wool workers. There he found many English men and women who had been imprisoned for their Quaker practices; most were farmers, some of whom were indigent. When Sharp sought to speak with Hammond on their behalf, the governor refused to see him, whereupon Sharp sent him a letter on 4 October. In it he protested that a hundred people could gather "in drinking and madness" with "scarce a protestation testyfied against them," whereas the authorities oppressed the godly, giving the Gaelic Irish cause for laughter. Sharp complained as well of the conditions in which the Friends were held, citing the "uncomly" lack of privacy for men and women and the hardship for wives and children whose husbands and fathers were jailed. He implored Hammond to release the Friends with the assurance that they would appear at the next quarter session. Reminding the governor that he had "time and opertunity to doe Good in [his] place both for the Lord and the country," Sharp asked him to "wash [his] hands From persecuteing the true English protestants." Noting that he paid his taxes and customs duties, employed the indigent, and contributed to Ireland's welfare, Sharp signed his letter, "a lover of mercy & truth and a hatter of Oppression."[6]

In the ensuing years Sharp unselfishly assisted a number of Friends in trouble, sometimes after receiving their personal appeals, sometimes at the behest of Quaker meetings. One of the most difficult and long-running cases involved John Goodbody, a father of eight children and a convert to the Quaker movement around 1670. Incarcerated at Philips-town, King's County (Offaly), in 1671, he came to Sharp's attention as the result of an appeal from Edward Taverner, a fellow prisoner. For refusing to pay tithes on a mill at Ballyboy, "which [had] never paid any," Goodbody had been arrested on a complaint from the minister Thomas Coffey. When the subsheriff gave Goodbody two weeks to get his affairs in order before going to jail, Coffey sent his son and a servant to the chancellor to complain, hoping he would fine the high sheriff. Taverner urged Sharp and other Friends in Dublin to block this attempt "or else It is Like to be a great Hinderance to our future enlargement," specifically recommending that they seek the assistance of Taverner and Goodbody's landlord, Thomas Crookshanks, Sir William Petty's steward, and of John Reading, the solicitor for the late high sheriff in the Court of Chancery. Taverner also pressed Sharp to consult with such prominent Dublin Friends as Robert Turner and Samuel Clarridge, and to sell his wool and sheepskins for him.[7] In November 1672 the six-months meeting appointed Clarridge and John Savage, also a member of the Dublin meeting, to handle the cases of Taverner and Goodbody when they came before the bishop of Meath. After Goodbody had been excommunicated for his refusal to pay tithes and for his alleged contempt, Sharp drafted a petition to the lord chancellor on his behalf.[8]

Despite the efforts of Sharp, Clarridge, and others, Goodbody was still in prison in November 1676, at which time the national meeting delegated Clarridge and John Gay to seek the help of Petty and Henry Jones, bishop of Meath, in procuring his release. The meeting also appointed Sharp, Fuller, Holme, and Thomas Starkey, a Cheshire-born "gentleman" living at Abbeyleix, Queen's County (Laois), to investigate whether any "Lawfull means" were available to "preserve and recover his right," presumably to the mill, which was now being contested by a widow. The meeting was willing to pay up to £5 to acquire her interest in the property and to investigate ways to raise additional funds if required.[9] These efforts appear to have been successful, though Goodbody remained behind bars. Sharp then wrote to Coffey on 18 January 1677, lecturing him on the wrongfulness of tithes. Tithing had ceased, Sharp insisted, when Jesus abolished the Jewish priesthood, and Christians were commanded to give freely even as they had received freely. In response to Coffey's contention that tithing was a matter of obeying a state law, Sharp retorted: "As to the law of the nation unto which wee are as timely or passively obedient, not For Wrath but Conscience Sake, which thou Seems to build upon more then . . . [the] Gospel in this case; i do not see such a great matter . . . on thy side, as to Soe Violently opress a poor Family, where it is for matter of Conscience." Had the apostle Peter ignored his conscience, Sharp added, he would not have preached "a new doctrine" to unbelieving Jews. Sharp thus built his case on a combination of biblical exegesis and compassion, relegating legal obedience to a manifestly inferior status.[10]

Coffey paid no heed to this plea, but later the same month the Leinster provincial meeting asked Sharp and Clarridge to work for Goodbody's release, if necessary by seeking legal remedies. Sharp's efforts may have helped to persuade Coffey to relent, for in the late spring of 1677 the latter agreed to forgive his share of the tithes owed by Goodbody and the costs of prosecuting the case. But Goodbody remained in jail, eventually prompting the justices of the peace in King's County to petition the bishop of Meath for his liberation so the county did not have to continue his maintenance. The same month the half-yearly meeting instructed Sharp, Fuller, and Turner to continue to assist Goodbody, and the Leinster meeting issued a comparable directive the following February. In the meantime the meetings in the province of Ulster collected £4 10s. for his relief. At last, Sharp and his colleagues were apparently successful, for Goodbody seems to have received his freedom in 1678 after seven years in prison.[11]

Sharp's activities on behalf of jailed Friends increased in the later years of Charles II's reign as the government repressed dissidents following the recall of the earl of Essex, the duke of Ormond's return as lord lieutenant, the security threat posed by the Bothwell Bridge rebellion in Scotland, and the conservative backlash resulting from the disclosure of the Rye House plotting.[12] Among the cases with which Sharp was most active were those of the husbandman John Watson of Kilconner, county Carlow, Daniel White of Killabban, Queen's County (Laois), and Samuel Watson of Fennagh, county Carlow. Between 1679 and 1683 this involved Sharp in a variety of inquiries and appeals to such entities as the Hanaper of Chancery (the department into which fees were paid to seal and enrol documents), the consistory court of the diocese of Meath, and the Privy Council. As a result of Sharp's petition to Ormond on the three men's behalf, which cited their lengthy incarceration and the distraint of many of their possessions, the duke referred the case to a judge of assize at Carlow. The defendants' refusal to take oaths regarding their distrained property compounded their difficulties, but perhaps at Sharp's suggestion they sought to have their cases decided on merit, not their refusal to swear. In May 1682 the six-months meeting advised White and David Watson to have their legal counsel draft a petition to the lord lieutenant, his deputy, or the Privy Council and give it to Sharp, Turner, and the tanner Joseph Sleigh, who had instructions to provide further assistance. When the cases were still pending in November, the meeting directed Sharp, Sleigh, and Starkey to seek the advice of Fuller, John Burnyeat, and the Cork merchant Francis Rogers. The following month the Leinster provincial meeting instructed Sharp to consult with an attorney—something Irish Friends normally did only if necessary—concerning a decree promised to Samuel Watson at the Carlow assizes, and if he still had difficulty obtaining the signed document, to speak directly with the judges.[13] By March 1683 Sharp was successful, whereupon the Leinster meeting instructed him to petition the lord deputy and Council on other Friends' behalf. Now at liberty, White was to assist him by searching episcopal court records for data that would enable Sharp to "know how to Expresse the matter" in his petition, a draft of which Edmundson, Fuller, White, and others were to examine the following day. The agencies and officials with whom Sharp dealt, his role in drafting documents, and the rapidity with which the Leinster meeting expected him to prepare a petition manifest the Quakers' respect for his legal skills as well as his commitment to this work.[14]

Sharp assisted Edmundson himself after the latter had been imprisoned and excommunicated in 1682. When Edmundson's landlord, Edward Loftus, Viscount Ely, interceded for him, William Moreton, bishop of Kildare, summoned Edmundson to his court. Burnyeat and Sharp stood at the door as Edmundson debated tithing with the bishop in the presence of ten or twelve clerics. In a discussion that lasted three hours they also talked about the ministry, worship, and the nature of faith. Edmundson insisted he was suffering illegally under a Henrician act (32 Henry VIII, c. 7) that did not apply to him, for he had refused to tithe as a matter of conscience, not, as the statute specified, because of an "ungodly and perverse will and mynde." Not having a copy of the act and wanting Edmundson's views in writing, Moreton ordered him to appear at the court's next sitting. In an assessment perhaps shared by Sharp, Burnyeat observed that he had never been "better satisfied with a Day's Work in all his Life, the Testimony of Truth being so over them." It was probably at this point that Moreton referred the case to the justices, whereupon Sharp wrote to a Colonel Warnford to examine the allegations against Edmundson. At the court's next session, Moreton ordered the sheriff to discharge Edmundson notwithstanding the fact that he refused to attend services in the Church of Ireland. Sharp was apparently not present this time.[15]

During the same period Sharp willingly helped other Friends, particularly by drafting petitions and other documents as well as by personal meetings with ecclesiastical and judicial officials. On behalf of James Wasly (or Wastly, Wisely), a member of the Moate meeting, Philip England, and James Ryan, all of whom were in prison on writs of excommunication, he drafted petitions to the archbishop of Armagh, the bishop of Meath, and the chancellor of the consistory court in the diocese of Meath.[16] He also prepared petitions for Friends in county Wexford and elsewhere. When Quaker sufferings intensified in the early 1680s, the Leinster provincial meeting asked Sharp and Sleigh to seek the advice of the second-day meeting in London as to whether excommunicated Friends could take legal action; the response indicated that some defendants in England had halted proceedings by filing pleas, as Friends in Ireland were already doing. In the spring of 1683 Sharp and James Taylor met with the chief justice and another judge on behalf of suffering Quakers in county Carlow; sympathetic "beyond Expectation," the chief justice promised to ask the clergy in his circuit to reduce their legal actions against the Friends. Speaking for other Quakers, Sharp conferred with the bishops of Ferns and Raphoe as well as assorted landlords, judges, and magistrates.[17] When the opportunity arose, the Friends sought to obtain the release of jailed colleagues by citing technical flaws in the legal proceedings, as in 1684 when Joseph Boardman was incarcerated under a *significavit* (a certificate obtained by a plaintiff citing the alleged offense) and a writ, at least one of which referred to him as Joseph Moony. The six-months meeting directed Sharp to get copies of both documents. After the recorder of Dublin advised Sharp that the sheriff in this case could be sued for false imprisonment, the half-yearly meeting asked Sharp to obtain the Council's judgment.[18] Thus by the early 1680s the Friends were making considerable use of Sharp's legal talents and access to a wide range of officials, some of whom were at the center of Irish government. Clearly he enjoyed a degree of respect in such circles and must have carried himself appropriately. Over time, these contacts contributed to the gradual acceptance of the Quakers by some in the political nation.

In addition to his endeavors on behalf of Friends in travail, Sharp served the movement as a public Friend commencing in 1674. Armed with a certificate from a monthly meeting, a Quaker could embark on "truth's service" as a traveling minister. Some of these public Friends came to Ireland from England on preaching missions, as did John Banks no fewer than a dozen times beginning in 1668. Irish Friends ranged throughout Ireland or traveled abroad, as did Edmundson, who went to the West Indies in 1671 and on to the American mainland the following year.[19] As their excursions took public Friends to Dublin, Sharp regularly met them and often received letters from them after their departure. On occasion he helped to coordinate their itineraries, as in the summer of 1676 when Samuel Burgis, Oliver Sansom of Berkshire, and Thomas Briggs were journeying through Ireland.[20]

Sharp's first recorded trip as a public Friend occurred in September 1678. He went to Ballinakill, Queen's County (Laois), shortly after Thomas Curtis, the shoemaker Thomas Atherton, and the Westmorland husbandman Stephen Hubbertsty, and participated in a meeting there before accompanying Curtis to Rosenallis. His journey then took him to Mountmellick in Queen's County and Athy in county Kildare before his return to Dublin. While together, Curtis sought Sharp's advice concerning his future travels. Four years later Sharp was on the road again, this time visiting the north with Clarridge and William Bingley, a London cloth merchant; the latter subsequently thanked Sharp for his "good company," but humorously noted that the goldsmith George Gregson of Lisburn, county Antrim, a Quaker stalwart in Ulster, "saith he is not Beholding to You for your company because you stayed So Little a time there."[21] Sharp's visits were thus welcomed. Although he provides little detail about Sharp's work as a public Friend, the Quaker historian Thomas Wight of Cork observed that "in his public testimony he was many times zealously concerned for the convincement of strangers, being gifted for that service, having a good understanding, a ready utterance, and a clear way of delivery."[22]

Sharp was also involved in providing material support to public Friends during their journeys. In May 1679 the Leinster provincial meeting appointed him to a committee of four to examine traveling Friends' needs and to report on the funds required to assist them. Four years later he served on another provincial committee, this time to advise the women of the Dublin meeting concerning the provision of linen and other cloth to public Friends. In 1686 this became a standing committee, charged to convene every six months, to consider the need for stockings and cloth, and to authorize the women to disburse money for such items.[23] Service on this committee enabled Sharp to track the movements of Friends in the ministry.

While serving as a hub for traveling Friends, the Dublin Quaker community periodically experienced internal tensions, some of them concerning morality and religious belief. The most notorious of these involved Clarridge's sexual liaison with his maid and his ensuing attempt to cover up the scandal. When Clarridge discovered she was pregnant, he sent her to England, where she gave birth, telling the midwife she had a husband and that the delivery had come unexpectedly while she was traveling. At the behest of the Dublin men's meeting, Sharp wrote to Clarridge in 1676, urging him to repent and provide a full confession; if not, the meeting would issue a testimony condemning his and the maid's actions. Their conduct was "in direct despite to that Spirit of Grace that God had planted in every mans heart to instruct and guide him into all truth." In Sharp's judgment Clarridge was now a lover of darkness and "a bed of ease." He wrote again to Clarridge during a visit to England, noting that Clarridge had ceased to attend the Dublin men's meeting and admonishing him to "mind the Lords work in thy own heart in perticuler and in the meetings in general." The tone was congenial, reflecting Sharp's desire to see Clarridge make his peace with the Friends.[24] When Clarridge refused to repent, sought the support of unnamed Quaker ministers who reportedly knew nothing of his background, and made the reputation of Dublin Friends "stink in England," Sharp became embittered. In May 1677 he complained to Briggs that Clarridge's defiance of the Dublin meeting was in keeping with his previous behavior, and he denied Clarridge's charges that the meeting had not dealt with him openly and without malice.[25]

The Clarridge scandal not only created misunderstanding between unnamed Quakers in England and those in Dublin but also caused friction among the latter. In November 1677 Francis Rogers and others publicly argued with Sharp in favor of condemning the meeting's proceedings against Clarridge, prompting Sharp to retort in writing, not least because he thought "many Flatterers" would report the dispute to Clarridge, thus encouraging his defiance. The latter's apologists had spoken in defense of his character and accused Sharp and his supporters of being "like Oules [owls] in the Desert that knew not When good coms," to which Sharp replied that Clarridge's goodness was presently hidden, and that "as the Lord discovers it to me, which i desire, so i shall own it and him therein." Referring to a larger issue, Sharp averred that the meeting could not disavow its earlier condemnation of Clarridge without violating the consciences of its members. "That is not the way to have peace amongst us, & it will streng[t]hen the hands of evil doers."[26] When Rogers replied the same day, insisting his statements had been truthful, Sharp reaffirmed his position while declining Rogers' invitation to air their differences before their coreligionists. "To Jangle i have no Desire," Sharp insisted, though he was manifestly unwilling to compromise.[27]

The Clarridge case caused dissension in other ways as well. Accused of having had sexual relations with the same maid, one John Huggs faced interrogation by the Dublin men's meeting. Although admitting he had been "too Familier with her," he contended he was "clear of acting the bad Act" and expressed regret for having condemned the meeting for its proceedings against the maid. In a separate case, when a delegation of Friends visited Ann Savage and found her "hard and Stif," she retorted by criticizing Sharp, Turner, and others. As Turner "Laid more load on her own head," others joined in condemning her wicked ways, to which she replied that the meeting would not have dealt with her in this manner had she been wealthy and influential like Clarridge.[28] Perceived reticence to deal firmly with Clarridge thus fanned social resentment.

Although Clarridge ultimately submitted to the Dublin men's meeting, the episode was traumatic for Sharp. In its aftermath he was not persuaded that Clarridge had been truly repentant, and he admitted to Robert Stepney that "many Times the Bitterness of the cup of the Tryals and exercises have made [me] ready to say, my God, my God why hast thou Forsaken me?" At the Leinster meeting's urging, the Dublin Friends sought to resolve their internal discord over the scandal in May 1678, determining "to watch against the enemy that sowes dissention & strife amongst Godes people." Sharp's name headed the list of signatories, among whom was Clarridge. Members of the women's meeting, including Sharp's wife Ann and Clarridge's spouse Anna, also signed the statement.[29]

Notwithstanding the attempted resolution, ill will poisoned relations for years. As late as 1682 some members of the provincial meeting argued that those who had committed "Gross Wickedness" should not attend the men's meeting when the latter was engaged in "the Lords buisness" until its members had unanimously agreed on their return. Clarridge was consequently excluded from the business portion of the provincial assembly until such a time as the Dublin men's meeting readmitted him. Sharp drafted the order, which reflected his tough stance on dealing with Clarridge.[30]

While the Clarridge scandal raged, Sharp became embroiled in a dispute in 1677 over the treatment of John Marshall, a member of the Lisburn meeting. Because Marshall had allegedly been critical of "the power of God" in George Gregson, the six-months meeting discussed the matter, and Marshall, for the sake of harmony, condemned himself. Dublin Quakers then signed a lengthy statement denouncing the spirit of darkness that had threatened to destroy their unity through backbiting and false accusations. Sharp had never been persuaded of Marshall's guilt, and when Marshall subsequently admitted he had denounced himself simply to keep peace, Sharp insisted that his own name be removed from the statement of condemnation. In an unusual move, the national meeting allowed signatories to withdraw their names but simultaneously permitted people who had not hitherto signed to add theirs. It was an obvious gesture to prevent the issue from causing an even deeper rift.[31]

Sharp participated as well in the most serious challenge to Quaker unity in the restoration period, the Story-Wilkinson dispute. This controversy had originated in England essentially over the growing centralization of power, and it manifested itself in disputes about the nature and role of women's meetings, hostility to mandatory written testimonies against tithes, an insistence on silence while Quakers were praying or speaking, a limit on the number of Friends who could attend business meetings, and not recording papers of condemnation without consent of the guilty parties. The fissure deepened when John Story, John Wilkinson, and their followers established their own business meeting in May 1675. Two years later, in June 1677, the yearly meeting of ministers banned worship services in the homes of Quakers who had participated in schismatic business meetings.[32]

Sharp collected documents concerning the dispute, including testimonies against Story and Wilkinson by prominent leaders in England, the parley near Sedbergh that attempted to effect a reconciliation, a statement from the two men expressing regret, and Wilkinson's letter to Friends in Wiltshire.[33] One of Sharp's principal sources of information was his former father-in-law, Thomas Curtis, who, with his wife Ann, had supported Story and Wilkinson when they met with George Fox and Thomas Lower at Worcester Castle in January 1675. On 10 March 1679 Curtis wrote to Sharp and his wife protesting "a multitude of Lyes, slanders and false accusations" against Story and Wilkinson, and blaming young preachers of both sexes who could not "tell how to Be quiet." During his recent trip to Ireland, Curtis had also heard spurious charges that he had accused Fox of attempting to establish popery in England. The alleged source of this rumor was the Dublin linen draper James Fade, but he professed his innocence and support of Curtis. The latter told Sharp that many Friends wanted a reconciliation, failing which "all these differences will be made much higher than ever they were."[34] After their colloquy with Story in April, William Penn, George Whitehead, Alexander Parker, and nine other Friends, hoping a reconciliation was possible, urged all Quakers to "be exercised towards him," "for the Bringing of him nearer to his Brethren who are in the ancient fellowship." Perhaps influenced by this report, Irish Quakers showed their support for Fox at the six-months meeting in May 1679 by appointing a committee of six men to collect reports of Curtis' unsavory comments concerning the dispute to anyone in Ireland and submit them to the Leinster meeting. Curtis' letter to Sharp of 10 March clearly fell into this category.[35]

Caught between his friendship with Curtis and the support Fox enjoyed among most Irish Friends, Sharp pressed for conciliation. On 13 May 1680, while he was in England on business, he wrote to Story, asking him to attend the next yearly meeting in London and to seek peace by offering to take its advice as far as his conscience allowed. He also urged Story to invite his followers to be present in "the same Spirit of forgiveness and peace." Should Story be unable to attend, Sharp requested that he send the meeting a conciliatory letter. This was not an easy missive for Sharp to compose, for he had a deep respect for Story's role in the Quaker movement: "Dear John I acknowledge my Self but young In comparison of thee, and thou hath been an honourable elder in the church." He went on to describe himself as a worm compared to Story, but he also felt an urgency to clear his conscience, for this spiritual conviction was "a stronger impulse on my spirit then [any I] had since my first convincement as I remember, though I have always been backwards to lay any on the Lord (as to others) knowing that God will own what is of himself."[36]

About the same time, Sharp wrote to the yearly meeting at London, appealing for an end to the recriminations that had become commonplace since its denunciation of Story and Wilkinson in June 1677. Sharp deplored the confusion that plagued Quaker meetings, with some members wearing hats during prayer while others did not. He was no less displeased with those who interrupted fellow Quakers while they were speaking, and with the partiality with which members of a dominant group expelled its opponents from a meeting. "Ought not gospel order be used to all equally without respect of persons lest the Issue prove that one or two, eight, or one half of a meeting may cast out the rest? Consider the consequences of it." Meetings, he concluded, should be in essential unity before they pronounced judgment on any of their members.[37] Sharp's statement may have been quietly shelved, for on 17 July William Gibson wrote to him from London, indicating he had shown the letter to Fox; Sharp himself had shared it with Penn. Gibson advised that it "be laid by," for making it public would not accomplish Sharp's purpose. Story and Wilkinson, explained Gibson, had already been subjected to "Gospel order and a great Long and tender travail." A year and a half later, in November 1681, Story died. Two of his diehard supporters, a Quaker couple in Reading, reported his death to Sharp, adding that they had hoped Story and Wilkinson's opponents would repent and not "deck themselves with what they have known of Truth, and go a whoring after other lovers."[38] Sharp must have read about Story's death with a sense of pensiveness and sadness, knowing his hope of effecting a conciliation had ultimately failed.

Indeed, Story's followers, including Thomas and Ann Curtis and Benjamin Coale, kept his cause alive. In April 1685 Coale protested to Sharp that Sansom and Burgis had been complaining about him to Sharp and others, "a work too frequently practised by them tending rather to Stir the Coals of contention and Division then true unity amongst Friends." Sharp was still following the dispute in late 1691, when John Blaykling reported to him about continuing divisions at Reading.[39]

Story was barely in his grave before another, less acrimonious controversy disrupted the Dublin Friends. This dispute involved the works of Jacob Boehme (1575–1624), the German mystic whose writings were studied by such early Friends as Thomas Taylor, William Smith, and Benjamin Furly, but whose view of the Spirit within was different from the Quakers' distinctively Christian concept of the inner light of Christ. Boehme contended that three principles permeate the universe: divine wrath, divine light, and the external world or "visible word." Creation is not God's simple historical act but a continual process represented by the three principles. To the extent that God is the source of these principles, Boehme appears to have made the deity the author of evil. Yet the first two principles, which permeate nature, are spiritual and dualistic, giving nature the potential to be both good and evil. The struggle between good and evil is acted out in every godly person, and those who knowingly choose the good and possess the knowledge of the three principles can attain perfection.[40] Quakers such as John Perrot and John Anderdon read Boehme's works but eventually condemned his tenets. Anderdon likened Boehme's assertion that divine light permeates natural objects to Catholic teaching in that such objects became "'*Mediums like Sacraments*'."[41]

In December 1681 the Dublin men's meeting dispatched several members to visit Thomas Smith, John Beckett, and Christopher Marshall, who possessed copies of Boehme's books and were espousing his tenets "and other principills and Imaginations." The meeting was particularly concerned with their contention that God's wrath and the devil's actions are one "in nature & property," a thesis Beckett had developed in a paper. The three refused to recant. On 3 January 1682 the same meeting instructed Sharp and Turner to write to Sharp's brother-in-law, John Crabb, who had "been somthing Levened with that spirrit of theyrs." In fact, they also wrote to his father, Thomas Crabb.[42]

When Beckett and his colleagues, including his brother James, continued to affirm Boehmist principles, the Dublin men's meeting commissioned Sharp and three others on 28 March to draft a paper condemning those who "Runn into faulse Liberty under any pretences whatsoever & Runs from Truth into Errors." The testimony was read in the Bride Street meetinghouse in April. Signed by the Sharps and thirty-eight others, it denounced "the blasphemous principles & disorderly practices" of the Becketts, Smith, and Marshall, who had been enticed into "Confused, antichristian, Antiscriptural, Imaginatory and Blasphemous dark principles." Such teachings, the testimony claimed, were conducive to carnal liberty or "Ranterisme" and rendered the cross of Christ ineffectual. Young people were especially urged to heed this warning and beware of the "Luciferian spirit [that] leadeth out of the lowly truth" as well as "Exaltedness of mind and high Imaginations." Shortly thereafter, the meeting heard from John Crabb, who acknowledged that he had lent books owned by Beckett to others, but he refused to recant his allegiance to Boehmist views and condemned the meeting's actions against Beckett and his compatriots. The Friends then declared they had no unity with him, though he continued to participate in Quaker meetings. On 6 June the men's meeting unanimously agreed to charge Crabb to remain silent in meetings for the foreseeable future, failing which the Friends would publicly testify against him.[43] Theological controversy thus disrupted Sharp's extended family, undoubtedly causing him consternation.

Beginning in the late 1670s Sharp plunged into religious controversy with adherents of other religious groups. Among them was his neighbor, a Church of Ireland cleric, the Rev. Mr. Gobourn, to whom Sharp wrote in April 1678 on the Friends' behalf, explicating their views of the gospel ministry and the duties of ministers and messengers of God according to the prophets, Christ, and the apostles.[44] Sharp's disputes with the Catholics, especially Thomas Gormagan and Michael Archer, are discussed in Chapter 10, as is his debate with William Joseph over the Quaker practice of allowing women to speak in meetings. After three Presbyterian ministers, including William and Gideon Jacque, "blazed abroad" a spurious report about Friends circulated in Ulster by "a wicked girl," the six-months meeting appointed Sharp and four others to compose a refutation, and asked Friends in the north to draft a certificate denouncing the rumor.[45]

When the Dublin alderman and goldsmith Enoch Reader attacked the Friends for their refusal to conform in matters of religion and to take the oaths normally required for membership in the corporation, Sharp came to their defense in January 1680. He had adjudged Reader to be a magistrate "of some conscience," but now he accused him of violating the Quakers' right of conscience by denying them the benefit of law if they refused to conform. Moreover, he argued that no law prohibited the arrangement whereby some Friends enjoyed the freedom of the city in return for paying entry fines and other fees. "It is not the oath [that] makes free but the grant on consideration, the consideration being performed, and again the benefit of our freedom is city Duty." To reject this arrangement was to void a legitimate covenant under pretense of law. Many statutes and customs, averred Sharp, could not always be upheld in good conscience. To illustrate his point he cited a statute that prohibited giving alms to beggars, but the law of reason, he maintained, justified such assistance if a beggar would otherwise perish before reaching a town. Furthermore, common and civil law must be tempered with equity and mercy, the very principle on which the Court of Chancery rested.[46]

Much of Sharp's appeal to Alderman Reader dealt with the Quaker case against oaths. They bound men, Sharp contended, to perform their official duties, yet many broke their vows when it was advantageous to do so. He also questioned the necessity of oaths, for even without an oath every person was bound to render to Caesar his due. "Election makes an officer," not an oath. Eruditely, he went on to cite an impressive array of sources to buttress his case, including such biblical verses as Jeremiah 32:10, Matthew 5:34, and James 5:12; such patristic scholars as Tertullian, Clement of Alexandria, Origen, Chrysostom, and Athanasius; the church historian Eusebius; the martyrs Justin and Polycarp; the medieval reformer John Wyclif; Erasmus' commentary on Matthew; and John Foxe's *Acts and Monuments*. Sharp chided Reader, reminding him that Catholics had refused to respect tender consciences in "the First protestant reformation," but the Friends expected better treatment from Protestants. The Quakers, after all, had not been disloyal to king, country, or city. Insisting the Friends did not want Reader as their enemy, Sharp nevertheless deemed him "one of the chief against us to enjoy the city grant except one or two Self concerned who are parties and Judges." The blame for any denial of the Quakers' "Just right," he insisted, would rest squarely with these critics.[47]

Reader and his allies were unsuccessful in repressing the Quakers, for in May 1682 the six-months meeting reported to the yearly meeting in London that Friends throughout Ireland suffered little for any reason apart from a few prosecutions for not paying tithes. Their numbers, in fact, were growing. Late in the year Burnyeat noted talk of enforcing the laws against nonconformists in Ireland, but Quaker gatherings were "large and full."[48]

Burnyeat correctly reported a growing desire in some conservative circles to execute the laws against dissent, but this concern was directed almost exclusively toward the Presbyterians[49] and was largely the result of stories about a Presbyterian plot against the monarchy—rumors that were sufficiently alarming to prompt the Dublin city council to send an address to Charles II in April 1682 pledging to defend him and the Church of Ireland against all associations and threats. Quakers were feeling the pressure by late 1682, and in January 1683 the Leinster provincial meeting decided that at least two Friends should attend the assizes and quarter sessions in every county to assist members who were in trouble.[50]

Disclosures of the Rye House plotting in June 1683 induced the government to tighten security in all three kingdoms. Sharp would later describe the leading conspirators who lost their lives—Lord William Russell, Algernon Sidney, and Arthur Capel, earl of Essex—as "eminent statesmen." In Ireland the Scottish Presbyterians were the primary ob-

jects of concern, but nonconformists of all persuasions were affected. As
late as 24 July Burnyeat noted reports that meetings would be dispersed,
but added that no action had yet been taken. If suffering did come, he
opined, it would "work for good through Trying our Spirits, Faith, and
Patience, so that many may come to know themselves, and the Lord and
his Power also better thereby."[51] Shortly thereafter, the government ordered dissenters in Dublin to cease holding services in their meetinghouses. Francis Marsh, archbishop of Dublin, summoned Sharp and
told him the Quakers must cease assembling, but this, Sharp insisted,
they could not do. When the Friends alone refused to comply, the earl
of Arran, the lord deputy, wrote to Ormond on 4 August, explaining
that the Quakers have "no particular teachers to give warning to";
hence he thought they would probably continue to meet. Although Arran did not consider the Friends a security threat, on Sunday, 5 August,
the mayor of Dublin dispatched the marshal to the Quakers' meeting.
When he found Burnyeat "declaring Truth," he ordered him "to come
downe," but Burnyeat retorted: "We are met together to worship God
and not in contempt of authority, and therefore we desire our liberty."
Although the marshal arrested Burnyeat, the meeting continued,
prompting the marshal to take the schoolmaster Alexander Seaton into
custody and order the rest to disperse; however, they "kept quiet in
their places" until the usual time to adjourn. Appearing before the may-
or, Burnyeat was asked why Friends refused to submit as had other nonconformists, to which he retorted: "What they do, will be no Plea for us
before the Judgment-Seat of the Great God." The mayor committed him
to the Marshalsea prison. The same day the marshal and his assistants
apprehended Sharp, Clarridge, John Bourne, and James Taylor as they
were leaving the meeting and took them before the lord mayor, who
had them incarcerated in the Marshalsea. On the 7th Sharp and Clarridge were released following an order from Arran, and Taylor and
Bourne were free by the 9th. The earl of Longford had confided to Ormond that the Quakers were "somewhat obstinate," though he expected Arran's "prudence . . . [to] bring even those unreasonable bruites
to owne & submitt to Authority."[52]

On 9 September 1683, a month after their release, Sharp and Clarridge called on Arran to seek freedom for imprisoned Friends, whereon
the lord deputy told them "he had a greater Love for us, than any other
Dissenters, because he believed that we did mean honestly." Burnyeat
and the other Friends in the Marshalsea subsequently appealed for their
release to Arran, who consulted with the Council and then liberated

them in early October; Burnyeat and Seaton were out on the 10th. At that point Burnyeat wrote to a Quaker in London, "I have not heard that Friends in any part of this Nation are medled with."[53] When Sharp, Burnyeat, and five others reported to the London yearly meeting in May 1684 at the behest of the six-months meeting, they said essentially the same thing.[54] Yet Friends continued to face persecution for refusing to pay tithes. Subjected to what they deemed unreasonable fees in episcopal courts, they suffered as magistrates seized goods worth more than they owed. When this happened to Quakers in the Wexford area, the national meeting instructed Sharp and six others to prepare a statement detailing their losses for presentation to the judges and others, and to draft a petition to the lord lieutenant and Council indicating many families faced ruin unless the government redressed these grievances.[55]

About this time, Sharp wrote an undated address to the king on the Friends' behalf. They honored the monarch and rendered him his due, Sharp maintained, yet though they were innocent and industrious they were often imprisoned and had their possessions distrained. Sodom, he pointedly noted, would have been saved had five innocent persons lived there, a clear allusion to the Quakers' conception of their role in Charles' realms. "Does not their Christian profestion press people to peace and holyness?" he asked. "By their industry is not thy Revenues encreased, thy people bettered and nothing bad but Good infused into thy peoples minds by them." The Friends' only offense, Sharp concluded, was worshiping God, and they should therefore be unmolested.[56]

Sharp experienced one other manifestation of anti-Quaker hostility in these years, namely, the violence to which Friends were subjected because they declined to observe Christmas, insisting that all days were the same in God's eyes. Refusal to celebrate this holiday was not unique to the Quakers, for strict Puritans had long objected to merrymaking, sports, and bell-ringing on that occasion. Those who protested Christmas festivities typically kept their shops open, provoking retaliation from traditional revelers. For refusing to close their shops at Christmas, Friends in Ireland as in England experienced rough treatment from the crowds. Following what Burnyeat described as "very rude" behavior by "the Rable" in Dublin at Christmas 1683, the Dublin men's meeting delegated Sharp and Clarridge to ask the lord mayor the following December to charge the constables to keep the peace. Nevertheless men and boys stoned Quaker shops and houses on Christmas day, whereon the men's meeting deputed Sharp and Clarridge to report the offenders to the mayor and seek their punishment. Sharp did not carry out these instructions, perhaps owing to illness, but Clarridge and the innkeeper Roger Roberts did. As we shall see, however, the Quakers continued to be the targets of overzealous revelers for years to come.[57]

By the time the age of Charles II ended in February 1685, Sharp had established himself as a prominent figure among Dublin Friends. Since the early 1670s he had boldly sought relief for incarcerated Quakers— drafting petitions, conferring with magistrates and others, and seeking legal remedies. A public Friend since 1674, he made his first recorded preaching trip in 1678, visiting meetings in east central Ireland. He knew and corresponded with public Friends who visited Ireland and undoubtedly served as a fount of information on their journeys for members of the Dublin and Leinster Quaker communities. In most of the internal controversies that disrupted those communities he adopted a conciliatory stance, as in the disputes surrounding Marshall, Story, and Wilkinson. In two controversies he found himself in a difficult position because of the involvement of his former father-in-law Thomas Curtis, a supporter of Story and Wilkinson, and his brother-in-law John Crabb, who expressed interest in Boehme's tenets. In the scandal involving Clarridge, however, Sharp did not seek conciliation; on the contrary, his resolute disapproval of Clarridge's sexual misconduct and prevarication so troubled Sharp that he was one of the last to accept Clarridge's full restoration to Quaker fellowship. On moral issues Sharp was unbending. Commencing in the late 1670s, he took up his pen to defend Quakers from their external critics, notably a Church of Ireland cleric, Alderman Enoch Reader, and a group of Catholics. By 1685 Sharp's stature among the Friends was firmly established, thanks especially to his efforts on behalf of jailed Quakers, his conciliatory endeavors, his strong stand for moral behavior, and his contributions as a public Friend.

4

"Taking Up the Cross"

Toleration, the Magistracy, and the Time of Troubles

THE ACCESSION OF the Catholic James II to the throne in February 1685 set the stage for nearly seven years of dramatic change culminating in the time of troubles and massive suffering for Friends. Sharp, very unlike Fox in his willingness to assume municipal office, established himself as a leading Quaker in Dublin's government and then, during the war, exercised significant responsibility in providing relief to his stricken coreligionists. During this period, as we shall see in the next chapter, he also acquired a position of leadership in the weavers' guild, thanks in part to the new king's policy of religious toleration. Before the disruptions caused by the war, Sharp, with an insatiable appetite for work, made the most of his opportunity to engage in municipal and guild government.

Before his death Charles II had decided to replace Ormond as lord lieutenant with Henry Hyde, earl of Clarendon, and the duke accordingly left Ireland in February. Until Clarendon arrived the government was in the hands of Arthur Forbes, Viscount Granard, and Michael Boyle, archbishop of Armagh, both of whom were preoccupied with security issues, particularly the activities of dissident Scots in northern Ireland and Scotland. Their concerns were not baseless, for in May the earl of Argyll and his supporters invaded western Scotland, and the following month the duke of Monmouth's forces landed at Lyme Regis in Dorset. Ireland generally remained calm during this period, partly because the government took adequate security precautions in the north and partly because it treated both nonconformists and Catholics with relative leniency. The Sharps were probably unsettled in July when Irish Catholics, on learning of Monmouth's defeat, burned his effigy in Francis Street and set fire to stools and chairs in the High Street. Nevertheless, political, religious, and economic conditions were reasonably favorable until mid-1686, prompting relatively few people to emigrate from Ireland.[1]

The Quakers were rather optimistic at James' succession. Sharp observed that "the Best sort of protestants trusted God, [and] believed he was sufficient to preserve them to himself; they Looked not for worldly Interests and places of profit, and . . . had the King been a turk or heathen they were of the primitive christians faith to be subject to them as Caesar, and to be subject to God as God." For the Friends the first two years of James' reign was a time of sporadic though relatively minor persecution. William Edmundson plausibly attributed this intermittent harassment to the unsettledness of people's minds under the new regime. Anticipating a crackdown on Protestants with a Catholic on the throne, some officials disrupted Quaker meetings and arrested Friends, including Edmundson, but their incarceration was brief. Returning to Ireland, Burnyeat attended large, peaceful meetings in Dublin and Ulster. At the six-months meeting in Dublin in May 1685, he witnessed "a very great Appearance of Friends out of the Country; many say, they have not seen so many ever before." So crowded were public meetings in Dublin that the meetinghouse could not accommodate all who desired to attend. Burnyeat pointedly contrasted the openness in which the Friends gathered with the behavior of other Protestant nonconformists, who, he said, "shrink and hide," and rail at Quakers who "do not flie into holes as they do."[2]

The Friends did what they could to persuade the government to treat them tolerantly. On 3 November 1685 George Whitehead gave Clarendon, who was still in London, a select list of Irish Quakers whom the earl might receive in groups of two or three when they had occasion to seek relief. Clarendon assured him they would be as free to see him as Whitehead had been. Three days later Fox wrote to Friends in Ireland, asking that two or three call on Clarendon after he arrived in Dublin, and suggesting appropriate names.[3] I have found no record indicating which Friends visited Clarendon, though Sharp may have been one. In any event he continued to contact other magistrates on behalf of suffering Quakers. In January 1685 he was awaiting "a perfect accompt" from Daniel White of Friends who had suffered at the assizes for refusing to pay tithes; Sharp had been under instructions to present this material in a petition to the judges or the lord lieutenant and Council, but the Leinster provincial meeting, perhaps anticipating a change in the government, suspended this plan on the 5th. In November of the same year the half-yearly meeting delegated Sharp and others to speak with a judge on behalf of Elizabeth Cuppage, who had been excommunicated and faced imprisonment, and with a Church of Ireland minister and an official in an ecclesiastical court on behalf of Wicklow Friends charged with failure to pay tithes.[4]

The continuing need for Sharp's services in this area throughout 1686 indicates that Quakers still faced persecution even in this relatively tolerant period. In February the Leinster provincial meeting deputed Sharp and Burnyeat to write to the meeting for sufferings in London on behalf of three Quaker men imprisoned on the Isle of Man, asking English Friends to persuade the earl of Derby to intercede with the island's governor for their release. Three months later Edmundson sought Sharp's assistance after receiving an appeal from John Hull, who was experiencing legal difficulty in the diocese of Cork. In August the Leinster meeting dispatched Sharp, Edmundson, and Francis Randall of Randall's Mills, near Enniscorthy, to the assizes at Clonmel to seek the release of the husbandman Gershon Boate of Borrisoleigh, county Tipperary, whose father, Gerard, had been Charles I's physician; Thomas Starkey went in Randall's place, and the three men attained their objective. Sharp took the occasion to visit other meetings on his journey. The same year William Brownlow of Ballyhagan, county Armagh, asked Sharp to take his petition for release to William Smyth, bishop of Raphoe, who reportedly thought Brownlow and others had been liberated, and edit the document to alter anything Smyth found objectionable.[5]

Conditions worsened in the summer of 1686 owing especially to outbreaks of violence between Irish soldiers and Dublin citizens, and to talk among the Gaelic Irish about recovering their lands and subjugating the English. Trade declined, investments fell, and emigration began to rise, although the numbers of those leaving Ireland remained comparatively small. In March, Gaelic Irishmen had killed some of Sharp's cattle at Killinure, Queen's County (Laois). Like the subsequent attacks on cattle by the "Houghers" that began in county Galway in the early 1710s, this act was probably motivated by resentment against the use of land for grazing rather than tillage. More trouble erupted later in 1686 when Irish soldiers prohibited the popular commemoration on 23 October of Protestant deliverance in the 1641 uprising and again on 5 November of the Gunpowder Plot, extinguishing bonfires and breaking windows in the mayor's house, thereby inciting riots in which some people died. Rumors circulated of a mammoth English conspiracy to cut Irish throats at night, and in January 1687 three Irish men robbed a Quaker named

Gay—probably Penn's comrade John Gay—and murdered his female servant in Dublin, a crime for which they went to the gallows in April.[6] There is no record of the effect of all this on Sharp, but the following May Edmundson wrote to him and Burnyeat concerning his confrontation with dragoons at his Mountmellick home. The commanding officer had denounced Edmundson as a traitor and a rebel when he refused to feed soldiers who were to be quartered in his house. Although he eventually allowed two dragoons to use his best room and fed them oat bread, fresh milk and butter, cheese, and boiled veal, they scorned the food, verbally abused him, and caused him to fear for his life. Edmundson requested that Sharp and Burnyeat convey his protest to the earl of Tyrconnel, the new lord deputy, warning that quartering troops in the countryside would force many people to leave their employment.[7]

On 11 April 1687, one week after James had proclaimed the declaration of indulgence in England, Tyrconnel reissued it in Ireland, officially providing toleration to dissenters. Responding to the lord deputy's request that nonconformists submit declarations of gratitude to the king, the Dublin men's meeting drafted a statement and sent it to Friends throughout the country for approbation. When the document was ready, a delegation that included Sharp, John Edmundson (William's brother), Roger Roberts, and Abraham Fuller presented it to Tyrconnel in early July. Expressing their gratitude in the declaration, the Friends described themselves as "tyed to the King, as with a threefold Coard that cann neavour be broeken: which is greater then all outward Bonds."[8]

The indulgence's impact in Ireland was less immediate than might have been expected, the claim of one Friend notwithstanding. "After such an hard Fight of Affliction, through many Persecutions and Tribulations," he wrote, "the Churches began to be at outward Peace, and have their Aggrievances in some Measure redressed." Yet at the six-months meeting on 9 and 10 May 1687, the delegates complained that Friends in several places were suffering because of their refusal to take oaths when wills were proved, the actions of episcopal courts against those who refused to pay tithes, and the quartering of sometimes abusive soldiers in private homes. The meeting deputed Sharp, Burnyeat, William Edmundson, Rogers, and four others to draft a petition to the lord deputy seeking redress of these grievances, and several of them presented it to Tyrconnel or his secretary.[9] This appears to have been delivered prior to the declaration of thanks in July, and was probably the undated document in the Sharp Manuscripts addressed to James II from

Sharp, Fuller, Edmundson, Randall, Trafford, and John Tottenham. Referring to the recent national meeting, it thanked the king for providing liberty of conscience, professed the Quakers' loyalty, and then recounted their grievances.

> Notwithstanding the great distractions In this Kingdom the generality of our friends have kept in their places and employments, yet they have been made a very great spoil of, so that many of them and their families are already ruined. And many more in several counties are spoiling daily by robberies and outrages.

The petitioners entreated James not to credit accusations against the Quakers without first giving them an opportunity to defend themselves.[10]

By the summer of 1687 the religious atmosphere was sufficiently encouraging for either Sharp or the merchant Amos Strettell to urge public Friends in England to visit Ireland, adding that there was now a "great openness in the Country." Nevertheless, Quakers continued to suffer and Sharp's assistance was still required. Boate had needed his help in the late spring, and in November Sharp and Starkey consulted with the lord chief justice about the imprisonment of Thomas Cuppage, a member of the Moate meeting, and subsequently sought, with the assistance of Henry Hillary of Wexford, a writ for Cuppage's release. When the mayor and deputy recorder of Carrickfergus denied legal redress to Thomas Calvert of Ballyhagan, county Armagh, to recover a debt because he had been excommunicated, the national meeting directed Sharp and Starkey to draft a petition to Tyrconnel and the Council on his behalf, noting that such actions impeded commerce. Sharp and Starkey took their complaint to the lord chief justice, who agreed to hear the case and make an example of the Carrickfergus magistrates because they had improperly used a sentence of excommunication in an inferior court. The meeting also asked Sharp to obtain professional legal advice in the case.[11]

The six-months meeting noted in November 1687 that Friends facing prosecution for their refusal to pay tithes required the assistance of well-qualified Quakers at assizes and quarter sessions. Each provincial meeting therefore received directions to appoint suitable Friends in every county to attend assizes and sessions to aid their coreligionists. Moreover, the same national meeting called on each provincial assembly to ensure that at least six qualified men were designated to seek relief from the government as necessary, a practice that had been adopted when the six-months meeting was founded in 1668, but had mostly lapsed.[12] Besides representing the Leinster and six-months meetings in such a capacity, Sharp continued to write petitions on behalf of suffering Friends, including Edmundson, Joseph Boardman, and John Barcroft of Ardkill, county Kildare, in the late 1680s.[13]

While he was aiding Friends in legal difficulty, Sharp became embroiled in several matters involving Church of Ireland clerics. In the spring of 1686 William King, then rector of St. Werburgh's, Dublin, preached before Tyrconnel and the Council, reportedly accusing the Quakers of denying Christ's divinity and assorted other charges. At the behest of the Dublin men's meeting Sharp, Burnyeat, and Starkey called on King to ascertain if the charges were true, but he denied them.[14] Earlier the same year another Anglican minister, John Hollin, had begun attending Quaker meetings, claiming to be a Friend. The apparent propaganda value was more than outweighed by the fact that Hollin was living with a woman to whom he was not married. Claiming she was only his housekeeper, Hollin reluctantly promised to "put her away" if the Friends insisted. This indeed was their resolve, but Hollin agreed to do so only if he ascertained that her husband was still alive in England; if not, he intended to marry her. Deeming Hollin's actions contrary to their principles, the Dublin men's meeting testified against him. In May he told the meeting he would dismiss the woman when he found another housekeeper, but by July the Dublin Friends had discovered that Hollin had deserted his own wife in England and that the housekeeper had abandoned not only her husband but her children. If this were not enough, Hollin maintained a "tippling house" and was himself sometimes inebriated. When the Friends asked him to give up the alehouse because it dishonored "truth," he disputed their judgment. Finally, on 29 July 1686, the meeting publicly disowned him.[15]

Less than a year later, on the very day James issued his declaration of indulgence in England, 4 April 1687, the Dublin assembly responded affirmatively to a Protestant petition asking that dissenters be exempt from the oath of supremacy. James subsequently decided to recall Dublin's charter and issue a new one, including a provision that those who refused to swear could simply state their fidelity to the king and the corporation. When the government expressed interest in including Friends in corporations, the Dublin men's meeting commissioned Sharp and Clarridge to inquire of the attorney general which charters would be formulated first. If it were necessary to submit any names prior to the six-months meeting in November, Sharp and Clarridge were to consult with Burnyeat, Seaton, Amos Strettell, Roberts, and four others.[16]

When Dublin received its new charter in November, ten of the twenty-four aldermen were Protestants, including two Quakers, Sharp and Clarridge; fifteen of the forty-eight burgesses were also Protestants. Sharp was admitted to office upon his affirmation of loyalty. Friends also served as aldermen at Cashel, Cork, and Limerick. Looking back on this in 1691, William King would complain bitterly that James II's government had encouraged "the most Obstinate and Perverse Sectaries, ... shewing them Favour according as they were most opposite and refractory to all Ecclesiastical Discipline and paying their Dues to the Clergy." This, he averred, was "one reason of their peculiar Fondness of Quakers," whom they appointed aldermen and burgesses, using them to destroy ecclesiastical discipline.[17] Presumably this was how many Church of Ireland stalwarts viewed the new charter and its consequences in late 1687.

Beginning around this time, the Friends enjoyed relatively easy access to Tyrconnel. A list of nineteen Quakers with such entree included five from Dublin, namely Sharp, Burnyeat, Starkey, Roberts, and Atherton. Among the others were Edmundson, Fuller, Rogers, Trafford, and Randall. On 12 November 1687 Edmundson reported to Fox that he and others had called on the lord deputy and chancellor several times, and that "they are redy to heer us."[18]

The Friends' participation in the magistracy and on governing bodies raised questions of appropriate conduct. Consequently, in November 1687 the six-months meeting directed Burnyeat and John Watson to draft a statement advising Quakers engaged in such activities "to keep to the truth in every thing, that the honour thereof may be cheifly in their eye & that no Just offence may be given by them." The resulting document urged Quaker officeholders "to keep low, tender and watchfull in all things, upon all occasions, in all Societies or Assemblys," not least because many of their colleagues would have no knowledge of the Friends' principles. Burnyeat and Watson advised Quaker officials to wait for the Spirit's counsel in their hearts, whereby they could "be a good savour" among the other magistrates and work for justice. As in other areas of life, fidelity to the truth and its simplicity was crucial: "Be carefull to keep the Testimony of the Truth, in the true self denial, through taking up the Cross in keeping out off such words, Customs,

Gestures & Garbs as are not agreeable to the simplicity of the truth, nor doth answer the plainness of our holy Profession."[19]

Fox too weighed in with advice in a letter to Edmundson on 28 November, admonishing Quaker officeholders not to take or give oaths or to wear the traditional gowns and "strange Kind of habits." When they met with other officials, they were not to remove their hats. Nor were Quaker magistrates to participate in banquets for mayors, aldermen, and common councillors, but they could attend meals for the poor inasmuch as the latter were unable to reciprocate. Fox counseled Quaker magistrates to render justice to all, punish malefactors, preserve each person's rights and property, and disturb no one's "divine right or liberty, for the good, Just, holy and Righteous law of God preserves all both In their divine right and Liberty and in their Natural Liberty and property." Finally, Fox wanted Quaker aldermen and burgesses to caucus in order to present a common front. Edmundson apparently shared Fox's letter with Sharp, who preserved a copy among his manuscripts.[20]

Sharp also saved a copy of Fox's subsequent letter to Edmundson, dated 3 February 1688, which exhorted Quaker officeholders to remove the yoke of tithes. Let everyone who desires a clergyman "to say amen and turn his hour Glass, and Lay his cushion, and will have a meeting house" pay voluntarily. The gospel should be supported without charge according to apostolic doctrine, Fox argued, but "as long as their is a national priest held up by a National maintenance of tithes and offerings every sect will strive to get that mony Law," that is, mandatory tithes. If the government summoned Friends to court for refusal to pay tithes, Fox insisted that Quaker magistrates not sit as judges, for in so doing they would condemn themselves. Again he urged Quaker officeholders to caucus, at which time he wanted Edmundson to read aloud both this letter and its predecessor.[21] Both epistles were read in March 1688 to the Leinster meeting, which then forwarded copies to the other provincial assemblies and the six-months meeting. When the latter convened in May, it directed Edmundson, Burnyeat, Roberts, and three others to consult all Quaker magistrates who were present.[22]

During his tenure as an alderman Sharp was supposed to attend sessions of the Dublin assembly, but many aldermen and burgesses failed to fulfil this responsibility, and commencing in late February 1688 an alderman faced a fine of 2s. 3d. for each absence. Judging from their committee assignments Sharp and Clarridge took their responsibilities seriously. The latter was involved in implementing the assembly's decision in November 1687 to provide the city's first regular system of night lighting—the use of lanterns and candles between 5:00 and 10:00 p.m. during the winter to prevent "mischiefs and inconveniences." Both men were members of a committee that contracted for the removal of dirt, ashes, and filth in city streets, and in September 1688 Sharp was one of six aldermen, sixteen councillors, and five other magistrates appointed to audit the municipal accounts, a task any nine of these people could undertake.[23] Sharp also served on a committee that prepared a recommendation to the king for the establishment of a ballast office. By 1688 the Liffey had silted up to the point that the channel was no longer passable, even for small boats, except during spring high tides. To dredge the channel and keep it open the assembly wanted seamen to obtain their ballast solely from the channel bottom rather than the banks, hence the desire for a ballast office. In September 1688 each alderman was responsible for collecting voluntary subscriptions in his ward to pay for dredging. The onset of revolution and war, however, precluded founding the ballast office.[24]

In other actions during Sharp's tenure as an alderman, the assembly, following Tyrconnel's recommendation, limited the number of hackney coaches in Dublin to eighty and charged each an annual fee of 50s., with the proceedings going to the municipal workhouse. In December 1687 the assembly also authorized the disbursement of £20 *per annum* to fund a school where children of the poor could study mathematics. Sharp's signature appears only once in the aldermen's minutes, namely, when he and a dozen others affixed their names to the discharge of the merchant John Rogerson as an alderman in March 1689 because he had moved to England. With the lord mayor, recorder, and eleven other aldermen, Sharp also excused the alderman Michael Lincoln from serving as lord mayor because of his advanced age in return for a fine of £50.[25]

A more detailed picture of the municipal government's concerns and personnel can be reconstructed from the corporation's book of accounts, though no entries survive from 27 September 1687 to Michaelmas 1691, which includes Sharp's aldermanic term. Nevertheless, the entries detailing disbursements for fiscal 1685–86 (the last such data before the gap) offer a reasonable view of the range of matters that would have occupied Sharp and his colleagues a few years later. The city budget was sizable, with income having risen from nearly £1,537 in 1665 to £2,871 in 1687; the average during the period 1683–87 was £2,821. In 1691 the city coffers amassed £3,673, and between 1693 and

1706 the average would rise to approximately £4,992, a reflection of urban growth and inflation.[26]

The disbursements for fiscal 1685–86 covered both the mundane and the ostentatious, or so it probably seemed to Sharp when he became intimately involved beginning in 1687. While some personnel costs were for functionaries and essential workers, others paid for ceremonial figures, namely, the bearer of the great mace (£25), the sword-bearer (£25), the city drummer (£4), the city trumpeter (£7 16s., including livery), extra trumpeters for special occasions (£9 15s.), and ten city musicians (£20). The recorder received £35, the clerk of the council £4, the lord mayor's porter £8, the porter at the Exchange £10, the Tholsel's janitor £4, and the city's blacksmith £5. The corporation paid one beadle £10 plus a bonus of 40s. for his "extraordinary and diligent attendance" on the mayor, while the other beadle earned £5 15s.; the outlay for both included their livery. Leaving the lord mayor aside, the city expended slightly more money for ceremonial personnel than officials and municipal employees—a clear indication of ritual's importance as a manifestation of the city's stateliness and a device to enhance civic loyalty among its residents.[27]

Non-personnel matters ranged from repairs and routine maintenance to charity, legal concerns, the apprehension of various malefactors, and purchases for special needs. Maintenance costs included disbursements to repair the Exchange's dials, to glaze the Wood Street schoolhouse windows, for carpentry work at Wood Quay, for the maintenance of seats and cushions for city dignitaries at Christ Church, to repair the gate and clean the walks in St. Stephen's Green, for repairs on the Donnybrook and Essex bridges, and for paving work. The city made outlays as well for supplies, such as coal, candles, maps, brooms, flowerpots and flowers, herbs, timber, newsletters, and cloth for its livery and the municipal court. (Sharp may have sold this cloth to the city; the supplier is normally not identified, though in fiscal 1702–1703 the book of accounts records that the city paid him £6 6s. 9d. for green cloth for the Tholsel.) Among the special purchases were a clock for the Exchange, sixty sycamore trees for Oxmantown Green, three dozen "Turkey-work" chairs for the Tholsel (of the kind condemned by Sharp and the Quakers for personal use), and a coat of arms for Clarendon when he received the freedom of the city. A modest £24 15s. 9d. was expended for charity, of which £18 went to six widows. In contrast, law suits and attorney's fees required disbursements of £195 3s. 6d., and a further

£12 was used to pay jurors summoned from county Meath to hear two trials in King's Bench between the city and county of Dublin over a disputed boundary. The authorities dispensed an additional £4 5s. to arrest several people who had been "trepanned [entrapped] on board Shipps [in the harbor] bound for America."[28]

A final category of expenses related to special civic occasions of the sort in which Sharp may have participated during his aldermanic term. These included the celebrations to commemorate James' accession and coronation as well as the monarchy's restoration in 1660. The traditional ceremony of riding the franchises (discussed in the next chapter) required £7 10s. plus £4 for the trumpeters. It was also customary for the lord mayor, aldermen, sheriffs, and others to view the water supply at Templeogue, southwest of the city, which required an outlay of £4 4s., plus coach hire and a further £10 10s. 3d. for dinner on this occasion. The city government also funded various special "treates," including one for Ormond, one for the committee responsible for the accounts when it entertained the duke at the Tholsel, one for the city council, and yet another for those who arranged for Newgate's repair.[29] In addition to these occasions, several of which were replete with pageantry, the lord mayor would have conducted other, less formal dealings in relatively opulent circumstances, for he had a very substantial personal budget "towards Support of the dignity of the Kings Sword in [the] yeare of his Mayralty"—£500 for Sir John Knox in fiscal 1685–86.[30] If Sharp was uncomfortable amid such surroundings, he did not shy away from active participation in the work of the assembly and its committees.

Sharp was especially interested in the problem of the poor, whose numbers were increasing in Dublin. Indeed, throughout the country slightly more than half the population lived at the subsistence level. In March 1669 the Dublin assembly had complained that the city was "much annoyed with beggars," who reputedly dishonored it. To remedy the situation the assembly proposed to banish beggars from other areas and establish a hospital to care for Dublin's indigent. By the time it opened in 1675, the hospital was in fact a free school, with no provisions to assist needy adults.[31] The aldermen directed the city recorder to locate land for a workhouse in April 1682, but nothing came of this, and in January 1684, when the poor were experiencing severe distress because of inclement weather, the aldermen called on ministers and churchwardens to exhort their parishioners to donate coal for the indigent. Several years later, in December 1687, Tyrconnel and the Council recommended founding a public workhouse on Dublin's outskirts to put able-bodied beggars to work and assist the impotent. Faced with insufficient funds, the assembly suggested that money might be saved if inhabitants assumed responsibility for cleaning the streets in front of their homes. In addition, the assembly set aside £740 of the £840 received from the toll on corn (wheat) for the workhouse. Sharp and Clarridge served on the committee to oversee the workhouse. When the city was still short of funds five months later, the assembly recommended that the next grand jury seek the necessary money from those inhabitants of Dublin who could afford to pay, and it authorized the workhouse committee to appoint undertakers, overseers, and workers.[32]

The coming of revolution and war sidelined efforts to build the workhouse. Meanwhile Robert Parker, master of Bridewell, the house of corrections, articulated a plan to employ beggars at carding, spinning, weaving, knitting, beating hemp, and similar activities according to their abilities until they could post security to leave Dublin. He offered to donate the clothing they made to boys at the hospital. Because the assembly lagged in its funding of Bridewell, however, he warned that he would provide bread for the impotent only if he received his arrears. In response to his request that Bridewell be fitted with small sheds in which the indigent could toil, the assembly asked the lord mayor, the sheriffs, Aldermen Sharp and Reader, and four burgesses to see that this was done.[33]

It was almost certainly during Sharp's tenure as an alderman that he drafted a proposal to deal with Dublin's poor. Although the document itself apparently has not survived, Crabb briefly summarized it, noting that Sharp discussed the causes of poverty, proposed reforms to reduce the number of beggars, and submitted his plan to the lord mayor.[34] Perhaps inevitably, the problem continued, and in the spring of 1695 the assembly complained bitterly that many sturdy mendicants in Dublin sent their children at night to beg at doors, crying piteously and disquieting the residents; those who refused to donate risked being robbed. Two years later the assembly again protested about the "swarms" of beggars, but not until 1699 did the city begin constructing a workhouse. Whatever its fate, the city acquired other property in 1703 at a cost of £740 4s., and the duchess of Ormond laid the foundation stone in October. Funded by a tax on Dublin householders and completed in 1706, it was caring for more than 300 impotent poor and older orphans by 1707.[35]

Revealing a keen sense of civic-mindedness, Sharp's service as an alderman thus provided him with an opportunity to focus on various problems facing the city, ranging from night-lighting and the need to dredge the river channel to establishing a school for children of the poor and regulating the number of hackney cabs on the congested streets. The gravest problem—the growing number of indigent people—was the one with which he was most concerned, though the onset of revolution and war overshadowed his proposed reforms. The government recognized his financial expertise when it appointed him to audit the accounts. His rewards for service were largely intangible and must have been measured in prestige and whatever inner satisfaction he derived from contributing to the debate over municipal problems. In April 1688 the assembly did decide that the children of the lord mayor, recorder, aldermen, and burgesses could be enrolled without entry fines to trade in the city. The enactment included Sharp's sons, Isaac, Joseph, and Jonathan, as well as Clarridge's children, Lydia, Anne (or Anna), and Benjamin.[36]

Sharp was in the midst of his aldermanic term[37] when William Prince of Orange invaded England in November 1688 after months of planning and pledges of support from the "immortal seven," Sir Henry Sidney, Admiral Edward Russell, Richard Lord Lumley, the earls of Devonshire, Danby, and Shrewsbury, and Henry Compton, bishop of London. With William's acquiescence James fled to France the following month, leaving behind considerable mob violence, most of it directed against Catholics. Reports of Catholics massacring Protestants in Ireland were widespread, as were fears that disbanded Irish troops in England would go on a bloody rampage. The specter of disorder and violence undoubtedly helped to spur William and Parliament to reach a constitutional settlement, and on 13 February William and Mary accepted Parliament's offer of the crown and assented to the Declaration of Rights. In Ireland, however, Catholic support for James was strong, and Tyrconnel established control of Dublin and most of the south. Fearing a repetition of the violence of 1641, some Protestants fled to England or Scotland, while others sought safety in the walled towns. Burnyeat was among those who contemplated flight to England, but he finally decided that only his son should go. Other Protestants remained loyal to James in 1688 and early 1689, but switched their allegiance after the Jacobite Parliament repealed the Restoration land settlement in June.[38] Sharp apparently gave no serious consideration to fleeing.

Like other Protestants the Friends experienced considerable disquietude in the early months of 1689. They had met peacefully and sometimes in large numbers the previous year, and the Leinster provincial meeting was confident enough of the future in January 1689 to plan the sites of its forthcoming gatherings. Burnyeat later recalled that "many Testimonies came from Friends of sundry Meetings, for all to mind the Lord's preserving Power, and not to let Fears take hold of them, as it did of others, who knew not the Lord." But he also likened people's hearts to troubled waters. As the conflict unfolded, Joseph Pike observed that English people in Ireland lived in constant terror, fearing a recurrence of 1641.[39]

As the climate of fear and violence intensified, many people armed themselves and seized control of fortified places. On 25 January 1689 Tyrconnel and the Council issued a proclamation condemning such actions as riotous assemblies, likening them to high treason, and ordering those who had occupied fortified sites to withdraw. The following month he attempted to disarm Protestants in Dublin and commandeer serviceable horses.[40] But the government's troops were themselves part of the problem, particularly when quartered in the citizens' homes. Edmundson and his family again suffered at their hands, as soldiers assaulted and attempted to trample him, threatened to burn the house, shot his dog, and smashed his windows. Two months later, on 11 March, Edmundson beseeched Sharp to ask the lord deputy to transfer two companies quartered at Mountmellick, not least because a third company was also stationed there. Between them they threatened to exhaust the supply of hay, which would lead to the death of cattle in the area. To a Quaker in America a distressed Sharp described how Friends and others were robbed at night, their "houses broaken up [and] their cattle driven away to the ruining [of] many thousand Families."[41]

In the north, Protestants organized themselves in armed associations in Sligo and Ulster, prompting Tyrconnel and the Council to order them to disperse in March 1689. Arriving in Dublin the same month, James issued a proclamation on the 25th affirming the free exercise of religion in Ireland and commanding all Irish subjects in Scotland and England to return within forty days. At their next six-months meeting in May, the Friends sent an address to James thanking him, pledging their loyalty, and, noting that many of them had been despoiled, seeking his protection.[42]

The time of troubles lasted until the signing of the so-called Treaty of Limerick in October 1691. Jacobite forces besieged Derry from April 1689 until William's naval force relieved the city on 31 July, the same day his troops defeated the Jacobites at Enniskillen in county Fermanagh. In Sharp's judgment the misery inflicted on the people of Derry constituted divine retribution for their repudiation of a Quaker who had gone there a year earlier seeking their repentance. Williamite forces captured Carrickfergus later in the summer, and William himself landed with 15,000 men at Belfast in June 1690. "We all expected action," Sharp recalled. On 1 July William engaged and defeated James' army at the river Boyne. The days that followed brought turmoil to Dublin. Sharp described what happened when James' fleeing troops arrived in the capital:

> Fear possesed them, yet the[y] had account that king William was Killed, which made them run through this city with very great Shouting. The protestants [were] kept as prisoners or so close in their houses. They were not suffered to peep out, but in danger of Being shot. However it was Shomberg [who] was killed in the fight, and the news of the enemies persuing and their fear made them hastily leave the city. Some say Some of the Romish clergy desired liberty to Burn the city and he [James] would not grant it.

On 4 July James fled to France, having received shelter from Friends such as Francis Randall of Wexford on his southward journey.[43] The story that he met Sharp in Dublin before he took ship cannot be confirmed. Fighting continued until the Irish defenders of Limerick, the last Jacobite stronghold, were ready to negotiate peace. Most of James' remaining troops, some 12,000 in all, received permission to embark for France.

Sharp wrote an account of the war, including its economic impact. "The clouds and Darkness long gathering hath been great, the adversity and calamity long and heavy, and still many are in great distress where the Burdens of the armies are," he observed. James had commandeered tallow, wool, leather, and hides and required manufacturers to supply him with cloth at a loss. Sharp was among those who suffered financially because of such practices, on one occasion, for instance, having to provide a tun of tallow valued at £42 for £30. Yet he and fellow Quaker merchants did so without protest, prompting other Protestants to accuse them of supporting the Jacobites. To this, Sharp retorted that the Friends for reasons of conscience could not "be concerned in wars nor Incouraged it; we have not assisted on any such account, but are altogether clear; we wisht King James well and Looked on it [as] a great Judgment that he was given up to that principle and council, and so it was a Judgment to the nation."[44]

Evidence of Quaker suffering during the time of troubles is both ample and widespread, though this was not a period of unrelieved persecution. On 2 August 1689 James, professing his satisfaction with the Friends' loyalty, placed their families, lands, and possessions under his protection and exempted them from the penalties imposed on disaffected Protestants in previous proclamations. Moreover, in a proclamation dated 31 December 1689 he confirmed his tender of liberty of conscience and directed commissioners of oyer and terminer to punish those who because of indiscreet zeal had usurped his prerogative by impeding the exercise of such liberty.[45] In his journal Burnyeat confirmed the existence of a considerable degree of religious freedom during the time of troubles, observing that meetings were often large, sometimes because they attracted other Protestants whose ministers had fled. Apart from the areas occupied by warring troops, Burnyeat enjoyed unimpeded movement on his travels until his death in September 1690. He was careful to distinguish, however, between freedom of worship, which the Quakers enjoyed, and the suffering they sustained because of the military conflict. "Their Trials have been very great, and the Dangers, as to appearance, dreadful; yet Friends have kept to their Habitations, trusting in the Lord, and following their lawful Concerns and Business."[46] During the war's final throes, Sharp traveled to England on business in the spring of 1691, and Clarridge was also there.[47]

Through his correspondence Sharp helped to monitor the war's impact on Friends throughout Ireland. His papers contain accounts from Quakers at such places as Lisburn, Lurgan, and Ballyhagan in the north; Cork and county Wexford in the south; Limerick in the west; and Maynooth in county Kildare. Sharp used some of this material to petition the government for relief. Because he enjoyed access to James, as did Edmundson, he may have personally presented a petition from the Friends of county Armagh to the king; dated 12 April 1689 it described the seizure of their cattle, horses, and tools as well as some of their wheat and household possessions. The following month the six-months meeting appointed Sharp and thirteen others to draft a petition to James citing the extent of Quaker losses, which in Leinster alone had exceeded £900 by that point. When Sharp, Edmundson, Fuller, Randall, and Trafford delivered it to the king, he promised to protect the Friends. Sharp was probably also responsible for submitting a petition from Quakers at Edenderry, King's County (Offaly), to the lords justices seeking relief from the quartering of soldiers and the imposition of allegedly excessive charges.[48]

Sharp played an important part in the compilation of records concerning the sufferings. In May 1689 the national meeting instructed each provincial assembly to prepare an account of all "the Spoyles and Roberies Committed on them in these distracted times" and submit it to the next six-months meeting. The Leinster provincial meeting in turn asked each constituent member to provide such data. When the national meeting convened in November, it delegated Sharp, Strettell, or Thomas Winslow to calculate Quaker losses, whether from robberies or expropriations for the king's forces. Sharp, Burnyeat, Edmundson, and Fuller then drafted an address to James, noting damages of more than £7,000 in Munster and Leinster. When Edmundson, Burnyeat, and Randall presented the document to the king, he responded sympathetically.[49]

Nevertheless the depredations continued, as did Sharp's activities on the victims' behalf. After Cavan burned, the Friends there appointed Sharp to write to the provincial meeting on their behalf, seeking material assistance. The Dublin men's meeting sent £3 but also had Sharp and the merchant Alexander McClellan ask the victims to move to Dublin if they could not subsist in Cavan. In March 1691 Sharp also disbursed money and collected secondhand clothing and linen for Quakers whose houses had burned at Edenderry. For the Dublin men's meeting Sharp compiled data on suffering, as he did for the six-months meeting. When the number of Quakers needing relief became too great for the national meeting to handle as a body in May 1691, it appointed five committees; Dublin's comprised Sharp, Roberts, and John Stevens. The same meeting asked Sharp, William Edmundson, and two others to report the "many callamityes" experienced by Irish Quakers to the yearly meeting in London, and it instructed Sharp to provide copies to the provincial assemblies.[50]

The reports to Sharp manifest a wide variety of suffering at the hands of soldiers and robbers, or "rapparees" as they were known in Ireland. Such people, reflected a dismayed Jacobite captain, "having overstocked themselves with other men's cattle . . . destroyed millions throughout the kingdom only for their hides or tallow, and sometimes only to exercise their malice, leaving the carcasses to rot in the fields." In the north the seizure of agricultural implements made it virtually impossible to plant crops. Travel to meetings was hazardous because of rapparees and sometimes impossible owing to troop movements; at times, meetings had to move from one location to another because of the fighting. Even when the roads were clear, some Friends could not attend meetings because troops had commandeered their horses; when a Quaker at Lisburn protested such expropriation, a soldier stabbed him. The seizure and en-

suing slaughter of cattle for food left victims without the means to re-
plenish their herds. At Ballyhagan William's troops seized barns, fences,
sheds, and even part of the meetinghouse for fuel.[51] Landlords who insisted that rent be paid and relentless efforts to collect tithes compounded the distress. Even during the time of troubles Sharp's services
were needed to seek relief for Friends punished for their refusal to pay
tithes.[52]

By May 1691 Quakers estimated their losses at nearly £40,000 because of the Gaelic Irish alone, excluding the impact of free quarter and
damage inflicted by James' fleeing supporters. Because many Friends
lost everything, relief was essential. Two years earlier the London yearly
meeting had asked the meeting for sufferings to present Irish Friends'
needs to their coreligionists in England and Wales, but as late as November 1690 the Irish Quaker community still had sufficient means to
care for its own. Sharp and Trafford consequently asked the meeting for
sufferings to reserve its "charitable benevolence" until it became necessary.[53] That time came in May 1692 when the six-months meeting accepted £600 from English Quakers, who also donated an additional
£150 to Friends in Ulster; an English Quaker's legacy provided a further
£60, and Friends in Barbados sent £100. English Quakers gave £1,060
more by November and an additional £3,222 10s. in early 1693. As
generous as they were, these gifts amounted to a small fraction of the
total losses sustained by Irish Friends, which may have reached
£100,000.[54]

An unknown number of Quaker refugees fled to Dublin during the
time of troubles, though the city experienced a scarcity of bread in the
autumn of 1689 and high prices for wheat, meal, wool, leather, and
other commodities. Sharp was still an alderman when the lord mayor,
Sir Terence McDermott, reported to James that on the aldermen's recommendation he hoped to set prices for many goods and directed the
guilds "to call theire respective Halls and consider of their respective
Wages & prices of their Comodities [which had been] advanced to a
greevance, and the reasons of their Exactions in the sale thereof." The
most serious problem, McDermott believed, was the scarcity of bread
and beer, especially for journeymen, followed by the high cost of such
goods as wool, tanned leather, tallow, butter, and fresh fowl. Pending
royal approval he intended to impose prices for a range of foodstuffs
and goods, including bacon (3½d. per pound); choice beef, veal, mutton, and pork (2d. per pound); lesser quality meat (1½d. per pound);
fresh butter (4½d. per pound); wool (10s. per stone); tallow (£27 per

tun); candles and soap (4d. per pound); ale (2d. a quart); "Good Marsh beer" (3d. a quart); jack and plain boots (18s. and 12s. respectively); women's leather shoes (2s. 8d.); and heavy footwear for soldiers and others (3s. 4d.). Meat deemed "not Merchantable" was to be confiscated and donated to the poor. Not surprisingly, Tyrconnel complained in February 1690 that the necessity to mint large quantities of copper coins had forced the government to pay treble the value of the goods it needed.[55]

The city suffered as well from a breakdown in military discipline. In November 1689 rampaging soldiers wrecked vacant houses, kicking down doors, pulling up floors, breaking glass, and smashing shutters, rails, and wainscoting. According to a Jacobite officer, the disciplinary collapse stemmed from the fact that half of James' troops in the city were "almost naked by reason of the badness of their clothes and the blankets, and starved for want of firing, having none but what they stole with the utter ruin of many good houses, and of all the hedges, bushes, and trees about Dublin." By the spring of 1690 James had directed Protestants in the city to provide free quarter to French troops while Catholic residents were obliged to do the same for Irish soldiers. Although conditions in the city were grim, Sharp helped to provide refugees with bedding, clothing, education for the children, and apprenticeships for young people. In the summer of 1690 the Dublin men's meeting appointed a committee of four, comprising Sharp, Roberts, Inman, and Amos Strettell, to administer assistance to needy refugees in the city.[56] For all its problems, Dublin provided welcome relief from the depredations of rapparees and warring armies.

In the capital the Quakers continued to face hostile and sometimes violent treatment at Christmas. In November 1688 the Dublin men's meeting deputed Sharp and Clarridge to ask Tyrconnel and the lord mayor to provide protection from "the dainger of spoyle & damage that usually have & may be don" during the Christmas season because Friends refused to shut their shops. The Dublin meeting dispatched Sharp and Clarridge with the same request two years later, but to little avail. Soldiers and constables closed many shops, but some Quakers made little protest, prompting the Dublin men's meeting to complain "that there has been to much an Intimation to aveyd the Cross: & not standing in the Councell of Truth to beare a testymony for truth against those supersticions of popery." On the other hand, the same meeting cautioned its members not to oppose the government rashly. Shortly before Christmas 1691, the Dublin men's meeting instructed Clarridge and the smith John Hutchinson to speak with the mayor about anticipated violence, and similar efforts would be made in ensuing years.[57] By their refusal to close their shops at Christmas the Friends called attention to their unique testimony and suffered the consequences.

The time of troubles had an obvious and devastating impact on the material possessions of many Friends, prompting some to flee to the colonies or to return to England or Scotland. Sharp was undoubtedly aware of declining attendance at weekday meetings in Dublin, for in January 1691 the Dublin men's meeting had to request members to sit together in the middle of the building. Besides the confiscation and destruction of their goods, Friends sustained damages in other ways, as when Quaker manufacturers had to make clothing for the Irish army at a loss, or when Quaker landlords in Dublin lost their rents because of James' Act of Repeal. Sharp claimed to have "lost per the Act of Repeal the use of near prairies and had no Rent for two years—£80 per annum, besides debts." His home in Queen's County (Laois) was burned and his livestock were seized or destroyed, though by 1694 he had rebuilt the house and restocked the thousand-acre estate. During the war he would also have suffered from the disruption of trade within Ireland as well as a decline in the export trade owing at least in part to privateering and the use of ships to transport troops rather than commercial cargo.[58]

Like Sharp, many Friends maintained a spirit of fortitude in the face of trying circumstances. In April 1689 the women's meeting at Lurgan resolved to "stand firm and Stedfast without wavering," and the same month their counterparts at Limerick reported they were "more near and loving to each other, and Zealous for the truth, so not worse but bettered by this day of exercise as having no refuge to Flee unto but retiredness of heart, mind and spirit to the Lord." Presumably the spirits of Irish Friends would have been uplifted by Fox's letter of 10 January 1691, which clearly revealed the extent to which their sufferings had moved him.[59] But the women from Limerick were right: In the end, the time of troubles strengthened the Friends and provided the experiential foundation on which they built in the ensuing decades. Substantial credit for this achievement must go to Sharp, whose resolute efforts on behalf of suffering Quakers helped them through these trials.

5

"What Truth Makes You Free to Do"

The World of Guild and Colony

THE GUILD CULTURE in which Sharp increasingly immersed himself was nearly as all-encompassing as the religious movement that claimed his higher loyalty. In certain aspects they shared basic concerns, including their respective commitment to uphold standards of behavior, educate youth, conduct their business in regular meetings, and care for the indigent, especially unfortunate members of their own groups. In other respects they diverged, as in their views on oaths, obeisance to the powerful, the Church of Ireland, and bearing arms. To function effectively in both cultures was therefore a considerable challenge that required a certain degree of what Joseph Ward has aptly called "giving and withholding allegiance,"[1] a process that helped to shape Sharp's sense of identity and community. Had he repudiated the guilds because of their periodic conflict with Quaker tenets and standards of conduct he would have imperiled his opportunities for success in the business community. Consequently he bided his time, increasing his involvement in the weavers' guild as opportunity presented itself, until ultimately he became its master and a long-term member of its council.

The initial step had come in September 1672 when the Dublin assembly admitted him to the freedom of the city. Simultaneously he received permission to attend meetings of the weavers' guild, though his refusal to take the required oaths precluded him from membership. Not until 1678–79 do guild records list Sharp as a quarter brother (along with ninety-six others). In May 1692 he would reflect that at some point in Charles' reign he had been "admitted free and dispenced with only for saying the contents of a free mans oath and promising to be true to the King and corporation," but he was confusing his acceptance as a quarter brother with his subsequent admission to full membership.

The guild's "Book Generall" clearly indicates that he was admitted as a free brother on 2 May 1687.[2]

As part of the program of remodeling charters, in February 1688 James II ordered Dublin guilds to renew theirs. Because the weavers' guild opposed the surrender of its charter, Sharp, at his corporation's behest, conveyed its views to Tyrconnel. Although he won a delay, ultimately the government warned the weavers to take out another charter or it would grant one to Catholic weavers who were not members of the existing guild. In Sharp's words, the corporation, "being very unwilling to Loose their Rights, house, plate &c Agreed a long petition (desiring many priviledges) should be put in and to get as much as would be granted them, which was Done."[3]

Meanwhile, the guild had learned in March 1688 that those who were unwilling to take the oaths could promise allegiance to the king and obedience to the master, wardens, and corporation. Signers of such a statement would be "granted free." A number of prominent brothers affixed their names to this statement on 26 March, beginning with master George Spence and the wardens, followed immediately by Sharp. Normally the annual election for master and wardens in this guild occurred on 25 March (or the next day if the 25th was a Sunday), but in 1688 the information about the election in the "Book Generall" follows the entry of 26 March dealing with exemptions from the oaths, suggesting that the election may have occurred later than usual. The election was unusual in other respects, for Sharp, it seems, was a last-minute candidate; his name comes at the end of the list of masters' candidates, following that of Samuel Peacock, who had been the fourth and last candidate. However, Peacock's name was lined out and Sharp's inserted. On swearing-in day, 1 May, Sharp appears to have assumed the mastership, for the entry for that date in the "Book Generall" lists him as such. Yet someone (probably the clerk) subsequently crossed out his name and added it to the ensuing list of ninety-six free brothers. The same person then named Thomas Whitlock as master, but the latter attended only the first quarterly meeting. Whitlock's tenure must have been very brief, for there is no record of his disbursements or receipts and no audit of his accounts. When Spence's accounts were audited on 5 July 1688, the balance of funds was transferred directly to Sharp.[4] Thus Whitlock's tenure cannot have been more than two months and probably did not extend beyond the first quarterly meeting. Since the guild records do not refer to substantive internal divisions at this time, the decision to switch from Sharp to Whitlock and then back again may have been tactical. Guild members may have thought that Sharp, by now an alderman and a prominent example of the royal policy of indulgence, could negotiate better terms for the new charter.

In any event, Sharp was master when, on 17 September, the guild unanimously agreed to accept a new charter and to reimburse Sharp and his wardens for any expenses incurred in obtaining it. Ten days later they petitioned Tyrconnel, noting he had previously told them he thought the cost would not exceed £20. When it became apparent that the expenses could be triple that amount, the guild obtained Tyrconnel's pledge to limit the cost to £14 plus the attorney general's fees.[5]

The new charter, which was ready on 3 December, named Sharp as master, the attorney general having rejected his request not to continue in office. Sharp had cited his reluctance to serve simultaneously as master and alderman, though holding both offices was not uncommon, as well as his objection to swearing and administering oaths. To this the attorney general retorted simply that the weavers' clerk could tender the oaths, and Sharp thereupon "promised the Substance" of the oath to be loyal to the king and true to the corporation. A handful of brothers declined to take the oath because they had previously done so, but on 10 December the corporation resolved that all weavers who had been free brothers "& doe Scruple to take the oath may be admitted by Signeing to Subscription in this book [the 'Book Generall']. . . . The Contents of the Same is to be true to the King, & this Corporation."[6]

The refusal of one of Sharp's colleagues, Thomas Bond, to take the oath in 1688 became an issue in the attack on Sharp by Joshua Bows, a lapsed Quaker, in 1692. (For more on this attack see Chapter 10.) Sharp had assumed that Bond and others would subscribe a statement embodying the substance of a brother's oath, but Bond and several others refused to compromise. Concerned about the diminishing role of Protestants, Sharp asked Bond "to continue [in] the corporation as much as he could, protestants . . . being serviceable, that the army was by the government to have the greatest number of papists and every corporation." Bows subsequently charged that the statement Sharp had asked Bond to sign undermined "the protestant Interest," and that those who had repudiated "Lord Anthonys commands" were incarcerated and forced to pay £14 or £15 for their release. However, Sharp denied the accusation, insisting that as master he had never fined or imprisoned anyone.[7]

Sharp continued as master until the autumn of 1689. In mid-August Lawrence Eustace, one of Sharp's wardens, defeated his closest competitor, Miniard Lynn, who had briefly served as Whitlock's warden, by a single vote to become master-elect. One of Eustace's first acts was to select auditors for Sharp's accounts on 1 November, with Sharp naming the others the same day.[8] In all, Sharp had been master for sixteen to nineteen months; only one other clothier, Captain John Sporle, who served two successive terms between 1703 and 1705, had a longer tenure during Sharp's years in the corporation.

When Sharp moved to Ireland, Dublin was the home of the merchants' guild and seventeen trade guilds (compared to perhaps seventy-eight or seventy-nine in seventeenth-century London); the oldest, the merchants' guild (or Trinity Guild) may have been established as early as 1190. Guild life was thriving in seventeenth-century Dublin. As corporations, the coopers (1666) and feltmakers (1667) were in their infancy when the Sharps arrived, and six other guilds—the cutlers, painters, paper-stainers, and stationers (1670), the bricklayers and plasterers (1670), the hosiers and knitters (1688), the curriers (1695), the brewers and maltsters (1696), and the joiners, ceylers (ceiling-makers), and wainscotters (1700)—sprang up during his years in the city. Although the last of the Dublin guilds—the apothecaries—dates only from 1747, well after Sharp's death forty years earlier, he witnessed and participated in the last great flowering of guilds in Dublin.[9]

The guild with which Sharp was intimately involved, the weavers', had received its charter from Henry VI in 1446. Before 1682 this corporation, like most of the others, leased its (unidentified) meeting place, for which it paid an annual rent of 20s. The tailors had their own hall, which they built in Back Lane in 1583, and the merchants convened in the Tholsel. While the bakers leased space in St. Audoen's College and the feltmakers at the Crown Tavern in Wood Quay, other corporations met in rooms above the city gates, among them the tanners and the cutlers, painters, and stationers (St. Audoen's Arch), the barber-surgeons (Pole Gate), the glovers (St. James' Gate), and the smiths (Ormond's Gate, virtually adjacent to Sharp's house). Some guilds temporarily rented space, as did the weavers, who met in the Tholsel in October 1686, and who allowed the cutlers, painters, and stationers to use their new hall in 1694–95.[10] Sharp would have been party to the unanimous decision of the guild when it asked its council in May 1681 to consider erecting a hall on waste ground in the Lower Coombe belonging to a Dr. Sturdivill. The building was completed the following year at a cost of £209, which the corporation had to borrow. Two years later the merchants' guild moved from the "middle room" in the Tholsel to the "great room," henceforth known as Trinity Guildhall, with its wainscoting and painted ceiling decorated with gilded festoons and parquetry. In the ensuing years other guilds built their own halls: the barber-surgeons in Smock Alley in 1690, the shoemakers in Cook Street in 1698, the tailors in Back Lane in 1706 (after demolishing their Elizabethan structure), and the goldsmiths in Werburgh Street in 1709. The weavers appointed a fifteen-member committee (which did not include Sharp) to manage and let their new hall.[11]

As master of the weavers' guild Sharp assumed responsibility for guiding its administrative affairs and supervising its finances. The weavers were typical in having a single master; only the merchants, with approximately 400 members by 1679, had two as well as a "Mayor of the Staple." Because of their small size, the cutlers, painters, and stationers also differed from the weavers by insisting (from 1677) that each master serve two years; those who had previously held the office for twelve months were required to do so again for only one year. This provision remained in force for the cutlers, painters, and stationers until 1704, when a member could be elected to a second one-year term only if "there shall Be No Brother Proper or Convenient to be chosen." Members of this guild seem to have imposed tighter restrictions on their masters than did the weavers, for the former fined a master or warden 38s. for going into the country or to England during his term of office without license, and commencing in 1704 an incoming master had to post a bond (set at £100 the following year) for the money, plate, and goods belonging to the guild; should he refuse, the guild's council placed the possessions in a trustee's care.[12]

During his term in office a master had the assistance of wardens, normally two in number, though the weavers (in the early 1690s) and the feltmakers for a time had four. Sharp never served as a warden. Like the master's term, a warden's was typically one year, though the cutlers, painters, and stationers employed a two-year term as they did for their masters. Wardens were normally senior members of a guild, although in 1701 the feltmakers opened the office to younger colleagues, including journeymen. Wardens who neglected their duties or were absent from meetings without legitimate excuses could be fined or even removed from office. Masters and wardens were usually excused from serving on juries or assizes during their tenure in office. The weavers expected their wardens to collect fees from the quarter brothers, including Sharp before he became a full brother in 1687.[13]

The weavers were typical in electing their masters and wardens each year, normally on 25 or 26 March. Owing to unsettled conditions during the civil war, elections occurred in August in 1689 and July the following year before returning to March in 1692. Normally four candidates stood for the weavers' mastership each year, though there were six each in 1685, 1705, and 1706 but only three in 1686 and the first election in 1698. From 1676 to 1682 the number of members voting for master's candidates rose from thirty-eight to sixty-four, with forty-five as the average. When Sharp ran, he garnered forty-five votes, handily defeating his three opponents (including the future master Richard Falkiner), who together attracted a mere fourteen supporters. In the difficult years of 1689 and 1690 the number of voters dropped to thirty and thirty-four respectively, but the guild quickly recovered and in the period 1695 to 1706 the average was nearly seventy. The high and low occurred in the same year: A mere thirty-three cast their votes for three candidates in March 1698, but the winner, Thomas Litton, opted not to serve. A new election occurred the following month in which 104 votes were cast and Israel Mitchell emerged victorious. Guild records provide no clues about why the number of voters varied so widely in the 1698 elections. The weavers selected their wardens at the time of the mastership elections, typically choosing from among three to six candidates, though nine stood in 1693 and 1694, and seven in 1703. A guild member who failed to appear and vote on election day was fined 5s. Corporation accounts indicate that at least some elections involved special expenses, such as the £2 15s. spent at the Sun Tavern in 1685.[14] Elections in the other Dublin guilds were comparable.[15]

Like their London counterparts, Dublin corporations allowed members to avoid office by paying fines.[16] In 1679, for instance, Sharp's associate Christopher Lovett paid £12 to be exempt from all guild offices for life. When the government imposed the Test in 1682, two weavers who had been elected wardens, Thomas Bond and Richard Roaper, paid fines rather than take it, possibly because they were dissenting Protestants. Escaping the fine was nearly impossible, though there was some leniency. After Moses Mark was elected master of the weavers' guild in 1692, he failed to appear on swearing-in day and was mulcted £10; the guild remitted this when he proved he had been "wind bound in England," though meanwhile it had selected another weaver for the office. In 1698 Thomas Litton's colleagues took pity on him when he declined to serve, reducing his fine of £10 by half while insisting this was not a precedent; they also stipulated that he must provide his guild associates with a "treat."[17]

Whereas most refusals to officiate were probably due to business considerations, poor health, advanced age, or family obligations, some objected for conscientious reasons. This was the case with the weavers Bond and Roaper, who refused to take the Test, as did the cutler Henry Coleman (in 1701). The oaths of supremacy and allegiance and an oath of office were customary prerequisites to assume office as master or warden, but there were exceptions, as in Sharp's case. The stationer Joseph Howse and the cutler Jonathan James paid fines of £20 and £5 respectively in 1677 for refusing to take the oaths, and a feltmaker who did not take them after being selected as an assistant faced a fine of £5.[18] Further difficulties arose with the imposition of "the little oath" beginning in 1698. This oath, which the weavers' guild conspicuously copied on the inside front cover of its "Book Generall," averred that it was unlawful to take up arms against the monarch on any pretense, and that it was traitorous to have recourse to weapons "by his Authority" against his person or those with royal commissions (as occurred during the civil war of the 1640s). The extant records of the weavers' guild do not indicate whether this oath posed problems for any of its officers, but Tryall Travers, a warden-elect in the merchants' guild, was excused from serving because he could not subscribe; he was fined a guinea and exempted from the wardenship in perpetuity, though the corporation insisted his case was not a precedent.[19]

As a master, Sharp was responsible for oversight of the financial records. Although he could call on the wardens and clerk for assistance, ultimately he was answerable for the accounts' accuracy. At the conclusion of his term in office, a former master named two or three auditors and the new master a like number to examine the ledgers. Sharp selected three men, all of whom had been masters themselves, namely, Nicholas Taylor (1677–78), Daniel Falkiner (or Faulkner, 1678–79), and George Spence (1687–88). Completed on 29 November, the audit showed receipts of £88 14s. 2½d. and disbursements of £97 3s. 5½d., leaving the corporation owing Sharp £8 9s. 3d. Because of the civil war, the money with which Sharp had to work was considerably less than that of his predecessors in the period 1681–1688, when receipts had averaged £183 10s. 8¾d. and disbursements, £135 4s. 8½d. His successor, Lawrence Eustace, fared even worse, with receipts of £55 2s. 7d. and disbursements of £71 6s. 3d. Conditions improved after the war, with average income of £107 8s. 4d. and expenses of £92 15s. in the period 1692–1694. Still, in 1706–1707 (during which Sharp died), master Nathaniel

James had receipts of only £95 7s. and outlays of £84 13s. 11d.[20] Audits in other guilds operated comparably.[21]

The weavers seem to have had no disputed audits during Sharp's years in the guild, but the cutlers, painters, and stationers had to resolve a disagreement between its auditors by a vote of the members. The most serious complaint originated with an unidentified group in the merchants' guild that petitioned in early 1663 about a breakdown in "this once renowned Corporation" because of empty coffers resulting from alleged embezzlement by masters.[22] Accurate record keeping and the expeditious rendering of accounts were a crucial aspect of every master's responsibilities. Sharp knew this not only as a master but subsequently as an auditor of Isaac Sales' ledgers in May 1706, probably his last major assignment for his company.[23]

Like other masters Sharp had the assistance of a clerk and beadles. In the London livery companies the clerks and senior beadles acquired a fair amount of influence, partly because they, unlike the masters and wardens, had much longer tenure; partly because they were best placed to serve as the society's collective memory; and partly because so much business was done by the expanding guilds through written communications, with which the clerk was extensively involved. Clerks and beadles in the smaller Dublin guilds probably had less influence, though the records provide few clues. In Dublin corporations, selecting the clerk was the responsibility of the master and guild council. The weavers paid their clerk £2 *per annum*, but in 1685 they gave masters discretion to lower or raise the salary (to a maximum of £4 *per annum*) based on the clerk's performance. The weavers' clerk received fees to perform some of his duties, including preparation of the master's accounts, for which he earned 5s. As established by Sharp and his guild brothers in 1695, the other fees indicate the range of the clerk's responsibilities: 4s. 6d. to indenture an apprentice, 3s. 6d. to swear a brother, and 6d. to prepare a certificate for someone becoming free of the guild, to enrol a free brother's child, or to register a quarter brother.[24]

Dublin guild records provide only scattered references to beadles' responsibilities, though the bricklayers and plasterers were undoubtedly typical in expecting them to aid the masters and wardens in performing their duties. Another common task was summoning members when their attendance was required beyond the regularly scheduled meetings. Their counterparts in England were primarily messengers, often selected from among junior members who would thereby have an opportunity to

meet other colleagues and acquire a solid understanding of company affairs. English guilds also employed beadles who had lost their own
shops and fallen on hard times—a form of poor relief. Sharp and the
Dublin weavers used the beadleship in a variety of ways. The principal
or senior beadle, Robert Gaunt, who received an annual stipend of £6,
participated as a guild official on ceremonial occasions, carrying a
gilded or painted staff. He had a salaried assistant, who received £4 *per
annum*. But for most beadles in the weavers' guild the office seems to
have been essentially honorific and intended as a means of raising revenue. In the years preceding Sharp's mastership such beadles were elected
and then fined 40s. on assuming their nominal office. During this period
the number chosen each year ranged from one or two to eight. This pattern continued in the 1690s, though in 1692 Sharp and his colleagues
appointed the unusual number of eighteen beadles. Another peak occurred in 1703, when the guild named twenty-one beadles. Sharp may
never have served as a beadle, but his fellow Quaker Patrick Grumley
did in 1694–95, and the Quaker Joseph Inman paid his beadleship fine
in January 1692. Samuel Clarridge, who joined the weavers' guild in
February 1704 (and had dealings with it no later than December 1686),
was on a list of forty-four members appointed to the beadleship for
1704–1705, but he died before assuming office. Throughout Sharp's
years in the corporation the most unusual fine for beadleship was imposed on William Fownes in 1695, to wit, "the value of fifteen pounds
in plate for the use of the Corporacion . . . one silver tankard, Six Silver
spoons & one silver spoon gilt with gold weighing in all forty eight
ounces and four penny Weight."[25]

Generally, both men and women could acquire full membership in a
guild. Those, such as Quakers and Catholics, who refused to take the
required oaths for reasons of conscience could be quarter brothers,
paying a stipulated fee every three months though barred from holding
guild office. This was the status Sharp attained in 1678–79. In the more
tolerant atmosphere of James' reign, the weavers' guild, as we have
seen, admitted Sharp as a free brother in May 1687, six months before
he became an alderman. At that point the number of free brothers was
107, of whom four or five were women. The number of free brothers
had generally been on the rise, having been sixty-six in 1675, reaching
121 in 1683, and then dropping back. Partial records for quarter brothers in this period indicate the number ranged from ninety-eight (1678)
to seventy-eight (1682 and 1684). The nadir for free brothers occurred
in 1689, during Sharp's mastership, when the number declined precipi-

tously to fifty-seven (all men), probably reflecting the flight of many masters to England when civil war erupted. But recovery was rapid, with eighty-nine free brothers in 1690 and 111 in 1692.[26]

In January or February 1672 Clarridge petitioned to be admitted into the freedom of the merchants' guild, "or that such rule may be given whereby he may, during his life have the liberty of exercising his trade in this City [Dublin] without interruption." On payment of a fine of £5 and a quarterly fee of 2s. 6d. he received the free exercise of his trade for life. This was the first time the Trinity Guild had granted such a petition, and the same may be true of the weavers' action in Sharp's case. Eventually, in 1691 Clarridge successfully petitioned the merchants' guild to terminate his quarterage payments after he paid his beadleship fine like the full brothers.[27]

Entry fines varied widely. Whereas Clarridge paid only £5 as a quarter brother, admission to the merchants' guild as a full brother entailed a fine of £30, after which he owed a token quarterly fee of 6d. In marked contrast the entry fee in the cutlers, painters, and stationers' guild was only £4, and in 1692 the members decided to waive even this fee in select cases if the master, wardens, and council deemed fit. The same corporation accepted plate, paintings (including one of William III), and gloves for the master's wife as payment. Even by the standards of the cutlers, painters, and stationers, the weavers imposed light fines— normally 23s. to 30s. during Sharp's mastership—and they could be tendered in installments.[28]

Although the institution of quarter brothers enabled corporations to admit Catholics, there seems to have been little enthusiasm for doing so. As early as 1662 the Trinity Guild resolved to impose a fine of £100 on any brother who took a Catholic apprentice, and during the Popish Plot scare the same corporation enacted a prohibition against admitting Catholics as quarter brothers. Those already in the Trinity Guild who were "not free of the City [were to] be removed out of the protection of this guild and suppressed from trading." Around the turn of the century the cutlers, painters, and stationers' policy was ambivalent. In 1699 this guild denied the application of Luke Dowling, a stationer, to become a full brother following his indentured service because he was a Catholic, but the corporation allowed him to become a quarter brother, plying his trade during its pleasure by paying 4s. and quarterly payments of the same amount. Yet three years later the same guild ordered one of its members to discharge an apprentice because he was a Catholic, and in 1703 the lord mayor himself directed that the stationers dismiss an apprentice because he was a papist. The extant records of the weavers' guild provide few clues as to its inclusion of Catholics. During the mastership of William Wise (or Wyes), guild officials used corporation funds to record the names of Catholic apprentices in February and March 1698; this may have been done as the result of a directive from the city government, for the senior beadle delivered the names to the Tholsel in March. The same month the corporation purchased a copy of the Act for Banishing All Papists Exercising Any Ecclesiastical Jurisdiction, and All Regulars of the Popish Clergy (9 William III, c. 1), which required all designated Catholics to repair to Dublin or other specified towns and await transportation. Sharp and his guild brothers registered Catholic apprentices again the following year, and during Captain Sporle's first term as master (1703–1704) the corporation compiled a list (which does not survive) of Catholic weavers. Of 129 younger brothers in 1706, only one was a Catholic.[29] Perhaps the presence of Quakers such as Sharp, Grumley, Inman, Joseph Deane, and Henry Flower persuaded the weavers' guild to be more tolerant of Catholics.

Guilds carefully regulated their apprentices, or at least attempted to do so, insisting they be individuals of good repute and demonstrate this by appearing before the master and wardens of the appropriate corporation before being indentured. The cutlers, painters, and stationers, for instance, stipulated that a prospective apprentice "bee of a good Conversation and of the Protestant Religion." Recorded by the guilds' clerks, the indentures were supposed to be for at least seven years, but violations occurred. In 1692, the weavers, probably overreacting to the decline in their numbers during the civil war, were accepting many apprentices for shorter terms. Whether Sharp was among those who did so is impossible to ascertain. Simultaneously some weavers were taking excessive numbers of apprentices, prompting a protest in the guildhall in May 1692 that shorter terms and inappropriate numbers of apprentices damaged the trade by training more weavers than it could sustain. The problems had not been corrected by March 1704, when the Irish House of Commons unanimously resolved that it was prejudicial to the weavers' guild for any master to have more than two apprentices at a time or to release them in less than seven years. Guild members who did not properly enrol their apprentices had to pay fines, and the cutlers, painters, and stationers additionally rendered any indenture void unless it had been duly registered. In the mid and late 1690s the fine for an offending weaver was 6s. 8d.[30]

On completion of the term of indenture, an apprentice able to show requisite ability could pay a fine and be admitted to fellowship in the guild as a journeyman. Each corporation had its own regulations governing journeymen's behavior.[31] During the 1690s Sharp and his colleagues enacted various rules governing journeymen, including a prohibition against any master hiring another's journeyman without first ensuring that the latter was no longer obligated to his employer. In an attempt to safeguard the quality of old and new draperies, the weavers in March 1692 unanimously agreed that henceforth no master would hire a journeyman until the latter produced a certificate from the corporation's master and wardens attesting to his or her "Suffitiencey of ... workemanshipp." Moreover, all journeymen already employed by guild masters had to obtain such a certificate; a master who failed to enforce this requirement faced a fine of 5s. for the first offense, 10s. for the second, and permanent expulsion from the weavers' guild for the third. Controls were further tightened in November of the same year when Sharp and his associates unanimously decided that henceforth every journeyman employed by a corporation member had to demonstrate his or her "well makeing of goods & Deportement" during the previous quarter to the master and wardens. The guild fined transgressors 1s. for the first offense, double for the second, and a sum deemed appropriate by the council for the third. When at least some journeymen had not appeared by February, the assembly dispatched beadles to warn masters to send them as required or terminate their employment.[32]

The master-journeyman-apprentice relationship reflected a principal raison d'être for any guild, namely, to limit the number of people practicing a given craft or engaging in substantive commerce. Guilds therefore punished those who intruded in their monopoly. The weavers prosecuted thirteen intruders in September 1686, and in the aftermath of the civil war, when enforcement had undoubtedly been laxer, Sharp and his colleagues unanimously directed the master to prosecute all interlopers immediately, with the costs to be borne by the corporation. The weavers made an intensive effort to locate intruders in February 1704, dispatching search parties throughout the city.[33]

The control of intruders included monitoring immigrants who wanted to pursue their livings in Dublin. Attitudes toward foreigners (technically all noncitizens) and strangers (immigrants from other nations) varied among guilds. Huguenot merchants who had fled to Ireland to avoid persecution successfully petitioned the Trinity Guild in 1695 for "free liberty of trading." No less accommodating were the bricklayers and plasterers who asked Protestant foreigners and strangers only to pay 20s., follow their bylaws, and take the required oaths. The feltmakers insisted that any foreigners admitted to their society also had to be sworn free of the city within three months, failing which they would lose the benefits of guild membership. Unlike these groups, the weavers' guild apparently had more problems with outsiders because of the large number of immigrant weavers. The year before Sharp assumed the mastership, his corporation decided to prosecute all foreigners (undoubtedly including strangers) who practiced the weaving trade without becoming brothers in the guild. After the civil war the guild heard complaints that some foreign weavers had taken two apprentices at a time for less than the standard term of seven years, thereby impoverishing the trade and encroaching on the liberties of the guild's freemen. In response to these remonstrations, ninety-eight foreign weavers agreed to take no more than two apprentices, and journeymen at most one until any apprentice was within a year of completing his term. Moreover, these weavers pledged to indenture only apprentices approved by the master, wardens, and clerk (or any two of them), and solely for the full seven-year term. They agreed to pay fines of £5 for the first offense and £10 for every subsequent infringement if they violated this agreement. The war with France and the repression of the Huguenots brought an influx of weavers into Ireland, sparking an intense effort by Sharp and his guild brothers to find and deal with them, especially in 1697–98.[34]

Dublin guilds also attempted to control hawkers. During Sharp's mastership the weavers cracked down on hawkers, including those who were immigrants. Guild officers examined cloth vendors, some of whom were women, and seized their wares if they were not in compliance with corporation regulations. If the merchandise constituted a consignment from a guild brother, the offender could retrieve it only by posting a bond to cease selling through unlicensed hawkers.[35]

Besides efforts to maintain its monopoly (which were not entirely successful), a craft guild took measures to uphold the quality of its products, again with mixed results. Members' varying degrees of proficiency accounted for some fluctuations in the quality of manufactures, but differences would have been more pronounced had the guilds made no attempt to enforce standards. Those found guilty of infractions faced fines or imprisonment at the corporation's discretion. The weavers preferred to mulct transgressors, whose offenses included using coppings (which formed conical balls of thread wound on a spindle in a spinning machine), utilizing nonstandard weights, and making inferior cloth, and whose fines typically ranged from 2s. 6d. (for irregular weights) to 11s. (producing substandard cloth and using coppings). However, Israel Mitchell, who would be elected master in 1698, paid a fine of 20s. eight years earlier for manufacturing poor cloth. "Even the elite," as Steve Rappaport observed of London livery companies, "found that the companies' regulations could not be broken with impunity." Indeed, cheaters were subjected to a degree of humiliation before their peers as well as sanctions. As a further aid in upholding standards, by 1686 the weavers' guild had acquired its own perch (a measure of 5.5 yards or 30.25 square yards) to gauge cloth, seeking to prevent fraud and "the ill makeing of goods." Funds to run the perch office came from fines of 9d. per loom imposed on weavers who were not citizens of Dublin and guild members.[36]

Within days after the end of Sharp's term as master, his guild stressed the enforcement of standards to quash the abuses inflicted on customers by free brothers and foreigners alike "through the willfull & Designed neglect in Makeing Broad Cloath, Serges & other Stuffes &c. Narrower & not so good and Substantive as really they Ought to be, which tends to the great Scandall & reproach of the Mannefactury in this Citty & Corporation of Weavers & Clothiers." Work on the detailed statement must have commenced while Sharp was master, and its sense of fairness and honesty would have suited his Quaker commitment. Beginning with the erection of another perch, the regulations, reflecting the Act for the True Making of All Sorts of Cloth (17 and 18 Charles II, c. 15), specify precise measurements for broadcloth, mixed serge, white serge, baize, farandams, double prunella, camlot, and corduroy. Henceforth weavers had to take all cloth from the mills to the alnage office for examination and, if acceptable, marking; cloth that failed to pass inspection went back to the mills. Fees were imposed for the various kinds of cloth examined by the perch official—for example, 2d. for a piece of broadcloth. Three years later Sharp and his colleagues revised the regulations by stipulating a length of thirty-one yards for serge and a maximum length of forty-two yards for worsted. Thereafter, serge had to be stored in the mills, not private houses. Finally, in February 1693 the guild appointed a committee whose duties included regulating the manufacture of old and new draperies. Among the seventeen members of this committee was Sharp, who had manifestly demonstrated his commitment to the maintenance of equitable standards. In contrast, the guild fined Sharp's Quaker colleague Patrick Grumley 3s. 4d. for manufacturing corduroy of less than regulation length.[37]

The masters and wardens of the weavers' guild expended a fair amount of time examining cloth and traveling around the city and its environs to inspect looms. Sharp would have undertaken this responsibility during his mastership. Scattered throughout the corporation's ledgers are entries for expenditures relating to these activities, such as the nearly 10s. spent by George Duxberry examining goods at some point during his mastership (1695–96) or the 28s. 9d. Anthony Wills expended to inspect looms while he was master (1700–1701). John Sporle's examination discovered "fraudulent" serge, the manufacture of which was a serious enough offense to prompt the society to show the cloth to the speaker of the House of Commons and the attorney general in January 1704.[38]

The illegal serge was probably detected because it lacked the seal imposed by the alnage office. Operational details of this office are rare before 1682, though the weavers' guild rented the seal in 1677–78 for £27 13s. It also leased an office for the alnager in 1680–81 at a cost of 25s. and paid £40 to have cloth sealed that year. In March 1682 the guild provided for the nomination of one or more persons to officiate in the alnage office, though he or they had to have the approval of the committee that managed the new hall (including the master and wardens, or any two of them). Effective that September each guild brother and any foreigner in Dublin who made old or new draperies had to pay the alnager to have their goods sealed. So lucrative were the fees that the corporation could rent the office to two men the following year for £146. In 1684 Matthew Kena, who would become master a decade later, paid the guild £60 for the right to seal all foreigners' cloth. At that time the corporation decided that the cloth of free brothers would be sealed without charge, though this seems either not to have happened or to have been short-lived, for they remitted £24 0s. 9d. for sealing in 1685. The guild itself was paying Sir Robert Reading £40 *per annum* during this period for rent of the office.[39] Intended to help maintain standards of quality, the alnage office, as we shall see, was periodically a source of bitter contention.[40]

Like members of other corporations, Sharp and his guild brothers discussed their standards and other business in quarterly meetings and in assemblies held at other times as needed. Guild charters allowed companies to fine brothers who absented themselves, but they seem to have enforced such provisions laxly. When imposed, fines were not necessarily inconsequential. In August 1682 three weavers, including the future master George Spence, were each fined 40s. for rejecting the beadle's summons to attend a meeting, and earlier the same year another weaver was mulcted 6s. 8d. for contemptuously leaving the hall during a meeting contrary to instructions. The possibility of determining attendance patterns in the weavers' guild depends on how one views some of the data in the corporation's Old Book of Brothers, specifically the lists of members' names and the accompanying columns containing "x's" and blanks. This information could pertain to the payment of quarterly fees, to attendance at quarterly meetings, or to both since fees, as George Unwin has indicated, were collected at such gatherings. *If* the "x's" indicate attendance, absences were commonplace. During Duxberry's mastership (1695–96) he and two wards apparently attended all four meetings, as did nine of the nineteen council members (including Sharp), thirteen of the twenty-seven brothers who had served as wardens, and twenty-nine of the seventy-two "Younger Brothers." Seven members of the council, eleven senior brothers, and twenty-eight younger brothers attended none of the four meetings. During the period 1695–1707, two of the twelve masters seemingly missed meetings, as did three of the twenty-four wardens. During the same period 42.6 percent of the younger brothers maintained perfect attendance, while 38 percent attended no meetings. Attendance records (if that is what they were) for the councilors and senior brothers merged in 1702, but in the period 1695 to 1702, 46 percent of the former and 47 percent of the latter attended all meetings, whereas 19.7 percent of the councilors and 30 percent of the senior brothers missed each of them. In the period 1702–1707, 48 percent of the councilors and senior brothers were at all meetings, but 38.9 percent attended none. Thus in the period 1695 to 1707, 56 percent of the councilors, senior brothers, and younger brothers apparently missed some meetings, whereas 19 percent were absent from all of them. Clearly, most of these people were not fined. Sharp seems to have been absent only once in the period 1694 to 1699, but then missed every session in the next two years before resuming regular attendance. He was present twice in 1705–1706 for the last time. Again, however, these calculations are tentative because the data may not refer to attendance. Elsewhere, we know that between October 1696 and January 1700 the average attendance of the cutlers, painters, and stationers at quarterly sessions was only 16.2; absentees were fined 1s., though all such were excused from the meeting in November 1698 for unspecified reasons. Absenteeism was also a problem in London livery companies.[41]

Much of the real business of the Dublin guilds, especially as they be-

came larger, was discussed in councils, essentially the counterparts of
the courts of assistants in London guilds. The weavers appear to have
first established theirs in September 1686, when the "full hall" appointed the master, two wardens, and fourteen brothers, including
Sharp, Matthew Kena, Isaac Healme, Nicholas Taylor, and Anthony
Spence, all of whom had been or would be masters of the guild. Sharp
presided over the council during his mastership and remained a member
until at least 1702 and probably 1705 or 1706.[42] Shortly after the end of
his mastership, the guild unanimously resolved that the council, con-
vening on a hall day appointed by the master and wardens, could enact
regulations "for the Good of the house & Corporation as to them Shall
be thought Most Expedient, and all Such Lawes so Agreed upon to be
put in Execution and to continue in force in as full and Ample Manner
to all Intents & purposes, as any heretofore made." Although the brothers intended the council henceforth to have twenty-two members, it averaged fewer than twenty in the period from 1695 to 1702.[43] Sharp's
service on this body from its inception to the twilight of his life indicates
that he was among the most senior, influential men of his guild and
deeply committed to its well-being.[44]

Besides the council, the weavers' guild utilized committees to deal
with some of its operations. In July 1685 the corporation appointed a
committee comprising the master, at least one warden, and thirteen others to serve as trustees for leases and other rights for its lands, tene-
ments, and holdings. Apart from the master and warden(s), membership
was for life. At least initially, Sharp was not a member of this committee, but its records (if they were kept) are not extant, and he would have
served on the committee at least during his term as master. As we have
seen, he was also one of the seventeen brothers, along with the lord
mayor and recorder, designated in February 1693 to sit on the committee to regulate the manufacture of old and new draperies. The committee's mandate also empowered it to formulate rules for guild members'
behavior and to look into "all sutch matters as Concerns the said Corporation or any thing releateing to the said Arte or Corporation."[45]

Guild business was also the subject of informal meetings involving
the master and various members at taverns throughout the city and
sometimes in private houses. Cryptic notations in the weavers' accounts
provide some indication of the wide range of business discussed in such
settings, including negotiations in 1692–93 to supply clothing to the
army and discussions between select guild members and foreigners in
1703–1704 about "Composeing Matters betweene uss." A meeting at

the Salutation Tavern in February 1694 concerned sealing, whereas another in October 1703 resulted in an agreement between the weavers and the master of the hosiers and knitters regarding an unspecified issue. The weavers' master sat down with the wardens and some of the councilors at the Black Swan in December 1693 to look over the petition they intended to present to the lord mayor regarding the "little oath," and in August of the previous year he met at the Fleece with the council and other brothers to discuss the earl of Meath's lawsuit against the guild. Sometimes these informal gatherings were essentially celebrations, marking the successful completion of corporation business, such as the annual audit, the collection of a major debt, or a trial's conclusion. On such occasions those present imbibed beer or "burnt brandy," supped on meat, tongue, and bread, and smoked tobacco. The records contain a few tantalizing glimpses of Quakers at these meetings: At a gathering in July 1703 the master, John Sporle, spent 3s. to celebrate an agreement on an unspecified matter that involved Sharp, and the following February Sporle laid out 6s. 6d. on Sharp and others to examine an account dealing with "indian goods." Sporle also met with Clarridge on unspecified business in February 1704. Generally the funds dispensed in these meetings did not exceed 10s., but there were exceptions, such as the 40s. 7d. spent on auditors and others at the Exchange in May 1693 or the 16s. disbursed after a trial in 1687–88.[46]

Among the subjects of these meetings, as we have seen, were disputes involving the corporation. When the earl of Meath filed a suit in August 1692 accusing the weavers' guild of intruding on his liberties, Sharp and his fellow councilors unanimously agreed that the society would be responsible for any charges incurred in defending it. The following April the guild appointed Sharp, three other former masters (Anthony Spence, George Spence, and Richard Falkiner), and two additional brothers to negotiate an end to the dispute with the tuckmillers. If they failed to reach a settlement, the guild authorized them to seek a legal remedy in consultation with its attorney. Negotiations were fruitful, resulting in an agreement to pay the tuckmillers stipulated fees for scouring and milling different types of cloth.[47]

The alnage office, founded in June 1666 under the terms of the Act for the True Making of All Sorts of Cloth (17 and 18 Charles II, c. 15), was a source of recurring controversy. Designed to assure uniform standards of length, breadth, and weight for all old and new draperies intended for sale, the statute required the alnager, his deputy, or his agents to inspect all cloth produced for the market, and to seal or mark goods that met specified standards; the alnager was to cut defective cloth at both ends and not seal it. The act set fees for the alnager to perform this service, such as 4d. per broadcloth; it also empowered him to search all ships, fairs, and markets, and (with a constable or other parish official) warehouses, shops, houses, and cellars. Unsealed cloth, apart from that intended solely for personal use by its maker, could be seized. The act further required clothiers to weave their mark "into the head end" of all cloth before selling it. Finally, the statute provided that the alnager could be prosecuted if he or his assistants were negligent in performing the designated duties. Because alnagers tended to be members of the weavers' guild, disputes over their activities were disruptive to the corporation, as in 1678 when the guild expelled the alnager Jacob Hudson by a vote of twenty to eight. Nine years later the house unanimously instructed the master to file a complaint with the government or otherwise prosecute Sir Robert Reading, a guild member, for his "opression" in running the alnage office. Again, in November 1690 Sharp and his guild brothers unanimously agreed that they should pay the legal expenses of any member fined or sued by the alnager in connection with sealing cloth or failing to have it sealed. Several hearings before the lords of the great seal ensued, and in January 1691 the council directed the master to have an agent in London submit a petition to the English Parliament, which was considering a complaint from clothiers there against London's alnage office. Approved by Sharp, master Thomas Whitlock, a warden, and three former masters, the directive intended that the petition ask the English Parliament to protect the Dublin weavers from harm by the alnager until an Irish Parliament could resolve the dispute. This course was not fruitful, and two months later the corporation, again without dissent, appointed Sharp and three other former masters—Anthony Spence, Matthew Kena, and Daniel Falkiner—to negotiate with Captain James Hamilton regarding the alnage office; the house agreed in advance to accept anything the committee could legally do to resolve the dispute, a striking demonstration of confidence in Sharp and his associates. But the alnage office remained a source of substantial friction, and in 1695–96 the guild members paid fines totaling £25 7s. 8½d. to carry on their suit in Parliament.[48]

Guilds had the power to sue, though in turn they could be the targets of legal action. The feltmakers authorized their masters, wardens, and assistants to use guild funds to defend the corporation against any suits brought against it and to impose a levy on members when necessary. Like the weavers, the cutlers, painters, and stationers had recourse to a special assessment when necessary. Sometimes the guilds had to resolve disputes among their own members, and the cutlers, painters, and stationers expressly prohibited brothers in Ireland from suing each other over debts of less than £2 without permission.[49] To some extent, then, guilds provided opportunities to resolve disagreements that might otherwise have resulted in formal litigation and contributed in some degree to damping social disruption.

Some disputes were sufficiently serious to necessitate recourse to attorneys. Indeed, the merchants' guild employed its own lawyer beginning in 1678 to handle all suits involving the corporation and to review its regulations with a view to revising those that violated the laws of the land.[50] During Sharp's career the weavers never found it essential to hire their own full-time attorney, but periodically they paid legal fees typically ranging from 20s. to 26s. Like London's livery companies, they sometimes needed a lawyer's services to draft petitions or to plead before the Privy Council. During Duxberry's mastership (1695–96), legal fees were especially onerous owing primarily to renewed controversy with the alnage office; the cost of a petition to Parliament, legal expenses, and related items during his tenure may have exceeded £40.[51]

Petitioning Parliament or other government entities proved to be time-consuming and sometimes expensive. During Anthony Spence's mastership, when the guild petitioned Parliament and the lord deputy, the process lasted at least six months and involved payments to attorneys, one of the secretaries and his clerk, an unidentified officer of the House of Commons, and that body's doorkeeper. Moreover, guild leaders had to rewrite the petition several times; given Sharp's legal background and his experience drafting supplications for imprisoned Quakers, he probably worked on the guild's petition. Altogether, this appeal to the government cost Sharp and his associates at least £9 13s. 4d. between November 1686 and April 1687.[52] Other petitions went to Parliament in 1687–88, 1695–96, and 1698–99; to the lord lieutenant and Privy Council in 1687–88 and twice in 1692, and to the lord mayor in 1695–96. Normally, the accounts do not refer to the subjects of the petitions, though one in 1687–88 pertained to the corporation's new charter, and several dealt with contentious relations with the alnage office.[53]

Besides formal petitions, leaders of the weavers' guild discussed their concerns with the politically prominent in informal meetings. Most of these were with the lord mayor—at least five during George Spence's mastership (1687–88) alone—whereas others involved the attorney general, the earl of Meath, and members of Parliament.[54] Unlike some other guilds the weavers did not make a habit of bestowing gifts on the lord mayor; I have found only one possible instance, namely, a piece of plate for the lady "meris" in 1693. The merchants' guild first gave the lord mayor a present—half a tun of claret "as an acknowledgment of their affection to him"—in January 1666, and the practice soon became a regular occurrence, with most gifts constituting plate or cash valued from £20 to £50; sometimes the corporation's arms were engraved on the plate. The largess presented to Sir Humphrey Jervis in 1682 was in part for "shutting down foreigners shops and . . . suppressing intruders." The tailors made such gifts six times between 1652 and 1660, and presumably continued to do so, though we cannot know this with certainty because most of their records were destroyed. The cutlers, painters, and stationers sometimes presented gifts, such as a painting in 1677 and a Bible with gold clasps in 1681.[55] Whether such presents curried favor, they clearly symbolized the intimate links between municipal government and the corporations.

Some guild members had additional contact with the lord mayors through their service on the common council. The Act of Explanation (1665) empowered the lord lieutenant and Privy Council to make regulations for all cities, and Dublin received theirs in 1672. Under these provisions the common council comprised ninety-six representatives selected by the guilds. Henceforth each guild elected double the number of representatives to which it was entitled, and from this group the lord mayor, in the presence of a sheriff and eight aldermen, designated those who would serve. Terms were for three years. Until now, terms had been for one year and councilors were selected from the nominees by the mayor and aldermen. Although the merchants' guild complied with the new regulations, it protested in November 1672, claiming the rules were "destructive to many charters and priviledges thereby granted to this City and the Several Guilds and corporations therein." The number of representatives fluctuated over time; the merchants had forty-two in 1680, whereas other guilds had two to four (as did the weavers in 1675).[56] Sharp apparently never served as a common councilor, though he undoubtedly discussed municipal affairs with weavers who did.

Like the municipal government and the Quaker meetings, the guilds played an important role in supervising conduct, disciplining offenders, and providing relief to the needy. The corporations possessed the authority to fine or imprison those who violated their regulations; offenders could be sent to the city prison, from which they could gain release by a warrant from the master and wardens of the guild whose rules they had disobeyed. Some corporations had their own stocks to punish wayward apprentices. Guilds additionally had the right to distrain the goods of those who refused to pay their fines. A corporation could also punish offenders by excluding them from the trade, as happened to three weavers during Sharp's tenure as master, and this was obviously an onerous penalty. To maintain civil behavior the guilds imposed penalties for speaking ill of a master or a warden. Judging from the extant weavers' records, this was not a serious problem for Sharp and his colleagues. Indeed, as we have seen, Sharp subsequently claimed that during his mastership he neither fined nor imprisoned anyone.[57]

Neither the municipal government nor the churches could satisfy the needs of the indigent, and the guilds, in keeping with their historic assistance to their members and families, continued to provide relief, although the record in this period was not impressive. Thanks to its wealth, the Trinity Guild was somewhat of an exception. When the city had to discontinue the construction of an almshouse in 1668 owing to insufficient funds, the merchants donated the fines of the brothers who received the freedom of the guild at the midsummer assembly. Seven years later it pledged £12 *per annum* for the support and education of four boys at the Blew Coat School, and in 1701 the merchants promised double that amount for three boys whose fathers were "decayed" members of the corporation. The latter act seems to have inspired the lord mayor in February 1703 to urge each guild to maintain at least one boy at the school, to which the cutlers, painters, and stationers retorted that they already had many of their own widows and children to support. Although the weavers' accounts do not record their response, there is no evidence in the ledgers to suggest it was favorable.[58] In Dublin the normal pattern of guild charity involved modest donations on a case-by-case basis. The weavers' ledgers show no commitment to long-term relief but instead scattered donations to the poor, especially widows in amounts typically ranging from 2s. 3d. to 20s. Alms went as well to indigent brothers in the corporation, to a few people identified only as poor distressed Protestants, and to bury the destitute.[59]

Although the charitable record of the Dublin corporations was not very substantive (apart from the Trinity Guild), they found funds for sometimes lavish displays of civic pageantry that underscored their communal solidarity, their prominent place in the city's social and political structure, and their commitment to social hierarchy. Such displays ranged from the occasional bestowal of honor on dignitaries to the ritual attendant on riding the franchises, but they also included the relatively simple dinners that were part of the guilds' corporate life.[60] As a member of the weavers' guild Sharp presumably attended its quarterly and assembly-day dinners, the cost of which normally ranged from 17s. 4d. in 1680–81 to £2 3s. 10d. in April 1706, though the increase was anything but uniform; a dinner in February 1687 had cost £2 9s. 6d., whereas another in January 1706 required only 27s. 4d. The financial records for Sharp's mastership are so incomplete that it is impossible to know how many dinners—if any—he hosted. The records rarely show where these festive occasions occurred, but at least two (both in 1686) were at the Morocco Tavern. The guild dispensed £3 0s. 3½d. for quarter-day's activities, presumably including the dinner, in November 1693, after which members went for wine to the Exchange Tavern (13s. 10d.) and "more that night" (1s. 3½d.). The weavers also provided dinner for select members at the conclusion of an audit.[61]

Coming as they did after a day of guild business in which the masters, wardens, and councilors attended in their gowns, the dinners and wine-drinking capped the day's activities with a festive, harmonizing spirit that probably helped to damp any rifts that had emerged in discussions of guild business. If Sharp followed Fox's guidelines for Quaker magistrates, he probably would not have worn a gown during the day's activities and possibly would have shunned the dinners, though strictly speaking the latter were not intended to honor the master, wardens, and councilors and might therefore have been acceptable to Sharp as a communal activity. But he would almost certainly have absented himself from those events designed to fete prominent people, including the formal welcome accorded to the duke of Ormond when he returned to Ireland in 1684 and the festivities, including fireworks and a ball, to honor General Ginkel in October 1691. When Ormond's son, the fourteenth duke, became lord lieutenant in 1703, the lord mayor ordered each guild to march to St. Stephen's Green on 12 August, fully armed and in its best apparel, "for the Granduer of the Citty." The duke and duchess reviewed the assembled guildsmen, reportedly pronouncing themselves "mightily satisfy'd therewith." The weavers were, of course, present (perhaps without Sharp), having marched to the beat of their drummers and the sound of their hautboys (oboes), their beadles and others bedecked with ribbons, almost certainly orange and blue, the society's colors. Including a contribution toward the cost of the fireworks, the weavers expended £8 12s. 2½d. for these festivities. The masters and wardens, resplendent in their gowns, and the common councilors, all on horseback, were present as well to welcome Ormond when he disembarked at Ringsend the following year.[62]

The celebration that feted Ormond in August 1703 reflected two prominent civic traditions, one of which had evolved from the Black Monday rite into a May Day ceremony, whereas the other was the triennial ritual known as riding the franchises. The importance accorded both of them was part of what Patrick Collinson has called "a new slimmed-down, secular and increasingly civic-cum-martial festive culture." Simultaneously these events blended effectively with the "new national, secular and dynastic calendar" analyzed by David Cressy.[63] No other observances in the city's life—not even the major holy days—were marked with such displays of civic ritual. In this milieu Sharp found a way to participate, at least in riding the franchises, without apparently doing violence to his Quaker principles.

With the municipal authorities, the guilds observed Black (Easter) Monday annually until 1676, when the lord mayor, caught unprepared by Easter's imminence, moved the ceremony to May Day. All brothers between sixteen and sixty (and their male servants) gathered at their halls or designated meeting places by 7:00 a.m., wearing their finest apparel, bedecked with ribbons in their guild's colors, and bearing their arms (typically pikes). With all guild members who were aldermen or sheriffs peers on horseback and garbed in their gowns of office, they marched, in order of precedence, with guild colors flying, drums beating, and (at least for the weavers) hautboys playing, to Cullenswood, south of the city. Beginning in 1676 they rendezvoused instead at St. Stephen's Green, closer to the heart of the city, enabling the parties to assemble later, at 9:00 a.m. For the occasion, the senior beadle, who rode on horseback and bore the guild's painted or gilded staff, sometimes received a suit, a cloak, a hat, stockings, and shoes. Once at the green the guilds erected tents where their members could obtain refreshments and, as necessary, shelter. In 1660 the tailors, perhaps typical of most guilds, served French wine, meat, bread, and beer. At least some celebrations included fireworks. Activities at the green lasted six hours, from 10:00 a.m. to 4:00 p.m., after which the guilds marched back to their halls and meeting sites. These ceremonies were expensive: the merchants' guild saw its costs rise from £15 in 1661 to £40 in 1666 and up to £50 in 1694. For a dinner associated with the ceremonies the weavers paid £28 in 1701. Members who failed to participate without authorization were fined: an absentee merchant paid 20s. plus 10s. per servant, whereas a weaver who failed to appear was mulcted 6s. 8d.[64] There is no evidence to indicate whether Sharp participated, though the martial symbolism would have discomfited him, and he certainly would not have carried a pike.

The ritual of riding the franchises, in which Sharp took part, was somewhat akin to Rogation processions in which clerics led perambulations around the boundaries of parishes, partly to assert their rights and liberties, and partly to secure divine blessing on the crops.[65] Riding the franchises was a secularized counterpart, led by the mayor at the end of July or in early August (whereas Rogation occurred in the spring) to demonstrate the authority of municipal government, demarcate the boundaries of that authority, and provide vivid symbolism of civic unity, as in the Black Monday or May Day ceremonies. Throughout the period, the franchises were ridden every three years with the possible exception of 1689, when officials may have canceled the ceremony because of the civil war.

Many of the day's activities echoed those of the Black Monday and May Day celebrations. The guilds assembled much earlier, however, gathering at their halls or meeting sites by 3:00 a.m. There the members mounted their horses, wearing hats blazoned with their guild colors; the cutlers, painters, and stationers, their head wear edged in gold, would have been particularly striking. Senior beadles, bearing their staffs and astride horses provided for the occasion, were smartly dressed. In 1701, for instance, the Trinity Guild purchased a new livery cloak of blue cloth "with narrow edging and a laced hat" for its younger beadle "that he may with credit and decency attend the brethren." At the same time the merchants purchased two new livery coats and two sets of equestrian trappings to enhance the corporation's "Grandeur." Each guild employed its own trumpeters for the festivities.[66]

As in the Black Monday and May Day observances, the guilds marched in the order of precedence established by their antiquity. Following the mayor and his party came the merchants, the tailors, the smiths, and the barber-surgeons. The weavers were fourteenth, just after the glovers and skinners and before the shearmen and dyers. The route of march was set forth in precise detail. Beginning at the custom house in 1704, the riders proceeded down Essex Street and Temple Bar, then on to Ringsend "to the Water-Mark, where the Dart is thrown." From here the route wound its way to Blackrock before turning westward to (Mount) Merrion. Leaving the garden at the rear of a red house, the marchers wended their way to Clonskeagh, through a mill there, and on to the Donnybrook Road, proceeding as far as a house with the sign of a "Curran-Tree." The mayor then led the guildsmen across the fields behind Mr. Leeson's and eventually to Bride Street, very near the Quakers' meetinghouse, and Bull Alley, where a Presbyterian congregation met. Going down Patrick Street, they passed the cathedral before reaching the Coombe, where many of Sharp's employees worked. Following the water-course, the marchers went to Dolphin's Barn, site of the Friends' new burial ground, and then northward to Cutthroat Lane, Bow Bridge, and Hospital Fields. After several crossings over the wall of Phoenix Park, the assemblage followed the boundaries along Stoneybatter, Grangegorman Lane, and the Finglas and Drumcondra Roads, over Ballybough Bridge to Clontarf. With the end almost at hand, the riders proceeded to the watermill at Raheny, where the brook marked the end of Dublin's liberties.[67]

The cost of riding the fringes was substantial. As with the Black Monday and May Day observances, the expenses grew considerably during this period, the merchants' guild paying up to £20 in 1683 and four times that amount in 1701. The weavers laid out £54 16s. 9d. in 1704 compared to £16 17s. 4d. in 1680. The principal expenditures were for a participants' dinner and the trumpeters. For two of the latter the weavers expended £3 13s. 6d. in 1680 and £5 15s. twelve years later. A dinner for ninety cost the weavers approximately £10 in 1692, whereas the merchants authorized the expenditure of up to £80 "for the entertainment of this Guild" in 1701. Sometimes the societies financed these expenditures by soliciting contributions from participants toward the cost of the dinner. In contrast the weavers expected their younger brothers to pay for the meal, the cost to each typically being 10 or 15s. Although Sharp was not a younger brother, he was one of fourteen members who contributed 10s. apiece in 1692. In 1704 Samuel Clarridge's name appeared on a list of more than forty younger brothers who were fined the same amount to pay for the observances.[68]

The guilds mulcted members who disregarded the summons to participate. The masters' accounts indicate that the weavers fined Sharp twice, in 1701 and 1704 (10s. each time), for failing to ride the franchises. The weavers' fine was identical to that imposed by the cutlers, painters, and stationers, though a warden in the latter guild who declined to ride in August 1707 had to remit double that amount.[69]

Guild records in this period say relatively little about religious matters, even in a municipal context. In October 1679 the Trinity Guild donated £30 to repair and beautify King's Chapel in Christ Church and to erect seats "fit for the grandeur of the Chief magistrate & officers of this City"—an interesting hint of the near supremacy of civic values in one of Ireland's most famous cathedrals. The following month the cutlers, painters, and stationers contributed a tenth that amount for the new seats, and the weavers gave £3 10s. four years later and 2s. in June 1704. The merchants may have been the only guild to have their own chaplain; they appointed Thomas Seele, vice-provost of Trinity College, in 1656 following a period when the corporation's religious observances had been neglected. Seele was succeeded in turn by John Glandee, minister of St. Michael's, in 1666 and Dr. John Finglas in 1706. The merchants, "decently dressed," traditionally accompanied their masters and wardens, garbed in their gowns, to Christ Church on Trinity eve to hear a sermon and then return to the Tholsel for wine and refreshments. Commencing in 1683, the cutlers, painters, and stationers allocated 20s. *per annum* to pay for a sermon preached to the guild members in a Dublin church on St. Luke's day (18 October) in conjunction with the swearing-in of a new master and wardens. A dinner in a tavern followed. During Sharp's days, the weavers had neither a chaplain nor, apparently, a traditional annual sermon. In a rare action the weavers expended 23s. for a sermon in 1701–1702. Sharp, we can be certain, was not among the weavers who were present, nor would he have worshiped in the guild-sponsored pews in Christ Church. By focusing on economic matters, the weavers' guild kept religion from becoming a disruptive problem.[70]

More so than for the overwhelming majority of guild members, Sharp would have found his membership in the weavers' corporation a source of tension. Its brotherhood, with its regular meetings, its code of conduct, its disciplinary procedures, its sense of obligation to the poor (however modest), its characteristic practices, and, for the masters and wardens especially, its distinctive garb, required a personal commitment not altogether unlike the religious society to which he belonged. Fortunately for him, the points of friction were relatively few: bearing arms in the observances that marked Black Monday, May Day, and riding the franchises; the oaths normally required of guild members; support for the established church, however modest; the instances when the corporations rendered obeisance to the politically prominent; and the gowns worn by guild leaders. Sharp navigated these shoals without causing shipwreck to his conscience or bringing disrepute to his fellow Friends.

Without guild membership Sharp would have been at a serious competitive disadvantage as a clothier, not least because of his inability to trade on the same terms as corporation members. No less significantly, his involvement in the guild brought him into close contact with men of political and commercial influence, among them several clothiers who served as lord mayor, including Sir Joshua Allen (1673), John Eastwood (1679), Sir Elias Best (1683), Sir Michael Mitchell (1691, 1692), and Francis Stoyte (1704). Among the other weavers' guild members were Sir John Davis, chief secretary to the lord lieutenant from September 1690 to March 1692, and Thomas Cooke, the city recorder. Through the corporation Sharp would have met and possibly done business with Colonel Richard Lawrence, a Particular Baptist who helped Ormond establish a linen manufactory at Chapelizod and served on the Council of Trade for many years.[71]

Above all, the guild's ongoing cycle of meetings and business enabled Sharp to function at the heart of a network of trade and civic activity, making the most of his contacts to become a wealthy man and in the process contribute extensively to the Quaker cause. As we shall see, his donations were especially crucial for the success of the Friends' building program; just as commercial development was an indispensable handmaiden of the Puritans' achievements in New England,[72] so was the financial success of Sharp and Clarridge in enabling the Dublin Quakers to thrive in the late seventeenth century. Sharp's attainments in business undoubtedly helped him gain access to political leaders whose aid he sought on behalf of suffering Friends. His prosperity in the commercial world must also have assisted Dublin Quakers achieve a degree of respectability that could not have been anticipated in the 1650s and 1660s. In turn, his career would have been an example of the degree to which a talented, hard-driving person could achieve economic and social success, and thus proof that social mobility was possible in the hierarchical society in which he lived. "By offering some promise of personal advancement," as Steve Rappaport has argued, "the existence of considerable opportunities for social mobility [through the guilds] established a consensual basis for the stratification system and thus played an important role in preserving stability"; this was no less true of late seventeenth-century Dublin than sixteenth-century London.[73] Sharp's involvement in the weavers' guild, then, had significance far beyond its impact on his personal fortune.

THANKS TO HIS WEALTH, Sharp, motived by both financial and religious considerations, could invest in colonization in America with other Friends commencing in 1677. His initial interest was in West New

Jersey, which the English had won from the Netherlands along with other territory in September 1664. Shortly before this, Charles II had granted his brother James a charter for all lands between the Delaware and Connecticut rivers and also Nantucket, Martha's Vineyard, and most of Maine. On 4 June 1664 James in turn deeded much of the territory to John Lord Berkeley and Sir George Carteret. The following February the proprietors issued the Concessions and Agreements of New Caesaria, more popularly known as the New Jersey Concessions, which provided liberty of conscience. Shortly thereafter, Friends and Baptists began establishing settlements along the Raritan River.[74]

In March 1674 Berkeley sold his share of New Jersey to the Quakers Edward Byllynge (or Billing), a former officer in George Monck's cavalry and now a London brewer, and John Fenwick of Buckinghamshire for £1,000. The two men soon became embroiled in a proprietary dispute so intense that Penn had to arbitrate. Fenwick received a tenth of the land and £500 with which to establish a colony. Byllynge, however, was deeply indebted to his creditors, having accepted responsibility in 1673 for the embezzlement of £40,000. Byllynge and his creditors, most of whom were Quakers, persuaded Penn, the London merchant Gawen Lawrie, and the Hertford maltster Nicholas Lucas to serve as his trustees. Byllynge, Fenwick, and the trustees then entered into a tripartite indenture, according to which 10 percent of the proprietorship was under Fenwick's control. Organizing their own joint-stock company, the trustees offered to sell a hundred shares at £350 each. One share entitled the purchaser to buy 5,000 acres of land from the Amerindians, and holders of less than a full share could acquire proportional amounts of property.[75]

In 1676 the trustees agreed with Carteret to divide New Jersey along the Delaware River from its source to its mouth at Little Egg Harbor. Carteret retained control of East Jersey, which comprised 3,000 square miles, while the trustees were responsible for West Jersey, an area of 4,600 square miles. In the ensuing years the trustees sold or disposed of most shares in West Jersey, primarily to Friends, many of whom were lesser merchants, artisans, and shopkeepers. Among the purchasers were such Quaker stalwarts as the cloth merchant John Bellers, the lawyer Thomas Rudyard, and the ship-captain Samuel Groome. Quaker immigrants would have been attracted in part by the West Jersey Concessions (March 1677), which Byllynge penned and which, like the earlier New Jersey Concessions, provided liberty of conscience for all.[76]

Sixteen of West New Jersey's original proprietors belonged to the

Friends' community in Ireland. Among them was the merchant Andrew Robeson (or Robinson) of Clonmel, county Tipperary, who acquired a full share, and Sharp's associate Robert Turner, who purchased half a share. No less than ten of the original proprietors from Ireland were residents of Dublin, including the merchants William Clarke, Samuel Dennis, and Mathias Foster, the shoemaker Thomas Atherton, the tanners Richard Hunter and Joseph Sleigh, the innkeeper Roger Roberts, the weaver Thomas Thackery (or Thackaray), and the serge-maker Robert Zanes (or Zane). The tenth was Anthony Sharp, who was part of a group of seven that together purchased one share in March 1677; his associates were Atherton, Clarke, Foster, Hunter, Roberts, and Starkey. Shortly thereafter, Sharp's group agreed with Turner and his associates (Thackery, Zanes, Sleigh, and the carpenter William Bate of Wicklow) to appoint Thackery, Bate, Sharp's nephew Thomas, George Goldsmith, and Mark Newby to found a colony. As the advance agent, Zanes, a widower, arrived in West New Jersey late in 1677 and subsequently lived in Salem as he prepared for the arrival of the first colonists from Ireland; they finally came in November 1681. Clarke emigrated in 1678 and was one of the first settlers of Burlington. Sharp chose not to emigrate, and, like Atherton and Hunter, sold portions of his land.[77]

The eventual success of New Jersey colonization makes it easy to overlook the initial doubts and disputes among the Friends concerning the wisdom of this venture. For unexplained reasons, Sharp seems to have followed the early plans with interest. In March 1677 Clarridge reported to him from London that he had discussed the proposed colonization of New Jersey with various Friends, including several of the principal proprietors. Some eminent Quakers in London, he noted, "Judges it may not Be a place to turn to that account as many think of." The proposed colony, Clarridge opined, was "not a thing Sought By them but forced on them, . . . to gett some of the Debts Due to them from Edward Billing." Yet other Friends perceived New Jersey as a place to find respite from persecution, for Yorkshire Friends had reportedly acquired ten shares with a view "to make one Shire of it and to have the whole government within themselves of their own consent."[78]

Some of the correspondence between Sharp, Clarridge, and perhaps others concerning the plans for New Jersey apparently does not survive. Before March 1677 Sharp had decided to invest £20 in New Jersey, but something Clarridge or another correspondent reported to him made him change his mind. On 10 March Clarridge explained that James Claypoole, a London merchant and West Indian trader, had already paid Penn £20 on Sharp's behalf, though Claypoole thought Penn would refund the money if Sharp desired.[79] On 23 April Lawrie wrote to Sharp, asserting that Clarridge's report—presumably the missing correspondence indicating difficulties—had been erroneous, which he now acknowledged, though Lawrie still considered Clarridge disingenuous.[80]

Sharp opted not to withdraw his investment in New Jersey, even in the face of continuing dissension within Quaker circles. While he was in London during the spring of 1680 he received a letter from Atherton, Foster, and Starkey asking him to speak with Lawrie about developments in West Jersey. Expressing regret that Penn was involved in this affair, they complained that its acquisition by Friends

> now appears more to Be put on by a sinister self end, and private Interest than a real Publick charge as Was pretended, of all which as also the great sufferings it hath Brought to many familys and reflection on the Truth it self. . . . We can Instance in many perticulars how far short they have been in performing not only with us that remain here but also those that Left good and Setled habitations with Disappointments they found there.

Blaming Lawrie for the dilatoriness with which colonization was proceeding as well as the difficulties encountered by colonists arriving in West Jersey, Atherton, Foster, and Starkey urged Sharp to consult with Turner concerning ways to persuade Lawrie of the numerous wrongs he had allegedly done and the need to make restitution. Emotions were running high, as reflected in Atherton, Foster, and Starkey's plaint that "the Simple hearted" had been "betrayed into This Business."[81] As requested, Sharp presumably discussed these concerns with Lawrie, Turner, and Roberts, but whatever he learned did not dissuade him from continuing his involvement in West Jersey.

Sharp must also have shown an interest in Penn's colonizing plans for Pennsylvania, for in April 1681 Penn sent Sharp, Turner, and Roberts a copy of his tract, *A Brief Account of the Province of Pennsylvania*. In the accompanying letter he noted his previous efforts to reprove "mischeifs" in government and the opportunity he now had to formulate a polity for his colony that would preclude inappropriate actions by himself and his successors. Penn sought the support of Sharp, Turner, and Roberts, insisting his plans had "a cleer, unintangled, & I may say, honorable bottom." They would, he hoped, "have a brotherly eye to my honest concern, & what truth makes you free to do."[82] In fact, Turner became one of the earliest purchasers of Pennsylvania acreage, as did Clarridge, Clarke, Thomas Holme, and Francis Rogers, but Sharp did not.[83]

During the same year that Sharp received Penn's tract, he and Turner financed a colonial expedition to West New Jersey led by Sharp's nephew Thomas, a wool comber who may have worked for his uncle in Dublin; he would become a surveyor and teacher in America. On 19 September 1681 a group of more than 100 proprietors and their representatives, families, and indentured servants sailed from Dublin in *The Owners' Adventure*. After spending the winter in Salem the settlers moved to Newton Creek. Sharp and his fellow proprietors received the Third Tenth, subsequently known as the Irish Tenth, the land between the Pennsauken and Timber creeks. In 1686 this territory would become part of Gloucester County. The group initially took possession of a block of 1,750 acres. Shortly after the colonists arrived in West Jersey, Sharp deeded his nephew a thirtieth of the share owned by his group of proprietors, or approximately 167 acres. A map drawn by Thomas Sharp in 1700 shows that the initial purchasers acquired tracts between Newton and Cooper's creeks, beginning with frontage on the Delaware River and extending inland beyond the Salem road. The Friends established a meeting at Newton Creek, south of Burlington and across the Delaware River from Philadelphia, in what is now Camden and Gloucester City. By 1686 the Burlington quarterly meeting had recognized the Newton group as a monthly meeting. The Friends worshiped in private homes, probably including that of Thomas Sharp.[84]

In November 1681, the same month that Thomas Sharp's group of settlers had arrived in West New Jersey, the province's first general assembly convened, formulated fundamental propositions to assure the right of the people and their representatives to exercise political power, and persuaded Samuel Jennings, the recently appointed deputy-governor, to endorse them. The assembly also elected commissioners to distribute and regulate the province's lands. In December and January these officials drafted twenty-two regulations, all of which received the approval of Jennings and the assembly. Attempting to prevent the establishment of large compact estates, the commissioners limited each purchaser to 400 acres of townland and prohibited anyone owning an eighth of a share or more from obtaining a grant exceeding 500 acres in a single location. Moreover, the commissioners insisted that the recipient of a grant of townland erect a building on it or forfeit the property. Once a prospective landowner had registered his deed he had six months to settle his property.[85]

Anthony Sharp, Robert Turner, and other Irish proprietors took strong exception to some of these regulations and the way in which they were formulated, specifically the actions of Jennings and the assembly without the prior consultation of all the proprietors. Sharp and his colleagues initially protested to Jennings and the commissioners on 15 August 1682, claiming that these men, though Quakers, intended to defraud the purchasers. Responding on 20 February 1683, Jennings claimed that most of the proprietors had approved his actions, and he affirmed his belief that it was unjust for a proprietor to engross expansive tracts of land without improving it at his own expense.[86]

Replying on 26 May, Sharp asserted that the Irish proprietors had not been consulted about altering the concessions, nor did they have prior knowledge of any regulation that could restrict purchasers from taking up their land, a reference to the provision that no one could possess his acreage without first obtaining an order signed by at least two commissioners. Sharp also objected to the prohibition against purchasers engrossing large tracts, averring that Jennings' "Judgment will reach to more considerable purchasers than us who are smal in comparison of such you serve under." He was irate that Jennings had not acted against those who "Ingross our money, and that would near have doubled since first paid by some of us." Indeed, he charged, some purchasers had made substantial profits with the money invested by the Irish proprietors. Sharp repudiated the accusation that the latter had unjustly profited from improvements made on their land by the settlers, and in his judgment any gain that had accrued was the result of agreements properly fulfilled. There was a problem as well with the amount of land acquired from the Native Americans, which Sharp deemed inadequate: "We are much disappointed in that we send over goods to take up our land so that if enough be not purchased of the Indians let all concerned be advised to send effects for that purpose." If the original agreements could not be fulfilled, Sharp deemed it reasonable to formulate new arrangements mutually, not impose them by the decision of some.[87] Essentially the dispute stemmed from the impracticality of involving absentee proprietors in the detailed decisions affecting land distribution in West New Jersey. For their part, Sharp and his colleagues in Ireland resented changes that limited the size of single tracts they could acquire and aspersions that they were unfairly profiting from the labor of settlers on their lands.

Another opportunity for colonial investment presented itself to Sharp in the summer of 1682, this time involving East New Jersey, the proprietorship of which Penn, ten other Friends, and the London attorney

Robert West, a Rye House conspirator, had purchased for £3,400 in 1682. The twelve proprietors decided to double their number, with each of the twenty-four owning an equal share. Among the twenty-four were Lawrie, Turner, the now solvent Byllynge, the Dublin merchant Thomas Warne, the apologist Robert Barclay, and James Drummond, earl of Perth. Initially at least, the twelve proprietors envisioned East Jersey as another haven for persecuted Quakers, especially from Scotland, but this prospect dimmed when thousands of acres in Pennsylvania unexpectedly became available to immigrating Friends. Moreover, Puritans hostile to the Quaker movement populated the East Jersey towns of Newark, Woodbridge, Piscataway, and Elizabethtown. Doubling the number of proprietors brought in more men interested primarily in investment opportunities. Others were probably involved because of political and religious disaffection with the Stuart regime. Besides Robert West, the proprietors included two other men who engaged in the Rye House plotting, namely, the attorneys John Ayloffe and Nathaniel Wade, both of whom, like West, were members of the Green Ribbon Club. So too was John Freke, an ally of the earl of Shaftesbury. Among the other proprietors were Sir Gilbert Gerard and Sir Henry Ingoldsby, who were supporters of the duke of Monmouth in the early 1680s. Interestingly, all six of these radicals were present at a proprietors' meeting on 4 July 1682 with such Quaker stalwarts as Penn, Rudyard, and Ambrose Rigge; these Friends, of course, had no involvement in the conspiracy.[88]

Whatever the reasons for East New Jersey's appeal to others, the Friends remained interested in establishing Quaker settlements there. The proprietors offered to sell portions of their land at a cost of £100 per 500 acres to those who purchased by 1 October 1683. As early as the summer of 1682, Sharp and Clarridge had written to Penn about acquiring a third of a share apiece. On Penn's behalf, Claypoole responded, noting that he had conferred with Rudyard and other proprietors. They insisted that Sharp and Clarridge "must advance £100 more or else you cannot purchase, which is £350 for cost, and £50 toward a stock for the general good, which every 24th part may advance." The transaction occurred in September, with Sharp and Clarridge each paying £133 6s. 8d. for a third of Warne's share. Clarridge sold a quarter of his interest to the Dublin attorney Thomas Sisson, a like amount to William Bingley, and the remainder to Sharp. Sharp retained his portion and subsequently purchased Sisson's holding, thus giving him 7/12 of

Warne's original share. In 1698 Turner, acting as Sharp's agent, redeemed Sharp's portion for 5,834 acres of unappropriated land. With subsequent dividends, this increased to 10,208-1/3 acres by 1740.[89]

Sharp was understandably interested in political developments that threatened the proprietors' authority. James, duke of York, had granted the twenty-four proprietors the right to govern East New Jersey, but in January 1684 his secretary, Sir John Werden, and the governor of New York, Thomas Donagan, discussed the reunification of New Jersey and New York. Several proprietors, including the earl of Perth and Sir George Mackenzie, lord register of Scotland, successfully protested, though James would revive the idea after he became king in 1685. At first, however, he confirmed the proprietors' rights both to the land and to the government. William Gibson conveyed this news to Sharp on 18 April 1685, explaining that each of the twenty-four proprietors—"the Standing Ballance of the government"—had a right to choose his representative in the provincial assembly. As co-holders of one share, Sharp, Clarridge, and Warne had to decide how they would cast their vote. Gibson inquired if Warne, who had emigrated to East Jersey in 1684, would represent their collective interest or whether all three would participate in the voting. Sharp's response has apparently not survived, nor has his letter (listed in Crabb's register) to Penn, Byllynge, and others in 1685 concerning affairs in East Jersey.[90]

In subsequent years Sharp maintained his interest in the colonies. As Penn prepared to leave London for America, he wrote to Sharp, Edmundson, and the Cork merchants Francis Rogers and John Hammond in January 1691, enclosing a copy of *Some Proposals for a Second Settlement in the Province of Pennsylvania* (1690), instructions for emigrants (probably *Information and Direction to Such Persons as Are Inclined to America*, 2nd ed., 1686), and recent correspondence from America. Penn's *Proposals* set forth his plans to found a new settlement in the Susquehanna valley, including a city some 100 miles west of Philadelphia. He offered to sell 3,000 acres in this proposed settlement for £100, holding out the hope that it would be the gateway to an enormous new colony being planned by Dr. Daniel Coxe of London that would extend from the western borders of New York, New Jersey, Pennsylvania, Maryland, and Virginia to the Pacific Ocean. Penn asked Sharp, Edmundson, Rogers, and Hammond to distribute the *Proposals* and the accompanying material "in the most likely and successfull manner you Shal Judge meet." The same letter went to three Friends in Norfolk and probably to Quakers elsewhere. Penn clearly considered Sharp one of his key contacts in Ireland for the dissemination of promotional material about Pennsylvania and possibly for the recruitment of settlers.[91]

In 1702 Sharp had an opportunity to purchase Susquehanna Manor from George Talbot, the surveyor-general of Maryland and cousin of Charles Calvert, Lord Baltimore. Claimed by Pennsylvania and Maryland, this land included the site of a proposed settlement on Octoraro Creek. (The creek empties into the Susquehanna River, and the land in question is now part of Cecil County, Maryland.) Talbot seems to have been interested in solidifying Maryland's claim to the disputed territory by selling portions of it to Quakers who would defend their interests against Penn's claims. When Sharp notified Penn of the offer, James Logan urged Penn himself to acquire the land: "If, instead of him [Sharp], thou canst purchase it for anything under £2000, if it contain what they say it does, viz., 6000 or 8000 acres, I do engage, if we have peace, to raise the money off one half of it." But Penn did not have enough disposable funds to purchase the land, and Sharp may have declined the offer because of the contested title. Shortly thereafter, in a letter to Logan dated 24 January 1703, Penn referred to Randall Janney's landholdings, part of which lay in territory claimed by Pennsylvania and Maryland: "But if that [land] should prove within [Lord] Balt[imore's] bounds I should make a Count[r]y for him, but I think to fasten that matter with ant. sharp."[92]

Although Sharp opted not to acquire Susquehanna Manor, he continued to be interested in his New Jersey holdings. On 11 September 1694 he wrote to his nephew Thomas, instructing him to "take up as much as possible [of his uncle's land] & set it off." Anthony also wanted Thomas to provide "a good Farme" for the latter's brothers, William and Anthony the younger. In his reply, Thomas was to tell Sharp what land he was dwelling on, what additional property he possessed, the number and type of cattle he owned, and, almost as an afterthought, how many children he had. Finally, Sharp inquired of Thomas "how much lande thou hast Taken up for me that Layes wast," the value of Anthony's land in West Jersey, and the price of acreage in East Jersey. Sharp had assigned Thomas responsibility to collect a debt for him and apparently remit the money to Ireland.[93]

Sharp's eldest son Isaac would emigrate to West New Jersey in 1700, where he settled at Blessington (now Sharptown). He also inherited his father's lands in East Jersey. (These in turn he bequeathed to his eldest son, Anthony, who in 1740 obtained the Board of Proprietors' approval to convey them to his brothers Isaac and Joseph, both of whom subsequently served on the Board.) Altogether, some 3,000 Friends left Ireland for America between 1682 and 1776, including others with the surname Sharp.[94]

Although Anthony Sharp never emigrated, his business acumen and extensive guild involvement enabled him to amass the wealth necessary to invest in colonial endeavors. That he did so for both financial and religious considerations is indisputable. Like such Quaker merchants as Joseph Hoare and Samuel Pike of Cork and Isaac Norris of Philadelphia, Sharp was more concerned with colonial land speculation than transatlantic commerce.[95] Yet the opportunity for profit never became subordinate to his personal values, as revealed especially in his protest of 26 May 1683 to Jennings. The latter's contention that Sharp and his confederates were unjust because they insisted that their agreement be honored stung Sharp to the core. In closing that letter he expressed his desire that Jennings and his colleagues in West New Jersey would enjoy prosperity "in that which is Just, and that the Just principle and wisdom from above may be loved and obeyed by us all."[96]

For Sharp, prosperity, rigorous economic practices, and the Quakers' simple faith were not contradictions but handmaidens. This principle guided him both in his colonial dealings and in his guild activities. In seeking to live by this principle, with its affirmation of the acceptability of commercial success justly attained, he helped Quakerism make the transition from the sectarian fringes to social respectability. This acceptance was manifest in Quaker participation in the Jacobean magistracy, the guilds, the transatlantic commercial network, and colonial partnerships, and, as we shall see in the next chapter, the Friends' ready access to political and ecclesiastical officials in Ireland. In helping the Quakers achieve this respectability, Sharp did far more in the Irish context than did Edmundson, and perhaps, through his commercial links to England and his investment in New Jersey, for Friends in general than did Fox.

6

"Timely Endeavours"

Forging a Stronger Movement,
1692-1704

IN THE DOZEN or so years following the conclusion of the revolutionary upheavals, the Friends engaged in a program of rebuilding
and expansion. William's triumph did not bring an end to Quaker sufferings, which continued to demand substantial effort from Sharp and
his colleagues. The refugee problem also required attention, not only
with respect to Friends dislocated in the war but also for coreligionists
who had fled to Ireland from England in search of a haven. Yet these
were also years in which Sharp and other public Quakers traveled extensively, bearing witness to their faith and building a network that
linked Friends throughout the British Isles and beyond. As the Quakers
solidified their organizational structure in this period they commissioned
a history of their movement in Ireland and made provisions to preserve
written testimonies to their leading members after their deaths. His
commitment to the Friends undimmed and his capacity for work un-
abated, Sharp was active in all these activities as well as ongoing attempts to monitor and influence parliamentary proceedings, especially
those concerning the possible exemption of Quakers from oaths. Sharp
was now at the peak of his influence among Irish Friends and did much
to shape their relationship with the regimes of William and Anne.

One of the first tasks the Friends undertook in the postwar period
was an assessment of the refugees' needs and plans. As early as November 1691 the half-yearly meeting had encouraged them not to settle in
remote areas where they would be unable to attend meetings, and the
following May the Dublin men's meeting instructed Sharp and others to
ascertain the state of Quakers who had sought refuge in the Dublin area
and whether they intended to return to their homes.[1] Friends in England
had pledged financial assistance for those in need, and in January 1692

Sharp and Starkey, at the national meeting's behest, reported to the meeting for sufferings in London that several local meetings in every province had been asked to determine the needs of each family deserving assistance and report to the half-yearly assembly. At that point, Sharp and Starkey noted that Irish Friends were still able to provide all the necessary relief. As reports of losses and requests for assistance mounted, however, Irish Friends, as we have seen, accepted more than £5,000 from English Quakers by early 1693.[2] In the ensuing months destitute Friends from England began arriving in Ireland, some of them debtors without the usual certificates from their meetings attesting to their good character. The Leinster provincial meeting asked Sharp and Thomas Trafford to contact the national meeting concerning this problem, and in November the latter body directed Sharp and Amos Strettell to write to the meeting for sufferings in London, asking that it provide money to indigent Quakers traveling to Ireland and that it report those who left England "disorderly or in Debt."[3]

Neither these problems nor their experiences during the time of troubles cast a pall over the Friends. After the six-months meeting adjourned in November 1692, Sharp and John Watson remarked that God's goodness had been "wonderfully Felt and enjoyed to our great Joy, comfort and confirmation," and that the delegates had parted in a spirit of unity. From Ulster, the timber merchant George Rooke notified Sharp and Watson the following January that Friends in his region were "generally well and Truth gets ground, meetings is large and [there is] a good openness among people," though some who professed Quaker principles were unwilling to suffer on that account.[4]

The return of peace to the kingdom did not end Quaker suffering. In November 1691 the six-months meeting directed Sharp, Clarridge, and Thomas Winslow to deliver a petition to the Council and lords justices seeking the release of Friends incarcerated for refusing to pay tithes. From time to time the Leinster provincial meeting found it necessary to urge qualified members to attend assizes and quarter sessions to monitor proceedings against Quakers and to render assistance to the latter.[5]

Given his extensive record of activity on behalf of imprisoned Friends, Sharp was probably present at some of the assizes and quarter sessions. Among the fellow Quakers he assisted was John Lancaster, who had been jailed at Naas for declining to pay tithes on a mill at Castlewarden, county Kildare, and subsequent court costs. The Leinster and six-months meetings deputed Sharp and others to seek his release by appealing to the bishop of Kildare, the priest who had filed the complaint, other ecclesiastical officials, or even Archbishop Michael Boyle, and to employ "any other meanes according to Truth for his Liberty."[6] In 1694 and 1696 the national meeting instructed Sharp to consult with or petition Boyle on behalf of Friends who had been incarcerated in Ulster on tithes charges, and in 1694 the same body asked Sharp and two others to meet with Archbishop Marsh of Dublin or Sir John Topham on behalf of Christopher Cheater of county Wicklow, who had been imprisoned for contempt of the bishop's court. Sharp's reputation was again manifest in November 1703 when the parliamentary committee—in a departure from its usual business—appointed Sharp and John Hoope to ask the Ulster provincial meeting to assist four Quakers from county Cavan who were being prosecuted in an episcopal court.[7] As part of their efforts to conduct business in a more orderly way, in November 1696 the national meeting stipulated that Friends who suffered for their refusal to pay tithes should first apply to the appropriate priest for redress, then to the bishop, and finally to the justices of the quarter sessions or assize. Seeking legal advice was acceptable, and in 1700 the six-months meeting sent Sharp and Gershon Boate to obtain the opinion of a proctor in a bishop's court concerning the tithes charges against William Roberts, a "gentleman" of Cullenswood, county Dublin, who had been jailed at Maryborough, Queen's County (Laois).[8]

By the mid-1690s the number of imprisoned Quakers was not large. The six-months meeting reported to the yearly meeting in London in May 1695 that it knew of no imprisoned Friend in Ireland, where magistrates reportedly held Quakers "in pretty good Esteeme." A year later a similar report, compiled by Sharp and two others, noted only two Friends behind bars. Thereafter the numbers fluctuated slightly: six in 1697; none in 1698; six in 1701.[9] Although the number of incarcerated Quakers was small in these years, many suffered because of fines and distraint of goods for refusing to remit tithes and church rates. The national meeting calculated these losses at £1,949 3s. in 1699 and £2,050 15s. 2d. in 1700, with approximately 60 percent sustained by Friends in Leinster. The financial penalties subsequently declined, to £1,204 15s. 7½d. in 1703 and £1,134 18s. 3¼d. in 1706.[10]

Harassment of another sort continued to disrupt Quaker life during most Christmas seasons, and Sharp was still prominently involved in seeking redress. The Friends achieved some success in 1693 and 1694 following appeals to the ranking officer of the regiment in Dublin to order his troops to behave; Sharp and Alexander Seaton even had the pleasant task of transmitting a letter of appreciation to the commander after the 1693 Christmas season. The Dublin men's meeting was also sending representatives to seek protection from the lord mayor, the seneschal of the earl of Meath's liberty, and others. Although these officials "promised very fair" in 1695, the "rabble" again subjected the Quakers to abuse. "A rude rabble of Some hundreds of men and boyes came with great Sticks and Stones, Some of them three or four pounds weight," and smashed the glass in Thomas Ashton's shop as well as the upstairs windows, a mirror, a clock case, iron window bands, and a lattice. The crowd similarly broke windows in the shops and upper floors of George Rooke, the tallowchandler Samuel Baker, John Stevens, George Newland, and John Hutchinson, and hurled stones and dirt into the shops of Amos Strettell, the merchant Robert Smallman, and Richard Sealey. The following year Sharp, Rooke, Amos Strettell, and Smallman therefore petitioned the lords justices, who ordered the lord mayor to curtail such rowdiness. In 1697 the Dublin meeting sent members in pairs to seek the assistance of the lord mayor, the earl of Meath, and Lord Drogheda (whom Sharp and Clarridge approached), but the resulting promises to help had little impact as revelers smashed numerous windows in Quaker houses and shops.[11]

Protesting such behavior became routine for Sharp on the eve of the Christmas season. By 1701 an exasperated Dublin meeting dispatched Sharp, Amos Strettell, and the merchant James Pettigrew (or Petticrew) to beseech the lord mayor to issue a proclamation directing masters of families to confine their sons and servants to their homes. Although the mayor received Sharp and his colleagues courteously, he insisted he had no precedent to issue such a proclamation. Friends, possibly including Sharp, also made the same request of the lord lieutenant, the earl of Rochester, but he agreed only to ask the major general to order his troops not to harm the Quakers. Notwithstanding these efforts, on Christmas day 1701 "a great Rabble Came into Meath Street to the meeting house pretending that a Schoole was kept there and threw stones in a violent manner and broke the glass windows." The following year the Friends persuaded the mayor to issue a proclamation ordering the "rabble" not to gather "in a tumultuous manner to shut friends shops" on Christmas day, and for this Sharp and Amos Strettell thanked him in early January. The precedent was a fortunate one for the Friends, and Sharp and his colleagues cited it in ensuing years with some success.[12] Records of the Dublin men's meeting suggest that the officials and military officers to whom Sharp and his colleagues appealed each year treated them with civility and even sympathy, thus implying that the Quaker representatives handled themselves with proper decorum and probably enjoyed the respect of those whose aid they sought.

Recording sufferings was an activity in which the Friends had engaged since 1653, and in the ensuing decades Irish Quakers evolved stricter procedures to keep such records. In May 1672 the six-months meeting named three men from each province to prepare lists of incarcerated Friends, including data concerning when, where, and why they had been jailed. Six years later the same body directed each provincial assembly to review the records submitted by the men's meetings to ensure their completeness before forwarding this material to the national meeting.[13] The meetings' efforts notwithstanding, some Quakers were remiss in submitting accounts of their suffering, perhaps because they were paying tithes and church rates, as some Friends in England were doing. The meetings repeatedly admonished their members to provide the required information,[14] and in May 1695 the half-yearly meeting complained that accounts of sufferings were not arriving "in good Order." It thereupon exhorted Friends who had "money taken out of their Shop Boxes on account of Tyths or Preists maintanance or repaire of worship houses [to] beare a faithfull testimony against such proceedings." Several times the national meeting instructed Sharp to correspond with William Williamson of Ballyhagan, county Armagh, who was responsible for recording the sufferings at the national level, but this was an area in which the Quakers seldom required Sharp's services.[15] When, for example, Williamson died in 1700, Sharp did not serve on the committee of nineteen that reviewed his records for errors. Nevertheless, he was at the six-months meeting in November 1697 when it enjoined the provincial meetings to maintain a record of the time each Friend spent in prison "for Truths Testimony" and how she or he gained release. The following May he was again present when the six-months meeting recommended that a qualified person in each women's meeting receive reports of sufferings, which were then to be examined by the men's meeting and forwarded to the provincial and ultimately the national assemblies. Seeking even greater accuracy in reporting, the national meeting in May 1699 called for uniform language in accounts of sufferings.[16]

Another indication of the Friends' determination to impose greater order on their movement was the renewal of visitations in 1691. The half-yearly meeting in November 1692 had each provincial body appoint one or two Quakers from every local meeting to inquire into the latter's management "as in Relation to worship or concerning publique friends or Testimonies borne in Meetings." The Leinster provincial meeting complied the following month, designating two members of each local group, with instructions to provide advice and admonition if they found anything amiss.[17] The records of the Leinster meeting for May 1694 contain what appears to be an early report of such a visitation. Dublin Friends found a general willingness to seek God and a receptivity to truth, but reports from such places as Edenderry, Wicklow, and Carlow were less sanguine.[18] A few days later the six-months meeting further structured the visitations by directing each provincial body to consult every quarter with the two visitors to each local meeting, "that soe a right understanding may bee had how all things are among Friends, & advice may bee given where needfull, for the helping & strengthening of one another." The capstone of the system occurred at the national level, when eighteen or nineteen representatives from the provincial assemblies convened at the time of the six-months meeting to discuss "the Mannagement of Church Government," in part with public Friends.[19]

The public Friends themselves were more carefully monitored after the time of troubles. In December 1692 the Leinster meeting instructed members desirous of traveling "in the Service of Truth" to inform their respective men's meeting or its elders to obtain assistance and advice. The following November a committee of twenty-one, which did not include Sharp, submitted a statement on the ministry to the six-months meeting. In it they directed public ministers not to speak at great length in their own meetings, for this, they said, was conducive to dull formalism rather than the life and power of the Spirit. Simultaneously, however, the committee pleaded with members of local meetings not to talk at length when visiting ministers were present, leaving little time for the latter to testify; "instead of the best wine to come at last, a Generall flatness hath come over the Meeting."[20]

The Leinster provincial meeting added stipulations concerning female public Friends and the necessity of recording visits to remote regions. Concerned about "proudlike, unsettled Girles or Lasses" who accompanied Quaker women as they traveled from meeting to meeting, the Leinster delegates insisted in September 1698 that henceforth a "staid, sober, plaine" woman accompany a female public Friend. Nearly three years later the same body urged traveling Friends to submit accounts of their journeys to Amos Strettell, with special attention to places where meetings had been settled and the times they met.[21] The intent was to provide this data to public Friends embarking on trips in the future.

Although visits by public Friends from England were welcome, their activities sometimes posed problems. Ten to twenty Friends accompa-

nied John Banks and John Lancaster on their travels in 1694 though it
was harvest season. The following year the Dublin men's meeting expressed dissatisfaction that two of its members, who were accompanying traveling Friends in Ulster, had been away from their businesses so
long; this, they opined, was "evile service."[22] Expense could also be a
factor, especially for the provision of horses. In 1692 the Dublin men's
meeting converted a building on its Meath Street property into a stable
for the steeds of traveling public Friends. When the latter had completed
their itineraries, the horses had to be disposed of, and in the interim the
Dublin meeting had to absorb the expense of their upkeep (£5 4s. in
September 1700).[23]

An Irish Quaker who intended to travel as a public Friend had to obtain a certificate from her or his meeting, as did those who hoped to accompany him. Sharp and Amos Strettell prepared such a certificate for
George Rooke in 1698 when he planned to visit meetings in England.[24]
After Sharp informed the Dublin men's meeting that he had "a concerne
on his spirit to goe for Hollend in Truth['s] servis," it prepared a certificate which Sharp himself helped to draft. Dated 21 May 1695 and addressed to Friends in the Netherlands, it carried the signatures of eighteen colleagues.[25]

Shortly thereafter, Sharp sailed for England, narrowly escaping two
privateering vessels in the Irish Sea. After visiting Liverpool and London
he and Samuel Baker obtained a pass from the government on 7 June to
go to the Netherlands. They sailed from Harwich six days later, only to
be forced back to port by contrary winds. When the weather improved
Sharp sailed to Edam, and was in the Rotterdam area by 7 July. From
there he wrote to his wife, telling her of holding a meeting where the
Baptists usually gathered at Groningen, and outlining an itinerary that
would take him some 200 miles to Friedrichstadt in Schleswig via Bre-
men and Hamburg. He was with the Quaker community in Friedrichstadt on the river Eider by 17 July, after which he journeyed to Harlin-
gen in the Netherlands. From there he wrote to Ann on 1 August of the
love and goodness of God he had experienced on his trip, and he took
this occasion to send his greetings to Rooke, from whom he had received a letter on 30 June. Returning via Amsterdam and Rotterdam,
Sharp was in London by 31 August; again he wrote to Ann, seeking to
comfort her with "many Loveing, Tender and precious expressions,"
and thanking God for a happy, comfortable journey. He sent her yet
another letter on 7 September, this time from Marlborough, expressing
his intention to be at Holyhead in three weeks to embark for Dublin.[26]

Sharp made other trips as a public Friend, though none so ambitious as his foray to the Netherlands and Schleswig. With James Fletcher of Cheshire he attended meetings in Ulster, including Lurgan and Hillsborough, county Down, in the spring of 1696, and reported that Tories were fomenting trouble in the region. In September Sharp and John Watson visited Cork, and the following January Anthony was at Wexford, though perhaps only on business.[27] That summer he journeyed to Scotland and northern England, reporting to his wife from Edinburgh that Scottish Quakers were compelled to meet in the streets. After visiting a number of Scottish meetings Sharp crossed the border into Cumberland, where he worshiped with Quakers near Carlisle. From there he went to Swarthmore, expecting to meet Edmundson, with whom he was now estranged for reasons that will be discussed shortly. He missed Edmundson, however, and subsequently traveled to Holyhead via Lancaster to board a ship for Ireland. By 27 September he was in Cork in time to attend the Munster provincial meeting, and from there he made his way to Dublin by way of Cashel, Longford, Durrow, and Abbeyleix, stopping long enough to participate in the Leinster provincial meeting.[28] Sharp apparently traveled to England as a public Friend in 1699, for the Dublin men's meeting prepared a certificate at his behest. The following year he again toured Ulster, visiting meetings at Lurgan, Monaghan, Charlemont, Ballyhagan, Antrim, Grange, and Coleraine. As far as we know, this proved to be his final journey as a public Friend. Coincidentally, the following year the Leinster meeting, noting the shortage of qualified preachers, resolved that at the next national meeting "some be stirred up to their duty in Answering that Service."[29]

Besides his work as a public Friend, Sharp was active during the postwar period in several endeavors designed to preserve a historical account of the Quakers. This involved the recording of testimonies, the publication of collected works by authors who had recently died, and the preparation of several histories. Quakers had long recognized the value of deathbed statements and testimonies about deceased Friends. In 1673, for example, the six-months meeting had made provisions for the printing and distribution without charge of Rebecca Stevens' deathbed testimony, the cost to be borne by the national meeting. The usefulness of such testimonies stemmed from their power to move people spiritually, as with the statement of George Hall, the national meeting's scribe, who had died in October 1680; many Friends who heard it were "much tendred." When Abraham Fuller's son Joseph died in 1687, an account of "how the Lord visited him by his power a little before and near his departure" was printed and distributed to each Quaker family in Dublin.[30]

Postwar efforts to provide the Quaker movement with more structure included the preservation of testimonies to public Friends. Such records had not been systematically maintained; hence in May 1695 the six-months meeting charged each province to compile a collection following the death of a public Friend, noting when he or she died and appending whatever statements any Quakers contributed. In November the provinces submitted the names of deceased public Friends to the national meeting, which passed them to the Dublin men's meeting for recording in a special volume. By May 1696 it was apparent that the inclusion of all the testimonies would be too bulky; hence the six-months meeting authorized Dublin Friends to condense them, though noting that local groups could record the unedited testimonies in their burial books.[31] The task of abbreviating the testimonies fell to Sharp, Roberts, Ashton, and Amos Strettell. A further step in this process of regulating the recording of testimonies occurred in January 1703, when the Leinster meeting requested that a dying Friend's witness be submitted to the local meeting and then to the provincial assembly, after which it would be forwarded to London if deemed appropriate.[32]

As well as editing testimonies, Sharp wrote several. Following Burnyeat's death in September 1690, Sharp, Amos Strettell, and others prepared statements and sent them to the morning meeting in London. So many testimonies about Burnyeat arrived that the morning meeting had them edited into three documents, one each from London, Cumberland, and Ireland. The printed testimony composed by Sharp and his colleagues described Burnyeat as "one of the Archers of Israel, who could shoot to an Hairs-breadth, to the wounding of the Hairy Scalp of the Wicked one, and the putting of the Lord's Enemies to Silence."[33] After the tanner Peter Fletcher, a Cumberland native, died on 29 June 1698, the Dublin men's meeting asked Sharp, Ashton, Amos Strettell, and John Chalmers to expand Rooke's testimony to Fletcher as they thought fit. Ultimately Sharp and ten others signed the testimony, saluting Fletcher as a man "of few words but savoury." The most difficult testimonies for Sharp to write must have been those for his wife Ann and his son Jonathan in 1706. After hearing them read, the Dublin meeting ordered that official testimonies be drafted for Ann and Jonathan and entered in the national record.[34]

No less important were efforts to publish the works of recently deceased Friends. Following Burnyeat's death, Sharp and his colleagues shipped copies of his books and manuscripts to the morning meeting in London. When Fox died, the London yearly meeting asked Friends to submit the titles of his works in their possession; responsibility for compiling the Irish list was assigned to the Dublin men's meeting by the six-months meeting, though Sharp did not serve on the Dublin committee that undertook this task. In 1698 the London yearly meeting requested Irish Quakers to locate copies of Fox's works it did not have.[35] A similar effort was undertaken to collect the writings of Thomas Loe in 1698, though Dublin Friends found only his epistle to Jane Pildren.[36]

Sharp was more directly involved in the collection of materials for two Quaker histories. In May 1698 the national body asked monthly meetings to gather data concerning the rise and progress of truth, including information about who had introduced the Quaker message in an area; the first converts and the sufferings to which they were subjected; the names of both temperate and persecuting magistrates, and the judgments inflicted on the latter; the names of public Friends and the dates of their calling; and "what faithfull men there were and good Examples that had not a publique Testimony that served in their Generation according to Truth." The motivation behind this effort to collect historical data was probably Willem Sewel's request for information about the earliest Quakers, which Thomas Eccleston in London had passed to Dublin. Referring explicitly to this appeal, the Dublin men's meeting appointed Sharp in December 1699 to collect the provincial assemblies' responses. He, Ashton, and Amos Strettell then edited them and forwarded the material to London.[37]

In response to another request from the national meeting in May 1700, the Leinster meeting assigned two Friends from each monthly group to gather the material, including data on the establishment of assemblies for both worship and church affairs, accounts of backsliders, and "remarkeable passages of Sufferings or hardshipps, as well as favour showne." Sharp would have been among the elder Quakers whom the Dublin men's meeting deputed to talk with a committee of eight about their recollections of the Quaker movement's rise in Ireland. At the behest of the Dublin men's meeting, between November 1700 and February 1701 Sharp, Ashton, and Amos Strettell drafted an account of the rise and progress of the Quaker movement in the city. All of this material was submitted to Edmundson, and ultimately to Thomas Wight, who prepared the final manuscript for *A History of the Rise and Progress of the People Called Quakers in Ireland*. Sewel's more comprehensive work, *A History of the Rise, Increase and Progress of the*

Christian People Called Quakers, was published in Dutch in 1717 and English in 1722.[38] The efforts to compile and publish accounts of their history demonstrate the respect of Sharp and his coreligionists for the past, the significance of their traditions and practices for the shaping of future thought and action, and their maturation as a community determined to preserve its distinctive identity.

The sense of common purpose notwithstanding, the postwar years were not without their tensions. This was certainly so for Sharp, not least because of his recurring conflicts with Edmundson. Trouble between these twin pillars of Irish Quakerism dated back at least to December 1687, when Sharp had professed his innocency with respect to the unspecified but "Unhappy Differrence" between the two at the provincial meeting at Rosenallis, Queen's County (Laois). "Their other unhappy Differrence"—also unspecified—commenced about the same time according to Crabb. The disaffection between Sharp and Edmundson surfaced again in late 1695 when the latter told J. S. (Joseph Sleigh? John Stevens?), a confidant of Sharp's, that he had "drunk a cup of Sour Wine," an expression of his displeasure over the close relationship between Sharp and J. S. The latter refused to discuss the matter with Edmundson, whom J. S. thought was "resolved to make partyes for he Seemed to be Full of Bitterness."[39] Some of the dissension may have been rooted in Edmundson's outspoken criticism of "great Trading" and a high regard for materialistic things. When God called the first Friends "to be a People," such concerns, Edmundson believed, had been devalued, "but as our Number increased, it happened that such a Spirit came in among us, as was among the Jews, when they came up out of Egypt; this began to look back into the World, and traded with the Credit which was not of its own Purchasing, striving to be great in the Riches and Possessions of this World."[40] Did similar criticism provoke a defensive reaction in Sharp, who was one of the wealthiest merchants in Ireland?

The deepening rift between the two men provided the background for the proposed discussions between them at Swarthmore in August 1697. Sharp had consented to the meeting "as Far as his Freedom in the truth would allow him," but Edmundson failed to appear, as previously noted.[41] Three months later, Sharp and others complained that Edmundson had been making critical comments about fellow Friends in public meetings at which non-Quakers were present, notwithstanding requests that he cease this practice. When Sharp's protests to the Dublin and Leinster meetings did not dissuade Edmundson, Sharp laid his grievance before the national assembly in November 1697. In response to a question from the delegates about what action the Dublin and Leinster bodies had taken, Sharp replied caustically that "justice could hardly be had Where W[illiam] E[dmundson] was concerned." Seizing the opening, Edmundson insisted that the meeting hold Sharp accountable for casting such aspersions, but the latter averred that he had meant only to criticize the Mountmellick representatives, not the entire assembly. Several delegates implored Edmundson "to consider the Efect of such personall reflection that it tended not to edifie the Church nor convince others but to harden them and Sow discord amongst Brethren." Before he left the meeting Edmundson made some (unrecorded) remarks that satisfied most delegates, but he ignored entreaties to reconcile with Sharp, who was reportedly willing to forgive him. Crabb later reflected that Edmundson hunted Sharp as Saul had pursued David.[42]

In December a group of ministers and elders from the Dublin men's meeting visited Sharp with a request from the Leinster assembly that he explain his critical remarks at the last national gathering. He took the occasion to reiterate the history of his complaints against Edmundson's disparaging remarks as well as the failure of the meetings to end this provocation. Never, he insisted, did he intend to say that justice could not be obtained in these meetings "in a generall Way." This defense satisfied the Dublin delegates, who concurred that Edmundson had treated Sharp in a "disorderly, unbrotherly, Unchristianly, and unfreindly" manner in public meetings at such places as Dublin, Castledermot, Clonmel, and Mountmellick, offending Friends and scandalizing truth.[43]

The Dublin elders and ministers found that Sharp's criticism of the Mountmellick meeting had only been partially justified, for although Edmundson was one of its members, the others had cleared themselves of Edmundson's accusations. Nevertheless, some Mountmellick Quakers had opposed Sharp's plan to visit Scotland as a public Friend, probably because of the unresolved tension between the two leaders. Moreover, when Sharp rose to speak during the Leinster provincial meeting at Moate, Edmundson left the room and some of his supporters stood and occasionally interrupted Sharp.[44] Early in 1698 the Dublin men's meeting discussed the dispute, though Sharp was unable to attend. He wrote to the meeting on 7 March, insisting he would have been there to clear himself of the unjust charge had not an "urgent Occasion" necessitated his absence.[45] At root, the cause of the discord between Edmundson and Sharp must have been a personality conflict, perhaps the result of an unspoken competition for leadership, particularly of the Quaker movement in Leinster, as well as Edmundson's critical remarks about the wealthy. There was no hint of controversy between the two men over doctrine, polity, or worship.

The quarrel between Sharp and Edmundson seems to have terminated in 1698, perhaps because Penn interceded during his visit to Ireland that spring. Certainly he drew large crowds, as attested by both the six-months meeting and the bookseller John Dunton. In their report to the yearly meeting in London, Penn and his two companions, John Everett and the lawyer Thomas Story of Kirklinton, Cumberland, commented not only on the peace and unity that characterized the six-months meeting but also on the dispatch with which differences were settled and means found to prevent them in the future.[46]

The tensions between Edmundson and Sharp may also have been pushed into the shadows or perhaps dissipated altogether owing to attacks on the Friends by John Plimpton, a General Baptist artisan in Dublin. In 1698 he published three works against the Quakers: *Ten Charges Against the People Called Quakers*, *A Quaker No Christian*, and *Quakerism: The Mystery of Iniquity Discovered: In a Brief Dialogue Between a Christian and a Quaker, by Way of Supplement to My Former Papers Exhibited in Dublin Against Them*. Apparently only the last of these works is extant. A refutation of the *Ten Charges*, entitled *Gospel-Truths* and dated at Dublin on 14 May 1698, was written primarily by Penn, with the assistance of Sharp, Story, and Rooke. A simple broadsheet, it contains eleven brief statements, each supported with scriptural citations. *Gospel-Truths* amounted to a succinct primer, asserting the Quakers' belief in universal atonement; the necessity of obeying Christ's light to obtain justification, which nevertheless is not earned by righteous works; the inward light of Christ in every person; a repudiation of formal worship in favor of that performed through the Spirit; a rejection of the vain customs and fashions of the world; observance of the inner (Spirit) baptism and the Lord's supper, with tolerance for those who conscientiously practice the traditional rites; and respect for government as a divine ordinance, with Friends having a duty to submit, either by obeying its dictates or suffering the penalty for noncompliance. The authors took exception to the traditional doctrine of the Trinity, preferring instead to assert "that there are Three that bear Record in Heaven; the Father, the Word, and the Spirit; and these Three are really One, 1 John 5.7."[47]

Penn and his colleagues attacked Plimpton in other works as well.

Sharp independently refuted Plimpton's second or third tract. Entitled *Dirt Wip'd Off, Being a Return to J. Plimpton's False and Dirty Charge Against W. Penn* (1698), it may not be extant. With Story and Everett, Penn composed *The Quaker a Christian* (Dublin, 1698), which rebutted Plimpton's *A Quaker No Christian*. On 26 May 1698 Penn alone completed *Truth Further Clear'd from Mistakes* (Dublin, 1698), which reprinted the eighth and ninth chapters of his *Primitive Christianity Revived* (London, 1696) on Christ's death and the salvation of humankind, and added new material. The latter includes a concise statement of the prevailing Quaker position on the trinitarian debate: "Such as desire to lessen the Credit of our Perswasion with sober People, Represent us to deny the Trinity at large, and in every sense, tho' we only reject School-Terms, and Philosophical Definitions, as Unscriptural, if not Unsound, and as having a Tendency to Fruitless Controversie, instead of Edification and Holiness among Christians."[48]

Early in the summer of 1698, while visiting his comrades and estates in Cork, Penn provided a copy of *Gospel-Truths* to Edward Wetenhall, bishop of Cork. Wetenhall had hoped for a subsequent meeting with Penn to discuss the points raised in the broadside, but he was absent when Penn returned later in the year. The bishop therefore published a critique of *Gospel-Truths* in July 1698, asserting that the Friends were beyond the pale of Christianity and must "Repent and Return" to biblical principles. Penn replied in *A Defence of a Paper, Entituled, Gospel-Truths, Against the Exceptions of the Bishop of Cork's Testimony* (London, 1698), as did Sharp in an unpublished work that apparently does not survive. Crabb provided a brief synopsis of Sharp's retort but unfortunately found it too tedious to transcribe. He summarized four points, beginning with the Quakers' belief in God as the creator of heaven and earth who rules the universe in wisdom and holiness, sustaining and witnessing to all by his mercy and judgment. Secondly, Sharp reiterated the Friends' conviction that God speaks to humans through Christ, who enlightens every person and makes it possible for each to believe in and obey the light. The final two points summarized by Crabb were Sharp's affirmation of the divinity of Father, Son, and Spirit, and of a universal atonement.[49]

Sharp engaged in several other controversies in the postwar period. Among these were a refutation of the Muggletonians; a reply to an anti-Quaker polemic by Joshua Bows; a debate with Thomas Adams of Coleraine over such issues as immediate revelation and predestination; a defense of Quaker doctrine against an attack by Charles Whittingham of Wicklow; and a literary exchange with Robert Cook of Cappoquin, county Waterford, who left the Friends to find the "true" church. These debates, which are discussed in Chapter 10, had concluded by early 1695. After that date Sharp would record his views on spiritual and doctrinal matters in letters of counsel, but he engaged in no further religious debate, at least in writing.

He was, however, embroiled in two final disputes, both in 1701. The first of these, essentially another internal Quaker rift that had much to do with personality conflicts, achieved notoriety when it became the subject of a London newspaper story. According to this account Sharp and John Beck, also a public Friend, had "fallen out & raile one against another soe that Friends are divided." Alarmed Quakers in London sought an explanation from the Dublin men's meeting, which instructed Sharp and Amos Strettell to send a copy of the meeting's testimony against Beck for his disorderly marriage. The Dublin meeting also informed Friends in London that no greater difference existed between Sharp and Beck than between the latter and the rest of the group.[50] The fact that the author of the newspaper report singled out Sharp not only attests to his stature in Dublin Quaker circles but also suggests that some Londoners would have recognized his name and found the story of interest.

The final controversy was a bitter legal battle that could have cost Sharp £4,100 had he lost the case. Before the commissioners for forfeited estates, assorted witnesses for Thomas Pue accused Sharp of accepting more than £2,000 from Major Teague O'Regan in 1689 or 1690, providing him with lodging, and meeting in his home with Colin Kennedy, Sir James McClellan, and Lieutenant Bourk, all of whom were presumably Jacobites. Pue's witnesses could not agree on details, and Sharp marshaled his own witnesses to prove he had neither accepted money from nor provided lodging for O'Regan. More witnesses would have testified on his behalf but they were Quakers who could not swear. In his own defense Sharp declared "that if any man of Credit (not Such as they that had Sworne against him) would prove that Major Regan lodged at his house or was acquainted with him, he would give them his life and all that he was worth." On 15 September 1701 the commissioners not only dismissed the charges but also ordered Sharp to prosecute Pue and his witnesses for subornation and perjury, which he did in the court of King's Bench. The judges sentenced two of them to prison for six months and fined them £40 apiece, half of which was payable to the crown and half to Sharp. One of the two also had to stand in the pillory before the commissioners' court, where onlookers pelted him with eggs, potatoes, and dirt. Warrants were issued for the arrest of three others, but their fate is unknown.[51] The Friends were ordinarily chary of lawsuits, but Sharp clearly saw this as a justifiable exception, partly because he had been ordered to prosecute the offenders by the commissioners, but perhaps partly owing to his sensitivity about the Quakers' reputed sympathy for James during the time of troubles. Such suspicions were not helpful as the Friends endeavored to work with the Williamite regime in the postwar years.

The unwillingness of some of Sharp's servants to testify on his behalf in the O'Regan case owing to their principled opposition to oaths underscored the depths of Quaker opposition to this practice, especially in Ireland. As Abraham Fuller and Thomas Holme argued, the Friends believed oaths were "but Figures of this inward Bond or Covenant, confirmed by the Oath of God in the Seed of Abraham, which the True Christians are of, who witness the Substance and End of all Oaths without, and of Strife, Doubts and Variances that occasioned the Oaths." Yet early modern British society relied extensively on oaths, not only to determine the truth in judicial proceedings but also to assure the obedience of subjects to rulers and tenants to landlords. Oaths had both a political and a religious context, as reflected most obviously in the oaths of supremacy and allegiance. Because they refused to take oaths the Friends faced fines and imprisonment and they could be excluded from jury service and government office as well as from proving wills, suing to recover debts, or testifying in court. During James' reign, however, the government at various levels had made efforts to accommodate the Friends, permitting them, as we have seen, to serve in corporations if they would attest their loyalty.[52]

William and Mary's government was inclined to treat the Friends tolerantly, and in 1691 the English Parliament approved legislation abrogating the oath of supremacy in Ireland and permitting the Quakers to make an affirmation instead of taking most other oaths. Eleven Dublin Friends, including Amos and Abel Strettell, Smallman, Fade, Deane, and the merchant Edward Webb, took advantage of this opportunity to obtain the freedom of the city after they subscribed the declaration and the freeman's oath and paid the entry fines. Between 1692 and 1695 an additional sixteen Friends followed suit, as did twenty-three more between 1696 and 1706. The Friends had to pay special fees every year, thereby giving the municipal government a small source of additional revenue.

Most were charged a token 12d. *per annum*, though Sharp had to pay five times this amount.[53]

In February 1692 the Dublin men's meeting named a committee, whose members included Sharp, Clarridge, Roberts, and the Strettell brothers, to sign and seal certificates for Friends who subscribed declarations as provided by the new law.[54] The statute did not exempt Quakers from oaths in law courts, but in 1692 the English Parliament took up a bill that would have allowed affirmations in this arena as well. In a spirit of cooperation, the yearly meeting in London expressed a willingness to use such phrases as "in the sight of God," "in the fear of God," "before God," or "in the presence of God," but Irish Friends were not inclined to compromise. In September the Dublin men's meeting sent Sharp, Clarridge, and Gay to Viscount Sydney, the lord lieutenant, with a petition (which Sharp drafted) seeking liberty of conscience and exemption from all oaths; Sydney promised to do what he could for the Quakers. Because nothing had happened by the time the half-yearly meeting convened in November, it appointed a committee of nineteen, including Sharp, to urge the Council to act on the petition. When they discovered the Council was not sitting, the delegates instructed Sharp, Starkey, Ashton, and Winslow to take up the issue of the petition when it resumed.[55]

When it convened, the Council summoned a Quaker delegation that included Sharp, Starkey, Ashton, and the schoolmaster John Archer, a member of the Limerick meeting, to discuss the petition. Francis Marsh, archbishop of Dublin, wanted to know the basis for the Quakers' assertion that the king and Parliament had provided liberty from oaths in England, to which Starkey retorted by referring to the Act of Toleration and the poll tax legislation. Sharp added that several other statutes did the same, but he apparently did not cite them. When William Moreton, bishop of Kildare, asked Sharp if he had sustained losses of £500 for refusing to swear, he answered negatively but insisted that some Quakers had. To Marsh's assertion that the angels swore, Sharp retorted: "All the Angels Worship christ who commands not to Swear at all." Henry Jones, bishop of Meath, attempted to break the impasse by proposing an alternative declaration, such as "in the presence of God" or "before God and the World." Although Starkey apparently found this appealing, Sharp was unyielding, insisting that "wee are allways in the presence of God and must needs be true." Judging Sharp mistaken, Jones asserted that only "promisary" and vain oaths were prohibited. Evading the real issue, Sharp reminded Jones that the law banned vain oaths, whereupon an exasperated Jones told the Quakers that their consciences were mistaken and for good measure called Sharp a fool. Starkey attempted to elevate the debate by reminding the Council that everyone would ultimately be accountable to another judge, and he called attention as well to the understanding that God had given him. Unwilling to shift the debate into this area, Jones focused again on oaths: "You say christ forbids all Swearing; do you believe he practised himself what you beleives he Forbids?" Starkey thought not, and Sharp quickly added that Christ had come to fulfil the law. Although Jones claimed he could prove Jesus had sworn, Sharp countered that Quakers believe he never did. Again at an impasse, the disputants concluded their discussion with an exchange about Christ's divinity.[56] The episode is significant as a revelation of Sharp's uncompromising opposition to an affirmation as the alternative to an oath, but it also suggests that his debating ability was not particularly impressive.

Sharp's opinion of oaths was exemplified on another occasion, which Crabb neglected to date. T. S.—almost certainly Thomas Starkey—had been cited before the lord chancellor, who insisted he was bound by law to swear before giving evidence. On Starkey's behalf, Sharp began by complaining that the Friends had been subjected to considerable injustice because of their refusal to take oaths, and urging the chancellor to act on their behalf before the Quakers were destroyed; he was, Sharp contended, bound by his office to render justice. "The law doth not absolutely tye up a Chancellor to the Rygor of a ceremony to doe injustice therein, or hinder justice, for that would be contrary to it self, for the law is not made to destroy any but to preserve." The oath itself, Sharp averred, was not the substance of either justice or the law; its purpose was solely to assure that people testified truthfully. If Friends told the truth, they fulfilled the intent of an oath even if they did not take it. After all, there were no oaths when God created the first humans. Quakers, he concluded, should not "lose the benifit of the Law that by birth accrues to every person born Subject of England in justice & truth because, for Conscience Sake toward God, they cannot Swear."[57] This belief provided the foundation for Sharp's conviction that not even an affirmation was requisite or conscionable; the word of Friends must be accepted simply because their consciences bound them to tell the truth.

In November 1692 the six-months meeting discussed the proposed affirmation and found the compromising position of English Friends unacceptable. Over the signatures of nineteen members, of whom Sharp was not one, it sent a letter to the meeting for sufferings arguing that a declaration of truth be accepted instead of an oath, and that Quakers be required to use only the "yea" and "nay" recommended by Jesus if possible. Irish and English Friends continued to communicate about this issue, with Sharp and Starkey serving as the Dublin meeting's designated respondents.[58] This assignment strongly suggests that Sharp was influential in shaping the stricter position of Irish Friends.

The divisions among Friends over the proposed affirmation may have been a factor in Parliament's procrastination in passing legislation on this matter until early 1696. Meanwhile Irish authorities had permitted the Quakers to subscribe a declaration instead of taking an oath associated with the poll tax. The Dublin men's meeting even had Sharp and Amos Strettell inquire of the poll tax commissioners in December 1695 if Friends could produce certificates attesting they had previously subscribed such a declaration instead of making new ones, but the commissioners rejected this proposal.[59]

Spurred on by George Whitehead in England, the king threw his support behind a parliamentary bill that would permit Quakers to make a simple affirmation in lieu of an oath: "I, A. B., do declare in the presence of Almighty God, the witness of the truth of what I say." The Affirmation Act (May 1696) fanned the smoldering embers of division among Friends over what constituted an oath. Politically, the debate was sensitive because the king's supporters were now demanding not only the usual oaths but also adherence to an Association recognizing William as the rightful monarch and requiring all officeholders under the crown to swear to avenge his assassination should it occur. The English House of Commons had instituted the Association following disclosure of an assassination plot in February 1696, and on 1 April of that year the Dublin aldermen instructed churchwardens, sidesmen, and overseers to go house-to-house obtaining subscriptions to the Association and recording the names of Protestants who refused to comply. Moreover, in Dublin, Quakers seeking admission to the freedom of the city now had to sign the Association as well as make the affirmation stipulated in the new statute.[60]

The affirmation was a major topic of discussion at the national meeting in May 1696, when Irish Friends decided they could not subscribe because it included the Lord's name. Better, they concluded, to suffer if they could not profess their loyalty using only Jesus' "yea" and "nay." With respect to the Association, the representatives, noting that Quakers in most parts of Ireland now had to sign the document, pro-

fessed their agreement with a statement about the affirmation prepared
by their colleagues in London. This permitted those who could make the
affirmation with a clear conscience to do so, but insisted that others
should not be compelled to use it. The delegates appointed Sharp, Edmundson, and Trafford to draft a postscript to the English declaration
that could be presented to the government by the six-months meeting if
necessary. The postscript professed the unity of Irish Friends with their
English colleagues concerning the Association.[61] Whitehead was irate
when he learned of the half-yearly meeting's refusal to accept the affirmation. When Rooke conveyed Whitehead's displeasure to Sharp, the
latter wrote a lengthy letter dated 29 August explaining the Irish position, but the document seems not to have survived. When the six-
months meeting next assembled, in November 1696, it unanimously reiterated its decision "to keepe to Christs plaine words in matters of Affirmation and Negation in earthly Affaires." At the assembly's behest,
Sharp, Rooke, Wight, the merchant Joseph Pike of Cork, and Robert
Hoope (or Hoopes) of Lurgan informed the London yearly meeting of
this action.[62]

Sharp and his associates refused to retreat from their strict position
on the affirmation. In August 1697 the Leinster provincial meeting recommended that each of its constituent bodies remind its members not to
accept the affirmation or sign a declaration instead of an oath, and it
also authorized Friends who were present at the next parliamentary session in Dublin to inform members of Parliament that Quakers could not
sign any declaration that included "the sacred name of the Lord."[63] Six
months later, on 12 February 1698, the Leinster meeting, noting that
the last session of the English Parliament had approved a bill to secure
the king's safety (7–8 William and Mary, c. 27) with a provision for
Friends to sign a declaration of loyalty, directed Trafford, Rooke, and
Amos Strettell to inform the yearly meeting in London that Irish Quakers remained unanimously opposed to such a declaration because it incorporated the Lord's name. Instead they proposed "that timely endeavours may be used to ease our tender Consciences therein," and that
a delegation of Friends from the Dublin meeting make their position
known to the lords justices and Privy Council. Less than two weeks
later, on 23 February, the Dublin men's meeting dispatched Sharp and
Amos Strettell to consult with Judge Coote about obtaining a declaration "in such easie words as may not pinch upon the tender conscience
of any Friend," but Coote advised them not to meddle in this matter for
the present. Responding to a request from English Friends for further

discussion of their differences over the affirmation, the six-months meeting in May appointed a delegation of seven (not including Sharp) to go to London if necessary.[64]

Because of their refusal to accept the affirmation, many Irish Quakers had their poll taxes doubled. Consequently in May 1698 the six-months meeting delegated Sharp, Boate, Trafford, and Thomas Pearce, a prominent member of the Limerick meeting, to seek relief from the lord chief justice, other judges, and the speaker of the Irish House of Commons. When they had not undertaken this assignment by the time the Leinster meeting convened in June, the latter asked Sharp, Trafford, Amos Strettell, and James Hutchinson of Knockballymagher, county Tipperary, to do so and to convey the results to Friends throughout Ireland. There is no evidence to indicate whether they fulfilled their commission, but the problem in any event remained unresolved, for in July the Leinster meeting ordered its constituent groups to maintain records of those who suffered for refusing to subscribe the declaration associated with the poll tax.[65]

The six-months meeting decided in November 1698 to reiterate its principles in an address to the Irish Parliament and the lords justices. Signed by Edmundson, Trafford, Hoope, Wight, and Boate, it reaffirmed the Friends' principle of living peacefully under a government ordained by God. Their refusal to subscribe the declaration did not stem from disaffection to the king and government but from "a tender Scruple of Conscience" because of the inclusion of God's name. Although some Quakers had previously subscribed the declaration, their consciences were troubled because it was too similar to an oath. Now, "wee are ready to declare Our Selves in as full words as are Contained Either in the Declaration of Fidelity or that against the Pope and his Supremacy under any Penalty you shall think fitt (the Sacred name of God not being therein)." The address went on to complain that Friends were wrongly accused of having lent money to James and clothed one of his regiments.[66] Sharp neither signed this address nor was a member of the delegations that presented it to Parliament and the lords justices, but he was one of the twenty-two Friends who wrote an epistle to Irish Quakers imploring them to stand together in supporting the address.[67]

Although the address was read in the House of Commons, Parliament offered no relief. The Friends remained adamant in their refusal to subscribe the declaration, even when the government distrained the goods of those who refused to pay the double tax. The financial impact can be seen in the steep rise in the annual value of distrained goods (including those seized from Quakers who refused to pay tithes and church rates), from £554 11s. 2d. in 1692, to £887 1s. 6d. in 1695, to £1,710 18s. 11½d. in 1698, and to £2,000 2s. 9d. in 1700. In the hope that elections for a new English House of Commons in the summer of 1698 would result in a more sympathetic attitude toward the Quaker position, the six-months meeting was prepared to send a delegation to London in 1699, but nothing came of this.[68] In November 1700 the national meeting was again willing to send representatives to London to attend both Parliament and the yearly meeting; Sharp was not among the dozen Friends, including Roberts, Winslow, Wight, and Pike, who were to make this journey if needed.[69]

More than a year later, in February 1702, a group of Friends gathered in Dublin to discuss the affirmation. This group too wrote to London, offering to send a delegation to explore the issue. Sharp was among the twenty-seven men who signed this letter, which restated the longstanding opposition to any declaration that included God's name. However, the authors noted that some Irish Friends were now prepared to sign the declaration, though they refrained from doing so for fear of offending other Quakers.[70] The day after sending this missive, Irish Friends received a report from London concerning a parliamentary bill to renew the Affirmation Act. Sharp and his twenty-six confreres responded the next day, 9 February, expressing concern that English Friends had not objected to the bill and articulating a sense of futility about sending a delegation. If English Friends could not persuade Parliament to amend the bill, Sharp and his cohorts thought it would be preferable for the bill to fail rather than be renewed in its existing form.[71]

In fact, English Friends were not of one mind regarding the affirmation, for Westmorland Quakers opposed it, as did Friends in northern Scotland. Sensitive to such concerns, including those of Irish Friends, English Quakers proposed the following wording:

> You shall declare or Speake the Truth, the whole Truth, and nothing but the Truth in the present Case according to the best of your knowledge, and that the friends Answer may be Yea, or Yes, which forme may be Applyed Mutatis mutandis to other Cases, which the Affirmation may reach unto.

Should this be unacceptable, alternative wording was suggested:

> I A. B. do sincerely and Solemnly declare and Affirme that in the matters to which I am now Called to give Evidence I will Speake the Truth, the whole Truth, and nothing but the Truth, according to the best of my knowledge.

English Friends were clearly willing to accommodate the scruples of Sharp and his confreres, but the conciliatory move came too late to enable them to approach Parliament with a united front. Nor was it necessarily the case that Quaker unity would have persuaded Parliament to use alternative language. In any event, Parliament renewed the act in 1702 (13–14 William III, c. 4).[72]

Sharp almost certainly sided with the majority in the Leinster provincial meeting (only one person dissented) in March 1704 when it ordered that the Friends' "tender Scruple of refuseing the Affirmation" because it mentioned God's name be "recorded in its season in the written rise and progresse of Truth." They obviously deemed this an important episode in their history. Wight devoted two paragraphs of his third chapter to this issue in the 1690s, stressing the attainment of unity among Irish and English Friends in 1696.[73]

Long before the affirmation controversy the Irish Quakers had manifested concern about their relationship with Parliament and the magistracy. As early as November 1673 the six-months meeting had decided to record all petitions to the king, lord lieutenant, and Council as well as all conciliar orders concerning Friends. The same meeting also called for the preservation of copies of all Quaker applications to judges and magistrates as well as their directives concerning Friends.[74]

After the time of troubles the Irish Friends took a more active role in monitoring and attempting to influence government policies. James' declarations of indulgence and the Act of Toleration had raised their expectations of better treatment at the authorities' hands, but they were wary that their enemies might succeed in curtailing such limited freedom as they had come to enjoy. In the fall of 1692 the provincial meetings (probably including Munster) designated agents to attend the Irish Parliament when it resumed sitting. The Leinster meeting named six men, including Sharp, Clarridge, and Trafford, and the Ulster meeting three; Munster was definitely participating by 1697. By that time the Leinster meeting asked each of its constituent groups to send two representatives who were responsible "to Advise concerned friends when any extraordinary Occasion may Appeare that they may Come up and Consider what may be done." When the national meeting convened while Parliament was in session, it dispatched agents to monitor parliamentary proceedings. During the ensuing years the number of people appointed to undertake this task varied: Leinster sent three each from Dublin and Mountmellick and two apiece from Moate, Newgarden, Wexford, and Wicklow in the fall of 1703; in early 1705 the same meeting selected thirteen people, and the national meeting added another four from each province and five from Dublin.[75]

The parliamentary committee's records, which are reasonably full for the period 1703 to 1705, reveal Sharp's extensive involvement in its work. Among those with whom he served were Amos Strettell, the committee's leading member, and Ashton, Baker, Newland, Cuppage, Brownlow, Barcroft, Hammond, James Hutchinson, and John Watson. Shortly after the opening of Queen Anne's first Irish Parliament on 24 September 1703, the lord chief justice requested a meeting with Sharp to report that "he had made Interest with Severall of the Lords" and thought it was now possible for Parliament to pass an affirmation bill akin to the one recently enacted in England. Expecting an expression of gratitude from the Friends, the chief justice was offended when Sharp and Boate, who accompanied him, registered their opposition. It was a principled if shaky commencement of the Quakers' relationship with the new Parliament.[76]

In the months before this Parliament adjourned in March 1704, Sharp and his colleagues consulted with a wide range of prominent political leaders, including two lord deputies, Major-General Thomas Erle and the earl of Mount-Alexander; the earls of Meath, Inchiquin, and Londonderry; Lords Charlemont, Coningsby, Ely, and Lanesborough; the chancellor of the Exchequer, the clerk of the Privy Council, and the speaker of the House of Commons; the archbishops of Armagh, Dublin, Cashel, and Tuam; and the bishops of Down and Connor, Kildare, Meath, Ferns and Leighlin, Elphin, Clonfert, Waterford, Killaloe, Ossory, Limerick, and Killala. Sharp personally met with the archbishop of Dublin and Lord Lanesborough, and possibly others.[77]

During the first session of this Parliament the committee expressed an interest in a wide range of bills, including those dealing with the growth of Catholicism, church rates, tithes, the suppression of profanity and blasphemy, imposition of the abjuration oath (on clergy and others), and the valuation of houses in cities and corporations (which was intended to prevent an increase in clerical revenue). The parliamentary committee was also interested in an address to the queen seeking permission for merchants in Ireland to export linen directly to the American colonies. Sharp and his colleagues quickly recognized that the popery bill (enacted in 1704 as 2 Anne, c. 6), which severely restricted Catholic rights to acquire land, did not threaten Quakers, but the committee was sufficiently concerned about the bill for church rates to send Sharp, Boate, and John Hoope to consult an attorney.[78]

Understandably, the bill that most concerned the committee pertained to the collection of tithes. In preparing its case against this bill the committee amassed records of Quaker suffering, including data for Leinster in the period 1700–1702. Sharp drafted a brief against the bill, explicating four reasons to oppose it. First, he contended that the clergy sought to enable "every ill minded Tythe taker to ruine & destroye us," for they had already distrained more in kind than the tithes were worth. He noted as well that even some rapparees were collecting tithes. Secondly, whereas existing law empowered the bishops, following "a definitive Sentence," to have justices of the peace arrest and imprison those who refused to pay tithes, the new bill would give a suer the option of obtaining a warrant for distraining goods or jailing the offender. This, Sharp believed, would result in more tithe-farming and encourage tithe-holders to inflate their value. Thirdly, although the bill claimed it would reduce the frequency of excommunications, Sharp disputed this inasmuch as it would enable church courts to excommunicate by the new and simple procedure of taking a party's failure to appear as his or her guilty plea. This would harm those Quakers who ignored summons, seeing no remedy for relief in a court appearance. Finally, Sharp averred that the bill threatened the Friends' liberties as well as their families because it would enable a tithe-holder to take out a warrant to have Quakers incarcerated and another to seize their goods while they were in prison. Because tithe-payments were due more than ten times a year, this bill would enable Friends to be sued virtually every month by tithe-farmers.[79]

The committee assiduously opposed the tithes bill. Consultations with many prelates "had good Efect," and some bishops insisted they were not interested in persecuting Quakers. Moreover, the temporal lords approached by committee members expressed a willingness not to punish the Friends if the bishops did not. But when some prelates urged the Council to support the tithes bill, the committee employed the solicitor general, Richard Levinge, to appear before the Council on the Friends' behalf. On 30 November Boate and Rooke called on Ormond, who received them with kindness and accepted a petition signed by Sharp, Boate, John Watson, and Amos Strettell. If the bill were enacted, the petitioners claimed, "its like to ruine Soe many English Familys as wee are in this Nation, & therefore of great Disadvantage to the Queens & true protestants Interest in this Kingdome." The Friends requested and received a copy of the bill and an opportunity to have Levinge plead their case to the full Council, which he did on 13 December. Perhaps partly because of the sustained Quaker opposition, the bill made no further progress in this session.[80]

Sharp's final service on the parliamentary committee occurred in the months following Ormond's reconvening of Parliament in February 1705. Three bills—the pending one on tithes and others on manufactories and marriage—concerned the Friends. In March, when the committee dispatched several of its people to consult possible sympathizers, Sharp and Thomas Duckett met with Stephen Ludlow, who seemed receptive to the Quakers' case, and Abel Strettell had comparable success with Levinge and Sir Thomas Southwell. With six others, Sharp, Duckett, and Strettell responded to a committee request to draft a document incorporating the Friends' case against the tithes bill. Among the dozen reasons were several cited by Sharp in 1703, the last of which was expanded into a warning that someone refusing to pay tithes could be financially ruined by twenty or more suits a year because small tithes were staggered. The drafters evoked the threat of popery and financial loss, claiming the bill would enable Irish Catholics who served as churchwardens, constables, valuers, and tithe-collectors to weaken the Protestant interest and distrain animals needed by the poor to pay their rents. The document also complained that the bill would allow a knavish tenant who wanted to leave his landlord "to gett one of his Sort to take his Tythe & So willingly come under the Lash of this bill, that he may defraud his Landlord of his Rent." Sharp and his coauthors also adduced legal reasons against the bill: It included no provisions for farmers to complain to justices of the peace if tithe-takers were vexatious, nor did it empower justices to intervene if distraints were excessive. Finally, the drafters appealed to anticlerical sentiment, contending it was unreasonable for the clergy to become more severe in collecting tithes at a time when many conscientious landlords "finde themselves concerned to make Considerable abatements of their Rents." Moreover, Sharp and his associates warned that if this bill passed and proved to be oppressive, it would be difficult to remedy because historically the clergy had been reluctant to yield anything, even for the public good.[81]

In the ensuing weeks the committee pressed its case. Sharp and Amos Strettell met with the Whig Alan Brodrick, speaker of the House of Commons, who promised to consider the written statement they left with him. Members also consulted with Privy Councilors, among whom the earl of Drogheda was the responsibility of Sharp and Winslow. Although noting that he had supported the Quakers on this issue, Drogheda could not attend the Council meeting because of illness, but the lord chancellor, who met with Amos Strettell, invited Friends to attend the Council session. Levinge, the earls of Meath and Abercorn, and others were sympathetic to the Quakers. Sharp and Winslow also sought the assistance of Brodrick, who thought the bill would fail and declined to accept a fee from the Friends, and John Foster, the recorder of Dublin, who agreed to appear before the Council on their behalf. Meanwhile, Sharp, Winslow, the Strettell brothers, Duckett, and ten others reviewed the latest version of the bill and drafted another statement opposing it. Like its predecessor, it reiterated the view that, if passed, the bill "carryes the face of utmost ruine Particularly to us the Said people, & to the Protestants in Generall."[82]

The committee records say little about the manufactories and marriage bills, both of which the Friends opposed. It is difficult to ascertain why they might have been against a bill encouraging the manufacture of hemp and flax unless they were displeased by the competitive disadvantage of its provisions to enlarge houses of correction for the dressing and preparation of hemp and flax at the counties' charge, and to require each town to establish a spinning school. Another bill, which was not enacted, encouraged the consumption of Irish-manufactured items in Ireland. From the minutes it is impossible to tell which of these bills the Friends opposed. In any event, Sharp and Ashton consulted with Foster about a manufactories bill, but he concluded that it did not affect the Quakers and would not pass. After the committee decided it was a threat, Sharp and Amos Strettell went to see Foster again, while other members conferred with Ormond, Meath, and the attorney general.[83]

Intended to stop clandestine unions, the marriage bill proposed that couples could only be wed by legally authorized people using the rite incorporated in the Book of Common Prayer, and only after the publication of banns. Because this clearly threatened Quaker marriages, Amos Strettell found some sympathy when he spoke with the attorney general and the solicitor general in late March. When Strettell and Sharp showed a copy of a Quaker marriage certificate to the lord chancellor, he adjudged it "very Sollemn" and seemed to approve of it.[84] None of the three bills had been passed at the time of Sharp's last recorded activity on the parliamentary committee, which met at his house on 5 April 1705,[85] nor were they enacted during the remaining years of Anne's reign. Apart from that of Amos Strettell, Sharp's service on the parliamentary committee had no peer.

In the affirmation controversy's early stages, Irish Friends expressed a willingness to send representatives to monitor the proceedings of the

English Parliament, but it is unclear when the first group did so. By January 1705 the Ulster and Munster meetings had each appointed two Friends to travel to London for this purpose, and the Leinster meeting named eight, four of whom were to go when needed. Sharp was not among them.[86]

Advancing years did not temper Sharp's interest in the political realm, especially as it had an impact on Friends. Moreover, he seems to have continued to enjoy respect from non-Quakers, particularly commencing in the late 1680s. In 1700 the lord mayor-elect of Dublin sought Sharp's advice on how he should govern the city. Sharp's response manifested a simple but potent standard of ethical conduct, the heart of which was the principle that "the Honour of god is to be minded and the Good and Well Fare of the people." As Solomon recognized, the most requisite trait in a magistrate is the wisdom to rule well; God, the author and provider of wisdom, must therefore be called on for guidance. To rule effectively one must fear God and shun vice by practicing virtue, and to facilitate good government magistrates must lead by example, manifesting justice, eating and drinking in moderation, and subduing excess, debauchery, and contention. The good magistrate must cherish peace, virtue, and "Kind neighbourhood" as well as remain sensitive to the needs of the indigent. Sharp placed a premium on inner qualities as opposed to material accomplishments: "As it is a comly sight to behold a clean cyty and the Streets Sweet, so it is much more excellent that the people be clean." Although some would oppose this emphasis on "Sweet," virtuous living, Dublin's "best sort" would commend the mayor, and some would even emulate his standards. Sharp could not let this opportunity pass without concluding with the iteration of a fundamental Quaker principle: "To obtain the power of doeing Good as well as Saying or commending Good, is to beleive in and obey that good Spirit of God in the heart, he being the Fountain of all Good, and First principle of all true Religion." Cognizant that high office embodied an almost irresistible temptation to haughtiness, Sharp added—almost as an afterthought—that God would teach the humble.[87] Here, then, was Sharp's prescription for political success—a standard of conduct almost eloquent in its simplicity and perhaps nearly impossible to attain.

Sharp's last known proffer of political advice was unsolicited. In the spring of 1704 the French and the Bavarians began to threaten Vienna with the aim of driving the Holy Roman Empire from the Grand Alliance. In a brilliant strategic maneuver John Churchill, duke of Marlborough, marched his British, Dutch, and German forces 250 miles from the Low Countries to the Danube. There, at Blenheim in August, he destroyed two-thirds of the French army and captured its commander, Maréchal Tallard. For the first time, Louis XIV's forces had experienced total defeat, though the war itself was a long way from being over. Nearly three weeks after the battle, Sharp wrote to Marlborough, insisting the victory was the Lord's, for all power derives from God. He moved quickly to lay the foundation for an appeal to the earl to work for liberty of conscience in the Empire. Without faith, he argued, there can be no true worship of God—no pleasing the divine. Because faith is a divine gift that no human can bestow, no one should attempt to coerce people in matters of worship contrary to the dictates of their faith and their consciences. "Pretended Dominion over mens Faith is against God, and for which his judgments have been and is now against potentates and will be more if they doe not repent." Having achieved such a spectacular triumph for the Emperor Leopold I, Marlborough, advised Sharp, should press on him the importance of granting liberty of conscience to the Hungarians and other non-Catholics in the Empire.[88]

The expression in this letter of Sharp's interest in international Protestantism is rare among his writings; indeed, the only other substantial indication was his continental trip as a public Friend. Yet there is nothing surprising about this international dimension in Sharp's thought, for many Protestants in the British Isles had for decades been alert to their coreligionists' plight in such places as France and Savoy, partly because of newspaper reports. Moreover, Fox wrote to Poland's King John III on behalf of Friends in Danzig.[89] What is unusual was Sharp's decision to write to a prominent general seeking his intervention on behalf of persecuted Protestants. Penn, he hoped, would transmit the letter to Marlborough.[90] Whether he did, we do not know.

For Sharp the postwar era provided an opportunity to engage in a more thorough structuring of the Quaker movement, the more deliberate preservation of its records and the writing of its history, the continued defense of its principles against attacks by critics, and the Friends' ongoing involvement in the political process, notably by monitoring parliamentary proceedings and attempting to sensitize members of Parliament to Quaker concerns. Sharp was a constructive, leading force in shaping Quaker policy and participating in the movement's work. This was the period of his greatest engagement in the work of a public

Friend, and it was ultimately in that capacity that he proffered his views on civil magistracy to a lord mayor-elect of Dublin and pleaded with Marlborough to intervene with the Holy Roman Emperor on behalf of persecuted Protestants. During this period Sharp was at the zenith of his influence in the Quaker movement, helping it complete the transformation from sect to protodenomination.[91]

7

"That Truth May Be Clear"

The Meetings and Their Work

THE FOCAL POINT of much of Sharp's religious activity with other Friends was the cycle of monthly, provincial, and national meetings, in all of which he played a prominent role, helping them to conduct their business, record their activities, communicate with other meetings, and manage their finances. His coreligionists valued his business expertise, legal background, and organizational skills, much as they looked to him to deal with magistrates and clergy of the established church in the pursuit of their affairs. Adept at institutional matters rather than in rhetorical skills, Sharp manifested extraordinary skill in helping the Quakers develop a polity more characteristic of a church than a sect.

Monthly meetings antedated Sharp's arrival in Ireland, the first having been noted by Thomas Loe as early as August 1660 at Cork. The monthly meeting, which typically comprised local or preparative meetings, was a cornerstone of the Quaker movement. Here the Friends dealt with such basic matters as the time and place of worship, care of the needy, disciplining the wayward, the building and upkeep of meetinghouses and burial yards, and the collection and disbursement of funds. Here too lay the primary responsibility for recording births, marriages, deaths, testimonies, and papers of disownment and condemnation. Members of the local meeting, explained Sharp, "wait upon the Lord, to have their hearts real unto the Lord, to hear him, to mind his buisness and affairs of the church in that place that truth may be clear and of a Good report and all evil don away that the strong may be encouraged and the weak strengthened & evill and bad condemned that Unity may be preserved and all may be in good order in that place."[1]

Despite the nomenclature, in Dublin such meetings convened biweekly. All adult Friends in good standing were expected to attend, but those whose conduct was questionable faced banishment. In 1699 unrepentant Quakers who had engaged in an illicit sexual relationship were prohibited from attending monthly meetings and serving as public Friends. By the early 1700s the Dublin meeting had begun to interview those who had expressed an interest in participating in its activities. In July 1706, for example, Sharp and Samuel Baker, acting at the behest of the men's meeting, talked with Francis Russell about his conduct, explained Quaker standards of behavior, and concluded that he could be admitted to the monthly meeting.[2] Over a period of more than two decades the Dublin meeting periodically appointed Sharp, with others, to determine why some members were not attending meetings. Those who lacked acceptable excuses and continued to miss meetings for worship faced condemnation in a formal testimony. One of those whom Sharp investigated, Jonathan Taylor, had been absent because of problems with a wayward apprentice so severe that he (unsuccessfully) sought the assistance of the justices of the peace to remove the young man from his service; however, the meeting did not adjudge this a valid excuse and ordered Taylor to resume attending.[3]

Besides setting times and places for worship, the monthly meeting monitored conduct at such assemblies. This could include such behavior as sleeping during meetings or arriving late,[4] but oversight extended as well to what people said in meetings and how long they spoke. By December 1679 Joan Pildren was again provoking concern by her unorthodox behavior in assemblies, and the Dublin men's meeting therefore dispatched Sharp and Roger Roberts to request the next women's meeting to counsel Pildren and Catherine Jackson about their "Imaginary Spiritts." If they refused to submit, the women's meeting was to refer the matter back to the men. Jackson subsequently agreed to remain quiet in meetings, but only as long as the Spirit did not compel her to testify, whereas a defiant Pildren refused to confer with the women's meeting, "for she had speakeing Enough already & . . . she Should but Trouble Friends & Friends Trouble her." Ann Sharp and Eleanor Atherton reported Pildren's and Jackson's responses to the men's meeting. As in 1669, the Friends issued a testimony against Pildren, yet in 1686 she was again disrupting meetings. This time Sharp and his confreres ordered that the earlier testimonies concerning her be read again in the meetings, yet she refused to acknowledge herself "to be in any disorder but doth impudently Justifie herselfe in all that she hath done."[5] In another case, the men's meeting dispatched several members, possibly in-

cluding Sharp, to Chapelizod in February 1693 for the purpose of asking Sarah Johnson to subject herself to public Friends' judgment concerning her speaking in public meetings.[6]

Men did not cause similar concerns by speaking with unrestrained
spiritual enthusiasm in the Dublin gatherings, perhaps because they
were subject to different social constraints, or possibly owing to gender-
based variations in religious experience. Despite the difficulties with the
religious exuberance of some women, the Dublin men's meeting demonstrated no reticence to approve women as public Friends. On the same
day the men sent Sharp and Roberts to consult with the women's meeting about Pildren and Jackson, they deputed Roberts and James Taylor
to tell Ann Sikes, who was about to become a public Friend, that she
should do so only if "it bee in the Authority of the power of God, and
. . . will Doe good." She agreed to act responsibly.[7]

From time to time Sharp and the other members of the Dublin men's
meeting held special services. They did so in July 1684 to remind
Friends of the danger of frequenting alehouses and engaging in light discourse, and to urge masters and mistresses of families to oversee the behavior of their children and servants. Young people and servants were
expected to attend some of these special meetings, a number of which
were devoted to their edification. Dublin Friends were pleased with the
results, "the Lord owning the same," the minutes note in June 1700,
"by affording his divine tendring power." The same month, husbands
and wives gathered for a special meeting, and later that year the heads
of families assembled, again with beneficial results. Although the men's
and women's business meetings normally convened separately, members
of the two sexes sometimes sat together in meetings of worship, for in
June 1696 the men's meeting had to admonish Dublin Quakers that it
was "necessary and decent" for them to be segregated. Yet they assembled together in May 1701 at the women's request and were pleased
with the result.[8] During the Sharp era the Dublin Quakers were relatively flexible and innovative in their willingness to congregate for special purposes.

Much of the work of the Dublin men's meeting involved correspondence and record-keeping, areas in which Sharp performed nearly her-
culean service. For at least a quarter of a century he and several others
acted as scribes, writing letters, recording testimonies and papers of
condemnation, and corresponding with other meetings about Friends
who had relocated, young people who intended to marry, and similar
matters.[9] A sampling of Sharp's scribal activities illustrates their nature

and broad scope. In 1678 he and Turner communicated with Quakers in Limerick and Cork about Rebecca Gotely's behavior in "relation to truth or otherwise"; she proved to be a woman of ill repute who had become impregnated in her husband's absence. The following year the men's meeting commissioned Sharp to draft a statement explaining its manner of recording marriages, take the document to the women's meeting for a reading, and explain it if necessary. When the men's meeting wanted to know if Friends in Kilteel and Drogheda were still refusing to pay tithes in 1692, it asked Sharp and Amos Strettell to obtain a report. Yet another example of Sharp's wide-ranging scribal duties occurred in 1700, when he and Strettell dispatched copies of the wills of the Essex Quaker William Williams and his wife to the meeting for sufferings in London to determine the status of some Irish land Williams had bequeathed to the Friends.[10]

Perhaps no records were more important for the Friends than those that detailed their suffering, for these reflected their self-proclaimed identity as a persecuted community. This identity was clearly manifest in the title Abraham Fuller and Thomas Holme gave the first published overview of Quaker persecution: *A Brief Relation of Some Part of the Sufferings of the True Christians, the People of God (in Scorn Called Quakers) in Ireland* (1672). The title of William Stockdale's supplement, published eleven years later, continued this theme: *The Great Cry of Oppression.* So too did the expanded history of Quaker persecution by Holme and Samuel Fuller, Abraham's grandson, issued in 1731 under the title, *A Compendious View of Some Extraordinary Sufferings of the People Call'd Quakers, Both in Person and Substance, in the Kingdom of Ireland.* Suffering was a hallmark of the Quaker community, and the intense sense of shared injustice bound Friends together. The record of affliction was no less important as a polemical device that potently contrasted the persecutory practices of the Church of Ireland with the radically different usages of the apostolic church. Stockdale articulated this dual purpose of a historical account of persecution in the epistle to *The Great Cry of Oppression:* "Our intent in publishing this Book partly is to make known to the Rulers, and Magestrates, and others, the oppression and great sufferings which we endure: . . . and also that people may see that the Teachers of this age are none of Christs Ministers, who are found walking contrary to the commands of Christ, being called of men Master, and preaching for hire; and also contrarie to the practice of the Apostles and primitive Saints, for they laboured with their hands, and coveted no mans Silver, Gold, or Apparel . . . ; neither did they make spoil of peoples goods as these Teachers do, who have made their spiritual war a carnal war."[11]

As part of his service to the monthly meeting, Sharp, as we have seen, helped to compile data on suffering. This was hardly a new development, for such records date from at least 1653, but over time the Irish Friends regularized the gathering and preservation of this information. The six-months meeting took an important step in May 1672 when it appointed three men from each province to compile lists of incarcerated Friends. The following year it directed this group to review reports of distress and prepare them for recording, and it also insisted that every instance of suffering be registered at Dublin before it was recorded in a provincial or local book. Five years later the national meeting reminded each men's group to chronicle local instances of persecution and then report them to the provincial assembly; the latter was responsible for seeing that such accounts were accurate before forwarding them to Dublin. The movement for the standardization of records culminated in 1699 with a call for uniform language.[12]

Sharp's involvement in gathering and preserving data concerning suffering was extensive. For the period 1681–84 he compiled information about Friends whose goods had been distrained for refusal to pay tithes in the diocese of Ferns and Leighlin; Quakers, he reported, had not only been imprisoned but had also lost possessions valued at £173 15s. for failing to pay tithes worth £34 12s. 5d. Some Quakers were dilatory in reporting sufferings, perhaps because they had allowed sympathizers or family members to pay on their behalf. In 1683 and again in 1687, Sharp was among those the Dublin meeting assigned to contact Friends who had not reported their suffering. The problem was especially widespread in the latter year, when the men's meeting suspected that some Quakers might not have borne "their Testimony against Preists wages faithfully." Sharp assisted with the gathering and reporting of data, including its submission to the meeting for sufferings in London. As late as the summer of 1706, shortly before his death, he was one of the four Dublin men responsible for overseeing the chronicling of all Quaker tribulation in Ireland.[13]

The widespread disruption and misery caused by the time of troubles was understandably the principal reason for the Friends' determination in the postwar years not only to write their history but also to safeguard important documents. As early as November 1693 the Dublin men's meeting acquired a chest to hold legal documents such as leases as well as books (a practice familiar to Quaker guild members). At first the chest was kept at Abel Strettell's house in Meath Street, but fourteen months later it was transferred at his request to the Meath Street meetinghouse. Shortly thereafter the men's meeting charged Strettell and Sharp to see if "all Friends writeings be in the Chest that ought to be." Among those documents were statements by James Fade attacking Sharp, Clarridge, Ashton, Amos Strettell, and other stalwarts of the Dublin meeting. When the national assembly asked the Dublin men's meeting in 1694 to record its proceedings as far back as it deemed appropriate, the latter assigned the task to Sharp, Amos Strettell, Smallman, Archer, and Webb, or any three of them; perhaps because of other commitments, Sharp engaged in this work for no more than six months.[14]

Because of Sharp's business acumen, the Dublin men's meeting relied heavily on him to help with the management of its accounts and its contractual negotiations.[15] From at least January 1678 he acted as cotreasurer of the meeting, working in this capacity with such colleagues as Sleigh, Turner, and, commencing in 1683, Thomas Atherton and James Taylor. Sharp collected funds and dispensed them to pay rent, relieve the indigent, support apprentices, and ransom Quakers held as slaves by Muslims. When English Friends required financial assistance in 1684, Sharp and Amos Strettell took up donations in the Dublin area, and Sharp also handled funds for the relief of Quakers who had fled to Dublin during the time of troubles; by January 1691 he had disbursed more money than had been subscribed, prompting the men's meeting to instruct him to inform Friends that funds would be diverted from other areas unless more gifts were forthcoming.[16] Periodically the men's meeting commissioned Sharp to receive funds from the women's meeting and to audit its accounts, and in 1697 he helped to prepare the accounts for the Quaker schoolmasters in Dublin.[17] Sharp's own ledgers were audited, apparently without any problems. Indeed, in November 1692 Sharp requested the audit.[18] He was clearly a man with accounting skills as well as a person of integrity and a keen sense of service.

Sharp was also very active in the Leinster provincial meeting, which convened every six weeks. Held at such sites as Rosenallis, Athy, Wicklow, Castledermot, Moate, Carlow, and Mountmellick, the provincial assemblies necessitated a fair degree of travel by Sharp. These gatherings were, of course, the intermediary between the monthly and national meetings, and they served as well to articulate and deal with problems at the regional level. They were especially interested in disciplinary matters, though they also monitored the recording of births, marriages, and burials by the local meetings and concerned themselves with care of the poor, orphans, and widows. The provincial meeting was responsible for seeing that at least six qualified people attended the six-months meeting, which it provided with an account of Friends in the province who had suffered. Neatly encapsulating the activities of a provincial meeting, Sharp reflected that the delegates "waight upon the Lord to be directed, for the ending or doing such buisness of the Churches in that country or province, which the perticuler men and Womens meetings cannot doe or doe not doe, and to See as Brethren that all is Well in that county or province, and to encourage the church to take care of their own; and the general [meeting] will have the less care."[19]

With one exception, the character of people who attended provincial meetings did not pose a significant problem until the late 1690s. The anomaly occurred in May 1678 when Sharp asked the Leinster meeting if it was appropriate for someone to attend the assembly other than on business concerning himself if he refused to subordinate himself to his local meeting. Presumably he was alluding to Clarridge's refusal to acknowledge his sexual promiscuity with his maid, a matter that had deeply offended Sharp. To his query the provincial delegates responded that the Dublin men's meeting should advise the offender to subject himself to its authority, failing which the local body was to seek mediation from the national meeting.[20]

The basic problem resurfaced nearly two decades later, at which time the Leinster meeting informed its national counterpart that it was endeavoring "to prevent Raw and unfitt persons [from] sitting in men and womens meetings when mett about the Lords busines as also such that will not Referr their differences that so they may bee Ended by friends, or that Refuse to performe the Judgment given whether by A Meeting or persons chose for that purpose by the persons concerned or the Meeting." However, in July 1698 the Leinster delegates had to admit they had found no effective way to keep unfit people from attending men's meetings, especially those who displayed "great Charracters of Covetousnesse and Earthly mindednesse." The following year the Leinster delegates confronted the same question Sharp had posed in 1678, namely, whether someone who had been spiritually enlightened and had subsequently defiled himself in an illicit sexual relationship was fit to attend business meetings if he denied his offense. Perhaps Sharp had again raised this issue; certainly he would have concurred with the delegates' judgment that such a person should be excluded until he repented to the satisfaction of Friends.[21]

The problem of unsuitable people attending meetings for business and discipline remained unsolved, for Sharp and his compeers had to deal with it twice in 1700. Concerned that one or more people who were at the provincial meeting in January had not conformed to "Gospell Order," the representatives charged the monthly meetings to prevent such individuals from attending, especially at the provincial level. In October the provincial assembly recommended that the monthly meetings exclude any member, whether male or female, from participating in sessions "to adjudge others" unless he or she was subject to the meeting's authority. This last recommendation had been sparked by one or more cases involving Friends who had refused to accept judgments against them by their meeting.[22] Given the strictness favored by Sharp as early as 1678, his support for these actions is virtually certain.

By the late 1690s conduct in meetings had become a sufficiently serious problem to require the provincial assembly's attention. Indeed, those who attended the meeting at Castledermot in January 1698 referred to the "Injurious Consequences" that had resulted from "hott, Rash, Irreverent Appearances" in recent business meetings by unnamed people. The delegates, presumably including Sharp, therefore recommended that each meeting remind its members of the importance of meek, quiescent behavior. They also exhorted Friends to eschew "Extreames in speaking" and debate, and to talk one by one, not simultaneously.[23] Clearly, divisive speech and a breakdown in decorum plagued at least some meetings in Leinster.

The minutes for 15 February 1702, when the delegates gathered at Carlow, provide an idea of the size of the Leinster provincial meeting. On that occasion fifty-six men and twenty-two women came together—a dozen each from Wicklow and Dublin, including Sharp, along with twenty-seven from Mountmellick, eleven from Newgarden, nine from Wexford, and seven from Moate. They first congregated at 6:00 a.m. on Friday, prior to the commencement of the business meeting, to "consider the Lords wonderfull kindnesse towards us every way and particularly in that acceptable work and service of Close Order and holy discipline that many are called unto."[24]

As in the Dublin men's meeting, Sharp served the Leinster assembly as a scribe and treasurer. He corresponded with other meetings, sometimes about the "clearness" of Friends who had moved from one place to another. In 1697 the Leinster representatives assigned Sharp and five colleagues the task of editing the meeting's proceedings from 1679 to 1692 prior to their transcription into a bound volume by the Dublin schoolmaster Thomas Banks. The meeting must have been satisfied with their work, for it subsequently renewed the commission for later proceedings. In 1688, when Robert Turner, who was then in Philadelphia, wanted an epistle conveyed to the provincial meeting, he sent it to Sharp.[25] From at least 1678 Sharp diligently helped to prepare the accounts for the provincial meeting, working with Sleigh, Atherton, and others, and commencing in 1700 he audited the provincial accounts maintained by his fellow merchant, Edward Webb.[26] The province no less than the Dublin Quaker community utilized Sharp's talents extensively, particularly in the preparation and auditing of its fiscal accounts and in the editing of its proceedings.

Because the national meeting convened in Dublin from its origin in August 1669, it was less onerous for Sharp to participate in its sessions than in those of the scattered provincial meetings. Penn's Irish journal suggests that Sharp was at the six-months meeting in November 1669; unfortunately the earliest minutes date only from May 1671, and the first list of participants appeared in November 1673. Sharp attended at least twenty-two of the thirty-two meetings that occurred between the latter date and May 1689. Records are incomplete from November 1689 to May 1695 (though meetings were apparently not held in November 1689 and May 1690); he participated in at least seven and probably all ten of these gatherings. Between November 1695 and November 1698, the last meeting he is known to have attended, he missed only one gathering. When he participated, he was, of course, a member of the Leinster delegation, the size of which varied from an average of nearly eleven in the 1670s to twenty in the period between November 1695 and November 1698, with the smallest being six (November 1673) and the largest twenty-seven (May 1692). Although he remained active in the provincial meetings until almost the end of his life (certainly as late as February 1702), for unexplained reasons Sharp may never have attended a national meeting after November 1698, at least not as a delegate. Physical infirmity does not provide an adequate explanation, for the national meetings were in Dublin, and he continued to travel well after this date to provincial assemblies in other locales. Perhaps he opted to step aside at the national level, participating in the meetings for worship but leaving the conduct of Quaker business to younger people as well as some of his longtime associates. Many people were present at the half-yearly meetings as worshipers; in May 1680, for example, between 200 and 300 people attended, though most of them were at the worship service rather than the business session.[27]

Each province was supposed to send at least six representatives, though more were welcome to attend. Between November 1673 and May 1689 the Leinster delegation averaged fifteen, approximately twice the size of the Munster and Ulster delegations. The numerical preponderance of the Leinster delegation was considerably less in Sharp's late meetings (November 1695 to November 1698)—an average of twenty representatives per meeting compared to thirteen for Munster and fourteen for Ulster. The meeting's decisions were based on consensus rather than voting, but the size of the Leinster delegation undoubtedly gave its views added weight, especially in the early years.

As in the local and provincial meetings, the quality of people participating in the national gatherings became a problem beginning in the mid-1690s. Delegates to the half-yearly meeting in November 1687 had made clear their expectation that representatives would be the leading men in each province. Indeed, such stalwarts as Burnyeat, Abraham Fuller, Holme, Turner, Starkey, Sleigh, and Francis Randall as well as Sharp represented Leinster. In the postwar years Quakers who lacked their monthly meetings' full approbation attended the national assemblies, provoking the delegates in May 1696 to take steps to bar "disorderly, unfitt, Raw persons and such as frequent not their owne particular men and womens Meetings." Henceforth, at the beginning of the half-yearly meeting one Friend from each province and one from Dublin were appointed to exclude from the business session those who lacked the approval of "sensible freinds that know them." Before this time, a paid doorkeeper had apparently undertaken this task. A year later the national meeting delegated the authority to appoint excluders to the provincial and Dublin meetings, with the latter now asked to name two persons.[28] There is no evidence that Sharp served either to exclude unfit people or as a doorkeeper, though the Dublin and Leinster meetings in which he was active took those responsibilities seriously.[29]

The national meeting's decision in May 1696 to ban unfit people from participating may have been occasioned by their disruptive behavior, for the same assembly stipulated that delegates must "sit downe orderly" and speak audibly one at a time. Some were leaving before all business had been transacted, prompting the Leinster assembly and the Moate men's meeting to instruct their representatives to remain until the national body had finished its work.[30]

A greater problem, which might have personally involved Sharp, was the conduct of commercial transactions by Friends during the national meetings. As the most prominent Quaker businessman in Ireland, Sharp almost certainly would have been approached by colleagues engaged in commerce and manufacturing, yet those who participated in such discussions rendered Friends subject to criticism from outsiders. Consequently, in November 1683 the delegates, deeming it "a great inconveniencie" when Quakers pursued their business interests during the meeting, admonished them to avoid such practices because they were a distraction from spiritual concerns, a hinderance to "the service of Truth," and "an occasion for some to Judge that Friends are Covetous minded." Delegates must have continued to pursue their commercial interests, for subsequent meetings found it necessary to reiterate the admonition. In May 1697 the delegates expanded their exhortation by adding a prohibition against bringing merchandise or cattle to Dublin at the time of the six-months meeting. Commercial transactions nevertheless continued, inducing the representatives in November 1699 to request Dublin Quakers to report offenders to their local men's meetings. As early as 1691 the half-yearly meeting had urged monthly meetings to discourage discussions of worldly affairs immediately before and after gatherings for worship, and the Leinster meeting reiterated this exhortation in June 1704.[31]

Sharp left no account of what transpired in a national meeting other than his observation that emissaries were "to See that all things be Well through the churches of the said Nation, and what else the Lord shall put in their hearts, so that what Difficulty cannot be ended at county and provintiall meetings is to be ended at the Nationall meeting." Oliver Sansom provided a detailed description of a six-months meeting that convened in November 1676, when Sharp, Holme, Turner, Abraham Fuller, and three others comprised the Leinster delegation. The meeting began at 9:00 a.m. on Wednesday, the 8th, with a period of worship that lasted more than an hour. After a break the representatives, including eight from Munster and seven from Ulster, reconvened to consider church affairs, "but the power of the Lord brake forth so mightily amongst Friends in many testimonies, prayers and praising the Lord, that there was no time to enter upon business that day, and so the meeting broke up." The delegates gathered on Thursday morning around 9:00 and discussed their spiritual business for nearly six hours before adjourning until 4:00 p.m. What "a precious heavenly time it was," Sansom recalled. After their break the emissaries reconvened to resume their business, but as on the previous day, mundane considerations were swept aside by a tide of spiritual devotion "whereby many mouths were opened to declare of the goodness of the Lord, and to offer up prayers and praises to him."[32]

The delegates devoted much of Friday and Saturday to their business, most of which they conducted in a spirit of unity. A disagreement between several Friends temporarily disrupted the harmony, but others worked diligently and successfully to resolve the issue, the nature of which Sansom did not record. Once the controversy had been settled, "the Lord's presence was preciously enjoyed, and his power was over all and brake forth through many vessels, in testimonies, prayers and praises," presumably including contributions from Sharp. Because of this renewed burst of spiritual fervor, the assembly could not finish its business until Saturday evening. Two large public meetings for worship took up most of Sunday, and Friends from outside Dublin began leaving for their homes on Monday. "A very heavenly season it was all the time that the Friends were together," Sansom concluded.[33] John Banks, who was at the same meeting, wrote a similar though much abbreviated account.[34]

At the half-yearly meetings Sharp and his compeers dealt with a wide range of subjects basic to the movement's ideals and operation, including matters of worship and service, weighty cases of discipline, the articulation and implementation of standards of conduct, and the supervision of collections and disbursements. The delegates were also concerned with the construction and maintenance of meetinghouses and burial grounds, the monitoring and recording of Quaker sufferings, the publication and distribution of printed materials, and the oversight of Quaker schooling. The national meeting communicated with its English counterpart, submitting an annual report on "the affairs of Truth" in Ireland commencing in the early 1680s and sending emissaries to the yearly meeting in London starting in the late 1690s. Sharp never undertook this duty, though colleagues such as Edmundson, Wight, Roberts, and Rooke did.[35] With Amos Strettell, Boate, Wight, and others, Sharp prepared reports to the yearly meeting in London concerning incarcerated Friends; the number discharged in the preceding twelve months and how they obtained their release; those who died in prison; the deaths of public Friends; the number of meetinghouses built and new meetings established; the progress of the movement, especially matters of education and standards of conduct; and the "signall Judgments" that had befallen persecutors.[36]

Sharp dutifully served the six-months meeting as both a record keeper and a treasurer. In the early 1680s he handled monies remitted by the provincial meetings, communicated with English Friends concerning their need for financial assistance during the Tory Revenge, and sent them funds. When English Quakers reciprocated by donating money to Irish Friends who suffered during the time of troubles, Sharp disbursed £3,222 10s. to the provincial meetings in a single year. On behalf of the Dublin men's meeting he also provided an account of the public charge to the national assembly.[37] Sharp handled some of the official correspondence for the six-months meeting as well as keeping custody of its proceedings. He must have been embarrassed in 1692 when the minute-book could not be located, causing Winslow and Archer to go from house to house among the Dublin Quakers searching for it; one of Sharp's maids, it turned out, had mislaid the volume. The proceedings were recorded following the conclusion of each national meeting, and those portions relevant to the provincial bodies were copied and sent to them; in November 1696 this responsibility fell to Sharp and Amos Strettell.[38]

Utilizing his business experience, Sharp devoted considerable time to the construction and maintenance of meetinghouses and to the leases for the property on which they stood. Long before Sharp moved to Dublin, the Friends had relocated from a house near Pole Gate to Bride's Alley (now Bride Road) in 1657. Quaker records refer to Bride's Alley and Bride Street, which intersected with the former; apparently they used houses, possibly adjoining, in both streets.[39] They worshiped at Bride's Alley until 1687 and at Bride Street until 29 September 1692, paying £12 *per annum* for the lease. In March 1692 Sharp and Clarridge sought an extension of the lease for two or three more years, but the owner demanded an increase of 25 percent in the rent and a twenty-one-year agreement, prompting the Friends to terminate their lengthy association with this building.[40] Periodically their tenure had been problematic, as in 1681 when they considered moving because of noise in the area, including a musician's distracting sounds. On occasion people hostile to the Quakers threw stones at the meetinghouse, breaking windows and endangering worshipers.[41] The Friends were responsible for maintaining the building, including repairs to the roof and floor as well as routine cleaning. They also made some improvements, adding shutters to the rear windows in 1678 and special accommodations for children in 1683. Responsibility for the latter rested with Sharp, Fade, and John Newby, who commissioned a new room or "office" adjacent to the meetinghouse, with access by a common casement through which children could pass by climbing up and down steps. This proved to be too noisy, triggering complaints from some members and a suggestion that access to the children's room be provided through the adjoining property of John and Elizabeth Burnyeat, but the Burnyeats vetoed this proposal.[42] Thus the Bride's Alley complex was insufficiently commodious for all of the Friends' needs.

In November 1677 the half-yearly meeting appointed Sharp, Sleigh, Fade, Turner, Roberts, and Mathias Foster to find another meetinghouse or a site on which to build one in Dublin or Oxmantown, with the cost to be apportioned among the provincial meetings. The committee settled on a house in New Row, which ran southward from Ormond's (later Wormwood) Gate. Adjoining Sharp's house, the site was owned by the alderman John Knox, who agreed to lease the property—an interesting case of cooperation between the Friends and a local magistrate who was obviously willing to accommodate them. The new building was not without problems, for in 1680 provisions had to be made to drain water from the structure. Tensions surfaced, moreover, owing to the cost of leasing and maintaining both the Bride's Alley and New Row properties, and the Dublin men's meeting complained in 1680 that it was paying more than its fair share of these expenses. The national meeting resolved in May 1682 that the costs be apportioned on the following basis: 37.5 percent to Leinster, 35 percent to Munster, and 27.5 percent to Ulster.[43]

The New Row site never proved to be very satisfactory, not least because of the disturbances caused by others in the area and the ability of such people to overhear the Quakers' debates. In January 1683 the Dublin men's meeting decided to transfer its sessions back to Bride's Alley. Four months later the construction of a drainage ditch that passed under the New Row building resulted in an objectionable "Noisom Smell." The six-months meeting therefore resolved to have Sharp and Roberts find a site on which a new meetinghouse could be erected.[44]

By November 1683 the two men had located property owned by William Brabazon, earl of Meath, in Brabson's Liberties, Meath Street, on which the national meeting planned to build not only a meetinghouse but also "such Conveniencies ... as may yearly bring in some profit." Sharp and Roberts were instructed to negotiate for a lot at least 50 feet wide and 120 feet deep and a lease of at least sixty years, and "to inspect whether the Interest be sure." They reported to two representatives for each provincial meeting, including Abraham Fuller and Francis Randall for Leinster. These six were in turn responsible for communicating with the local meetings in their respective provinces. Because the half-yearly meeting did not want "to lay a tye upon Friends Concerning the said Building," it solicited contributions. Gifts were collected by the local meetings, forwarded to the provincial assemblies, and finally sent to Sharp and Roberts.[45] Besides serving as national co-treasurer for the building fund, Sharp collected donations from members of the Dublin meeting. The Friends leased the property from the earl in Sharp's name. On the site already stood several houses, apparently of recent construction, which the Quakers hoped to rent to some of their own. Responsibility for arranging these rentals rested with Sharp, Ashton, and two others.[46]

Donations toward the estimated cost of £600 were slower in coming than Quaker leaders had hoped, though the province of Leinster alone had subscribed the impressive total of £445 13s. 6d. by December 1683, of which nearly half—£211 8s. 6d.—came from the Dublin meeting and an additional £108 19s. 6d. from Mountmellick. Sharp, who gave £30, was easily the most munificent benefactor, followed by Roberts and Fade at £10 each, and Ashton and the miller and tanner Joseph Thomas at £8. Clarridge, Fuller, Amos Strettell, and the merchant Samuel Randall each donated £6. Altogether, 116 members of the Dublin meeting contributed.[47]

Construction commenced in 1684. The national meeting made Sharp, Starkey, and John Tottenham responsible for obtaining the requisite legal documents. By May 1685 the outlay for the building had exceeded income, forcing the six-months meeting to suspend construction; nearly £548 had been spent by November of that year. At the ensuing meeting, in May 1686, the delegates decided that construction should resume, that the debt should be defrayed, and that the provincial assemblies should determine how to raise the £250 deemed necessary to complete the building and clear the debt. Once the structure had been finished and the debt paid, the Friends expected to clear approximately £20 *per annum* from the rental houses on the property. A committee of nine, including Sharp, Randall, and John Watson for Leinster, was appointed to work with the provincial meetings to raise the money. With Fuller's assistance, Sharp was also responsible to reconcile any differences between actual construction costs and the terms that had previously been agreed.[48]

Whatever work had been done on the meetinghouse in 1685 must have been limited to site preparation and perhaps the erection of a foundation, for not until May 1686 did the six-months meeting appoint

Clarridge, the carpenter Thomas Bell, John Newby, William Williamson, and two others to prepare a model of the building. Oversight of construction was the responsibility of Clarridge, Roberts, and Thomas, who reported to the Leinster meeting.[49] Both as a member of that body and as one who lived near the construction site, Sharp probably monitored the building as it was erected. Meanwhile the Dublin men's meeting commissioned him to prepare an account of what each member had contributed toward construction costs so that those responsible for collecting the remainder knew how much people still owed to fulfil their pledges.[50]

On completion in 1687 the Meath Street meetinghouse had exterior whitewashed walls sixteen-feet high, gabled ends, and a slate roof. A stone pillar approximately a foot square and sunk deep in the ground helped to support the lower floor. The wall of the building adjoining a garden owned by Sharp contained four (later five) windows, and another wall included four more. The building had two fireplaces, wooden floors, and a gallery. An upper story provided space for the women to gather as well as for small groups and for storage.[51] In the ensuing years the Quakers made various modifications, beginning with the raising of the gallery, where public Friends sat, one foot in 1688; for this, Sharp, as treasurer, paid 31s. 5d. The following year the Friends bricked up the two lowest windows at the western end of the building, perhaps because they had been tempting targets for vandals. A second, smaller gallery was added in 1698, suggesting either an increase in the number of public Friends or the growth of the meeting itself. Children sometimes sat there as well, prompting the meeting in 1704 to add a rail to prevent them from falling. Three years earlier, Sharp, Abel Strettell, and the merchant Joseph Hanks (or Hankes) had orders to see that a seat with "A pretty high rayle" was built next to the gallery both at Meath Street and in the new meetinghouse in Sycamore Alley.[52] Sharp must have been knowledgeable about construction and maintenance, for in 1693 the Dublin men's meeting appointed him, Thomas, Roberts, and Thomas Bell to "view & search" the meetinghouse for defects and have them repaired.[53]

Although the Meath Street meetinghouse had been completed in March 1687, bills were still due the following year. The Munster and Ulster provincial meetings had agreed to pay £50 and £40 respectively towards the necessary £250 necessary to complete the building in 1686 on condition that the income from the houses on the property be used to retire the debt and reduce their portion of the national meeting's expenses in the future. By May 1688 Sharp had computed the final account for the structure, but as late as September of that year the Dublin Friends were asked to pledge enough to pay the remaining debt and give the money to Sharp.[54] Although the meetinghouse belonged to all Irish Quakers, the Dublin meeting accepted full responsibility for upkeep and repairs because it enjoyed the greatest use of the building.[55]

To meet expenses the Friends leased some of their Dublin properties. As early as November 1686 the six-months meeting instructed Sharp and Roberts to arrange a lease for the New Row meetinghouse; they found a renter who was willing to pay £10 *per annum* to use the structure as a warehouse. When the Meath Street building was ready the following March, the Friends disposed of the Bride's Alley meetinghouse to Fade after adding a partition and making repairs.[56] Whereas some meetings used their upper floors or attics to house the elderly, the Leinster and Dublin meetings pondered the possibility of renting the rooms on the Meath Street building's second story, a decision left to Sharp and Roberts. Those rooms, they calculated, were worth £30 *per annum*, for which the Dublin meeting assumed responsibility. As late as November 1696 this space, which Quakers from Dublin and other areas were using, had not been leased, for at that time the Dublin meeting asked Sharp and Abel Strettell to reexamine the possibility of renting it to someone.[57] The Friends obtained additional income by renting houses on their properties, including some bequeathed by George Gregson, and Sharp periodically helped to negotiate the leases and audit the rental books.[58]

Sharp also had a major part in negotiating leases for their meetinghouses and accompanying properties. He originally held the lease from the earl of Meath for the Meath Street properties in his own name; he renewed this lease in the fall of 1692 "for three lives renewable for ever, at a years Rent, within three moneths after the fall of any Life."[59] In January 1694 the earl, Sharp, Roberts, and Clarridge agreed that Amos Strettell would be named in the lease as trustee, and that the three lives would be those of Sharp's son Isaac, Roberts' son Isaac, and Clarridge's son Benjamin. Strettell thereupon made a deed of trust to Leinster Friends for the meetinghouse.[60]

After the Quakers opted not to renew their lease for the Bride Street property in September 1692, they leased a site on the eastern side of Sycamore Alley—now Sycamore Street—between Essex Street and what is presently Dame Street. The land was a waste parcel formerly used as a garden and enclosed with stone and brick walls; the lease included an alley providing access to the property from Sycamore Alley. As in so many other cases, Sharp helped to negotiate the terms and had the task of announcing that henceforth the Friends would no longer gather in Bride Street. The lease was taken by Abel Strettell and John Hutchinson but made over to Sharp, Amos Strettell, Ashton, Baker, Peter Fletcher, and the tallowchandler Richard Middleton as trustees for the meeting. For use of the Sycamore Alley property they paid £6 10s. *per annum*.[61] As a result of the Friends' decision in 1703 to secure stable leases for all of their properties, including meetinghouses and burial grounds, Sharp and the Strettell brothers obtained from Thomas Pooley, the Sycamore Alley landlord, "a Lease for Lives" at the current rent of £6 10s. *per annum*, renewable at that rate for a fee of one year's rent when one of the designated people died; there was also an initial fee of £40. Concluded in the spring of 1705, the negotiations had lasted more than a year.[62] With Ashton, Abel Strettell, Stevens, and Newland, Sharp was also responsible for examining all other Quaker leases in the Dublin area, but they found everything in order.[63]

The Friends also relied on Sharp to deal with matters concerning the burial grounds. When Quakers at Lurgan needed advice about a proposed burial yard in 1678, the national meeting deputed Sharp, Fuller, Starkey, and Thomas Cooke of Cork to assist.[64] In Dublin the Friends interred their dead on land adjoining St. Stephen's Green. The Dublin meeting appointed Sharp, Turner, Roberts, Foster, and Fade in 1679 to survey this graveyard, examining the deed to ascertain "what ground wee have without the graveyard wall backwards and what else they see needfull to informe them selves of." When their inspection revealed that their holdings included a strip of land between four and five feet wide beyond the graveyard's rear wall, the meeting charged Sharp, Fade, and Sleigh to employ a mason to construct a new back wall encompassing this ground, not least to secure a drainage ditch which a grand jury had threatened to close. The new wall, on the cemetery's west side, was to be uniform with the adjoining north and south walls, and was to be no more than a foot within the lot line. If anyone sued the Quakers to halt construction, Sharp and his colleagues were prepared to defend their legal rights. In the end the new wall was some three feet inside the lot line, for in August 1680 the Dublin men's meeting agreed to lease the unenclosed property to Fade for thirty-one years at a cost of 5s. *per annum*, including the right to build on the wall as long as he made no windows or openings that overlooked the burial yard, cleaned the common ditch each year, and hauled away his own dung.[65]

The graveyard required constant oversight and recurring maintenance. Dublin Friends assigned two members to oversee the cemetery
for three-month periods; Sharp performed this duty twice, commencing
in July 1680 and May 1685. The Quakers laid out £10 11s. 2d. to pave
the side street adjoining the burial ground in 1680 and £2 11s. to pave
this or another street nearly two decades later; they also paved the
ground at the front of the cemetery in 1694, all of which would have
made access easier. However, the paving may have contributed to
drainage problems, which required attention in 1696.[66] The graveyard
wall periodically needed repairs, partly because of damage caused by
passing carts, and in 1704 the Dublin meeting paid £9 5s. to raise the
height of the wall two feet with brick. In 1703–1704 the meeting had
the gate enlarged and raised to a height of at least seven feet. To beautify the graveyard the meeting spent £2 15s. 6d. to plant thirty-seven
lime trees; Sharp and Atherton inspected the work before authorizing
payment. Fir trees were added in 1703, but most died and were replaced
with 150 new trees the following year. The meeting expressed concern
that these trees be carefully preserved and that no horses or cattle be
allowed into the cemetery to cause damage.[67]

Space in the burial ground was at a premium, perhaps as early as
1681, when the Dublin men's meeting instructed its grave digger to bury
no one without the group's approval. Acting at the meeting's behest, in
1693 Sharp and Clarridge explored the possibility of leasing a burial
plot behind the Meath Street meetinghouse, but nothing came of this,
probably because of the expense. Four years later, Sharp, Clarridge, and
others examined land owned by Roger Roberts in Cork Lane (now
Cork Street) near Dolphin's Barn, southwest of the city center; the
meeting subsequently leased this plot. To construct a nine-foot wall
around the land, the meeting solicited subscriptions totaling nearly £160
from ninety-nine contributors. Sharp and Clarridge provided the largest
donations, at £15 and £9 respectively, with other benefactors giving between 1s. and £6 apiece. The new cemetery was ready by May 1698,
and just in time, for the grounds near St. Stephen's Green were full. After Sharp, Clarridge, and Bell examined the new cemetery and found
everything in order, the meeting authorized its use, with corpses to be
interred in orderly rows.[68] The same year the Leinster meeting, in a
move that explicitly recognized the Friends' desire to be a distinct people and implicitly responded to finite spatial limits, unanimously resolved that those who "turned their back on friends in their life time"
could not be buried among Quakers.[69]

Like its predecessor, the new graveyard required both beautification and upkeep. In 1703 the Quakers planted 120 fir trees on their Dolphin's Barn property, but they had to appoint thirteen people to keep boys from damaging them during funerals. They also removed a stone adjacent to the wall which boys were climbing to gain entry to the graveyard when the gate was locked. To help with the cost of maintenance, the Friends sold grass cut from the grounds for 23s. *per annum*.[70]

As with other Quaker properties in Dublin, Sharp had a major role in negotiating and checking leases for the burial grounds. He also helped to draft a document giving one Martin Gregory permission to build a house abutting the wall of the St. Stephen's graveyard, subject to the condition that he "make no light towards Friends ground." The Quakers also permitted the son of a Dublin councilman to erect a stable adjoining the St. Stephen's wall as long as he had no windows opening on the graveyard and he removed the dung.[71]

Sharp's manuscripts provide virtually no information concerning his personal reaction to the rather onerous duties involving the construction and maintenance of meetinghouses and cemeteries, the rental of other Quaker properties, the negotiation and examination of leases, and the collection and disbursement of funds. Judging from the extant evidence, he performed all of these tasks diligently and without complaint. As the most generous donor for the Meath Street meetinghouse and the Dolphin's Barn burial ground, he was indisputably an influential figure among Irish Friends, particularly in Leinster, but he must have been effective in his business dealings on the Quakers' behalf or they would not have had recourse to his services so frequently and over so many years. In turn, he was obviously willing to donate both his time and his expertise, and to do so on such a scale that the motivation must have stemmed to a considerable degree from his spiritual commitment. Perhaps he also found gratification in the implicit acclaim such service and financial donations undoubtedly brought.

8

"As Truth Shall Direct"

Life in the Dublin Quaker Community

THE ORGANIZATION OF MEETINGS, the construction of meetinghouses, the maintenance of burial grounds, and the machinery
for the collection and disbursement of funds constituted the infrastruc-
ture of the Quaker movement. Sharp and his confreres would have seen
their real business as witnessing to the inner Spirit through the propagation of the gospel and a godly, disciplined life. Quaker missions and the
activities of public Friends played a crucial part in spreading the gospel,
but so too, in their eyes, did the education of the young and the publication and distribution of Quaker literature. In all these areas, Sharp was
deeply engaged, as he was in the meetings that articulated and upheld
standards of behavior, disciplining the recalcitrant, mediating disputes,
dispensing charity to the needy, and ransoming captives in foreign
lands. In carrying out such endeavors, Sharp and his compeers gave expression to the driving force of their faith and simultaneously built a society that sustained the Quakers for centuries to come as a minority
within yet another minority, the Protestants of Ireland.

The nature of Quaker education in Ireland before 1675 is unclear, although as early as May 1672 the half-yearly meeting had directed Clarridge to have 2,000 primers printed. Recognizing the need to find a
Quaker schoolmaster to establish a school in Ireland, the national
meeting in November 1675 charged each provincial body to ascertain
how many children "may be had to put forth to such a schoole." At the
national meeting's behest Thomas Holme and Francis Rogers contacted
English Friends to locate a suitable teacher with the intent of founding a
school in the Castledermot area. With Fox's recommendation, the English schoolmaster Laurence Routh arrived in the summer of 1677 and
settled at Trade's Hill, King's County (Offaly), where he received sup-

port from the Mountmellick meeting. When the number of students proved to be fewer than anticipated, the Leinster provincial meeting, beginning in 1679, had to provide a subsidy of nearly £6, of which the Dublin Friends paid £1 16s., the largest amount.[1] Fox also recommended Richard Gowith, whose services the national meeting assigned to Cork in 1678. Nineteen years later, Sharp assisted the Cork Friends in finding another schoolmaster in England, probably William Glenny, who taught reading, writing, Latin, and mathematics.[2]

Credit for the initiative to establish a Quaker school in Dublin goes not to Sharp but to Alexander Seaton, who had studied at Aberdeen University; in August 1680 the Dublin men's meeting accepted his offer to teach on a trial basis. He instructed his pupils in a house on the Bride Street property. In May of that year the six-months meeting had directed Rogers to ask Christopher Taylor, Richard Richardson, and Ambrose Rigge what books Quaker schoolmasters in London used, where they could be obtained, and the pedagogy employed to teach Latin, Greek, and Hebrew in a manner consonant with the Friends' principles. By the time of the next national meeting, in November 1680, Taylor and his colleagues had responded. Opting to follow the pedagogical methods used in England, the delegates directed all Quaker schoolmasters to attend the half-yearly meeting in May. Five—Seaton, Routh, John Archer, the Scot Patrick Logan of Lurgan, and Henry Rose of county Carlow—complied. After discussing the letter from London and the manuscript of a short textbook on spelling by Richard Jordan, they objected to "the Shortness of the Rules in these books lately put out by friends [in England], viz. Compendium trium Linguarum," and decided against publishing Jordan's manuscript because it was flawed and poorly organized.[3] Sharp had not been present when the national meeting decided to contact the Quaker schoolmasters in London, but he attended the meetings in November 1680 and May 1681, and thus presumably heard and discussed the schoolmasters' reaction to the report from England.[4]

Sharp was involved as well in the Quakers' assessment of *The Child's Delight: Together with an English Grammar* (1671) by the Presbyterian clergyman Thomas Lye, who ministered at Clapham outside London. In August 1680 the Leinster meeting denounced the book as unacceptable on the grounds of its offensive illustrations and language. Concurring, the Dublin men's meeting and the national assembly prohibited Quaker schoolmasters from using it. The Dublin meeting instructed Seaton to provide a copy of the order from the national meeting to Sharp or Roger Roberts, presumably for recording and distribution.[5]

By the fall of 1682 Seaton, apparently unhappy with his salary, was seeking release from his instructional duties, though Sharp and his colleagues in the Dublin meeting pressed him to continue until they found a replacement. In addition to stipends from the pupils, they offered to pay £5 *per annum* if he also served as the meeting's secretary. For a time, the number of students increased, at least in part because of the meeting's willingness to pay the expenses of children of the poor.[6]

In the climate of toleration during James II's reign, some Quaker parents began sending their children to non-Quaker schools. Owing to the unwillingness of Quaker schoolmasters to use "vain latin books usually taught by the worlde['s] people" because of their objectionable content, they failed to attract sufficient numbers of non-Quaker students to offset Quaker pupils who selected other schools. When some Quaker teachers began closing their schools, the six-months meeting ordered them to continue their instruction unless they obtained the approval of their local men's meeting to cease.[7]

Seaton may have been among those who temporarily stopped teaching; if so, he was again in the classroom in the summer of 1688, when the Dublin men's meeting increased his secretarial stipend to £7 *per annum* and established a committee of six to remind Friends every quarter to support their schoolmaster. However, the upheavals of the revolution forced the school to close, and by the late summer of 1690 Seaton had left for Scotland. At the behest of the Dublin men's meeting Sharp and Amos Strettell urged him to remain, but failing that, they asked him to recommend a successor.[8]

Although Seaton held out hope that he would return, in May 1691 the Dublin meeting offered the post to Archer with a secretarial salary of £10 *per annum* plus student fees. He must have declined, for in late 1692, on Seaton's recommendation, the Dublin meeting hired Samuel Forbes, an usher at Richard Scoryer's (or Scory's) school at Southwark. When Forbes insisted on a salary of £40 *per annum*, the meeting agreed to make up the difference between that amount and the pupils' fees. He began teaching in mid-March 1693 on the Meath Street meetinghouse's upper floor, charging each student 6s. per quarter. In keeping with the exhortation of the six-months meeting in May 1691 that all Friends should send their children to Quaker schoolmasters, Sharp and his Dublin compeers urged all Quaker parents in their region to enrol their

offspring in Forbes' school. They also disbursed £5 8s. to outfit the
school.[9]

But all was not well, for Forbes failed to meet the expectations of
some Quaker parents because he was "not soe good a writer as Friends
Expect." When some parents refused to enrol their children and others
withdrew them from the school,[10] the men's meeting dispatched Sharp,
Amos Strettell, and Joseph Deane to discuss the problem with Forbes.
Concerned about his contractual income of £40 *per annum*, the meeting
threatened not to renew its guarantee and warned him that he would
have to enhance the school's reputation to attract more students;
moreover, it insisted on lowering the fees to "the usual prices." Although the meeting had to supplement his charges by £18 14s. 11d. in
1693, not until 1695 did it alter the terms of the agreement, pledging
only £10 to supplement student fees. In return for the £10, the meeting
expected Forbes to serve as its recorder and teach the children of poor
Friends without charge. When he protested, it agreed to pay him £12
15s. 6d. but gave him six months' notice to find other employment.
Sharp was almost certainly among those who were "greatly dissatisfied
with [Forbes'] reflections upon Friends as well as not keeping his accounts well stated."[11]

With Amos Strettell and Robert Smallman, Sharp had the responsibility of finding a new schoolmaster. After Henry Molyneux declined,
they hired John Dobbs of Lurgan and Thomas Banks in June 1696.
They too taught on the upper floor of the Meath Street meetinghouse,
receiving stipends of £13 and £10 *per annum* respectively. By year's end
the number of pupils was still small, prompting Dobbs to announce his
intention to leave the following March.[12]

Faced again with the task of finding another teacher, Sharp and his
colleagues decided to provide training for one of their own young men,
James Whitehill's son, to become a schoolmaster. Sharp and Amos
Strettell arranged for him to study at the Dublin meeting's expense with
Gilbert Thompson at Penketh, Lancashire. Meanwhile Sharp, Strettell,
Clarridge, Smallman, and three others hired the Scot John Chambers,
who had lived with Robert Barclay's family, offering him £10 *per annum* plus half of the students' tuition. Banks continued to teach, receiving the other half of the fees, £4 *per annum* as the meeting's scribe,
and additional stipends from the national and Leinster meetings for
serving as their recorder.[13]

Sharp was increasingly involved in settling the school's affairs, and he
had a major part in negotiating a new agreement with Chambers in No-

vember 1697 according to which the latter undertook responsibility for running the school. Chambers hired an usher, or assistant instructor, to teach writing and arithmetic. Friends' children could study "fine writing" with Banks, whose wife taught small children to read, probably using a primer by Stephen Crisp and George Fox the younger, a thousand copies of which had been ordered by the half-yearly meeting in 1695.[14] Although more Quaker parents had promised to send their children to study with Chambers, he complained in November 1697 that insufficient numbers were doing so. The situation had improved by the summer of 1700, when Sharp, Abel Strettell, and several others found nothing remiss and concluded that the students were orderly and receiving "a sober education according to truth."[15]

Stable conditions were short-lived, for in 1703 Chambers resigned "to enter upon some business"; (he remained in Dublin until his death in 1713). Sharp and several others reached an amicable settlement with him but found themselves having to launch another search for a schoolmaster. Some favored Archer, who was offered relatively generous terms of £20 besides the students' fees and a rent-free house; however, Archer died before he could take up his post. A request seeking Gilbert Thompson's assistance in finding a new instructor proved fruitless, but in November Sharp and five others hired Samuel Fuller and James Whitehill. Faced with diminishing numbers of students, the school was again in trouble by 1704, though the Dublin meeting was sufficiently optimistic to add another schoolroom on the meetinghouse's upper floor. When Whitehill wanted to relocate to Penketh later that year, Sharp and others attempted to dissuade him on the grounds that he should "keep close to his business in teaching schoole & . . . keep lowe in his mind." In late 1706 Fuller too expressed a desire to leave, but by this point Sharp was no longer active in the school's oversight. That it had survived to this point, its almost endemic problems with schoolmasters notwithstanding, owed much to his involvement. The Dublin school was an exception to J. William Frost's depiction of early Quaker schools as "more or less fly-by-night affairs."[16]

Despite Sharp's determined efforts to keep the Quaker school in Dublin operational, he sent two of his own sons to Penketh to study with Thompson, which suggests that he too had doubts about the quality of instruction available in Dublin as well as the school's stability. In large measure the problems of the Dublin school stemmed from the Friends' inability to retain an instructor over the long term, but the teachers themselves were discouraged by the failure of many parents to support them. To some degree the Quakers' insistence that children not be raised "above their abilitys" exacerbated the problem. In March 1701 the Leinster provincial meeting reflected that "Sorrowful Experience has taught too many Parents" that their children sustained substantive damage by staying in school too long rather than engaging in physical labor, trades, or husbandry, all of which "may . . . be more Christian like and of better consequence" than excessive education. The same body determined that children should not stay in school longer than their intended vocations required, and the half-yearly meeting endorsed this view two months later.[17] At least some Quaker parents must have abbreviated their children's schooling, thereby undercutting, however unintentionally, the Dublin school's ability to thrive.

There can be no doubt that Sharp and his co-workers valued education. Dublin Friends paid the schooling expenses of children whose parents could not afford the fees, and in 1693 the Leinster meeting charged each of its constituent units to provide a schoolmaster. Some sense of the number of children studying in Quaker schools around the turn of the century is suggested by the national meeting's order for 3,000 primers, half of which were for the Leinster meeting, and twice that number of "prints" for hour books. The number of primers was 50 percent higher than a comparable order three decades earlier.[18]

In Sharp's last years the Irish Friends imposed greater rigidity on the curriculum. The emphasis had always been on "Educating Children in plainnesse," as the national meeting phrased it in 1705, or keeping "schollars in sobriety," as the Dublin meeting had insisted the previous year. In keeping with this ideal, in 1705 six Quaker schoolmasters submitted a report to the half-yearly meeting providing new guidelines for both the curriculum and educational objectives. For instruction in Latin, no longer were Quaker teachers to use *Aesop's Fables*, Ovid's *Metamorphoses* or *Tristia*, the colloquies of Corderius, or the works of Erasmus, Terence, Virgil, Horace, or Juvenal. Nor were they to employ any other books "treating of things not agreeable to Truth." Such views were in the spirit of the attack on vulgar expressions in Latin classics mounted by the Lancashire Quaker John Stubbs in 1660. For Dublin Friends, the list of acceptable texts included the Vulgate, Robert Barclay's catechism and *Apology*, the works of Cato and George Buchanan, the mystic Francis Rous' *Academia Coelestis: The Heavenly University*, Leonard Culman's *Sententiae pueriles* (a collection of Latin maxims), Castellion's colloquies, and a work on nomenclature, probably *Nomenclatura trilinguis Anglo-Latino-Graeca*, the sixth edition of which was published in 1704. Moreover, the national meeting appointed a committee "to make some Allocations in Rules and Examples" from William Lilly's standard grammar. Schoolmasters, the delegates opined, should neither correct their pupils in anger "nor for their Lessons, more then for untruthlike behaviour."[19] The emphasis, then, was less on educational content than on the inculcation of pious conduct, a goal in keeping with Sharp's own values.

Sharp was involved as well in a related educational endeavor, the apprenticing of young people. In the postwar years Dubliners were experiencing problems with masters who terminated apprentices before they had served seven years, thereby resulting in unqualified people receiving the freedom of the city. The Friends seem to have had little or no difficulty with this problem, though they were concerned with other aspects of apprenticeship. Chief among these was their desire to place apprentices with Quaker masters and to encourage Friends seeking apprentices to accord priority to Quaker young people. In 1701 the six-months meeting also expressed concern about parents who apprenticed their children to merchants and shopkeepers if they had insufficient financial resources to establish them in business once the apprenticeships had concluded. Four years later the national meeting condemned masters who bound their apprentices not to establish themselves in the same area after completing their terms; this prohibition, the delegates adjudged, was "contrary to the liberty and freedom of Truth and . . . [had] Appearance of Covetousnesse in it."[20]

Irish Friends demonstrated concern for the welfare of apprentices. In 1682 the half-yearly meeting stipulated that after apprentices had completed their term of service, their masters had to appear with them before the appropriate men's meeting, which had the responsibility of determining whether the conditions of the apprenticeship agreement had been fulfilled. Periodically the Dublin men's meeting placed the children of indigent Friends in apprenticeships, as in 1699 when it paid £6 to apprentice a widow's daughter to Thomas Banks' wife to learn how to teach.[21] To Friends, apprenticeships were a religious and social responsibility as well as a vehicle for the instruction of youth.

On behalf of the Dublin men's meeting, Sharp negotiated the terms of apprenticeships and mediated disputes between masters and apprentices. In 1683 the meeting commissioned Sharp and Atherton to investigate a quarrel involving an apprentice who had run away, allegedly because his master had abused him. Sharp helped to settle another case in which a member of the Mountmellick meeting, the clothier George

Pope, wanted to terminate his son's apprenticeship with a cutler who belonged to the Dublin meeting; the latter had paid the cost of the lad's apprenticeship (£5), and Pope had to reimburse the cutler before the Dublin Friends would consent to the request. Sharp sometimes had to deal with seemingly trivial matters, as with an apprentice accused of "Lying out of his Masters house at unseasonable times." Sharp and Ashton settled this problem by talking with the young man and persuading both his mother and his master to be more vigilant in supervising him. On another occasion the Dublin meeting dispatched Sharp and two colleagues to dissuade a father from placing his children on a ship, apparently as apprentices, "at such a distance from his house" as to cause a "Scandale to Truth." In all these cases Sharp's responsibilities reflected the Dublin meeting's confidence in and respect for his abilities and commitment to Quaker principles and probably for his experience as a member of the weavers' guild.[22]

No less important for the Friends' educational program was their publication of Quaker books, tracts, and epistles. Here too Sharp was engaged, both as a businessman whose expertise was useful in negotiating contracts with printers and distributing publications, and as an author and editor. Throughout the period Irish Friends depended heavily on their counterparts in England for printed materials, though Quaker works were being printed at Cork from at least 1670. In 1679 the national meeting commissioned a Cork printer to issue 450 to 500 copies each of two of Fox's epistles, but after that date, printers in Dublin handled most or perhaps all of the Quaker works published in Ireland, including a thousand copies of Fox's epistle to innkeepers and vintners in 1682. Irish Friends attempted to stay abreast of Quaker works issued in England, in part by contracting with their English colleagues in the spring of 1675 to obtain a dozen copies of every work they published.[23]

Initially the number of copies acquired by Irish Friends was small, sometimes fewer than fifty in the early 1670s. Yet even this early there was a considerably greater demand for some titles, such as Edmundson's *A Letter of Examination* (1672) and James Parke's *The Way of God, and Them That Walk in It* (1673); the half-yearly meeting ordered 469 copies of the former and 500 of the latter in May 1674. In time the demand for some works skyrocketed. Among the bestsellers were George Whitehead's *The Christianity of the People Commonly Called Quakers Vindicated* (1690)—5,500 copies in the 1690s; Penn's *A Key Opening a Way to Every Common Understanding* (1692)—3,500 copies in the same period; and *A Visitation of Love to All People* (1681) by the Bristol tanner Paul Moon, 3,000 copies of which were ordered in 1691. Quakers also purchased thousands of copies of Edmundson's epistle on marriage, and, notwithstanding its expense (2s. 2d. unbound), 2,000 copies of Barclay's *An Apology for the True Christian Divinity* (1678) in 1700.[24] A relatively small number of works made their way into lending libraries operated by the meetings, but individual Friends acquired the vast majority of Quaker publications and undoubtedly lent them to one another, as did Sharp. Apart from Friends who were engaged in polemical debate, Irish Quakers, unlike their counterparts in Philadelphia, limited their reading to the Bible and works composed by Friends, thus contributing to what Carla Pestana has called "their continued insularity." The Dublin meeting owned Fox's *Journal*, George Keith's *Immediate Revelation* (1668), Thomas Ellwood's *Truth Prevailing and Detecting Error* (1676), other works by Ellwood, and unspecified books by Edward Burrough. Sharp's name is not on the list of borrowers, but it was probably incomplete, and in any event he was wealthy enough to own copies of any books he wanted to read.[25]

Sharp contributed to the acquisition and distribution of Quaker publications in various ways. His business background provided useful experience to negotiate with printers, as he did for works by Fox, Burnyeat, and others. In his capacity as a treasurer of the national and provincial meetings, he dispensed funds for various books, and he helped as well with the task of allocating and shipping copies to the respective meetings. He also corresponded with the Quaker printer Tace Sowle (daughter of the well-known Quaker printer Andrew Sowle) in England concerning the possibility of obtaining copies of Barclay's *Apology* for Irish Friends, but the Dublin meeting decided it was less expensive to print the work in Dublin; Sharp helped to negotiate the contract, insisting that the copies "bee as well done as them in England."[26]

When the six-months meeting resolved in November 1681 to publish an account of the Friends' suffering in Ireland in the 1670s, it directed Sharp to make inquiries of a printer and report to the next meeting. He seems not to have done this, for Turner and Sleigh were subsequently assigned this task, yet in May 1682 the half-yearly meeting asked Sharp, Abraham Fuller, Stockdale, Williamson, and four others to compile an account based on reports from the meetings. This committee resolved that the sufferings would be grouped into two categories, one for declination to pay tithes and the second for all other offenses, including re-

fusal to take oaths, pay church rates, attend services of the Church of
Ireland, and observe holy days. When the material had been gathered in
1683, the national meeting appointed Sharp and Seaton to see the work
through the press, assisted by Burnyeat and Fuller if they were available.
The meeting gave Sharp £50 to pay for 500 copies. Not until 1685 had
the work—Stockdale's *The Great Cry of Oppression*—been completed
(though the title-page carries a date of 1683), at which time Sharp allocated copies to the three provincial meetings. A committee of four met
at Sharp's house in late 1697 to distribute the remaining copies. Although the book was published in Stockdale's name, Sharp had a significant role in gathering and probably editing the material as well as in
seeing the manuscript through the press and distributing the printed
books.[27]

Sharp shared responsibility for reviewing several manuscripts that
were candidates for publication. As early as May 1666 Quaker ministers who had gathered in London recommended that "faithfull &
sound" Friends review manuscripts before publication, but not until
1672 did the yearly meeting appoint a committee of ten to supervise the
press. The second-day meeting, established the following year, also concerned itself with such oversight, and after 1679 the meeting for sufferings was primarily responsible for printing and distributing Quaker literature. In Ireland, when the half-yearly meeting pondered whether it
should collect and publish the writings of Thomas Carleton (at his
widow's expense), it appointed Sharp, Burnyeat, Seaton, Fuller, and
Trafford to review them. Either their reaction was negative or they
failed to complete the assignment, for the question arose again in 1692;
at that time the delegates asked Sharp, Ashton, Archer, and three others
to examine the papers and print what they deemed appropriate at the
meeting's expense.[28]

Several times the Dublin and national meetings designated Sharp to
serve as a coauthor of statements that were at least semi-official in nature. The first instance occurred in November 1697, when the Dublin
meeting wanted to reprint Whitehead's *The Christianity of the People
Commonly Called Quakers*. First, however, it instructed Sharp, Roger
Roberts, Ashton, and Rooke to review the volume and write a preface if
necessary. Six years later the national meeting asked Sharp, Seaton, and
Wight to compose postscripts to William Morris' *Tithes No Gospel-
Ordinance* (1680), "setting forth as briefly as may be what is the Gospell Maintenance mentioned in Scripture, and the great disparity betweene it, and the Tything Ministry of this present Age." By May 1704

they had done so, but the half-yearly meeting deferred publication until an opportune time.[29] What Sharp wrote on this occasion was probably similar to his substantive testimony against tithes (discussed in the following chapter), which was subsequently incorporated in the unpublished manuscript "Memoranda Against Tithes" (1716) by Samuel Fuller, Nathaniel Owens, and others.[30]

Besides his involvement in education and publication, Sharp played a major role in the investigations that preceded Quaker marriages and assisted in drafting marital certificates. When a Quaker couple decided to marry, they had to express their intention to their respective men's and women's meetings, which then conducted inquiries to determine if the prospective bride and groom were free of obligations to others and, if young people, had parental approval. If the outcome of the inquiry was satisfactory, the couple's intention to wed was announced several times to their meeting(s), after which they pledged themselves to each other during a meeting. The Friends recorded such contracts in the meeting's register.[31]

Beginning in 1675 Sharp became embroiled in a controversy over whether the final determination of a couple's suitability to marry was to be made by the Dublin men's meeting or the provincial assembly. As Sharp argued in a letter of 27 November to Patrick Levyston, who believed that a prospective bride and groom were duty-bound to seek the provincial meeting's permission, this procedure required couples to travel as much as sixty miles to attend such a gathering, and the additional delays forced some to wait as long as three years to marry. Frustrated couples had filed complaints with the Dublin men's meeting, which wanted to render the final decision except in problematic cases. The latter would be referred to the Leinster meeting. The Dublin meeting was unanimous in its belief that inquiries should not be unduly prolonged.[32]

The issue was not resolved, for early in 1678 the Dublin men's meeting dispatched Sharp and three colleagues to the women's meeting preparatory to submitting a proposition to the provincial assembly. When a couple announced their intention to marry to the women's meeting, the men wanted the latter to "enter it as a presentation in a book," conduct an inquiry into their "clearness," and make the results known to the next men's meeting. Both meetings would then undertake a joint examination and allow the couple to proceed if nothing were amiss. The Dublin men's and women's meetings proposed that only cases in which couples were not cleared should be forwarded to the provincial level. Among the women who affixed their signatures to the proposition was Ann Sharp.[33] In fact, the proposal was unanimously endorsed. In arguing their case the Dublin meeting noted that several Friends had recently been wed by priests, citing "the hardness and charge and tegiousness of marridges among freinds." If the Leinster body denied this request, the Dublin meeting threatened to seek recognition as a provincial meeting in its own right.[34] The proposal sparked more debate among the Leinster delegates than the official records indicate, for Crabb observed that Sharp, who bore the primary responsibility for making the argument, returned from the meeting with a countenance "like death" because of the opposition. Nevertheless Sharp prevailed, for the Leinster assembly decided to approve the Dublin proposition if Fox had no objections.[35] Apparently he had none.

Sharp dutifully undertook his share of inquiries at the local and provincial levels on behalf of couples intending to wed, after which he drafted the certificates. The best known involved Burnyeat's marriage to Elizabeth Maine in 1683.[36] Sometimes the inquiries necessitated correspondence with Friends in England, as with Mary Lewis in 1672, when Sharp and Clarridge wrote to Quakers in Bristol, partly to ascertain if she had her mother's acquiescence. He also obtained information about Irish Friends seeking authorization to marry in England. Oliver Sansom, for instance, sought his aid when a Quaker from county Carlow wanted to marry one of Sansom's relatives in 1686. Besides the usual questions about the man's clearness to wed, Sansom asked Sharp to investigate his character and determine what his father would "do for him upon an outward account."[37]

Most inquiries were routine and turned up no impediments to matrimony, but occasionally difficulties arose, as in a proposed union between Abraham Fuller the younger and Elizabeth Smith, James Fade's daughter-in-law. When the couple announced their intention to marry in 1678, the Dublin men's meeting deputed Sharp and Atherton to ascertain Fuller's clearness and write to James Hutcheson, who apparently thought Smith had agreed to wed him. In fact, Hutcheson objected to the proposed marriage, but he insisted on taking his case to the Leinster meeting, contrary, complained the Dublin men's meeting, to "Gospell order" and "the practize of freinds." After examining the case, the Leinster delegates concluded that Fuller had not initiated his "proceedings ... according to truth," and it ordered him to condemn himself. After he had done so, he and Smith reiterated their intention to marry, whereupon the Leinster representatives charged the Dublin men's meeting to investigate a letter from an English Friend expressing his desire to marry Smith, whose mother thought she might have consented to do so. The Dublin meeting also inquired about "a Taylor [said] to have been about her." By April 1679 the investigation had been completed and the Dublin Friends gave Fuller and Smith permission to wed.[38] In this case the principle at stake was the Quakers' insistence that betrothals could not be annulled without a meeting's formal approval. Among Sharp's papers is the Dublin meeting's testimony against a couple in 1669 who had married before the woman had obtained such authorization. This "disorderly and abominable" practice, the meeting concluded, would bring "evil reproach" on Friends. With his keen sense of propriety, Sharp clearly subscribed to this belief.[39]

In matrimonial matters one of the most frequent problems with which Sharp and his colleagues had to contend was the marriage of Friends to people of other faiths. The Quakers routinely condemned such unions, expected offending Quakers to denounce their actions, and censured their parents. In Ireland the principal statement on this subject, a paper by Edmundson, was read to the half-yearly meeting in May 1680. Citing the first covenant, the law of Christ, and apostolic doctrine, Edmundson insisted that Friends must not intermarry on pain of loss of inheritance. He buttressed his case with a materialistic argument, warning Friends that non-Quakers sought Quaker spouses to obtain a share of their wealth. Another major theme of Edmundson's was the necessity to shun marriage by professional clergy; instead Quakers were to emulate Rebecca and Isaac, who wed without a priest (Genesis 24:67).[40]

Cognizant that several young Friends had recently married people of other faiths, delegates to the national meeting blamed this partly on indulgent parents, partly on stubborn youth. Following an intense discussion of possible preventive measures, the meeting resolved that parents who suspected their children were about to be wed by a priest or marry non-Quakers should inform other Friends so the latter might advise the young people. Indulgent parents faced admonition, and youth who defied these principles were not to receive their inheritances until they repented. The Sharps were not among the thirty men and twenty-one women who signed this statement in May 1680, but a year later Anthony was one of eleven Friends who subscribed it.[41]

Over the years Sharp acted in various capacities to uphold the prohibition on marrying people of other faiths. In 1670, for instance, the Leinster meeting charged Sharp, Turner, and two others to see that "truth be cleared" by insisting that a Quaker woman who had been wed by a priest fully condemn her actions. Five years later he wrote to Francis Nicholson, warning him not to debase truth and dishonor God by marrying an unbeliever.[42] On numerous occasions Sharp counseled offenders on this issue, helped to draft statements of condemnation, and read the latter to his meeting. One such testimony, which he signed with thirteen others in January 1697, disowned Margery Ottway for the double offense of marrying a non-Quaker less than three months after becoming a widow.[43]

Quakers who had professional clergy perform weddings undermined the Friends' reputation. In one such case, the Dublin men's meeting instructed Sharp in 1681 to ask a priest if he had married the schoolmaster George Richardson to Cisly Fade; although the priest professed to have a memory lapse, Richardson had no license to wed and the marriage was invalid anyway, but the meeting formally condemned him in a statement signed by Sharp and nineteen others. In 1682 Sharp and Peter Sleigh informed the Bristol meeting that Thomas Player had married by a priest and then abandoned his wife in poverty; he turned up again in Bristol, where he committed bigamy by taking another spouse.[44] One of the most stubborn offenders was Samuel Clarridge, who had married his second wife, Anna (or Anne) Raymond of London by a priest in 1662. After she died on 20 July 1700 he wed Frances Auldridge in 1702, again by going to an ordained cleric. When confronted by two Friends sent by the Dublin men's meeting, Clarridge admitted in writing that "hee did not well in goeing contrary to our order," but the meeting found this inadequate and insisted he must confess that he had wronged God. When Clarridge's second written statement proved to be ambiguous, the meeting deputed Sharp and Ashton to warn him that if he refused to confess fully and clearly, the Friends would disown him. Clarridge thereupon yielded in a statement dated 15 September 1702, but not without implicitly criticizing the importance Friends accorded testimonies of condemnation and denial:

> I believe assuredly that it is not papers that blotts out Sins and Offences Committed against Allmighty God. But it is the blood of the Immaculate Lamb of God that hee washeth the Soul withall that doth the work, for poor Mankind. Now Friends I do Confesse, I did amisse, and not well, in going contrary to the Law of God, and contrary to the Order of Truth in takeing my now Wife according to the Custome and Ceremony of the Church of England for which doing I have been sory in my very heart many a time and Season. . . . I am heartily sory I have troubled the upright hearted in this matter.

This did not satisfy the men's meeting, which issued its own statement two weeks later announcing that Clarridge was not yet received into fellowship because for many years he had repeatedly transgressed and "been an Exercise to friends." Only after he manifested genuine repentance, a "plyable temper," and humble deportment would he be restored to unity. Although Frances had attended Quaker meetings and seemingly professed truth, her involvement with Clarridge in this disorderly marriage prompted the meeting to conclude that "shee hath thereby plainly manifested her selfe not to be of us." The importance attached to this case is indicated by the fact that forty-eight Friends, including Sharp, signed the statement of 29 September.[45]

Their endeavors notwithstanding, Sharp and his colleagues were unable to staunch the practice of intermarriage. Sharp was apparently not at the business portion of the half-yearly meeting in November 1702, but he would have endorsed its affirmation "that none who have gained a good Report and Esteem in the Truth by their faithfulnesse to the same, may for sinister or worldly Ends, Encline or Endeavour to Match or Marry with or into Families, or with Persons, that through unfaithfullness to the Truth have not that Repute and Credit amongst friends as the honest hearted and rightly concerned have, there being an Inequallity in such Joynings in Marriage." The following month the Leinster delegates ordered the reprinting and distribution of 2,000 copies of Edmundson's paper on matrimony, some of which they were prepared to share with the Ulster and Munster meetings.[46]

Sharp and his associates took pains to prevent Friends from marrying in haste. In 1674 the Leinster meeting advised its constituent members not to approve marriage certificates too quickly, for "that which is good the Lord will bring to pass in his time." A meeting might ask a couple to "wait in the thing a while" until it felt "unity to arise," and those who were adjudged to have married with unseemly dispatch risked disownment by their meetings.[47] Quakers expected widows and widowers to wait a decent interval—a year, recommended Fox—before remarrying. In 1686 the prominent Ulster Quaker George Gregson asked Sharp to reissue Fox's statement, "For there is need for it." Curiously, however, Gregson requested that Sharp do this circumspectly "least some concerned may Judge It was I [who] was the mover of it." Like Fox, the Dublin and Leinster meetings deemed remarriage within a year of a spouse's death indecent and immoderate.[48] Among the more disagreeable cases requiring Sharp's involvement was one in which he had to defend the Dublin meeting after it had disowned a widow for her disorderly remarriage. On another occasion he and Amos Strettell had the awkward task of informing a Friend who had emigrated to Barbados and sought permission to remarry that his wife was in fact still alive, had debts in Ireland, and was of "verry foule and unseemly behaviour."[49]

Keenly sensitive to behavioral patterns that would cast them in a negative light, the Friends established standards of conduct that were beyond reproach. The Leinster provincial meeting instructed Sharp in 1677 to urge the national body to remind local men's and women's groups that single people intending to wed should not live together before marriage. A decade later, Sharp prepared a marriage certificate for a couple that had been "scandellous in keeping Company together at unseasonable times and giving occasion to people of the world to reflect [negatively] upon Truth," but only after they had independently condemned their actions. There had also been accusations that the man in this case, the Dublin alehouse keeper Thomas Wilson, had acted promiscuously with another woman, "who Claimed marriage of him."[50] Several months later the Dublin men's meeting dealt with a similar case, this time involving James Wilson and Elizabeth Weld, who had to condemn her "Scandallous foolish Carriage" with another man. James Wilson wanted to marry her, but only after seeking the meeting's consent. Given her past conduct, it was reluctant to approve; indeed, one can imagine Sharp raising his voice in protest, yet the members finally concluded that "friends do neither make marriages nor break them, and therefore as they Cannot advise him to proceed in his Intentions with her (fearing it will not Tend to his good) So they will not take upon them to stop their proceedings, but leaves it to themselves to weigh and consider according to the measure of truth in themselves, and so to do as they find Clearness in their owne minds." Notwithstanding the meeting's hesitation, the couple announced their decision to marry a month later.[51]

The Friends endeavored to prevent these problems and increase the prospects for stable union by cautioning their youth not to marry when they were too young and to obtain parental consent before matrimony. Martha Archer found it necessary to condemn herself in 1698 for having kept company without her mother's consent "with more than one young man at once in relation to Marriage," and for compounding her offense by consulting a conjurer. Complaining in 1701 that some Quaker youth were marrying too early, the Leinster meeting cast some of the blame on parents, who were warned to "Expect to be dealt with as Truth shall direct." The problem, the Leinster representatives concluded, stemmed at least partly from "unmoderation" and a desire to acquire wealth through matrimony.[52] The exhortations, of course, were not always heeded. Like other members of the Dublin men's meeting, Sharp was undoubtedly troubled by a 1701 case in which Peter Vousden and Rebecca Lloyd were asked to postpone their wedding because they were "very young & childish" and because of their relationship's brevity; when an ordained minister married the couple less than a week later, the meeting dismissed them as meaning "little to us, they haveing little vallue or esteeme for truth or us."[53]

In the early 1680s Sharp had direct experience in his own family with the difficulties that could result when young people contemplated matrimony. While still an apprentice, his brother-in-law, John Crabb, struck up a romantic relationship with Elizabeth Hawthorn of Ulster, reputedly leading her to believe they would be married. Crabb's decision to break off the relationship incited a controversy, with Gregson averring that Crabb had acted "knavishly" in "draw[ing] out the mind and affection" of Hawthorn. Crabb had already sought to shift the blame to Joseph Sleigh and others on the grounds that they had encouraged him to marry her during his apprenticeship, though they denied having done so. In the judgment of the Dublin men's meeting such encouragement would have constituted disorderly conduct and it therefore ordered the women's meeting to investigate.[54]

Because of the importance of maintaining the meetings' control over prospective marriages, especially those of young people for whom parental consent was a virtual *sine qua non*, the half-yearly meeting in May 1688 urged each provincial assembly to appoint emissaries to ask the bishop of every diocese or his chancellor to cease issuing marriage licenses to Quakers unless the latter could demonstrate parental consent. To this end, the Leinster meeting charged Sharp and Starkey to meet with William Moreton, bishop of Kildare, or his chancellor.[55]

Late in Sharp's life the Irish Friends took up the question of the marriage of cousins. Fox and the yearly meeting in England were on record as opposing the union of first cousins; in 1675 the yearly meeting, unwilling to embrace a standard less stringent than that of Judaic law, urged Friends to shun marriages between "near kindred." At the Leinster provincial meeting in February 1699, the delegates unanimously resolved that this meant a prohibition on unions between second as well as first cousins, with several members unsuccessfully arguing that even third cousins should not wed. Sharp's position in this matter was not recorded, but on behalf of the women's meeting his wife and Sarah Hutchinson reported the judgment of the men's meeting to local women's groups. Three months later the half-yearly meeting formally endorsed the ban on marriages between first and second cousins. The Leinster meeting further clarified the prohibition in 1706 by stipulating that a surviving spouse could not wed the first or second cousins of a deceased mate.[56]

The Friends' sense of responsibility, particularly for the young, extended to orphans and fatherless children. Sharp was at the six-months meeting in November 1696 when it reminded the provincial assemblies that Friends caring for orphans and fatherless children should "Carry an even hand towards them in their Education and usage, so as may Answere Truth." Periodically Sharp acted on behalf of orphans to ensure that their inheritances were secure. He did this as well for children whose fathers had died and whose mothers intended to remarry, typically insisting that such mothers provide portions for their children.[57] He assisted children in numerous other ways: obtaining an interest-bearing loan to provide income for one orphan, leasing houses built with funds left to another orphan, and arranging for the sale or lease of a New England house inherited from their deceased father by children in London. In 1701 Sharp and Amos Strettell contacted Quakers in Gloucestershire to arrange for the care of several orphans by their uncle, discharging the Dublin meeting of this responsibility. Following Burnyeat's death, the Dublin men's meeting commissioned Sharp and three others to inquire about an apprenticeship for his son and to ensure that his inheritance "bee Improved to his advantage."[58] When Joseph Deane died, the same group turned to Sharp and others to persuade Deane's father-in-law to relinquish money that belonged to the widow, Abigail née Chaundey, and her two children. On behalf of the Dublin meeting Sharp was among those who investigated the activities of executors to ascertain whether they were fulfilling their obligations to orphans and fatherless children in their charge.[59]

Concern for the well-being of orphans and fatherless children was a major reason for the Friends' substantive efforts to keep accurate records of wills and supervise their administration. In November 1673 the half-yearly meeting named Sharp, Fuller, Holme, and four others to a committee "to mind the Concerns of friends deeds of Gift, or wills, buriall places or the like." By 1685 the local meetings had assigned members to inspect wills and supervise the overseers or executors responsible for orphans' and fatherless children's estates; in that year the

Leinster meeting directed these inspectors to report to it each year and to submit sealed copies of all wills and inventories for recording in a provincial register. As we have seen, Sharp served as an inspector.[60] He contributed as well by helping to resolve disputes over legacies and to handle administrative details.[61]

One of Sharp's most important duties entailed keeping the Dublin meeting's register of wills and inventories. This body made its decision to maintain such a register in July 1684, antedating by more than three months the national meeting's recommendation that each local group keep such a book. The following February the Leinster provincial assembly selected one member from each meeting to maintain a register of wills and inventories, which it wanted kept as private as possible; for Dublin that member was Sharp. From this date until his death, Sharp was responsible for the Dublin book of wills and inventories, assisted by a supervisory committee comprising eight other members at its inception. The committee, which convened at Sharp's house, was meeting at six-week intervals by the early eighteenth century.[62]

A record of the committee's work is extant commencing 27 December 1704. Not surprisingly, Sharp was among its most active members and remained so to the end of his life, attending the meeting on 5 December 1706, the last one before his death. On behalf of the committee he worked with other members to obtain funds bequeathed to the Friends as a group or as inheritances to Quaker children. Sometimes this involved securing deeds as well as recording wills and legal arrangements for children whose widowed mothers were remarrying. One of the most substantive cases involved Susanna Brittan, who chose to marry James Peirson following her husband's demise. Sharp handled the legal papers for the committee in this case, which involved a settlement of £178 for Brittan's son John, and assisted as well by helping to arrange for the lease of land belonging to the boy. Sharp was also involved in monitoring the use of funds by Cumberland Quakers that had been bequeathed to Jonathan and Philip Burnyeat. Near the end of Sharp's life, these committee responsibilities seem to have been more than he could handle, for after his death the committee discovered that his books did not indicate into whose hands the legacy of the deceased Thomas Mills had been remitted.[63]

The responsibility for orphans, fatherless children, wills, and inventories vested in Sharp by the Dublin meeting was a testimony to the esteem in which he was held and his extraordinary capacity for administrative tasks. Because of his negotiating skills, the meeting also turned to him for help in resolving disputes. Dealing with these problems internally was intended to preserve harmony within the movement, to avoid presenting an image of fractiousness to the outside world, and to prevent unnecessary recourse to law courts. The Friends settled most disputes at the local or provincial level using *ad hoc* committees that typically numbered four to six people. Even before controversies reached this stage, Quakers were supposed to seek reconciliation with the informal assistance of two or three Friends in keeping with the Pauline exhortation in 1 Corinthians 6:1–7. Serious cases could go all the way to the half-yearly meeting, which in May 1676 appointed twelve men from Leinster and six each from Munster and Ulster to resolve such disputes following the conclusion of its sessions. Sharp, Clarridge, Turner, Starkey, Foster, Joseph Sleigh, and Abraham Fuller were among the Leinster referees. Two decades later the national meeting again took up procedural matters, resolving that Friends who refused to submit to arbitration or who rejected the referees' judgment would be barred from business meetings until they complied. It was probably at this time that Sharp prepared a statement urging Quakers to seek informal resolution of their disputes, failing which they were, as in the past, to refer them to their meeting. If either party refused to do so, the Friends, said Sharp, would adjudge the recalcitrant person "Stubborn and stiffnecked," and would exclude him or her from unity with the church. In such cases legal redress was not an option, "for its forbidden for Brother to goe to law with Brother."[64]

The subject of controversy was not recorded in many cases Sharp helped to resolve,[65] but judging from the extant evidence, the nature of the difficulties ranged widely. Among them were disputes involving unpaid debts, ownership of a watch, and unfair treatment as well as the quarrel between the younger Abraham Fuller and James Hutcheson over the right to marry Elizabeth Smith.[66] Other cases involved an apprentice who objected to relocating with his master to England, Fade's reported "abussing" of other Friends, an allegation of theft against three young women, and a spat between a Quaker couple and their son-in-law. Sharp also sought to mediate a case in which one party insisted on using two non-Quakers as arbitrators—"an Untruth-like practice," expostulated the Dublin men's meeting.[67] Quarrels could drag on, aggravating all parties and trying the forbearance of arbitrators, as in 1685–86 when Sharp and others attempted to persuade Roger Davenport to pay damages to another Quaker; after more than a year and several threats of condemnation by the Dublin men's meeting, Davenport acknowledged his "wilfulness and obstinacie against the Counsell and advice of friends of this meeting, and their patience in bearing with him."[68] The Friends invested considerable time in such quarrels in the hope of persuading offenders to reform by following the inner light.

Some sense of how Sharp might have approached these disputes is manifest in his letter to John Edwards dated 19 January 1680. A veteran Quaker preacher who had been imprisoned and fined for his work, Edwards was now embroiled in a squabble with other Friends who rejected his testimony and refused to engage in spiritual fellowship with him after he had accused the Quaker stalwarts William and John Edmundson and Richard Jackson of Mountmellick of hindering justice for a poor man. When the provincial and national meetings were unable to resolve the controversy, Edwards appealed to Sharp. "Dear John," Sharp replied,

> what can I do for thee or them; I cannot compel them, or perswade thee to do as I would have them and thee. . . . Thou knows what Differences have been amongst you; it had been really thy place as a minister (if so qualified) to have become as a child and not lett that fleshly will or kingdom Stood in thee which have much strengthned the same will and power in them against Thy will and power, but Instead thereof thou Should have washed their feet and put thy hands under them and have born for the Lord thy own and their Souls.

But Edwards had refused to assume the primary responsibility for the tensions or to shun strife and vainglory, submitting to his brethren in the manner of Christians in the primitive church. Sharp counseled submission, calling on Edwards to remember that God is the author of peace, not confusion. Moreover, "the church hath power in some Sence to bind offenders and loose them." Both sides, Sharp acknowledged, were at fault in this case, but he expected Edwards to submit "or none will Incourage Thee that is honest against christ's command, for the[e] ought not to strengthen differences against the church."[69] For Sharp, the group's wisdom and well-being had precedence over the individual; better to yield to a meeting's collective counsel than to persevere in a fractious course.

Sharp himself was a party to several disputes, at least three of which were financial in nature. The minutes of the Dublin men's meeting refer only to "some Difference" between Sharp and Winslow in 1692, but it was important enough for the appointment of six arbitrators—Amos Strettell, Thomas, Stevens, Ashton, John Hutchinson, and Roger Rob-

erts. In an earlier case, Robert Zanes had written from New Jersey in
1684 to complain that Sharp owed him money and compound interest,
but the Dublin men's meeting accepted Sharp's explanation that he had
treated Zanes fairly because the latter had refused to accept reimbursement in merchandise according to their bargain and had rejected Sharp's
offer to repay the principal plus simple interest.[70] In 1696 Abigail Deane
and her stepson Joseph Deane (not to be confused with her late husband
of the same name) complained to the Dublin meeting that Sharp had refused to honor a bill of exchange, but the Deanes, apparently afraid
they could not obtain a fair hearing in the meeting owing to Sharp's
stature, refused its offer to appoint mediators. The meeting in turn
warned the complainants that Friends who took legal action against
their coreligionists faced damnation. Abigail eventually decried her refusal to accept arbitration, but the men's meeting was not satisfied, demanding that she void all her dealings in this matter and permit Quakers to resolve her dispute with Sharp; presumably she did, but the terms
of the settlement were apparently not recorded.[71]

Sharp was the object of a complaint by Robert Boswell in 1695. An
adherent of the old Story-Wilkinson tradition, Boswell refused to remove his hat during prayer, which may have been a factor in causing
the dissension. The minutes of the Dublin men's meeting record only
that his accusations against Sharp were baseless and the result of prejudice. This was the judgment of the six Friends—Ashton, Thomas, Jonathan Taylor, Peter Fletcher, Roger Roberts, and Amos Strettell—who
heard the case. When Boswell refused to repent, the meeting publicly
denounced him.[72]

In a final case directly involving Sharp, Abraham Fuller protested to
the Dublin men's meeting in 1697 concerning a dispute between the two
men over land and asked that the Mountmellick meeting settle it. Professing his innocence, Sharp petitioned the Dublin meeting to resolve the
matter. When its preliminary efforts to effect a reconciliation failed, it
asked Sharp and Fuller to select a like number of arbitrators. Sharp concurred, insisting that the Dublin and Moate meetings each appoint four
"indifferent, uninterested persons" unrelated to the principals in the
case, and committing himself to accept the verdict. Dublin's representatives were Clarridge, Roberts, Thomas, and Joseph Hanks. This method
proved fruitful, and following a full investigation the eight arbitrators
found in Sharp's favor.[73]

Besides his work as an arbitrator, Sharp assisted the Dublin meeting
by helping to monitor Friends intent on relocating. Well before 1674 the

Quakers in Leinster had decided that Friends planning to move must inform their meeting and obtain its advice or risk estrangement from other Quakers. The half-yearly meeting made this the policy for all Irish Friends, and in May 1682 insisted that those intending to relocate obtain certificates indicating whether their respective meetings acquiesced; in the case of young or unwed Friends emigrating to America the certificates had to specify whether they were clear to marry.[74] Sharp helped to prepare some of these certificates and make the necessary inquiries before they could be granted.[75] When Friends moved to Dublin, Sharp sometimes had the task of obtaining references from the meetings they had left, as with Samuel Limeal, whom Irish Quakers suspected of "villanous practices."[76] Certificates were also used to check the relocation of people who would become a financial drain on the new meeting, but such efforts were not always successful. In March 1694 the half-yearly assembly protested to the Bristol meeting that some of its people had arrived in Ireland without certificates and means of subsistence, thus creating a financial burden on Irish Friends.[77]

Detecting discreditable people and thereby preserving the movement's reputation and spiritual integrity was a key reason for monitoring those who relocated. Among Sharp's manuscripts is a report from Quakers in Nailsworth, Gloucestershire, about Elizabeth Partridge, who wanted to join the Dublin meeting. She had never been "in the unity of Friends or in the least [been] accounted one," they averred, but she had attended Quaker meetings and had become "a reproach to Truth" because she "Kept company" with a man who also participated in their meetings, was a companion of her husband's, and supported her child.[78] Another letter in Sharp's collection, this time from Friends in Cork, warned about Richard Clemmons, a shoemaker who appeared to be a zealous Quaker but claimed the right to remarry because his wife had engaged in an affair and borne children by another man. Ignoring the admonitions of Cork Quakers, Clemmons "sought after a wife from one woman to another." After running up debts he fled from Cork, reportedly threatening to stab anyone who attempted to stop him. Sharp and Turner were asked to forward copies of this report to Friends in Wexford and Wicklow, and elsewhere if they saw fit.[79]

In several instances the Dublin men's meeting was reluctant to authorize requests to move. The peril of the proposed journey was its rationale in one case, but those involved had already committed themselves, and the Dublin meeting therefore directed Sharp and Roberts to write to them "according to the State of their Condition." Financial ramifications probably helped to account for the same meeting's reluctance to see the wealthy linen merchant Robert Turner emigrate to Philadelphia in 1683. When the meeting learned of his plans to move, it dispatched Sharp and Atherton to ascertain his reasons. Although Turner responded in writing, he refused to explain his motives in person, inducing the meeting to send Sharp, Burnyeat, Seaton, and three others to explain that it wanted him to part with Dublin Friends "in the unity of Truth." Before emigrating (with seventeen indentured servants), he transferred Quaker documents in his possession to Sharp.[80]

Like Turner, Sharp was, of course, a very wealthy man, and in the Friends' eyes this entailed special obligations, a sort of *noblesse oblige*. Delegates to the six-months meeting in May 1694 recommended that each meeting "stir up them that are rich (they being Capable of doeing great service for Truth) to discharge themselves faithfully therein every way." Sharp was among those delegates, who would undoubtedly have looked to him as an exemplar because of his opulence. Indeed, only three months earlier the Leinster meeting had urged its local groups to recommend that their prosperous members "be Rich in good works." Again the hand of Sharp was probably at work.[81]

Sharp's involvement in Quaker charitable work was substantial, although the level of his personal giving is difficult to gauge inasmuch as Fox had advised Friends in 1671 not to maintain registers detailing their provision of relief to the needy. Not surprisingly, therefore, poor relief accounts for the Dublin meeting date only from September 1700, when it began a ledger showing receipts (typically from biweekly collections) and disbursements. Generally, donors are anonymous, though initially Amos Strettell and Benjamin Head each contributed bonds worth £20 apiece and four others gave bonds valued at £15 each, the interest from which was used to relieve the needy. In September or October, Ann Sharp donated £10, and Anthony himself contributed £5 in the same period. The ledger shows no further gifts from the Sharps, but the record of donors is largely anonymous. Like her husband, Ann Sharp was active in the dispersal of relief; twice in the spring of 1701 she was reimbursed for dispersals of 6s. and 2s. 8d. respectively, and the following November the ledger indicates that the meeting entrusted her with 9s. 5d. to assist a poor woman.[82]

According to the ledger, the cash on hand was typically modest—21s. 3d. on 22 May 1704, for example—so that most funds were dispersed shortly after their receipt. In the period from 5 January to 21 December 1702, receipts, including interest on bonds (£3 18s.), totaled more than

£43. For 1706, the comparable figure exceeded £49.[83] Gifts normally ranged from 2s. to 24s. 6d. and took the form of cash or goods, such as coal or linen for shifts. One needy woman received assistance in return for cleaning the meetinghouse. Rarely did the Friends expect recipients to repay the money. The donees, who included indigent families as well as individuals, were not always named in the ledger. Often it simply indicates that donors made contributions "upon truths account."[84] We know considerably more about Sharp's dispensing of poor relief for the meetings than we do about his personal giving. Even if the latter was not on a scale comparable to his donations for the construction of meetinghouses, it may have been sizable. On at least two occasions English Friends wrote to him seeking assistance for needy people, which suggests that his philanthropic reputation was widespread.[85]

From at least the late 1670s Sharp disbursed monies to the needy for the Dublin and Leinster meetings. Sometimes he expended the money for specific purposes, such as the purchase of coal and clothing or the cost of a funeral or even a bath, but in other cases he and those with whom he worked either distributed money or had the discretion to assist in whatever way they deemed appropriate.[86] This charitable activity provided Sharp with an opportunity to assist people in a variety of circumstances: beef, mutton, and other foodstuffs for poor Friends on a ship in Dublin harbor awaiting the voyage to Pennsylvania; £5 to a needy Quaker who had moved to Bristol; assistance for the infirm and elderly; money to help a man find "a Livelyhood"; the loan of a horse; and relief for poor Friends who had relocated to Dublin.[87]

Requests for assistance were sometimes problematic. After totally supporting one needy Quaker for several years, the Dublin men's meeting had Sharp and the tallowchandler John Inglefield notify his uncle in Cumberland that in keeping with apostolic practice the relatives of the indigent should provide for them so as not to burden the church. When Friends in county Wicklow refused to aid a woman who had moved to Dublin unless Quakers there reimbursed them, Sharp and Newland explained that she was not a member of their meeting and was still primarily the responsibility of Wicklow Friends, for she had moved without the Dublin meeting's acquiescence; Dublin Quakers had hitherto assisted her only because of her poverty and "great suffering by her husband."[88] This attitude reflected the traditional English view that the primary responsibility for poor relief rested with the home parish.

Alleged spousal abuse was also cited by another woman seeking assistance, in this case a wife whose husband, though a professing

Quaker, had reportedly left her without cause; she appealed to George Gregson of Lisburn, who sought Sharp's aid in determining the facts, for the woman's husband was a hostler for Sharp's colleague, Roger Roberts. In the same letter Gregson warned Sharp about a man who had recently arrived in the Lisburn area, boasting "he would not take forty pound[s] for what he Would gett [in charity] among the Quakers." The Friends had obviously acquired a reputation for generosity, making it necessary to be alert for fraudulent requests for assistance.[89]

Sharp became embroiled in a controversy about alleged "Cheats" in 1677 stemming from his employment of Ann Cliff, a widow who had recently emigrated to Ireland with her sons. To keep her from begging, Sharp offered her not only a job but also money for food. One of Cliff's creditors in Nailsworth, Gloucestershire, Robert Silvester, thereupon wrote to Sharp on 9 April, accusing him of being "an encourager of Cheats." "I rather judge it to be foolish pity," he continued, "that hath just blinded thee," for God "admits not of willfull cheats." Silvester insisted that if Cliff and her son Thomas never repaid their debt, the blame would rest with Sharp. Silvester had not demanded their arrest, he claimed, knowing that Sharp would not "have Cheats to Suffer," but he expected Sharp to persuade her to pay what she owed; instead Sharp, he charged, "hast rather hardened her." He pressed Sharp to discharge his conscience by condemning Cliff's behavior, including her payment of money that should have been Silvester's to her son-in-law. Sharp had allegedly advised the latter to reimburse all her creditors except Silvester. Convinced that Cliff now "rest[ed] safe under [Sharp's] Wing," Silvester called on him to articulate her intentions and implied that he would take legal action to recover the money.[90]

Sharp responded on the 26th, denying he had encouraged swindlers. Turning first to Silvester's reference to Mary Penton, who had upbraided Sharp, he explained that he had attempted to help her recover a debt of approximately £8 from the tapster William Simkins, who was then in the Dublin prison and also had debts in England. Simkins offered to settle the obligation for 10s. in the pound, which Sharp recommended, but Penton demanded repayment in full. Shortly thereafter, Simkins died, leaving his widow and two children destitute and Penton with no opportunity to recover her money. Although Sharp insisted she did not blame him, she must have made disparaging remarks about him to Silvester or a third party.[91] Concerning Cliff's debt, Sharp told Silvester he would read his missive to the next men's meeting and let it be the judge. If the debt were owed to him, Sharp asserted, he would not have her arrested because she was poor; incarceration would only cause the debt to increase and impair Cliff's health. "I have dealt plainly with her," Sharp explained, "and not onely by my self." Although she had promised to make restitution to Silvester, Cliff had fled England because she feared Silvester would have her arrested.[92]

Silvester's letter included a reference to Sharp's treatment of Roger Gillet, whom Silvester denounced as another cheat. Gillet, of course, had aided in Sharp's conversion to the Friends, and Sharp was understandably sensitive to this criticism. While he was in Sharp's employ, Gillet had saved approximately £20 and gone into business for himself, but because he was "not of a capacity to drive a trade," he trusted others with his goods and plunged into debt. Sharp counseled him: "i had a Godly jealousie over him and spoke to him about it not Long before he [went] broke and i advised him to com to me and Work and pay all he owed," but fearing he could never repay his obligations, Gillet absconded. After the Sharps moved to Dublin, Esther saw Gillet, who burst into tears, presumably of shame. After two or three days of searching, Anthony found him: "i talked hard to him and he was as a dead man in Countainnance." At Sharp's urging, Gillet drew up a statement of his assets and liabilities, and gave power of attorney to his creditors to pay off his debts. Sharp also sought the advice of the Dublin men's meeting, particularly as to whether he should sue Gillet for debts owed to him. When the meeting left the decision to Sharp, he went to court, prepared to initiate legal action, but "being there i had a Stop within Myself that with Freedom should not proceed against him there, but i resolved to proceed with him other ways." Sharp left it to Silvester to decide whether he had acted properly, but he added that he had told Gillet he could never be clear in the eyes of God, the Friends, and the world unless he repaid his debts as far as possible and returned to England to "Offer up his body to his Creditors." Sharp had no objection to the punishment of fraudulent persons as long as the penalties were commensurate with the offenses,[93] but he was prepared to provide indigent people in difficult circumstances with a second chance to discharge their debts and reestablish themselves without facing incarceration, which would only inhibit their recovery. For Sharp, charitable relief included the capacity for reformation, both social and spiritual.

In the early eighteenth century the Irish Friends began to dispense relief on a nonsectarian basis, but during Sharp's lifetime charity was generally confined to needy Quakers. There were, of course, exceptions. When the lord deputy recommended collections to aid the indigent,

Dublin Quakers obligingly read his statements at their meetings, suggesting that Friends might donate "as they have freedom"; Sharp announced one such request in September 1687.[94] He was involved as well in providing relief to the penurious James Cunningham, who had been incarcerated with his son at Naas, county Kildare, in 1683, and turned to the Quakers for help. At the behest of the Dublin men's meeting Sharp and Clarridge told him they could not "stand by him as a friend," but they sent him 20s. Cunningham subsequently complained to the six-months meeting, which noted that those who knew him regarded him as "a Jangling contentious man & of a very scandalous Conversation . . . [who] hath procured sufferings to himself by his Contentious and unchristian Courses." The meeting dispatched Sharp, Roberts, and Richard Scot to inform him that it could neither accept him as a Friend nor "Countenance him in his sufferings least Truth should suffer thereby." Yet in 1687 the Dublin men's meeting agreed to give him another 20s. on the eve of his expected release, partly to enable him to purchase a necessary writ. However, Sharp had instructions to emphasize that this money was being provided out of pity, not because Cunningham was a fellow Quaker. The Dublin meeting was still giving him assistance in 1696, though it exhorted him to rely on his own kin.[95]

On three occasions in Sharp's life the Dublin Friends engaged in major relief efforts: the collection of funds to aid English Quakers in 1684–85, the receipt and disbursement of reciprocal help from England during and immediately after the time of troubles, and the collection of money from Irish Friends to assist the needy during the same period. Responding to the plight of English Friends during the so-called Tory Revenge, the half-yearly meeting in May 1684 appointed a committee of seven, including Sharp, John Edmundson, and Thomas Trafford for Leinster, to solicit contributions from the provincial assemblies. While the money was being collected, Sharp and Burnyeat corresponded with George Whitehead and Alexander Parker in London "in order to the disposing of it to the best advantage of our poor Suffering friends in England." By July 1684 Quakers in Leinster had pledged £400 17s. 6d., of which £120 9s. came from Dublin. Unlike his contributions for meetinghouses, which exceeded those of his fellow Quakers, Sharp gave only £4 to this cause, less than the £10 apiece donated by Clarridge and Samuel Randall or the £5 each subscribed by John Tristram and Abraham Fuller the younger. Burnyeat contributed £2 and his wife Elizabeth £1 3s. Altogether, 123 Dublin Quakers had made pledges by May 1684. Throughout the summer of 1684 Sharp was responsible for receiving the donations. The limited scale of his own gift suggests he was less interested in assisting the needy in England than in Ireland.[96] After the national meeting had considered further reports of Quaker suffering in England, it recommended another collection in May 1685. Sharp, Burnyeat, and Amos Strettell received these funds for transmittal to London. Leinster Friends pledged nearly £452, of which almost £155 came from Dublin.[97]

During the time of troubles the Dublin meeting received its first request for assistance—from Cavan—in January 1690. In the ensuing months it extended help as well to Oldcastle and Kilteel. At the behest of the Dublin men's meeting Sharp and Ashton inquired about the condition of Friends in Cavan, Drogheda, and other areas, and administered relief to Kilteel.[98] In November the Leinster provincial meeting, noting that Dublin Quakers had been succoring poor Friends who had fled to the city for refuge, recommended that £30 be raised from its constituent members, apart from Moate, where hardship owing to the war was a major problem. In six weeks, Irish Friends subscribed £37, of which the Dublin meeting pledged £15. All this and more paid the rent of distressed Quaker refugees in Dublin.[99]

As the depredations and war damages mounted, the meeting for sufferings in London wrote to Sharp and Burnyeat, offering £50 to relieve the needy. As directed by the Leinster meeting, Sharp laid this offer, which had since increased to £200, before the national meeting in November 1690, but a committee of ten, including Sharp, determined that Irish Friends could meet their own needs. By this point some two dozen families in Leinster who lived near the battlefront required approximately £70 in assistance, but Gregson had left a legacy of £50 for Leinster Friends (as he had for those in Munster), and Quakers in the province raised an additional £50.[100]

By January 1692 English Friends had again offered to help. The overture came at a time when Dublin Quakers were still assisting distressed comrades in their midst. On the 5th the Dublin men's meeting directed Sharp to release £10 for this purpose, with the women to dole out as much of this as they deemed necessary. At the Leinster assembly four days later, the delegates instructed each local meeting to determine what the "Condition of friends Impaired by the times is." Sharp subsequently reported the results of the inquiry in Dublin to the Leinster meeting.[101] Besides assisting the poor in its own midst, the Dublin meeting was asked by its provincial counterpart in the spring of 1692 to help Friends at Moate who were suffering because of the war. Although most members of the Dublin men's meeting were unwilling to provide the £30 requested by Moate Quakers, Clarridge, Sharp, Roberts, and the merchant Joshua Wilcocks were willing to lend the money if the six-months meeting repaid them in May; Sharp lent the smallest amount, £5, whereas Clarridge loaned the largest, £10.[102] Again, the limited scale of Sharp's donation, considering his wealth and his gifts for buildings, is striking; so too is his insistence on repayment from victims of warfare. There is more than a hint of occasional hardheartedness in his outlook toward those in need.

English Friends sent £600 to the half-yearly meeting and an additional £150 to Ulster in the spring of 1692. Sharp served on a committee of twenty appointed by this meeting to disburse the money as well as £60 bequeathed to Irish Quakers by Myles Gray. Of the £810, the committee channeled £297 to Friends in Leinster. They received an additional £42 5s. as their share of £100 donated by Quakers in Barbados. Dublin obtained only £20, which it used toward repayment of the Friends, presumably including Sharp, who had lent money to distressed Quakers at Moate. English Friends sent a further £1,060 later the same year, and Sharp again served on the national committee of twenty that apportioned the money, £460 of which went to Leinster. In early 1693 Irish Friends received an additional £3,222 10s. from their associates in England, and Sharp participated on a thirteen-member committee that allocated this munificent gift, £998 8s. 9d. of which was donated to the needy in Leinster. He also served on a committee of twelve appointed by the Dublin men's meeting to disburse its share of the money, and with Amos Strettell he drafted his meeting's statement of gratitude to English Quakers.[103] These were extraordinary sums for Sharp to manage, attesting again both to his business acumen and to the reputation for responsibility and integrity he enjoyed in Quaker circles.

Sharp assisted as well with the collection and disbursement of funds to ransom captive Friends in Algiers. Beginning around 1678, crews from Algiers and the Barbary States seized these victims and held them for ransom. Some, Fox would later report, were subjected to "great Sufferings and Abuses." Non-Quakers, of course, were also victims, and in 1679 the Dublin municipal government began soliciting contributions to redeem the prisoners. Among the Friends, in May 1680 the six-months meeting directed Thomas Cooke to ascertain what relief English Quakers had provided, and this information was in turn used as an example for provincial meetings in Ireland. Two months later the Leinster representatives resolved to raise £150, of which £45 was to come from Dublin, where the collectors were Sharp, Roger Roberts, and Joseph Sleigh.

Although donors with second thoughts received an opportunity to retract their donations in August, by November the Leinster Friends had amassed £232 0s. 2d. Approximately £523 was raised nationally.[104]

The London yearly meeting again sought help from Irish Friends for captive Quakers in Algiers in late 1684. Because Burnyeat, who received the appeal, was ill at the time of the national meeting in November, the delegates first took up the request in May 1685. Burnyeat, Sharp, and Amos Strettell had instructions to write to London to determine whether funds were still needed and to forward the response to the provincial assemblies. That summer the Friends learned that John Bealing had been a prisoner in Morocco for two years, and Sharp became involved in efforts to raise the £200 demanded for his release. At the national meeting in November a committee that included Sharp, Burnyeat, Edmundson, and Gregson recommended that a new collection be undertaken to redeem Quaker captives. Sharp, Fuller, and Francis Randall made the case to the Leinster meeting, which duly requested each local group to solicit gifts. On this occasion Sharp was not one of those asked to collect money in Dublin, perhaps because he was already so active in this cause at the provincial and national levels.[105] Nevertheless he and Amos Strettell handled the monies once they had been collected and forwarded them to England. Altogether, Irish Friends donated £281 13s. 6d. this time, of which £146 5s. 3½d. came from Leinster.[106]

Sharp's record of involvement in the community of Friends in Ireland is extraordinary. Because of his expertise in business affairs and the management of funds, Quakers at the national, provincial, and especially the local level looked to him for leadership and assistance. Much of the movement's business passed through his hands, particularly if it involved the collection and disbursement of money. He played a major role in the collection of donations to aid distressed English Friends in 1684–85, and he was no less active in allocating and disbursing relief funds for needy Irish Quakers during and immediately after the time of troubles. Handling substantial sums of money with skill and accuracy, he avoided any taint of scandal or miscalculation. As a wealthy man in his own right he donated to needy individuals, though his role in this sphere apparently was substantially less than his support for the construction of meetinghouses. He seems to have been more interested in giving funds to benefit the Dublin meeting in general than distressed individuals, yet the Dublin meeting's testimony to him after his death noted that he had not been "backward to communicate . . . [his riches] to the poor."[107] His philanthropy was known in England, and several times his generosity to debtors opened him to charges that he condoned cheats.

Sharp's business expertise was useful as well in negotiating agreements with printers to publish Quaker works, to maintain the Dublin meeting's register of wills and inventories, and to safeguard the rights of widows, orphans, and fatherless children. As a businessman he was a positive force in helping to manage the affairs of the Quaker school in Dublin, including the hiring of schoolmasters. Moreover, he was engaged in negotiating terms of apprenticeship, mediating disputes between masters and apprentices, and arbitrating conflicts between Friends. He was, of course, personally involved in several financial disputes, and though acquitted, he may have triumphed because of his reputation and influence more than the justice of his cause. Besides distributing Quaker books and pamphlets, he was a coauthor of several Quaker works and engaged to a limited degree in reviewing material before publication. Sharp helped to investigate couples prior to marriage, seeking to curtail unions between Friends and people of other faiths, and preparing marital and other certificates. All of this required a substantial expenditure of time and emotional effort, particularly in cases involving internecine tensions, physical and economic distress, and frustrations stemming from the unwillingness of some Quakers to embrace the movement's ideals. To have contributed in so many ways and to have been active and successful as well in his dealings as a wool merchant and a guild member point to an extraordinary level of energy, talent, and commitment.

9

"In a Lowly Mind"

Shaping and Enforcing Conduct

MORE THAN THEIR Quaker colleagues in England, Sharp and his fellow Irish Friends developed rigorous standards of conduct, especially in the period after the time of troubles when some Quakers were increasingly attracted to what their leaders deemed the ways of the world. In a less repressive society, encroaching secularism became a greater threat than legal repression. Sharp and his associates responded by articulating distinctive standards of conduct, thereby preserving the movement's strong sense of community, and introducing a system of home and shop visitations to inculcate and enforce them. As a shaper of these standards, Sharp must have practiced them, and indirectly they therefore suggest much about his behavior, his dress, and his home furnishings.

Irish Friends articulated behavioral standards in numerous areas, ranging from speech and sexual relations to indebtedness, inebriety, and recreation, but they also expressed a sense of what Quaker behavior should be. In 1694 and again in 1696, for example, the Dublin men's meeting dispatched Sharp and others to speak with James Fade's sons because their "untruthlike Carriage" and behavior reflected adversely on the Friends. Indeed, in 1681 Sharp and three colleagues had been sent to see Fade himself because his behavior grieved Quakers, but when he refused to acknowledge his faults, Sharp's delegation "Leaft him to have the matter Referr'd to the [Dublin men's] meeting if he thought good." Judging from the number of times the Dublin meeting appointed Sharp to deal with offenders, he must have been effective in counseling and admonishing, as in so much else. Among the cases with which he worked were Quakers whose (unspecified) actions in a bleaching yard were questionable in 1678, and a group of young men who met "to the hurting of one another," causing scandal in 1703. Most offenders promised to reform.[1]

Sharp and his colleagues expected Friends to speak in a manner conducive to "Truths Principles." The ideal, in the words of the Dublin men's meeting, was "a truthlik[e] conversation," not disorderly, scandalous, or wicked speech. A copy of a general epistle dated 28 October 1679 from the Dublin men's meeting in Sharp's papers deplores "all Light, wanton, foolish and vain Talk and Frothy Behaviours, and conversations, which doth not edify nor administer grace." The all-encompassing ideal of gravity in Quaker living was captured again by the half-yearly meeting in November 1693, when it proclaimed that "all Friends whether Young or old be weig[h]tly & solid, not airy & light in their discourse or deportment at all times, whether one among another or before other people, both in traveling upon the Road, in Inns, or elsewhere." Not surprisingly, some Quakers cited for unacceptable conversation were also prone to inebriety.[2]

The Friends were especially sensitive to slanderous speech because of the dissension it caused within the movement as well as the bad impression it made on outsiders, as when Ezra Thackery slandered Joseph Thomas and others "in the audience of severall great persons to the Scandall of Truth." In 1687 the Dublin men's meeting dispatched Sharp and others to rebuke George Zane for "bussying himself with a lying Report that was in the City some time agoe," an offense he acknowledged. Periodically the various meetings found it essential to ask any Quaker who heard a scandalous report about another Friend to ascertain its veracity from the rumor's subject before repeating the account.[3]

Sharp was involved in an earlier, enigmatic case concerning Elizabeth and George Danson of Rhode Island. After she complained to Fox about Quakers in Ireland, Fox sent several certificates about the Dansons to New England, presumably reflecting inappropriate conduct on their part. Elizabeth's agent, Katherine Vine, arranged to have those papers "Laid by" if the Dansons promised to cease their accusations; the national meeting appointed Sharp and Roger Roberts to review the correspondence Vine proposed to send to Rhode Island. However, the Dansons continued their "railing accusations," prompting the half-yearly meeting to retort in November 1679: "Be quiet & cease from thy evil doings and from thy railings and false accusations."[4]

Words, then, were important, and because the Friends attached so much significance to the necessity of speaking truthfully, they insisted that others accept their "yay" and "nay" without requiring oaths.

Sharp's position on oaths concurred with that espoused by Irish Friends, as summarized, for example, by the six-months meeting in May 1677: "To preserve the testimony of truth against swearing, it is the mind of the half years meeting that every friend have a care not to take an Oath nor seem to take an Oath, that the truth may not be dishonoured." In the same month Sharp and Burnyeat reproached John Gay on behalf of the Dublin men's meeting for having taken an oath in a legal context. They pointed out to him that he had long been "under a Convincement of Truth and that he had heavenly opportunitys to have his understanding fully opened and to be made Sencible of the Lords power, So that if he were not convinced of the evill of Taking an oath, it must needs be by reason of his unfaithfullness unto what was made manifest unto him." In other words, Sharp expected every mature Quaker to know that all oaths, including those administered in courts, were wrong, and he believed that this position had been reiterated often enough in Quaker meetings to leave no excuse for pretended ignorance.[5]

Sharp participated in one of the longest cases involving oaths by a Friend in this period. It originated when William Stanley of Galway took an oath in circumstances that are no longer known. The Leinster provincial meeting dealt with the case for the second time in April 1677, but when Stanley remained obdurate in November, the half-yearly meeting charged Sharp and Turner to admonish him in writing to clear the truth. Stanley later accepted an invitation to attend the Leinster meeting in February at Lehinch, where he denied having sworn vocally but admitted answering a question with his hand on the Bible. After the delegates rejected Stanley's argument that his action had not constituted an oath, Sharp and Turner drafted a statement denouncing all forms of swearing, including the ceremonial laying of a hand on a Bible or another book. In March 1678 the provincial meeting directed Sharp and Turner to ask Stanley to submit a statement disowning his action, but this he failed to do, and in June the meeting ordered Sharp, Abraham Fuller, and Francis Randall to prepare a testimony against swearing and send it to Stanley to see if he would condemn himself. The dispute dragged on, as Stanley refused any public denouncement of his deed, while the Friends procrastinated in the hope that he would renege. Had he done so, Sharp, Fuller, and Randall would have been among those assigned to review his testimony, but this Stanley refused to tender until November 1678. In his statement he admitted "takeing Councell of the Enemy in my owne heart, and consenting with my owne Carnall Reason for some time past" by taking an oath sundry times. Either this confession was deemed inadequate or he continued to take oaths, for in the spring of 1679 the Friends denounced his "disorderly walking."[6]

If a symbolic act in lieu of an oath was unacceptable, so, for most Irish Friends, was the use of a surrogate to take an oath. This practice originated by the early eighteenth century in connection with the probate of wills. In May 1705 the Leinster meeting commissioned William Edmundson and others to write an epistle to the six-months meeting expressing the discomfiture of some Friends at this practice. Although Sharp was not one of the five coauthors, the strictness of his views on other matters makes it likely that he was among those unhappy with the use of surrogates.[7] Indeed, he, Francis Randall, Trafford, and Starkey had written to William and Mary's government in 1691 seeking relief from provisions mandating oaths.[8]

Refusal to swear an oath made it difficult for Friends to engage in law suits. Quakers were not supposed to sue or have other Friends arrested, but some of them did so anyway, notwithstanding periodic admonitions from the national meeting. Moreover, the same body urged Quakers to avoid lawsuits against non-Friends, but those who believed they had been grievously wronged and therefore found "freedom to try the Justice of the Law against their adversarys" were first urged to seek the advice of their men's meeting or its elders.[9] In 1687 Sharp himself sued on behalf of the Leinster provincial meeting to prevent the double payment of ground rent. Sharp apparently had minimal involvement in legal disputes between Quakers, though the Dublin men's meeting deputed him and Abel Strettell to seek the help of the Devonshire monthly meeting in London to resolve a quarrel over an estate.[10]

Tithes posed a different type of legal issue for Friends. Opposed in principle to remit tithes to an established church whose spiritual legitimacy they challenged, the Quakers habitually found themselves in trouble for their refusal to render payment. The (incomplete) figures of Thomas Holme and Abraham Fuller for the period 1660–70 record sixty-six tithing cases in Ireland involving Quakers, with losses valued at £190 6s. 10d., or nearly £3 each.[11] Some Friends were inevitably tempted to remit their tithes or have someone pay on their behalf, thereby averting greater penalties in distrained goods or even incarceration. In an attempt to prevent this, the Leinster meeting in July 1680 resolved that each of its men's meetings would require those who had directly or indirectly paid tithes since their convincement to submit testimonies condemning their actions, and that everyone else should present written statements opposing the payment of tithes, "that it may stand upon Record for future generations." An account was also to be compiled recording the fate of all backsliders. Sharp had submitted his testimony by the time the Dublin men's meeting convened on 28 September, as had other prominent Dublin Quakers, including Turner, Clarridge, Ashton, Joseph Sleigh, and Roger Roberts. The testimonies eventually made their way to the half-yearly meeting in May 1681, when Sharp, Turner, Wight, Gregson, and three others accepted a commission to edit them.[12]

In his unusually full testimony Sharp made his case against tithes on the grounds that Christ had terminated both the old priesthood and the tithes that maintained it. In contrast, gospel ministers freely received their gifts and were exhorted by Christ to use them without charge. The apostles, moreover, frequently warned against the dangers of seeking material wealth. Sharp further averred that the Mosaic law neither directed Gentiles to pay tithes nor instructed Levites to receive them from such people. Finally, he rejected claims for mandatory tithing based on the nation's statutes, which were supposedly grounded on reason, the law of God, and custom. His refusal to pay tithes, he insisted, did not stem from contempt for the laws of his prince and nation but from his conscientious obedience to the command of Jesus and his church's precepts.[13]

Unlike some other couples, such as Robert and Martha Turner, Roger and Mary Roberts, Thomas and Eleanor Atherton, and Thomas and Esther Thackery, Sharp and his wife did not submit a joint testimony. In contrast to Sharp's, most testimonies are brief. That of the Turners is typical: "We doe hereby testify and declare thatt we never paid tithes or parish preists wages directly or indirectly, itt being Contrary to the Gospell day and Manyfestation of god in our Consciences & are perswaded we shall always deny to pay the Same. Soe in unyty we Subscribe." Amos Strettell's was to the point and terse: "I never payd any tithes or preists wages directly or indirectly but have a testymony in my heart against both paying tithes and receiveing of them." The theological depth of Sharp's statement is in marked contrast. The testimony of Samuel Clarridge and his wife Anna is different in its candid admission that they paid tithes when they were married by a priest, but not at other times.[14]

Although Sharp never went to prison for his opposition to tithes, ecclesiastical officials distrained his goods numerous times. The first recorded occasion was in February 1671, when the churchwarden of St. Catherine's confiscated two large pewter dishes valued at 20s. because

of Sharp's refusal to pay church rates of 12s., though one of these dishes
was subsequently returned. Three months later, while Anthony and Esther were in England, the churchwarden seized two large pewter dishes
worth more than a pound because the Sharps had not paid tithes of
12s.[15] According to the Dublin meeting's record of sufferings, between
February 1671 and June 1687 Sharp had £13 17s. 6d. worth of goods
distrained for refusing to pay £12 3s. 8d. in tithes and church rates, including a charge of 21s. 6d. for the bells of St. Catherine's. The confiscated goods were pewter ware and cloth, including serge and fustian.
Once, in May 1681, the minister of St. Catherine's purchased cloth
worth 25s. from Ann Sharp, but paid only 3s., claiming the rest was due
to him for his maintenance. Refusing the 3s., Ann demanded the full
price or the return of the cloth, but the cleric refused.[16] By way of comparison, Clarridge suffered distraints totaling £13 5s. 8d. between 1670
and 1688. Robert Turner's losses between 1673 and 1682 appear to
have been much smaller—only a total of 24s. is recorded—but on three
occasions the amount was not cited, possibly because, as in 1682,
Turner did not know how much money had been confiscated. Amos
Strettell suffered distraints of £2 13s. between 1683 and 1688, but twice
the figures connoted joint losses with Robert Smallman, whose average
forfeiture in the period was probably 6s. 7d. *per annum*.[17] This com-
pares with average distraints of approximately 16s. 4d. *per annum* for
Sharp (1671–1687) and 14s. for Clarridge (1670–1688). The reliability
of these figures depends, of course, on whether the record of sufferings
is complete.

During the period 1693 through 1706, officials expropriated items
worth £32 10s. 2d. from Sharp when he refused to remit tithes and
church rates worth more than £28. Cash and pewter were seized, but
church officials mostly took a variety of cloth, ranging from linen and
broadcloth to ratteen, serge, and worsted. On one occasion, in 1699,
Sharp gave the churchwarden 12s. when the latter falsely represented
that the money was for the poor when in fact it was for church repairs.[18]
During these years Sharp suffered considerably more than other prominent Quaker merchants, undoubtedly because of his greater wealth.
Whereas his average annual distraint during the period 1693 to 1706
was £2 6s. 5d., comparable figures for Amos Strettell were 19s. (£14 6s.
between 1692 and 1706); for Clarridge, 16s. 9d. (£8 7s. 7½d., 1691–
1700); and for Smallman, 14s. 7d. (£5 16s. 10d., 1693–1700).[19] The significantly larger distraints experienced by the Sharps reflect, of course,
their substantial personal wealth.

In addition to the losses he sustained, Sharp performed important services to uphold the Friends' testimony against tithing. They included conferences with those who had paid tithes, among them Thomas Goldby, who insisted he was incapable of walking "according to truth." Sharp and Burnyeat warned him of "the danger of giving such way to the Enimie of his Soul." They had a better response from John Baddely, who confessed that his conscience was troubled because he had paid tithes and had also asked his brother-in-law to remit them for him.[20] Sharp helped as well by assisting Friends who were in legal trouble for their refusal to tithe. This included intervention with those who had initiated prosecution as well as the ecclesiastical tribunals. When, for example, the Anglican minister at Blessington prosecuted William Lappam of Baltyboys, county Wicklow, in 1702, Friends persuaded the cleric to halt the proceedings if the officials in the bishop's court would waive their charges. Twice the Dublin men's meeting dispatched Sharp to seek their acquiescence, warning them that the Friends would not pay Lappam's prison fees if he were jailed, for that too was "A scruple of conscience to us."[21] During the time of troubles, Sharp and Trafford explained the Quakers' hostility to tithes to Tyrconnel himself.[22]

A small number of Irish Quakers ignored the peace principle and forcibly resisted tithes-collectors and magistrates seeking to distrain their goods, bringing condemnation from the half-yearly meeting in 1687. Violence occasionally transpired on other occasions, as in the revolutionary war when a Quaker and his wife took up arms at Bandon Bridge, contrary to "the peaceable principles wee profess." The national meeting ordered local Friends to investigate and report to Sharp. Quakers must have been tempted to defend themselves and their property when unruly mobs stoned them during the Christmas holidays, but the Dublin men's meeting condemned Quaker young men who did so in 1694–95.[23]

Occasionally various Friends lost their tempers and yielded to violent impulses. In 1682 the Dublin meeting sent Sharp and two others to read a paper of condemnation to Thomas Wilkinson, a servant prone to drunkenness and brawling, urging him to submit; if not, they threatened to read the testimony at the next public meeting. Five years later, Sharp and Roger Roberts achieved a reconciliation between two brothers, Ezra and Daniel Thackery, whose dispute had become violent, persuading them to condemn their actions publicly.[24] Sharp would have known about other cases of violent Quaker behavior and undoubtedly discussed them in the Dublin men's meeting. When Abraham Fuller the younger's apprentice seriously injured another man by throwing him on a counter, the meeting required the apprentice to reimburse the victim for his medical expenses. It also took firm action when one of its members fought in New Row on a market day, insisting that he denounce his actions in the same place they had occurred, explicitly confessing he had violated the Friends' "peaceable principle." He also had to provide the meeting with a copy of what he told the onlookers. In another case, when two Quakers argued in 1694, one struck the other, but the meeting deemed both of them guilty. Details are unfortunately lacking for one of the most intriguing cases, which occurred when Samuel Braithwaite hit a boy in 1699; the lad subsequently died, but Braithwaite claimed his blow was not the cause of death.[25] What, one wonders, did Sharp think of this tragedy?

Far more common among Friends was the curse of indebtedness. Neither borrowing nor lending was prohibited, though the ideal was "that friends be very carefull of going into debt or Run in Arreare of Rent, and that dealers be Cautious of trusting out their own Substance to prevent difference or trouble to the Church or their Executors and overseers after their death." Indebtedness was also dangerous because the borrower ran the risk of not being able to repay the loan and thus of breaking her or his word as well as harming the lender.[26] Yet the Dublin meeting lent money to its members, particularly if the funds were essential for the borrowers' subsistence. It advanced money to Patrick Naylan (or Nailen) in 1695 when a creditor threatened to take him to court, creating a spectacle that would have embarrassed the Friends. Three years later Naylan was again threatened, this time by creditors who wanted to imprison him for an unpaid debt of £10; the meeting lent him half that amount.[27] The meeting expected such loans to be repaid, though it sometimes had difficulty collecting the money.[28] The problem was more serious when money owed to non-Friends was not repaid, for this brought disrepute on the movement. When this happened, Quakers were admonished to settle their obligations, and in severe cases the meetings drew up papers of condemnation "to clear truth." In August 1690 the weaver John Peck testified against himself for having fled to England to escape his creditors, but he subsequently experienced remorse and returned to Dublin.[29] In fact, a number of cases involved Friends who had moved without settling their debts, thereby rendering intervention by the respective meetings essential.[30] By February 1696 the extent of Quaker indebtedness was rumored to be at least £2,000, but an investigation by the Dublin men's meeting fixed the total at less than a third of this amount.[31]

As an astute businessman, Sharp was regularly called on by the Dublin and Leinster meetings to resolve cases involving indebtedness. He reproved offenders, such as Edward Bonus, who left his wife and unpaid debts in England, attempting to defraud his creditors. Sharp inquired about excessive debts, arranged appropriate payments, attempted to track down debtors who had fled, and resolved disputes among creditors who sought their due from a deceased debtor's estate. When David Jones prepared to move to Barbados without paying his arrears, Sharp and Amos Strettell warned Quakers about him.[32] As an agent of the Dublin meeting Sharp loaned money to those in need, as in 1695 when John Plant received an interest-free loan of £6 to remit arrears to his landlord. When John Goodbody went into debt in the late 1670s as a prisoner for conscience, notwithstanding what he earned by weaving in jail, the Leinster meeting asked Sharp to monitor his affairs. Sharp was also involved in the case of John Redman, who had come to Dublin from Cork in 1688 without settling his debts. Despite his upright conduct in Dublin, its meeting refused to accept him until he produced a certificate from the Cork meeting. Sharp, Burnyeat, Clarridge, Ashton, and Thomas Bell consulted with Cork Quakers to arrange his return, which they expedited with a donation of £2 7s. Clearly, then, Sharp and his compeers were discriminating in their dealings with the poor, tempering fiscal responsibility with mercy.[33]

One of the more enigmatic cases involved a widow who owed an amount she reckoned at £105 to Amanah Orwett, though he claimed the debt was larger. Sharp believed the debt was recoverable because Orwett had a written record, but the widow wanted to settle for approximately 2s. in the pound. Orwett sought Sharp's further assistance while threatening to have the woman arrested if she did not pay.[34] Apparently no evidence of the case's resolution has survived.

Sharp played a role in the most spectacular case of Quaker indebtedness, which involved the linen draper James Fade. By January 1701 Fade owed his creditors £1,652; some of them were fellow Friends, among them Abel Strettell, Abraham Fuller, and Joshua Wilcocks. He was also in debt to Alderman John Page, a prominent municipal figure who would become lord mayor in 1703. To settle his financial obligations Fade had to sign over virtually all his possessions to six trustees, namely, Sharp, Page, Clarridge, Ashton, Abraham Fuller, and the merchant James Mitchell, who was also a creditor. In return for a pledge of reasonable subsistence, Fade assigned his extensive properties to the trustees in return for 5s. *per annum.* They included the ownership, in whole or in part, of some forty or more houses in Dublin, mostly in Bride's Alley, Great Butter Lane, and Patrick Street; Lord O'Bryan's Arms in Patrick Street and a share of The Pelican in Winetavern Street; and mills, malthouses, and stables in the city. The properties also encompassed a house and lot in St. Stephen's Green; Cullenswood Farm, south of Dublin, which the earl of Meath had leased; and various homes and malthouses in the suburbs, mostly near Young's Castle. Fade additionally had to surrender his gold, plate, silks, bonds, merchandise, and even bedding and linen; only his clothing was exempt. With the income from the properties and any debts owed to Fade (for which the trustees were empowered to sue), the trustees agreed to settle Fade's obligations. Once the debts were paid, Fade would have the use of his property and the right to dispose of his chattels. Sharp and his fellow trustees also assumed the obligation to pay £400 to Wilcocks as the portion of his wife, Elizabeth (neé Fade, James' daughter), and £50 to his son Issacher upon the latter's twenty-first birthday. Fade's children received smaller sums.[35] The extent of Fade's one-time wealth is no less impressive than the scale of his debt. His business relations with wealthy landowners such as Meath and Bernard Brown (with both of whom Sharp also dealt) and with a prominent municipal leader such as Page point to both an intricate commercial network in Dublin in which the richer Quakers were closely entwined and the increasing respect they enjoyed.

The standards of responsibility and honesty that underlay the Quaker position on the repayment of debt were fundamental to the Friends' understanding of how they were to conduct business, a subject that must have been of considerable interest to Sharp, the Irish movement's most prominent man of commerce. Friends exhorted each other not to engage in commercial dealings that exceeded their ability or financial capacity. Early in the eighteenth century the shopkeepers and traders who belonged to the Dublin meeting began to hold special sessions to encourage each other to be loyal to Quaker principles in their business dealings. The linen drapers, the clothiers, and the woolen traders and their spouses all followed with separate gatherings of their own.[36]

Some Dublin Quakers were less than forthright in their dealings. Among them was the miller Joseph Thomas, whom the men's meeting had to admonish to use scales and weights to measure corn when it came into and left his mill. Thomas was also the target of a complaint for allegedly harming a woman while she ground wheat at his establishment. In his testimony against himself Thomas referred as well to complaints that he had wasted corn (wheat) and malt, and allowed swine and horses to eat out of the hopper and sacks of grain. Other Quakers stood accused of embezzlement, overcharging for the grinding of wheat, and forestalling (withholding grain from the market to drive up prices). In 1702 the Leinster meeting, reflecting on "the generality of Goods of all sorts being made Sleightly, if not deceitfully," urged Friends throughout Ireland "to make good serviceable Goods Such as may Answer the Expectation of the Buyer, and wearer," and it exhorted Quakers to eschew "Oppression in Buying and Selling."[37] Leinster's action seems to have influenced the half-yearly meeting, for in May 1703 it directed all Friends "who Buy and sell upon Trust" to be mindful of "the End and Issue thereof," avoiding all covetousness and oppressive dealings. The Leinster meeting reiterated this theme in June 1704, admonishing dealers not to use the goods or money of others to purchase and sell on trust, for many had sustained considerable losses because of such practices, bringing reproach on Quakers. The following January the men's meeting condemned the linen draper Samuel Taylor for "wasting his own Substance, & Contracting a great deal of debts" as well as failing to keep his word and "using unfair Methods to get other peoples money and Goods." To "clear truth" he and his profligate wife had to acknowledge they were unfit to be accounted Quakers.[38]

The Friends' keen sensitivity to equitable business dealings was evident as well in May 1700 when the six-months meeting belatedly addressed the enigmatic issue of Quakers who had purchased cattle, horses, sheep, hides, and tallow in large quantities during the time of troubles to make substantial profits. Such practices, the meeting decided, had been unjust. On behalf of the Leinster provincial meeting, Sharp, Rooke, John Watson, and two others subsequently looked into the purchase of plundered goods and denounced those who were responsible. The Dublin meeting also launched an investigation to ascertain whether Quakers had purchased stolen cattle or goods during the upheavals, but of this it found no evidence. On the contrary, it noted that some Friends had refused goods in payment of debts if they suspected such items had not been honestly obtained.[39]

Sharp and his colleagues also had high expectations of Quaker landlords, whose rents for houses or lands were not to be excessive. In 1696, for instance, the Leinster provincial meeting exhorted all landlords "to be tender of the honour of Truth, and Ease of their Tennants and not to lett their Lands at too high Rates nor Impose Additionall Customes upon them." The Dublin meeting had problems with the earl of Meath, whose Quaker tenants in Meath Street suffered distraints in 1693 for allegedly not paying their rent. In fact, they had paid the countess dowager; hence the meeting dispatched Sharp, Deane, and Stevens to confer with the earl. His seneschal informed the delegation that if the tenants could prove their goods had been seized, they would receive credit toward their rent.[40] The unpleasant episode must have heightened Sharp's belief in the importance of just dealings by landlords.

Sharp contributed to the articulation and enforcement of behavioral standards, including familial and personal relations. Judging from Quaker castigation of indulgent parents, he would have been a strict father. In 1687 the Leinster meeting took up the case of John Edmundson, who wanted to assume care of his wife's granddaughter by a previous marriage, but it resolved to send the case to the six-months meeting rather than undermine the Friends' testimony "against parents indulging such Rebellious Children as the Childs mother is."[41] This case underscored the Friends' conviction that parental responsibility extends beyond the time when the child becomes independent. This principle was evident as well in the troubled history of Elizabeth Worrell, who came to Dublin from England and opened a shop, apparently without her father's approval. When she became enmeshed in debt, the Dublin men's meeting sent Sharp and Roger Roberts with a recommendation that she return to her father, failing which the meeting would ask her father to send for her. Perhaps owing to illness Sharp did not fulfil this responsibility, but Worrell told Roberts she would not relinquish her shop because it had been leased for a year. Within three months, however, she had closed it, leaving unpaid debts and "an evill savour," which the meeting duly disclosed to her father. After five months of searching, the meeting finally located her and proffered advice about the repayment of her financial obligations. Although Worrell refused to heed the counsel, the meeting waited almost sixteen more months, hoping for repentance, before publicly condemning her.[42]

Because of an irresponsible parent, tragedy struck the Dublin meeting in 1703. John Hind, who had moved to Dublin from England and "appeared like a friend" though of dubious conversation, carried a pistol on a journey into the countryside, ostensibly for protection against dogs, but when he returned he failed to secure the weapon. After his child found it and accidentally killed himself, the Dublin meeting admonished Hind but acquiesced to his request to inter the child in the Quakers' burial yard if Hind condemned himself in writing.[43] In this case, Sharp and his colleagues tempered their strictness with compassion.

Beginning in the late 1690s Quaker children who disturbed the meetings increasingly troubled Sharp and his confreres. Some were only playing outdoors during the meetings, but others were throwing rocks, breaking the neighbors' windows; the Dublin meeting appointed two men to prevent such behavior. In 1705 the same body assigned seven men to sit in the meetinghouse gallery to "Inspect the behavior of the boyes & young men, & if they doe see any who misbehaves themselves that they doe not faile to acquaint their Masters or Parents thereof." At the provincial meeting the following year, some complained of young people in attendance whose behavior was "lite," causing consternation to many. The provincial problem seems to have involved young women who were more interested in socializing than the work of the meeting, but all parties were reminded to behave appropriately.[44]

The proper conduct of young people extended as well to sexual matters. In 1703 the Leinster meeting found it necessary to caution its youth and others who had taken "a liberty of kissing each other" and keeping unsuitable company at times and places "more then what is holy." Even the appearance of evil had to be eschewed. After Sarah Carr and Elizabeth Sanders behaved scandalously in 1705 with two Trinity College students in Dublin alehouses, Sharp was among the eight Friends who signed a statement disowning them. Quakers expected parents to deal strictly with their children in sexual matters as in all else. Thus the Dublin men's meeting found it necessary to summon Richard Ballord in 1702 to answer accusations that his son, who still lived at home, had been guilty of sexual misconduct with several women. Confessing as much, Ballord acquiesced to the meeting's recommendation that he expel his son from home before the latter corrupted his siblings and dishonored the Quakers. Two years later Sharp and Ashton were asked to write a paper condemning Joshua Saunders of Kilteel, county Kildare, for having had sexual intercourse with his father's servant. Although Saunders confessed, he seemed "hard & unsenceable," whereas his father, Thomas, sided firmly with other Friends in censuring such conduct.[45]

Other Quakers known to Sharp succumbed to the temptation to copulate with their servants. The most notorious of these, as we have seen, was Clarridge, who impregnated Margaret Fawset and then sent her to England under an alias to have the baby. Sharp and seventeen others signed the statement denouncing his actions in April 1677, as others subsequently did, including Ann Sharp. The statement did not mince words: Those led by the Spirit, it averred, "cannot but beare testimony in plaineness against wickedness & ungodlyness in all, yea if committed within the threshold of our door, because all wickedness & ungodlyness is contrary to the nature of that heavenly Principle of Light and truth, which we profess." Although the half-yearly meeting investigated and even sent an agent to Broughton, Cheshire, to interview Fawset, who admitted Clarridge's paternity, he responded defiantly; however, he carefully avoided denying the accusations. Less than six weeks later, he reconsidered in a written statement to the national meeting. "My Spirit," he confessed, "hath & doth judge that Spirit that led me from the grace of God into wantonness, & it is in me Condemned, for it is for everlasting judgment & the Lake."[46]

The magnitude of the Clarridge case was such that the half-yearly meeting in November 1677 sent copies of a paper concerning it to London and Cheshire, where Friends read it to Fawset to see if she would provide additional information, including the identity of anyone else who might have been involved in this "uncleanness," presumably by attempting to help her and Clarridge keep his paternity secret. After Clarridge acknowledged the error of his ways, the Dublin men's meeting appointed Sharp and Roger Roberts to read his statement to the women's meeting in May 1678. Others related it to the national assembly. Clarridge's confession did not satisfy some, including Turner, Sleigh, and Thomas Thackery, who objected to his participation in the Dublin men's meeting that fall and threatened not to attend if he were present. Indeed, as late as January 1683 some Friends were still sufficiently troubled by Clarridge's "highness" that they expressed a desire to the national meeting "to see him more low, broken & humbled because his offences were great," though others thought he had adequately abased himself. Clarridge agreed to submit to the judgment of Edmundson, who ruled that he be permitted to attend Quaker business meetings as long as he lived as a Friend should, but he was not "to Judge, advise or Mannage things of truths affaires" without the members' acquiescence. The only exception was that he be allowed to speak "if something of necessity be upon his mind to deliver to the mens meeting which sound friends may Judge of for true."[47] This must have been a humbling experience for Clarridge, who, like Sharp, was one of the wealthiest and most prominent Friends in Ireland. But unlike Sharp, Clarridge found it difficult to accept the supremacy of the meeting over the individual.

Disputed allegations figured in other cases handled by the Dublin men's meeting, including one involving Robert Davis in 1706. Sharp and William Allen were supposed to investigate the charges of a woman who "threatned to lay a child" on Davis, but for unexplained reasons— possibly failing health—Sharp did not fulfil his responsibility. Allen and two others subsequently discussed the accusations with Davis and Alderman John Page, and although Davis denied paternity, the Friends did not believe him because he had given money to the woman. Moreover, Davis was a man of questionable conversation who spent time with women of ill repute and was accused of "fondling & toying with young women who come to his shop soe that the neighborhood make a discourse thereof." The Dublin meeting ordered him to repent and alter his behavior or be disowned. The same year the Dublin meeting believed allegations of paternity against James Hull because he too had given the mother money "to shut it [the scandal] up, and was also suspected of visiting bad houses," notwithstanding his attendance at Quaker meetings.[48]

The Dublin meeting had to deal with a variety of sexual offenses, virtually all of which Sharp would have heard about, and in a number of cases he had to treat with the alleged offenders. With four others he questioned the Dublin scrivener John Howard in March 1671 about his lusting after a young maiden; though Howard insisted he had not engaged in sexual intercourse with her, he confessed he had been "drawne to Embrace in my mind the Accursed Principles of Rantisme." In 1692 Sharp, Stevens, Thomas, Winslow, and three others investigated the scandalous conduct of Grace Newby and Joshua Bows and then drafted a statement of public condemnation. When Edward Swan behaved inappropriately with a woman on a voyage from England to Ireland in 1704, Sharp and Roger Roberts reproved him, but they found Swan "very dark" and possessing "little sence of his condition." Through further investigation the Friends learned he had married this woman in England by an Anglican minister, and Swan was consequently forced to denounce his actions.[49] In an earlier case, Sharp wrote to Bristol concerning Thomas (or John) Player, who had been wed by a conformist cleric, after which he left his wife in poverty in Ireland and moved to Bristol, where he committed bigamy by remarrying.[50] Sharp communicated with Galway Friends concerning the currier Samuel Neale, whose wife insisted on remaining in the west; although Neale provided her with ample financial support, he lived in Dublin with another woman. Sharp's efforts seem to have been unsuccessful in persuading her to join her husband.[51] Sexual scandal never tainted Sharp, though the Dublin

meeting had to cope with its share of sexual offenses. In matters involving sex, the Friends' standards were essentially the same as those
espoused by other Christian groups, but the Quakers seem to have been
more vigorous in enforcing them than was the Church of Ireland.

This was also the case with inebriety, one of the most common temptations to which some Friends succumbed. Among them was James
Fade. The most notorious case involved William Barnard, who went on
a ten-hour binge in the summer of 1683, drinking approximately thirty
flasks of wine, threatening to break one over a parson's head if he
hummed a tune, and attempting to kiss a maiden in a tavern. Not surprisingly, drunkenness was often accompanied by other unacceptable
behavior, such as offensive language, lascivious conduct, and unseemly
company. One such offender was the tanner Peter Robinson, the subject
of a condemnatory statement signed by Sharp and eight others in July
1704 for excessive drinking, spending time with a woman of ill repute,
playing bowls and cards, and staying out to unreasonable hours. The
heavy imbibing of another transgressor, William Keckwick, probably
contributed to his acknowledged abuse of his wife in his "hasty pas-
sion" as well as his "Lewd Carriages."[52] The Dublin meeting deputed
Sharp to treat with several offenders, including two Quakers who got so
drunk after a meeting that they could not ride their horses and thus remained on the road all night.[53]

Several cases involving Friends who operated unsavory alehouses
demanded the attention of Sharp and his associates. In 1681 he and
Atherton received a commission from the Dublin meeting to determine
whether Quakers who ran tippling houses or sold strong beer in their
homes also provided lodging for travelers and stabled their horses; if
not, the meeting frowned on their activities. Sharp and Atherton invited
two offending alehouse keepers to attend the business meeting, which
warned them of their dangerous ways. Eighteen years later the Dublin
meeting formally condemned Thomas Wilson and his wife for running a
disorderly alehouse where people drank excessively and disturbed the
neighbors.[54]

Just as the Friends deplored inebriety but not moderate alcoholic
consumption, so they accepted the modest use of tobacco. Indeed,
Quaker merchants in Pennsylvania were exporting it to the British Isles,
and in Ireland the merchants Joseph Pike and Samuel Randall decided
not to import it only because they were already wealthy and were chary
of appearing avaricious. Consumption was rapidly increasing in Ireland
in the late seventeenth century, with imports nearly doubling in two

decades, from 1.8 million pounds in 1665 to 3.3 million in 1686, excluding smuggled tobacco. Until the 1710s, tobacco was Ireland's leading import. The half-yearly meeting in 1695 advised Quaker artisans and tradesmen not to smoke tobacco in alehouses and taverns, and in 1699 William Edmundson urged Quakers to shun "Excessive Customary, uncomely smoaking of Tobacco." Two years later the Leinster meeting echoed this counsel with an admonition that "Truths limitts and bounds be observed in the use of this herb, both as to manner, quantity and season, that the service of it may not be abused." Rumors soon circulated that Friends opposed all use of tobacco, prompting the same assembly to deny this in January 1702 and call for each local meeting to launch an investigation into the perpetrators of this falsehood.[55] Judging from the extant documents, Sharp seems to have had nothing to say about tobacco, nor is there evidence to indicate whether he smoked it.

There is also a dearth of information about Sharp's attitude to assorted amusements, though as a leading member of the Dublin and Leinster meetings he undoubtedly shared their views on pastimes. The Quakers eschewed bowling and bull-baiting, and those who participated in such activities were expected to submit papers condemning their actions. In 1696 the Dublin meeting ordered Quaker children to cease taking cocks to school and throwing stones at them to make them fight, and the previous year it condemned the use of crossbows and guns by young people as inappropriate and dangerous; indeed, it urged a ban on crossbows and admonished Quakers to keep their children from access to guns and fowling pieces. Following an inquiry by the Leinster meeting into the use of greyhounds and other hunting dogs and hunting guns, the half-yearly meeting in 1704 concluded that young people who hunted with dogs or had greyhounds could be enticed "into hurtfull Company, and their minds into Vanity, and severall snares, whereby they are in danger to be drawn away from the Simplicity of the Truth." It therefore urged each meeting to prohibit such practices.[56]

Sharp undoubtedly concurred with pronouncements on other forms of amusement deemed inappropriate. They included some forms of music, such as "Reproachfull" ballads; indeed, in 1703 the merchant William Knox confessed he had been "hearing of Musick & said he was out of his place & Intended not to do the like againe."[57] Gambling and card playing were unacceptable, as was watching horse races, in part because the Friends adjudged such racing a form of vanity and oppression. Young people were admonished not to attend fairs "without real lawfull

business, nor to see vain shews, sports or pastimes nor to walk abroad
on first days because of the inconveniency and danger that may attend
it." Nor were Friends to ride "after an Airy flirting manner," ride
"abroad as if they want to see and to be seen," or participate in clubs.[58]
Although Robert Barclay endorsed gardening as one of the few "innocent divertisements" Quakers could pursue, Irish Friends imposed
limits, insisting that gardens be simple. "There is and may be great Superfluity and too great nicety in Gardens," the Leinster meeting cautioned in 1705; hence it urged its members to plant "in a lowly mind,"
keeping their gardens utilitarian and simple, "rather admireing the
wonderful hand of Providence in causeing such variety of necessary
things to grow for the use of men, then to please a curious mind."[59]

Sharp and his colleagues applied the ideal of simplicity to apparel
with increasing specificity in the decades following the time of troubles.
In an atmosphere of relative toleration, their intent was to preserve the
Quakers' sense of being a distinct people, not least because their garb
was their principal identifying mark in the minds of outsiders. Yet the
basic principle on which these increasingly detailed regulations rested
had long been espoused in Quaker circles, and Mabel Brailsford consequently erred in asserting that "the adoption of a distinctive costume
. . . assumed tremendous importance with the disappearance of larger
issues." On the contrary, the Quaker position on apparel was firmly
grounded in the movement's fundamental commitment to gospel simplicity, and the Friends worked out the details as part of their process of
defining and perpetuating their distinctive sense of identity. In May
1671 the national meeting approved a statement against "Needless
Fashions," and at the ensuing meeting in November the delegates listened to a paper in which George Fox exhorted Irish Friends to eschew
worldly fashions and "Keep to the Ancient Principles of Truth." The
message struck a responsive chord, for three days later Sharp, Turner,
Clarridge, Holme, and twenty-nine other men subscribed to a statement
by Gregson acknowledging that many Quakers had succumbed to the
"never settled fashions" of the world, which were vain and superfluous.
At the next half-yearly meeting, in May 1672, the delegates appointed
seven members to determine the local meetings' reactions to the recent
statements condemning worldly fashions.[60]

The Dublin meeting's earliest extant statement containing specific information about unacceptable apparel is found in a general epistle dated
17 March 1676. This document was among the manuscripts preserved
by Sharp, indicating the importance he attached to it. Indeed, he may

have been its principal author. In the context of a discussion of the applicability of "gospel order" to all the godly, the epistle exhorted Friends to treat everyone impartially, according no one favor because of "Gay gouldring [gold thread] or gay apparel." It cited Ezekiel 13:18, which condemned the sowing of pillows under armholes, a prophetic denunciation of vanity, deceit, and false prophesy, akin to builders who used untempered mortar or people who disguised the truth with flattery. Fancy clothing was objectionable because it detracted from the gospel's simple truth, enervated the Quaker testimony, and cloaked an individual in a manner that masked her or his true self. Sharp was one of the twenty-nine signatories of this document, thirteen of whom were women.[61]

The Quakers' interest in appropriate raiment intensified in the ensuing years. In November 1677 the half-yearly meeting instructed emissaries for each province to inquire about Quakers who dressed in a manner that detracted from the gospel. Three years later the delegates listened anew to the May 1671 testimony against "Needless fashions," which they wanted read again at the meeting in May 1681. Meanwhile, local and provincial assemblies were to act on it. Sharp probably heard Turner read the statement to the Dublin men's meeting in January 1681. However, little formal action was taken against offenders, who were apparently subjected only to exhortations to reform. In October 1682 Joseph Arnold admitted having worshiped in the Church of Ireland and "Joyning with the world in their fashions." He thus provided a neat juxtaposition of worldly worship and worldly dress, both of which the Friends shunned, at least officially.[62]

Certain Friends, especially young people, continued to wear fashionable attire. Consequently, in May 1685 the six-months meeting decided that the November 1677 pronouncement on clothing should be read every quarter in each provincial assembly, and that the elders should see that its advice was heeded at the local level. A year later the national meeting sent an epistle to the local men's and women's groups expressing concern that many youthful members and others were dishonoring truth by their attire and conversation, and directing elders of the meetings to see that previous testimonies on these subjects were frequently read and implemented. Parents who indulged such behavior by their children faced admonition. This epistle is noteworthy because it castigated Quakers who cut their hair and donned "great Ruffling Perrywiggs" as well as balding Friends who wore wigs of superfluous length. In keeping with this directive, the Dublin men's meeting appointed

Sharp, Ashton, Roger Roberts, and John Tristram to discern whether its members were adhering to the testimonies on raiment, superfluity, and indebtedness.[63]

The investigation of Sharp and his three associates was probably a key factor in the half-yearly meeting's decision in May 1687 to ask Quaker tailors to resume their conferences in order to assess whether any of them were making clothing "according to the vaine & changeable fashions of the world." Fourteen Quaker tailors plied their trade in Dublin at this point. The problem also involved cloth manufacturers and merchants, some of whom were selling striped cloth which various Friends found objectionable. Because of his own business this would have directly interested Sharp, who was a representative to the national meeting in November 1687 when it asked all Quaker cloth manufacturers and merchants to convene at the next six-months meeting and annually thereafter "to consider what is not fit to be made or sold by friends, viz. flower'd silks, stript stuffe or any thing else that may dishonour truth" or justifiably offend anyone. Complaints about indecorous cloth or attire were to be directed to this group rather than the six-months meeting.[64]

When the committee convened in May 1688 it comprised thirty merchants, clothiers, and tailors. Although Sharp's name is not on the list of members, he was one of the twenty-nine men who signed the pronouncement drafted by the committee calling for all Quakers to wear plain attire, and to make and sell unadorned things. "It will be commendable that all friends have the Truth Chiefly in their eye in all the said Clothes & goods in their deallings, makeings and wearings." The statement hints at some disagreement among committee members, for it strongly discouraged but did not prohibit the manufacture or sale of "draught, figured or stript work," including clothing decorated with images or drawing. The report also recommended that Friends employ Quaker tailors, for their potential customers were severely limited if they made only plain, unfashionable raiment.[65]

In the same month that the committee drafted this document, the national women's meeting, which also congregated in Dublin, sent an epistle signed by Ann Sharp and ten others to local women's groups throughout Ireland. In it they complained that some Quaker women ignored earlier testimonies concerning clothing and "still too much conforme to the vaine fashions of the world in wearing of Gownes or Mants with long Peakes, Dressing of their heads very high to make their hair be seen and wearing hoods with long flaps." The national women's meeting asked local women's groups to inquire into such abuses.[66]

During the time of troubles the Friends were largely concerned with survival and the provision of relief to victims of the fighting, the sporadic lawlessness, and the depredations inflicted by troops. Concern over apparel presumably continued throughout this period, though it must have been a subordinate matter. It surfaced again in January 1692—quietly enough—when the Dublin men's meeting sent Sharp and the skinner Evan Bevan to speak with the merchant William Hill about his sale of lace and ribbons. In April the same body commissioned Sharp and his associates who had formerly monitored clothing to draft a new report. By this time, according to Joseph Pike, most Quaker women, especially in England, were wearing silk clothing, though plainly colored, and other expensive garb. Quaker women in Ireland, Pike observed, never went to such extremes, at least in part because of William Edmundson's influence.[67] He could justifiably have mentioned Sharp as well.

In the decade 1693–1703, Irish Friends issued increasingly detailed guidelines for attire. With Ann Sharp playing a prominent role, the national women's meeting took the lead in this endeavor, a fact that should make us chary of any attempt to deny the influence and decision-making of Quaker women in Ireland in the late seventeenth century.[68] After reviewing reports from provincial assemblies, the national women's group, citing the problem of vain fashions and carnal customs, called on Friends to take a stand against every appearance of evil. Demurely referring to themselves as "helpmeets in the work & Service of the Lord," they called for female overseers to repress all superfluities in dress and home furnishings. Then followed the most detailed catalogue of unacceptable raiment hitherto produced by Irish Quakers. Included were headdresses with lace lappets hanging down on the cheeks, black and white pleated and welted bands, satin girdles, quilted or white fustian petticoats, painted calico frocks and aprons, all figured and striped woolen cloth, and mants lined with black or any other "very different" color. They also objected to scarfs more than two yards in length, hoods with long flaps, muslin aprons, "fine stays" that were visible, mants with narrow tails, and cloth shoes. Nor could women wear their hair piled high and powdered, or have coiffures with double borders of muslin or other fabrics.[69]

In subsequent years Ann Sharp and the other representatives at the

national women's meeting continued their campaign to restrict what
Quakers could wear. Scarfs could not hang below the waist because this
was fashionable. In 1702 the women endorsed the prohibition of the
men's meeting against the wearing of silk and "all those glittering halfe
silks which make a great show, and all light Colours in Garments."
They went on to ask Quaker women not to don the latest fashion in
hoods or "fine broad Stomachers with the Bosome open to be seen,"
and to eschew costly array, whipped linen, large handkerchiefs, and
fancy headdresses.[70]

During the same decade the men continued their emphasis on the importance both of plain garments and of employing Quaker tailors, but
they also became more specific in stipulating appropriate garb. The half-
yearly meeting exhorted Quakers to "beware of Running upon high,
lofty Fabricks to gratify a high, proud and Curious mind." Friends who
wore wide-skirted coats or men's campaign-style military coats were
asked to cease.[71] The tailors continued to gather, twice a year at provincial assemblies and normally once a year at national meetings. In May
1703 they issued a detailed statement recommending that men's coats
avoid "too much Compasse in the Skirts," large buttons or buttonholes,
false buttonholes, buttonholes near the bottom of the garment, and excessively large sleeves and cuffs. Straight coats, they advised, should be
open at the sides only for pockets. Vests should have necks and collars,
and breeches should "not be made too Strait with Buttons very farr up,"
for such a style was not deemed serviceable. The tailors announced their
intention to cease making women's riding coats with large shoulder
plates, deeming them neither necessary nor decent, and they thought the
coats would be plainer if the pocket holes were cut lengthwise rather
than horizontally.[72]

Gathering in 1701, Quaker shoemakers heard some of their number
admit they had manufactured fashionable shoes. Complaints to this effect arose two years later, prompting the half-yearly meeting to direct
provincial and local groups to investigate. As we have seen, the national
women's meeting had decried cloth shoes a decade earlier, and in 1699
it also opposed white shoes with red heels. Plain white shoes and the use
of heel blocks to enhance height were subsequently denounced.[73]

Given Sharp's prominence among the Friends, his membership on the
committee that monitored Quaker apparel, his signature on the May
1688 report on attire, and his wife's involvement with the highly detailed statements on Quaker raiment issued by the national women's
meeting, he and Ann must have dressed very conservatively. They must

also have spent a fair amount of time observing other Friends' attire and discussing appropriate garb. Moreover, they likely played an important role in shaping the increasingly rigorous standards of dress that distinguished Irish Quakers even from their compeers in England and Pennsylvania. In contrast, Margaret Fox castigated those who opposed colorful attire and stylistic variety as proponents of "a silly poor Gospel."[74] The Sharps would not have concurred with her judgment.

The Friends' treatment of household furnishings and decoration paralleled their handling of raiment, with pronouncements becoming more detailed, particularly in the less repressive conditions that prevailed after the time of troubles. Gregson's paper, which Sharp and thirty-two other men signed at the national meeting in November 1671, denounced not only vain fashions in attire but also the superfluous decoration of houses, which feeds "the lust of the eye (and therefore Must needs Minister into vanity and soe nott like to adorne the Gospell of Christ Jesus)." The mission of the Quakers appointed for each province by the half-yearly meeting six years later included inquiries to determine which members possessed extraneous household goods.[75] When this document was read again at the Leinster meeting in November 1686, the delegates responded by ordering home visitations to ascertain whether any Friends had "great shows of Shelves of Pewter or Brasse, or Turkey work Chaires of flourishing Colours and Images of Things," even if they were utilitarian. Such chairs were to be disposed of or recovered so they would "not appear to the satisfying, gratifying or Encouraging of the makeing or setting of such things up."[76]

After the time of troubles, Irish Friends launched a major campaign to eliminate elaborate furnishings. Pike provides a graphic account of the results at Cork:

> Our fine veneered and garnished cases of drawers, tables, stands, cabinets, scrutoires, &c., we put away, or exchanged for decent plain ones of solid wood, without superfluous garnishing or ornamental work; our wainscots or wood-work we had painted of one plain colour, our large mouldings or finishings of pannelling, &c.; our swelling chimney-pieces, curiously twisted bannisters, we took down, and replaced with useful plain wood-work, &c.; our curtains, with valances, drapery, and fringes that we thought too fine, we put away or cut off; our large looking-glasses with decorated frames, we sold, or made them into smaller ones; and our closets that were laid out with many little curious or nice things were done away.

In Dublin, the national women's meeting, in which Ann Sharp remained active, took the lead in providing more specific guidelines for home decorations and furnishings, much as they did for clothing and hair-styles. Their declaration of May 1693 denounced long calico curtains, bedroom curtains with fringes or ribbons, and children's linen with welts and needlework. A year later they added wall paintings, prints for hanging, large mirrors, and polished tables, stands, chests of drawers, and dressing boxes. Rooms, partitions, and mantles should not be painted, but if painting was essential, only plain, "civel" colors could be used. If wall hangings were necessary, presumably for warmth, they too had to be unadorned and hung only after consultation with the local meeting's elders.[77] The national women's meeting subsequently opposed "the rubbing of Roomes for the Satisfieing a Nice-mind" and called for the removal or recovering in cloth or leather of "Turkey-work Chaires and Cushions" because they were too colorful. They also recommended that Friends avoid table linens and damask.[78]

The men too were caught up in the spirit of prescribing simple home furnishings. Delegates to the national meeting in May 1694 asked the joiners, ships' carpenters, and founders in their midst to determine what they could appropriately make. These artisans concluded that chests of drawers should be plain, of one color, and devoid of "swelling works" (decorative protuberances). Tables and chairs were to be simple, free of carving, utilitarian, and not conformable to the latest fashions. Elaborate molding was not to embellish clock cases and beds, and all furniture and wainscoting were to be unadorned and of a single color. Carpenters were not to decorate ships with carvings or figures, founders were asked not to make images or other superfluous items, and saddlers were urged to manufacture plain saddles. Five years later the half-yearly meeting criticized unnecessary pewter and brass in kitchens.[79]

Unlike some wealthy Quaker merchants in Philadelphia during the eighteenth century, the plain-dressing Anthony and Ann Sharp would have lived in a house mostly devoid of color, its walls, floors, and furniture unpolished, its windows covered with simple hangings, its walls barren of paintings and large mirrors, and neither the furniture nor the mantles decorated with carvings. Chairs too would have no carving, and their covering would have been leather or a solid-colored, rather drab cloth. The ceilings would not have been adorned with carved plaster, which the Friends deemed superfluous. Yet the house was not without some color, for Sharp's will refers to both blue and green bed coverings. Notwithstanding Quaker recommendations to the contrary, when the Sharps dined, their table probably was covered with a linen cloth, for the will mentions damask linen. The Sharps used the recommended pewter ware, but Anthony's will also refers to plate. Their food may not have been "Rich and delicious," although the six-months meeting found it necessary to condemn such fare in 1699.[80]

The Friends applied the same standard of simplicity to their marriage ceremonies, childbirth, and funerals. Marriages, of course, took place during meetings and were similar to traditional handfasting, but the subsequent celebrations could easily become too convivial to suit the more sober Quakers. Following complaints of excess at a marriage supper in 1678, the Dublin men's meeting exhorted members to avoid superfluity and disorder, remembering "that solid way that may honour truth." Quaker marriages could make an impression on the outside world, as Burnyeat noted when he remarked on a large wedding in Dublin, after which many people referred approvingly to its gravity and solemnity.[81]

Among the manuscripts Sharp preserved was an epistle to single Friends composed in October 1680 by Richard Robinson of Wensleydale, Yorkshire, who deplored "the vain and foolish, untruthlike hissings, scoffings and wild Behaviours" and "the light, vain, profane, unclean, obscene, unholy, and unbeseeming gestures" characteristic of traditional weddings.[82] Following a Quaker marriage in 1681 there had been such "Feasting" that some Friends were disturbed, prompting both the Leinster and the national meetings to warn against such excess. Six years later the men's and women's meetings in Dublin had to deal with a wedding supper at the Bull Inn, where Quaker women acted immodestly by engaging in "wanton laughter and folly," pretending to put the bride to bed, unlacing her dress, pulling off her garters, and throwing her stockings "according to a heathenish Custome." Concerned about the maintenance of suitable decorum at weddings, the Leinster meeting decided in 1693 that two Friends in each local meeting would act as supervisors. A year later the half-yearly meeting cautioned against marital feasts and "all Airy, unsavoury discourse or deportment" in Quaker homes after weddings. More than on other occasions, Friends were to shun "outward decking or dressing" at weddings.[83] Sharp was probably among those Friends who were offended in early 1706 when a Quaker couple arrived at the meetinghouse in a coach for their nuptials. Even the language employed by a bride and groom had to reflect Quaker simplicity; the Dublin men's meeting required Samuel Fuller to state his intentions clearly on his marriage certificate in 1705 after he had offended by using "scholastick" words, namely, pledging his "Mutuall Love & Conjugal Fidelity during term of Life" instead of simply promising to be a faithful husband.[84]

A lavish marriage supper, reflected the Leinster meeting in 1681, was "like the worlds manners," and the national meeting concurred, advising Friends to avoid excessive food at marriage dinners. To prevent abuses, Sharp and his colleagues in the Leinster meeting opted in 1693 to appoint two members in each local meeting to supervise weddings.[85] But simplicity in marriage celebrations flew in the face of the customary conviviality. Not all non-Quakers responded as positively to this scaled-down festivity as did those to whom Burnyeat referred, and in 1695 the national body found it necessary to ask two Friends in each local meeting who were responsible for the oversight of weddings to explain the Quakers' disapproval of superfluity to guests who expected a traditional feast. The delegates also wanted to ensure that Friends restrained the scale of hospitality for the right reasons; hence they proposed that Quakers should "avoid makeing provisions at such a time as the vaine custome of some is, and not out of niggardliness nor Covetousness nor yeat for want of Affectionatness & civill Respect to our friends or Acquaintance[s]." The Dublin men's meeting went as far as deciding in 1700 that it was inconvenient to serve hot food at wedding meals, and the previous year the national women's meeting halted the practice of giving gloves at marriages because this distracted from the spiritual focus. Generally, Irish Friends celebrated their marriages with less festivity than their counterparts in America.[86]

Childbirth was another occasion when Friends shunned traditional customs, or at least were exhorted to do so. During the early 1680s some Quaker midwives had accepted the customary gifts from sponsors (gossips) at baptisms and refused to return them without a clear ruling to that effect from Quaker midwives in London. In response the London quarterly meeting explained that its midwives abhorred this practice because it obliterated the distinction between them and worldly midwives. In the same letter the London Friends also noted their opposition to midwives who dressed infants for baptism because this implied approval of the rite.[87]

As an active member of the national women's meeting as well as a woman who underwent multiple pregnancies, Ann Sharp took an interest in the behavior of midwives. She was one of twenty-nine signatories of a statement in 1697 that called for Quaker midwives to bear testimony against the world's ways and fashions, rejecting the gossips' money and refusing to participate in baptismal services, including dressing an infant for this rite. She undoubtedly paid heed in 1700 when the Leinster provincial meeting recommended that each local women's group take precautions to prevent "Superfluityes in and about womens lying in Child bed." The same year she and eight other Quaker women sent an epistle to the local women's meetings throughout Ireland recounting Edmundson's admonition "to take a narrow and Close Inspection into things belonging to our sex." Ann and her coauthors noted that at the time of childbirth Friends should "be Bowed under a deep sence of the great mercy and delivering hand of the Lord, and carefull to avoid all superfluities both of words, and other Extreames," including unnecessary company, a surfeit of food and drink, traditional spicecakes, and excessive speech, "All which is Judged to Border so near the worldes way and practice that they are a griefe to the tender hearted, and a dishonour to Truth."[88]

Born and wed without adornment, Quakers went to their graves in simplicity. As in the case of childbirth and marriage celebrations, this ideal ran against tradition, and not surprisingly the Friends sometimes ignored it. Thus in June 1679 Sharp and fellow members of the Dublin men's meeting stipulated that henceforth Friends walk no more than three or four abreast in funeral processions, the men preceding the women, and all moving in silence. The meeting appointed Sharp and Matthias Foster to see that these regulations were followed. When the committee of joiners, ships' carpenters, and founders convened in 1694, it decided that coffins had to be plain, with neither cloth coverings nor unnecessary folds of cloth. The same year the half-yearly meeting observed that some Quakers had "run into Superfluous Excess" at funerals by partaking of brandy, "strong-waters" (alcohol), cakes, pipes, and tobacco, all of which it adjudged unbecoming. By this time Sharp had apparently ceased to supervise funerals, for the Dublin meeting assigned that responsibility to George Pope, who was to see that Friends now walked only two abreast in silence. The same body decided that even wine could not be drunk at funerals without the approval of the meeting's elders.[89]

Notwithstanding these provisions, Quaker funerals continued to be less orderly than some Friends desired. In an epistle to local women's groups in 1699, Ann Sharp and thirty-five other delegates at the national women's meeting called for an end to the giving of mourning scarves and gloves at funerals, "there being some Occasion given for this Caution." Presumably this dispensation of charity had become so extensive that it detracted from the quiet solemnity the Quakers deemed essential for the occasion, and there may also have been some discomfiture because only the well-to-do could afford to dispense such gifts. Indeed, in 1701 the six-months meeting noted that the customary distribution of money from the deceased's estate had become distracting, but it left the time of dispersal to the executors even while reminding everyone that burials should manifest "as much stillness as may bee." Two years earlier the Leinster meeting, complaining that excessive eating and the consumption of alcohol at funerals were disrupting order, had instructed local groups to take steps to ensure "Solemnity and Solidity." In the twilight of Sharp's life, behavior at funerals continued to be problematic in Dublin, where women were cited for not walking two or three abreast and maintaining silence.[90]

To uphold these behavioral standards, with their pronounced emphasis on plain speaking, unadorned attire and home furnishings, a sense of separation from worldly ways, the eschewing of violence and uncivil actions, and fidelity to the gospel ethic, Sharp and his colleagues relied on a multifaceted disciplinary program. In 1673 the tone was embodied in a statement from Friends in London, including Penn, Crisp, and George Whitehead, against "Unsubject members." Much of it contained warnings against those who fomented division within the movement, but it also called for the severe reproof of "all Looseness and Disorderly walking and scandalous conversations and pratlers." Such admonitions were only to be as public as the offenses had been, for the intent was to reform the transgressors, not to harden them and provide an occasion for the Quakers' adversaries "to throw Dirt" on them.[91] The Friends, then, believed they had an obligation to counsel suspected offenders with a view to the "clearing of truth." This they did with reasonable circumspection and deliberation. In May 1682, in fact, the half-yearly meeting had to deal with seemingly unnecessary delays by the local and provincial assemblies in reproving the wayward, for dilatoriness had sparked criticism from non-Quakers. Fifteen years later the six-months meeting confronted the same problem, counseling its constituent groups to seek an offender's repentance even while avoiding unnecessary delay.[92]

Offenders were counseled, provided with an opportunity to submit a paper denouncing their offenses, and eventually disowned if they refused to do so. They were also subject to varying degrees of ostracism, including exclusion from business meetings (as happened to Clarridge), rejection of their monetary contributions, and termination of social intimacy. The national meeting in May 1699 approved one of the fullest statements on the treatment of transgressors:

> Its hereby Recommended to friends in Generall to be very carefull to beare a Testimony in their deportment toward Transgressors, and disorderly persons professing Truth, and have not Cleered Truth, nor given that satisfaction that Truth requires as also such as have been denyed, not to shew Intimacy nor familiarity in keeping such Company, nor frequenting their houses, Neither Entertaining them in friends houses with that freedom as faithfull friends, And that friends in the Ministry may be Cautious not to lay hands on such.[93]

As a public Friend, Sharp had to be especially chary of social intercourse with offenders.

Fully committed to the Quakers' strict behavioral standards, Sharp was active in their disciplinary work, admonishing malefactors and helping to draft testimonies against those who remained obdurate. This included a general statement in 1682 against all Friends who dishonored the movement by their disorderly lives. On occasion Sharp read testimonies of condemnation to the Dublin meeting, as in October 1683, when John Westrey refused to drop his erroneous charge that Friends were responsible for his fiancée's premature death. Periodically Sharp also read testimonies in which the offenders condemned themselves, presumably because they could not read or were unable to attend.[94] The submission and reading of such statements did not automatically restore malefactors to complete fellowship, for the meeting had to be certain the offenders manifested "a real sence of their sins and Godly sorrow and true Contrition for the same apparently wrought in them and manifested by their fruits."[95]

The obdurately recalcitrant faced disownment.[96] Again, Sharp was directly involved in some cases, as in 1704 when he and five others told the merchant Robert Ducker to clear the truth by an appropriate denunciation of his misbehavior or face public disownment. After Ducker's first paper proved to be inadequate, he submitted a second condemning his "loose scandalous actions." In effect, he was on probation when a constable apprehended him in a suspected brothel with two strumpets. Sharp and his colleagues tried to limit the damage to their reputation by disowning Ducker, though presumably they still hoped for his repentance. Besides Sharp's participation in specific disciplinary cases, he was one of eight Friends appointed by the Dublin men's meet-

ing in 1699 to examine papers of condemnation before they were recorded.[97]

Backsliders were the subject of special interest in 1680, when the national meeting requested each provincial assembly to prepare an account
of such people and the fates that had befallen them, presumably for edi-
ficatory purposes. The Dublin meeting could report a dozen, no more
than two of whom were women. Among the twelve was the weaver
Thomas Chandler, who succumbed to drunkenness and singing, became
ill with stones, and died in misery, wailing day and night. Another was
Thomas Warren, who fell into debt, betrayed the peace principle by becoming a soldier, and died in poverty. Once the data had been gathered,
the Dublin meeting commissioned Sharp, Seaton, Sleigh, and Turner to
draft a general testimony against backsliders.[98] On occasion Sharp counseled backsliders for his meeting. Among his manuscripts is a copy of his
letter to Marcus Lynch of Galway, who left the Friends and began
wearing a sword: "Remember therefore From whence thou art fallen,"
Sharp admonished him, "and repent and close unto thy first Love and
reject not the Lord and his love." For Sharp this attempt to reclaim
Lynch was part of his responsibility as a Quaker: "I shal discharge my
duty unto and for thee, and Leave the Issue unto the Lord." A sense of
urgency pervaded Sharp's message, for he remained persuaded of the
imminent judgment of God on the world: "If thou or many more should
oppose themselves against the Lord and his spirit in the work of reformation and regeneration the stone that shal fall upon such shal grind
them to powder; the Time is short that all shal return unto their long
home who then that hath dishonoured the Lord and his name shal stand
in Judgment."[99]

Nearly thirteen years later Lynch sent a letter to Clarridge and Elizabeth Huter for Friends in Dublin, expressing remorse for his backsliding
and dishonoring the truth. The Dublin men's meeting appointed Sharp,
Clarridge, and Burnyeat to encourage him to pursue truth and righteousness, insisting that "the Cross must be taken up against all the
temptations &c if he Expect to be restored."[100] His response, if he sent
one, seems not to have survived.

Sustaining the commitment of Quakers to their community's ideals
was easier than reclaiming them if they apostatized. This must have
been a primary motivation for the development of an increasingly active
visitation program. Well before such a program commenced in London
and New England in 1708, the first regular home visitations in Ireland
followed in the wake of the half-yearly meeting's instructions to local

groups in November 1677 to inquire into their members' conduct. The following April the Dublin men's meeting appointed four pairs of men, including Sharp and Roger Roberts, to undertake this task. The women too were soon engaged, for in May 1679 a letter from the national women's meeting signed by Ann Sharp and forty-seven others instructed each local women's group to select two members "of an honest life and good report" to examine families with a view to repressing pride and unessential things. The Dublin men's meeting expanded the scope of its visitations to include shops in 1681.[101] Although the Dublin minutes do not consistently record the visitors' names, Sharp appears to have performed this work on a fairly regular basis for a decade. Finally, in April 1688 the minutes note that he was replaced because he undertook so many other responsibilities for the Friends and was preoccupied with the public, presumably a reference to his guild and city activities.[102]

As a visitor it fell to Sharp to determine whether the Friends on whom he called were in compliance with Quaker directives on clothing, home decorations, and customs. Pike described a typical family visitation:

> We first sat down with them together; and, as we found a concern to come upon our minds, suitable to their respective states and conditions, we gave them advice and counsel, &c. accordingly; and particularly to keep close to the witness of God in themselves, and the gift and measure of his Holy Spirit. . . . And after we had spoken what was in our minds relating to spiritual things, we then proceeded to other things relating to conversation and behaviour, &c., as occasion offered. Then we read sundry rules of superior meetings, and spake the needful to those rules and advices, without partiality to any.

An undated manuscript by Sharp, probably composed while he was a visitor, served as a guide for those fulfilling this duty. Desirous of having Friends "circumspect and orderly in their things that they profess," he wanted visitors to pose a series of queries to the families on whom they called: Did they "Spare as much time from outward buisness to attend meetings Week dayes as well as first dayes?" Did they use few words in buying and selling? Did they wear plain attire and decorate their homes in simplicity? Did they avoid flowered and striped patterns? Did they "Keep their Words in Dealing" and stay out of debt? Did they educate their children in Quaker principles and plain speech, and did they send them to school or see that they were lawfully and honestly employed?[103] As Sharp and a fellow visitor sat in Quaker homes, these are the questions they would have posed, and the answers would have provided the basis for their report to the Dublin men's meeting.

In November 1686 the six-months meeting reported good results in some (unspecified) places, probably including Dublin, for Sharp and his fellow visitors in the city reported the following January that Quakers were "generally willing to condescend to leave off the use of Such things as are really offencive." The next year, when Sharp was no longer a visitor but would have listened to the report with considerable interest, the team observed that "where things has not been kept Cleare, there is hopes of Amendement, & that in the Generale things are pretty well."[104] In the years preceding the revolution, visitation results in Leinster were generally positive, though this was less so at Cork, Bandon, and Limerick. Among Sharp's papers is a letter from Rooke and Archer recounting that at Limerick they found many who verbally professed the Quaker message but repudiated it by their actions. This report must have saddened Sharp.[105]

Although the visitations apparently ceased during the time of troubles, they resumed in September 1691 with a directive from the Leinster provincial meeting and the appointment of four visitors, including Roger Roberts, Stevens, and Ashton, by the Dublin men's meeting. In late October the visitors observed that Friends were generally "soe Condescending, that they are willing to lay aside what was spoken to & Judged unnecessary." At the half-yearly meeting a fortnight later, the delegates called for the continuation of visitations to ensure observance of Quaker principles governing such matters as raiment, household goods, and commerce, with each provincial meeting to submit a report the following May. In fulfilment of this directive the Dublin visitors carried out another visitation in the early weeks of 1692. Again the results were encouraging, with reports that Quakers were willingly laying aside nonessential things, and that no one any longer made or purchased striped cloth to resell or to wear.[106]

Sharp was not among the visitors who were active in 1691 and 1692, though their work undoubtedly interested him. His wife was among the twenty-six signatories of an epistle from the national women's meeting to provincial and local women's groups in May 1692 calling for "Faithfull women" to resume visitations with a view to preserving "good Order." The women's renewed involvement was probably a major contributing factor to the heightened interest in visitations demonstrated at the national meeting the ensuing November. Concerned "for the honour & propagation of Truth, & the good & preservation of

Friends in Generall," the delegates called for each provincial assembly to appoint Friends to inspect every local meeting and each Quaker family, and to report to the next six-months meeting. Among the subjects of their inquiry was whether Quakers had attempted to acquire excessively large farms or had become involved in "Extravagancy of Tradeing or dealing of any kind."[107] The Leinster meeting subsequently delegated this responsibility to six men, one for each of its constituent groups; Sharp's former partner, Roger Roberts, served for Dublin. At the local level the Dublin men's meeting divided the work among ten men, an indication of the visitations' increased scope and probably of the Quaker community's growth in the city. Sharp was not one of the ten. The results of this visitation were again promising, and Roberts presented the report to the provincial body in March 1693.[108]

Meetings at all levels continued to be satisfied with visitation results throughout the spring of 1693, but in July the delegates at the Leinster assembly learned from their six visitors "of the Remissnesse of some that do not yet give up to Answer the desire of friends, And that they may Stand Cleare, and be more disintangled from too much Incumbrances that may prejudice others, or hinder their service for the Lord." The delegates responded with an expression of confidence in the visitors, whom they empowered to tell recalcitrant malefactors that their refusal to subject themselves to their meetings meant they were no longer "in Unity to Act amongst friends."[109] This determination to proceed forcefully with the visitations was reflected as well in the Leinster meeting's decision to appoint a second visitor for Dublin; Ashton thus joined Roberts in August. At the local level the mounting workload prompted the Dublin men's meeting to expand its corps of visitors to twelve by the addition of Sharp and Rooke in October.[110] After a hiatus of more than five years Sharp was again calling on Friends in their homes and shops to assess their compliance with Quaker behavioral principles.

Sharp's resumption of visitation duties may have been more onerous than his earlier period of service, for some Friends were now refusing to submit to the discipline of local meetings. Yet conditions had improved by April 1694, when Sharp and his co-visitors reported that they had found "things amended in many respects, and that their Endeavours have proved for the better to the Satisfaction of the Concerned." Visitors were calling on individuals as well as families and their servants, with queries about their spiritual and material conditions, their testimony against tithes, their attendance at meetings, and the extent of their response to previous visitors' advice. A report on the visitations signed by Sharp and eight others for the six-months assembly to England's yearly meeting in May 1694 was very sanguine, as was a companion account from the national women's meeting, signed by Ann Sharp and eleven others, to its counterpart in London. Female visitors were concentrating on those subjects "that more particularly belong to our Sex," such as clothing, household goods, and raising children.[111]

Throughout the rest of the 1690s the visitations continued to produce satisfying results, notwithstanding recurring accounts of misconduct by some, including "Guzling drinkers and Company keeping smoakers." The Leinster provincial meeting insisted in 1698 that such persons be excluded from all business meetings, including those at the local level.[112] Because Dublin visitors were unable to interview all the Friends on each visitation in the late 1690s, the men's meeting added two more visitors in 1699. By June a full visitation had been carried out with an encouraging outcome, most Friends having proven receptive to advice and promised to reform. In keeping with a directive from the half-yearly meeting, the Leinster assembly dispatched eight members to visit each local group in the late summer and fall of 1699 to inquire about doctrine as well as discipline. Some Friends in Leinster responded to the visitors—and to Quaker exhortations in this decade not to acquire excessively large farms—by donating tracts of land from their sizable estates to the needy; perhaps Sharp, who encouraged charity, was among the visitors who recommended that this be done, and possibly he even donated some of his own property. But the visitors also found it necessary to castigate those who had purchased cattle and goods if their prior ownership had not been definitively established, as well as those who had amassed material possessions and raised their children with a propensity to idleness and finery.[113]

An epistle from the Leinster women's meeting to the national women's group in May 1700 reflected the increased thoroughness of the visitations at century's end. The visits included "a more full and near Inspection into particulars Recommended from time to time in the severall yearly meeting Papers then formerly hath been with us." But by December the pressures of calling on all Quakers in Dublin were again too onerous for the visitors, to whom the men's meeting now gave discretion to concentrate on those who needed advice or admonition. Yet it also asked the women's meeting to send visitors to all Quaker families to ascertain if they were requiring their children and servants to engage in suitable work and to dress appropriately.[114]

At the Leinster meeting in December 1700 the delegates were troubled by reports of "such Nusances as are found more or lesse in most places amongst friends to the griefe of the upright in heart." The representatives therefore asked each local group to appoint a committee to conduct a "narrow Inspection" of such matters, especially pride and idleness, with the intent of eradicating them root and branch. In Dublin Sharp, the other visitors (including the women), and the public Friends convened in January to take up this charge. Any Quaker "who finds A concerne upon his, or her mind to come there, may . . . lay before said meeting any thing they know that is like to hurt any particular or the progress of truth in the generall." The resulting gathering must have resembled a New England town meeting or a cross between a modern group therapy session and a spiritual stockholders' meeting. Various matters were "closely spoken unto," and a report was subsequently delivered to the next men's meeting, which instructed the visitors to endeavor to rectify those things they found amiss.[115]

During the 1690s the Dublin Friends occasionally conducted visitations at Drogheda, where Quakers were less strict than their counterparts in the capital. In 1693 the visitors had to explain to the Drogheda meeting that it was not enough for transgressors to submit testimonies condemning their misdeeds; "fruits meet for Repentance" were also required before the errant could be received again into the meeting. When the Dublin men's meeting recruited members to visit Drogheda in 1705, Sharp, despite his advanced age, was one of the five volunteers. His interest in visitations thus remained strong to the end of his life. In carrying out this work he would have been mindful of a statement prepared by the Leinster provincial meeting in 1694 which noted that as persecutions had "formerly tryed & proved many, [so] now the Light searches & discovers all," especially through the visitations.[116]

Sharp's extensive involvement in the visitation program reflected the significance he attached to the maintenance of gospel order and the Friends' unadorned lifestyle. He was sensitive to the fact that outsiders judged Quakers by their distinctive principles and practices as well as their daily business dealings. Their word was therefore important, as were their speech and raiment, the furnishing and decoration of their houses, the shunning of excessive smoking and drinking, the repudiation of gambling, the avoidance of superfluity, and the confinement of sexual intimacy to marriage. Sharp counseled many Quaker offenders and knew about the offenses of a host of others, though neither he nor his wife was charged with any of these transgressions. Given his stature in the city as well as among Friends, had he violated Quaker standards in any significant way, someone would surely have castigated his behavior. Without such evidence we can imagine the Sharps, dressed in plain apparel, living in a simply decorated house, and regularly discussing the Friends' progress in upholding the stringent standards which the Sharps themselves played a major role in articulating. Few could have equaled them in the influence they exercised in shaping and enforcing the Irish Quakers' distinctive, strict lifestyle. Ultimately such strictness had an impact as far away as Chester and Lancaster counties in Pennsylvania, where the Friends' monthly meetings, so heavily influenced by immigrants from Ireland, were more strait-laced than those dominated by settlers from English meetings.[117]

10

"Generation of Vipers"

Sharp and the Lamb's War

FROM THEIR EARLIEST DAYS the Friends boldly challenged rival religious groups as an integral part of their "Lamb's War" against the forces of evil, both internal and external. The internal struggle was paramount, its aim, in James Nayler's words, being the formation of a new person and the redemption of those who believe in the Lamb of God. Indeed, God's "appearance in the Lamb . . . is to make war with the God of this world, and to plead with his Subjects concerning their revolt from him their Creator." This was a war to repudiate pleasures, profits, and ease, and to replace them with a life of faith and devotion to truth. "Christ hath a war with his enemies, to which he cals his Subjects to serve him therin against all the powers of darknesse of this world: and all things of this old world, the wayes and fashions of it will he overturn; and all things will he make new which the God of this world hath polluted, and wherewith his Children have corrupted themselves." Those who engage in this struggle do so, insisted Nayler, with spiritual weapons, arming themselves with the sword of the divine Spirit and shielding themselves in faith and patience.[1]

The propagation of this message of the Lamb's War propelled the Quakers into conflict with proponents of other religious traditions, all of which competed for souls with an intensity largely foreign to modern western society. This was a contest for empire by people who conceived of themselves as agents of the divine. Fired by the conviction that their views would ultimately triumph over all others, they dauntlessly confronted their opponents. For nearly all Friends after 1660 the weapons in the Lamb's War were spiritual—the spoken and the written word. Combat was typically in the form of disputation, whether face-to-face encounters in "steeplehouses," streets, and shops, or in tracts and epistles.

Because the Friends had no divinity schools or formal ordination, they lacked structural means to prepare themselves to enter the polemical arena as champions of "truth." As we have seen, however, they developed mechanisms to reduce the likelihood of unqualified people becoming public Friends or publishing their views. Over time, the Quakers developed a clear understanding of the necessity of limiting those who entered polemical debate. In November 1693 the half-yearly meeting asked the provincial assemblies to advise the local groups to caution their members not to engage in public religious disputations, either orally or in print, without first consulting "weighty Friends" in their meeting. Nothing of a controversial nature was to be published until it had been submitted to the local or provincial men's meeting. Three years later the six-months meeting found it necessary to revisit this topic, noting that some Quakers might possess hostile literature, "and notwithstanding the advice of Faithfull concerned Friends . . . may make an ill use of such Books to the prejudice and disservice of Truth, such friends not being subject to the advice and Counsell of friends." Offenders were barred from business meetings until they had adequately repented.[2]

Sharp was active as a Quaker polemicist and apologist, though apparently nothing he wrote was printed other than a broadsheet, of which he was a coauthor, and a related defense of William Penn, both in 1698. For the most part he was satisfied with disputing in person or through private correspondence. His polemic and apologetic works span nearly a quarter of a century, from February 1677 to December 1700, and he engaged critics ranging from Roman Catholics to lapsed Quakers and Muggletonians. Between them his epistles provide not only an overview of his theological tenets but also a manifestation of the zeal with which he engaged in the Lamb's War.

Sharp's disputes with the Catholics were triggered by the youthful Thomas Gormagan (or Gormogans), who began disrupting Quaker meetings in 1676. Finally a group of Friends, probably including Sharp, called on Dublin Catholics in early February 1677 to ascertain whether the priest and congregation approved of Gormagan's actions, and how they would feel if Quakers disturbed their services. After the Catholics admitted that Gormagan "Walk[ed] contrary to that discipline amongst them," he promised to stop disturbing Quaker meetings, but the following day he invited Sharp to discuss religious matters. Deeming Gormagan "a contrary Spirit" whose method was to ask and answer his own questions, Sharp declined the invitation rather than "Answer a fool in his folly." For Gormagan he had this advice: "I would have thee Learn to Know thy self, and Fear the Lord."[3]

On the evening of 12 February 1677, one of the Catholics, Michael Archer, came to Sharp's home to invite him and Francis Rogers to confer with Catholics at a house near the cornmarket. The discussion turned at once to Gormagan, whose disruptive activities Sharp recounted before explaining why he refused to meet with him. "Had he been under the sence of the Wait of Sinn and inquireing after the Salvation of his soul wee should be redy to inform and cherrish the good in all." Gormagan had prepared a response, which he permitted Sharp to see before he attempted to read it to a Quaker meeting, prompting laughter from Catholics who accompanied him.[4]

The Catholics to whom Sharp recounted all this shifted the subject by challenging Rogers and Sharp to demonstrate the basis of their calling to preach. It came from God, retorted Rogers, who compared those who doubted his message to the Jews who had opposed Christ. To the Catholics' rejection of the Friends' authority because they could not perform miracles, Sharp retorted:

> as Christ apeared outward in the body at jerusalem and cald disciples to him, so he did . . . outward miracles, that they and others might beleive in him, but now he apears inwardly in Spirit . . . ; yet the blind receives their sight, the deaf hears, the Dumb speak, the Leopars are cleansed, and the poor have the Gospel preacht to them, which miracles is now by Christ in us.

Outward miracles were no longer needed, Sharp insisted. He focused next on the power to preach which Jesus had bestowed on his apostles, a power they had not found lacking. He also noted Jesus' post-resurrection promise that God would send a comforter to his disciples who would lead them "into all truth," and the subsequent ability of Paul and the other apostles to turn people from spiritual darkness to light. The Catholics interpreted this to mean the Friends were claiming they alone were filled with the Spirit, but this Sharp denied, asserting that "a manifestation of the Lords Spirit is given to every one to profit withall." To each person is granted the ability to obey the Spirit within and thereby embark on a life of righteousness.[5]

The Catholics then approached the question of authority from another angle, averring that the Quakers' rejection of "the Worship of God" was tantamount to denying their earthly sovereign. Divine worship, countered Sharp, was a matter of acknowledging Christ's right to reign in human hearts as king, priest, and prophet, whereas Friends "doe own and are Actively or passively obedient" to monarchs and subordinate magistrates out of fear of their punishment as well as for conscience's sake. He went on to profess the common doctrine of obeying God rather than a magistrate if the latter commanded anything contrary to divine precepts, suffering as necessary like Daniel and the men in the fiery furnace.[6]

Authority was also at the root of the Catholics' contention that the Quakers' denial of their church, with its claim to apostolic succession, precluded them from salvation. The Friends, Sharp maintained, embraced the true church but denied that any of the apostles or other persons in the primitive church exercised lordship over it, for that was Christ's prerogative. Challenged to prove this, Sharp replied with a stinging rebuke:

> As John said to the jews who pretended to have abraham to their Father and to be the onely church of God, so may it be said to you he preacht, O generation of Vipers, who shall Forewarn you to Flee from the Wrath to com: bring Forth Fruits meet for repentance and say not in your hearts Wee have Abram to our Father, For God is able of these stones to raise up Children unto Abraham, and so tho you pretend to be of the Church, if you resist Gods Spirit in your Selves and Sin against God your name of church will not Save you.

Rogers and Sharp refused to let the Catholics take refuge in the doctrine of an infallible church, for Sharp forced them to admit that individual congregations could err. With this opening, he drove home his point that many churches could be mistaken, as were the Jews, "who accounted themselves the onely church of God." The Catholics, then, were like the Jews in erroneously claiming to be the only true church.[7]

Unpersuaded, the Catholics launched into a lengthy discourse on baptism by water and the doctrine of purgatory, but Crabb did not copy this portion of Sharp's record of the disputation, the original of which has apparently not survived. As the hour grew late, one Catholic made a lengthy speech accusing the Quakers of heresy, to which Sharp retorted that the latter had no obligation to consider Catholic doctrine since the Catholic church had so many characteristics contrary to those of the true church. Moreover, if the Catholics regained power, Sharp averred, they would resume their persecution of dissidents. This elicited a protest from the Catholics, who noted that some of their coreligionists had died at the hands of Protestants, to which Sharp countered that the Protestants must have been acting in self-defense.[8] Quickly he refocused the discussion on the marks of the true church, which he explicated in simple terms:

> Christ saith my sheep hear my Voice and the Voice of a stranger they will not hear, and his sheep are his Church and he is the onely shepheard of them; and its said the tree is Known by its Fruits; a bad tree cannot bring forth Good Fruit nor a Good tree cannot bring Forth bad Fruit. A Good man out of the good treasure of his heart bringeth Forth good things; a bad man out of the bad treasure of his heart bringeth Forth bad things.

Thus, in Sharp's mind Catholics could not constitute the true church by virtue of the lives they led. Instead of challenging this assertion the Catholics quibbled that Sharp had cited only one mark, but he countered that he had described "General marks." With the hour now approaching ten, the participants, obviously weary, went their separate ways.[9]

Several undated papers among Sharp's manuscripts were probably composed in the aftermath of this debate. One was a letter from Nicholas Nugent, a Catholic priest who claimed his institution possessed all the characteristics of a true church and therefore had to be accounted such. Sharp's response does not survive apart from Crabb's brief summation. Sharp repudiated Nugent's assertions on the grounds that the Catholic church contravened the primitive church in faith, doctrine, and conversation, for "the Holy men of god lived in a pure and undefiled Religion."[10]

The contrast between the marks of the true and false churches was also the theme of Sharp's letter to Dublin Catholics, especially Michael Archer. Sharp wrote, he said, "in Love to their souls." Again, the letter, which concludes with forty-two queries to Catholics, is not extant, but Crabb elsewhere recorded the themes of thirty questions, possibly the nucleus of the forty-two. These deal with such topics as the headship and foundation of the true church, the unworldly nature of Christ's kingdom, the defilement of the Roman church with pollution, Antichrist and his kingdom, the popes' "pretended intrest to Peter," the prophetic message in the times of the law and the gospel, the Roman church's burning of reputed heretics, that institution's "traditions and inventions" and its "profane" priests, the gospel as the new covenant of peace, and baptism by the Spirit.[11]

Less than two months after Sharp and Rogers debated with the Catholics, Sharp received a letter from William Joseph, a Catholic and probably a Dublin businessman who had been at that disputation, demanding to know why Quakers allowed women to preach, speak, and teach in their church contrary to Paul's precepts in 1 Corinthians 14:34–35 and 1 Timothy 2:11–12. Quakers, Joseph averred, should repent and unite with the Catholic church, outside which there is no salvation, or face divine judgment. The resulting debate, which took some strange turns and had several disagreeable moments, lasted more than two months in the spring of 1677 and briefly revived in March 1680. In a lengthy response that reveals Sharp's substantial familiarity with the Bible, he began by rejecting Joseph's exegesis of the Pauline passages in question. In 1 Corinthians 14:35, according to Sharp, Paul was only referring to women asking questions that should properly have been put to their husbands at home, while in 1 Timothy 2:11–12 he was writing of women who taunted and usurped authority over men, which the latter could not tolerate without admonishing such women to be silent and subordinate. Referring to Joel 2:28–29, Acts 2:17, and 1 Corinthians 1:13, Sharp insisted that women have the right to speak, pray, prophesy, and "Labour in the Spirit and in the power of God." He also cited the examples of Miriam (Exodus 15:20–21), Anna (Luke 2:36–38), Priscilla (Acts 18:24–26), Phoebe (Romans 16:1–2), and the women who announced the resurrection to the disciples (Luke 24:22–23). To his biblical case for the right of women to speak and prophesy in the church, Sharp added an experiential argument: "We have Witnessed the Lords presence in our meetings to our Souls comfort and refreshment."[12]

For a month and a half, Joseph did not respond, perhaps because he now believed Sharp was "Unlearned and unstable." He found no evidence to support Sharp's rather creative interpretation of the Pauline passages and rejected his citation of examples such as Miriam and the women who reported the empty tomb as irrelevant to the issue of women preaching. As the debate progressed, Joseph made it clear that he objected only to women preaching and teaching in the church, not to their praying, prophesying, or singing. But Joseph also broadened the debate, seizing on Sharp's passing reference to the coming of the Antichrist, "the Man of Sinn." Referring to James Nayler's infamous (and widely misunderstood) reenactment of Jesus' entry into Jerusalem, Joseph averred that "Neavour went any man so neer" to fulfil the prophecy of the man of sin.[13]

Sharp responded to Joseph's second letter, dated 30 May 1677, the following day. Clearly embarrassed by the Nayler episode, Sharp dismissed most of the story as false and "not soe nor owned by the

Quakers." Even if it were true, it would "onely Fasten on himself while disowned by the Quakers." Pausing only to insert a comma, Sharp attempted to shift the subject to the Catholics' persecutory actions: "How many Murthers, trecheries and Vile actions hath som popish committed, yet i would not lay perticuler mens Failings on the body, except they teach corrupt doctrines and stand by, own, allow of, and practice them."[14] Sharp obviously had no interest in defending Nayler, whose symbolic action was grist for the mills of anti-Quaker polemicists.

Sharp devoted most of his reply to the substantive issue of women's right to preach and teach, and to the underlying question of how the Bible is to be interpreted. For the Friends a correct understanding of Scripture requires the guidance of the Spirit within; indeed, the Quakers regarded the Bible as secondary to the inner light and deemed themselves, like the biblical writers, inspired by the Spirit's leading.[15] Thus Sharp could tell Joseph that the Bible must be understood by the same Spirit that enlightened its writers. "Wee own the Spirit of God to lead us into all truth, according to the Scriptures." Resolutely defending his earlier exegesis of women's right to preach and teach, Sharp cited 2 Corinthians 4:3 and Romans 1:16[–17], which deal with the limitation of revealed knowledge to believers; these passages, he argued, explain why such knowledge is hidden from some people. Women as well as men, he contended, have God's grace within them and must be allowed to obey its dictates. Chiding the Catholics for endeavoring "to quiet Gods Spirit in Women," he asked: "do they not the same in themselves?" In part he traced the Catholics' stance on women to their heavy reliance on Jewish ceremony rather than the Spirit.[16]

With "other buisness to mind," Joseph waited fifteen days to respond and then expressed interest only in meeting Sharp for a "private & Civill" discussion, the only condition being the right to bring a companion if Sharp had one. Firing back the same day, Sharp noted that he too had business to tend and expressed doubt that oral arguments could persuade Joseph if written ones had not. Sharp challenged him to prove his contentions that Quakers denied true prayer, that they endorsed Nayler's actions at Bristol, and that they allowed false prophecy; he also sought proof from Joseph that Catholic women praised God, prayed, and prophesied in the church as had Miriam and Anna. If Joseph could prove all this or admit he had lied, Sharp would meet with him: "If on these termes thou desirest my Company or in C[h]arity and Christian Love, canst com to me, thou shalt be Wellcom." Before sending this re-

ply, Sharp went on the attack in a postscript that asked if Catholics adjudged all who were not members of their church to be heretics, if it was
acceptable to execute heretics like murderers and other malefactors, and
if those who communicated with heretics would be damned.[17]

This time Joseph responded almost immediately, insisting that he
sought a personal meeting only to save the time and trouble of writing,
and again asserting that he opposed only women's teaching and preaching in the church, not their praying, prophesying, and singing. To provide Sharp with all the evidence would "be tegious work"; hence he reiterated his desire for a meeting. On the same day Sharp received this
letter in mid-June, Joseph and a colleague appeared at his house. In the
ensuing discussion Sharp reiterated his views on the right of women to
pray, prophesy, and praise God in the church, and averred that women
who admonished people to flee from evil and cling to the good could
teach, preach, and prophesy.[18]

Here the matter rested until March 1680, Joseph having given up his
quest for a substantive face-to-face discussion with Sharp. But the latter
could not forget the exchange and felt moved by the Spirit to write
again to Joseph. In the aftermath of the alleged Popish Plot he delayed,
not wanting "to write what was in my mind, and what wee hath before
discoursed, Lest thou or any should think i was Glad of an oportunity
to discourse your Weaknesses; i say, it looks more like an act of Ostentation than Charity, yet i can truly say had i don it, . . . twas no more
than was in my heart to doe before the late plott was discovered." Only
love for Joseph, Sharp professed, moved him to write. Returning to the
themes raised in the postscript to his letter of 15 June 1677, Sharp
wanted to know if Joseph regarded Protestants and others who rejected
papal supremacy as heretics, if it was lawful under Catholic doctrine to
execute all heretics, and if there were any Christians who rejected the
pope's authority. Answer plainly, Sharp insisted.[19]

Joseph accepted Sharp's profession of love while accusing him of referring to the Popish Plot to foment dissension. Just as Sharp had opposed attempts to tar the Quakers with Nayler's actions, so Joseph repudiated any effort to use the deeds of alleged plotters to cast aspersions
on Catholics. Sagely refusing to discuss the Popish Plot because it was a
matter of state, Joseph similarly would not be drawn into a debate on
the execution of heretics. Nor would he defend "every idle report"
Sharp heard.[20] The atmosphere of suspicion toward Catholics that pervaded the isles following the disclosures of Titus Oates and Israel Tonge
and the ensuing attempt of opposing political factions to fan the flames

with allegations from Irish witnesses made it imprudent for Joseph to resume his debate with Sharp.

The last word in the disputation therefore went to Sharp, who penned his response on 20 March 1680. Again he claimed he had proven that women could pray and praise God in the church, and with an unmistakable air of triumph he proclaimed: "Such as prophesie with the Spirit Speaketh to the Exortation, Edification and comfort of som, and therefor put away that Egyptian, Babylonish, prejudiciall Spirit of Enmity against the truth out of thy heart." Joseph, he charged, was ashamed to answer his queries about the punishment of heretics; tweaking his opponent, Sharp professed to be thankful that the inner light in Joseph had made him too embarrassed to embrace the Catholic position on the treatment of heretics. Sensing Joseph's vulnerability on this issue, Sharp drove home his point by referring Joseph to the annotations in the Rheims New Testament, specifically the second edition printed at Antwerp in 1660 by Daniel Veruliet. "The deeds and principles of Darkness cannot be hidden; if thou do not Know them examin your papist English Testament." Sharp had obtained a copy, for he cited specific references before taunting Joseph: "Tell me is this Your Doctrine or not?" If so, Sharp wanted to hear no excuses about matters of state. "Every consciencious man," he told Joseph, "is highly concerned to beware of your Doctrine, and Let it be hatefull to all the people, for no man would be so don by."[21] Like many other Protestants, Sharp had some familiarity with John Foxe's *Acts and Monuments*,[22] which clearly influenced his view of the Roman church as a persecutory institution intent on stamping out the forces of righteousness through bloody repression.

Understandably, the efforts of some Protestants to link Catholics and Friends would have stung Sharp. One of those who made such an accusation was the Congregationalist James Barry, minister of the New Row church in Dublin and a preacher at Thomas Court. He and Sharp apparently first crossed swords in 1685 when Barry accused the Quakers of sharing the Muggletonian tenet that God's physical dimensions are ascertainable. Knowing this was erroneous, Thomas Smith of Chapelizod related the charge to Sharp, who wrote a brief missive to Barry charging him with slander—but only after Smith had expressed a willingness to repeat his account to Barry's face.[23] Nothing seems to have come of this until the fall of 1687, when a major controversy erupted between Barry and the Quakers.

Once again Barry took the initiative, accusing the Friends of being "the Spawn of the jesuits" even as the latter were "the Spawn of the Devill." According to John Kelson, a smith of Bride's Alley, Barry called the Quakers "a bewitching and blasphemous, erronious people" who cheated God "of his right." This, Barry reputedly claimed, he would prove by a paper composed by Penn and cited by Sharp that sacrilegiously denied the resurrection of the dead. Both men, Barry allegedly charged, would "compass sea and land to make one proselite, and when they had done they made him two fold a child of the devil more then Before." According to Kelson, Barry then admonished his congregation to avoid all contact with this "bewitching, Hypocritical people."[24]

Sharp responded on 17 November 1687 after seeing a paper subscribed by Barry that accused him of denying a physical resurrection. Barry had based his charge on the report of two witnesses, whom Sharp censured for misrepresenting his views. The Friends, he averred, believe in the resurrection as well as eternal rewards for the saved and eternal punishment for the damned, but they do not concern themselves "with what Body we Shal rise"; like Paul, they believe those who make such inquiries are fools.

> For God gives it [i.e., the resurrected person] a body as pleases him; there is a natural body and there is a spiritual Body; it is sown a natural Body, it is Raised a spiritual Body; thou sowest not That which shal be; every seed bears it[s] own Body; they are as the angels of God; Flesh and Blood cannot Inherit Gods Kingdom.[25]

Barry also denounced the Friends for reputedly teaching the doctrine of perfection, a charge Sharp heatedly denied. Challenging Barry to identify a single Quaker who boasted of perfection, Sharp explained the Friends' conviction that God commanded nothing unreasonable, nor did he ask people to obey commands without providing them with grace that enabled them to respond. To assert otherwise, Sharp proclaimed, was to blaspheme a just and righteous God. Indeed, the Presbyterians' Larger Catechism, which embodied the negative view of human nature at the core of the Reformed tradition, did precisely this in Sharp's eyes.[26]

Sharp concluded by heaping scorn on Barry's criticism of the Friends' apparel and his ill-conceived proposal that Quaker books be consigned to the flames. "Had thou power I suppose Books Should not serve the turn, but the persons and the Books both Together, but it is the beast hath Short horns," an allusion to Revelation 13. Sharp's rhetoric was extraordinary: Given the power, Barry would burn the Quakers just as he wanted to incinerate their books. The very charge on which Sharp had concluded his controversy with the Catholic William Joseph was now hurled at the Congregationalist James Barry.[27]

Sharp and his colleagues challenged Barry to a debate in a place of his choosing or in the largest Quaker meetinghouse in Dublin. The topics would be resurrection, justification, election and reprobation, and "Perfection in Sanctification, as to Degrees attainable." Sharp promised the debate would be orderly, but Barry, unwilling to confront a predominantly Quaker audience, replied in a series of three papers, denouncing the Friends as people of little charity who stir up animosity, deploring their tenets as murky and uncertain, and accusing the Quakers of serpentine acts.[28] After listening to Barry's reply, the Dublin men's meeting appointed Sharp, Ashton, Burnyeat, and Amos Strettell to consider publishing a refutation or taking other appropriate action to clear the truth. Two weeks later the meeting approved a remonstrance and ordered that a thousand copies be speedily printed. Written by Burnyeat and Strettell, it was published in 1688 as *The Innocency of the Christian Quakers Manifested and the Truth of Their Principles and Doctrines Cleared and Defended from the Loud (but False) Clamorous and Base Insinuations and Wicked Slanders of James Barry*. They challenged Barry to prove four tenets: (1) the resurrection of the physical body; (2) justification by the imputation of Jesus' righteousness alone; (3) the believer's inability to attain perfection in this life; and (4) the doctrine of particular, unconditional election prior to creation. They also resolutely denied Barry's charge that they embraced Muggletonian tenets because they supposedly claimed to know God's physical dimensions. Barry drafted a reply, but the outbreak of the revolution forestalled publication, and his work was not printed until 1700.[29]

Sharp composed two pamphlet-length apologetic works, neither of which was published. The first of these grew out of a trip to the meetings in northern Ireland by Sharp and John Watson in January 1693. At Coleraine, county Derry, Thomas Adams and other non-Quakers took notes in a room adjacent to the meeting, following the conclusion of which Adams spoke with Sharp and Watson about immediate revelation. Adams was probably an English Presbyterian or possibly a Congregationalist; when asked by Sharp if he were a Presbyterian, he indicated that he was "not fully . . . one with them [but] there was nothing of Difference to make a breach." From the outset, the discussion had an ugly tone, for Sharp and Watson learned that on the eve of the Quaker meeting boasts had been made in Coleraine "of a rod laid in piss for us," and during the parley after the meeting Adams reportedly used in-

sulting language to boast about what he had done and would do to
Francis Howgill and Edward Burrough. As Sharp later recounted this
episode, he gave Adams a modest lecture on the evils of boasting.[30]

For nearly three hours Sharp and Adams dueled before an audience
of Quakers and others. Two themes predominated: The Friends' belief
in continuing revelation and their misunderstood doctrine of perfection,
according to which God does not command the impossible but gives all
people "a measure of his good Spirit to Instruct and rule them to do
what he requires." This, said Sharp, was "the new covenant, light, In-
grafted word, and Grace." Everyone is commanded to obey and has sufficient enabling grace to attain perfection by degrees, but many love
darkness, and their hearts are thus beclouded because of their rebellion
against the light. Sharp stressed that grace is universally present and
available to all:

> Every good man of himself cannot think a good thought much less do that
> which is good and perfect without the gift, and the Raiser up of every good
> thought and desire In man; it comes from God the father of light who is al-
> ways present to reprove man for Sin and Stir him up to that which he re-
> quires of him by his Saving grace, word and holy spirit which is Sufficient to
> enable man to obey and Serve God.

Yet, avouched Sharp, even the Friends, notwithstanding their receptivity
to the light, fail to attain perfection or feel bound not to boast of having
done so.[31]

The second principal source of disagreement between Adams and
Sharp was the doctrine of immediate revelation and the concomitant
question whether the Bible is the primary or sole authority in religious
matters. At Coleraine Sharp criticized the Presbyterians "for not believing they ought to wait for [Christ's light] and may enjoy it In this life to
guide them," and for asserting that immediate revelation had ceased. To
Adams the continuation of immediate revelation was tantamount to denying the Bible, the need for which would be nonexistent if the Spirit
were still revealing knowledge, but Sharp rejected this interpretation, insisting that Quakers deemed Scripture "a rule and director into all
truth." Simultaneously, however, he acknowledged that the Friends preferred the Spirit to the Bible or any other external medium "as the prime
Rule, chief opener, only abilitator to walk by and to worship God." The
Quakers, in other words, accorded primacy to the "Authour of faith"
over the written word, to the Spirit's immediacy rather than to interme-
diaries such as the Bible or ministers. Without the Spirit the Bible has no

efficacy, for Scripture is "a secondary Rule. . . . No man could know the Scriptures nor the things of God nor his own State and condition much less chuse the good and refuse the evil without the Spirit." Adams' insistence that immediate revelation had ceased amounted in Sharp's eyes to the Spirit's exclusion as a teacher and guide in the worship of God and the discovery of knowledge about the deity. Moreover, Sharp avouched that without immediate revelation there could be no genuine spiritual comfort, perhaps a recognition on his part of the acute anxiety that so often pervaded the early stages of Reformed religious experience.[32]

Disagreements over the nature of the light within led to an interesting exchange concerning the status of good people in non-Christian lands. Adams believed people have only a natural light (conscience) that by itself is inadequate to lead them to salvation; the elect receive an infusion of saving grace that enables them to believe. When the first Europeans arrived in the Americas, he maintained, they found the people ignorant of Christ, without whom there is no salvation. Referring to the Johannine gospel, Sharp retorted that the light of Christ enlightens everyone and "doth reprove them of evil and Shew them good." God, he averred, will accept those who choose the good even if they know nothing of Christ. Many such heathens, he told Adams, "hath more honesty then many of your pretended Christians."[33]

During their debate Adams, like Barry, linked the Quakers to the Muggletonians. Both groups, according to Adams, were "great pretenders" to the inner light, but Sharp would have none of this. Castigating Adams' doctrine of predestination, he likened this concept, with its delimitation of saving grace to the elect, to the Muggletonian view that restricted divine promises to the seed of faith. Sharp also rebuked both Adams and the Muggletonians for their spurious allegations, referring specifically to Adams' endorsement of Muggleton's charge in *The Neck of the Quakers Broken* (1667?) that the Friends were led by the Antichrist. Adams, charged Sharp, had selected the only passage in this book that suited his purpose, repudiating the rest and ignoring the Quakers' refutation of the book.[34] In fact, however, similar charges are scattered throughout Muggleton's tract, which includes assertions that Quakers are children of the devil, not God; that they are "the seed and nature of the lost Angel"; and that they are "the absolute spirit of Antichrist" because they have "jumbled the Father, Son and Holy Ghost together, and so instead of one person, [they] have gotten three persons, and yet never a person."[35]

The debate with Adams is important partly for the insight it provides

into Sharp's intellectual armory. At one point in the parley Adams referred to the account of Alice Driver in Foxe's *Acts and Monuments*.
Adams depicted her as "a great Boaster In thy Judgment," but Sharp
was quick to claim her as a proponent of immediate revelation who,
though formally uneducated, had the power through the indwelling
Spirit to confound the church's doctors, particularly on the doctrine of
transubstantiation. Sharp was also familiar with the Westminster Confession, which he cited to prove that Presbyterians rejected immediate
revelation, as well as the Larger Catechism, by which he documented
the Presbyterians' assertion that not all people receive sufficient grace to
enable them to obey God's commands.[36] He was at home as well with
both the Bishops' Bible (1568) and the authorized version of 1611 and
their annotations, as reflected in his sparring with Adams over the correct interpretation of Luke 17:20–21. During the debate Sharp also referred to various Quaker publications: Penn and Whitehead's *A Serious
Apology for the Principles and Practices of the People Call'd Quakers*
(1671), the same authors' *The Christian Quaker and His Divine Testimony* (1673–74), and works against John Faldo and Thomas Hicks,
probably Penn's *Quakerism a New Name for Old Christianity* (1672),
his *Invalidity of John Faldo's Vindication* (1673), and his *Reason
Against Railing, and Truth Against Fiction* (1673).[37]

A triumphant Sharp left the disputation, several non-Quaker observ-
ers having adjudged that he had proven his thesis on immediate revelation. After he returned to Dublin, however, he learned that Adams was
claiming victory, whereupon Sharp sent him thirteen queries. If conscience cannot lead people to salvation, how, he asked, could God be
"clear of the Blood of all men, many not having the Bible," and, if Adams were right, how could Christ have endeavored to save the unregen-
erate, all of whom were lost? Sharp wanted to know as well how people
could understand the Bible or things of God without the ongoing revelation of the Spirit, whether God commanded everyone to serve him or
only a remnant, and whether God ordered actions that were impossible
for humans to obey. His tenth question had been at the heart of their
recent disputation: "Is the Scripture a sufficient rule of life without the
Spirits Inlightening Teaching and Impowering? If not, immediate Revelation is not ceased and the Spirit as a rule and guide Into all truth
ought not to be Rejected."[38]

Although Adams opted not to respond directly to the queries, he exchanged letters with Sharp until September 1694. Sharp provided a reasonably full account of the controversy in his "Answer to Thomas Ad-

ams Letter of the Third of April 1694 Who Accounts It Erroneous to Believe the Immediate Manifestation of Christs Spirit in These Days." Dated 22 June 1694, the manuscript contains approximately 27,000 words.[39] It was never published, probably because the Quakers deemed Adams a minor figure whose views had minimal impact, and perhaps none outside the Coleraine area. The manuscript is also narrowly polemical, dealing with one unplanned parley, and it lacks thematic structure. Like so many other partisan writers of this period, Sharp and Adams indulged themselves by hurling odious epithets at each other, and this unfortunately detracts from the gravity of the argument. Although Sharp professed that he did not take "liberty with [his] tongue or pen but what is proper and modest," he characterized Adams as a busybody, an unbeliever, a writer of known falsehoods, a man blind to the truth, a person who was next of kin to the Muggletonians, a chained dog, and one who "used to Boast and Insult like Golia[t]h of old." Citing Adams' "contentious Brangling Spirit," Sharp pitied his ignorance of the truth and condemned his blind zeal. At least in part his arguments were a "Long Babble of many words, to little purpose."[40] Notwithstanding the time Sharp spent refuting Adams, he clearly had no respect for his Coleraine antagonist.

In the midst of his controversy with Adams, Sharp wrote another long work critiquing two sermons on Galatians 1:8 by Charles Whittingham, a minister of the Church of Ireland at Wicklow. Comprising approximately 21,000 words, this commentary was entitled by Sharp "A Defence of the Protestant Christian Religion as Professed by the People of God (in Scorn) Called Quakers." This work too was apparently never published, though the Dublin men's meeting on 19 December 1693 asked Ashton, Seaton, Archer, and Amos Strettell to examine it, and subsequently ordered copies made.[41] Whittingham had contended that the Quakers preached a counterfeit gospel and should be accursed in keeping with Pauline teaching (Galatians 1:8–9). He concentrated on seven topics: baptism, the Lord's supper, resurrection, perfection, the ministry, tithes, and immediate revelation. Sharp's critique constitutes his most substantive theological work and merits careful analysis. Judging from his preface to the reader, Sharp intended that his manuscript be published. Unless no copies of the printed work survive, the Dublin meeting must have thought otherwise, probably because Whittingham's sermons had not been printed. Little could be gained by publicizing his views or providing him with an excuse to publish his homilies.

In his preface Sharp enunciated several fundamental theses, the most crucial of which for the ensuing discussion was the proposition that the gospel's power and knowledge are received by degrees and through immediate revelation, not formal education. This enabled Sharp to explain why Paul temporarily retained the use of ceremonies and why gospel ordinances eventually supplanted "Shadows." Moreover, this principle led Sharp and other Friends to reject baptism by water and the physical celebration of the Lord's supper. He made it clear that Quakers did not condemn those whose consciences persuaded them to observe these ordinances in a physical manner, but he asked them "to consider if they are yet come to that one baptism of Christ, vizt: to be baptized with the holy-Ghost which the water was a figure of, and whether they are come to know a feeding on Christ, and to witness the Spiritual Supper to feed the Soul to eternal life which outward bread and outward water can never do." Christians, Sharp argued, must obey that which Christ and his apostles plainly teach in the New Testament, and they must separate themselves from non-Christians. Because Whittingham and his coreligionists espoused "popish Invention" in lieu of "the Seal of the New Covenant," upheld shadows rather than gospel ordinances, preached for material gain, and persecuted the godly, the Friends refused to accept them as gospel teachers. In short, progressive revelation led the Friends to spurn the traditional celebration of the sacraments, repudiate the professional clergy, and attest their fidelity to the gospel by separating from society, at least with respect to its materialism, covetousness, and oppression.[42]

Sharp challenged the traditional Protestant view of baptism on several points. Rejecting the common interpretation that the Jewish rite of circumcision was a figure (or type) of water baptism, Sharp averred that the former was the figure of the heart's spiritual circumcision. The prevailing view erred, he opined, by making one figure herald another. Similarly he refuted the idea that baptism by water is a sign and seal of the covenant, for the Spirit is the seal of the saints' redemption. Where in the Bible, he asked, does God command mutual engagements in the rite of water baptism? Where does Christ assert that such baptism is the sign of the new covenant and the means by which all believers should be admitted into communion with the deity? Where, indeed, does Christ mandate the sprinkling of infants? Sharp was willing to acknowledge that the apostles baptized by water, but, as the Baptists argued, the subjects of this act were believers, not infants incapable of repentance and faith. Such practices, including the use of godparents, were "popish Inventions."[43]

Sharp emphasized that the Friends did not repudiate any ordinance instituted by Christ. Jesus commanded his disciples to teach and then to baptize, but he said nothing about water. Indeed, Acts 11:15–16 makes it manifest, averred Sharp, that the apostles themselves were baptized by the Spirit.

> We do not understand that Christ baptized any with water, for his is the Substantial spiritual baptism, unchangable and is one, but his disciples did baptize Several In water, we do believe In honour to Johns manifestation, which was nevertheless to decrease and Christs to Increase, yet we do not find Such a stress was put on it, as that they would not be Saved or have any right to the gospel Without it.

John's baptism signified repentance and a belief in the coming messiah, whereas the apostles used water baptism in a figurative manner; it had no salvific power. In contrast, the baptism of the Spirit purges the flesh, gathers the wheat, and consumes the chaff with unquenchable fire. Thus, baptism by water and baptism by the Spirit must be clearly distinguished. As Paul contended, there is only one baptism, and for Sharp that baptism is spiritual. Because Whittingham conflated water and Spirit baptism, Sharp thought he should be ranked with Nadab and Abihu as men who "offered Strange fire not commanded of God" (Numbers 26:61).[44]

Sharp's views on the Lord's supper were also grounded in the conviction that Christian worship as instituted by Christ is spiritual in nature; hence the godly eat and drink spiritually. Jesus told his followers he would drink no more of the vine until he partook in his father's kingdom, clearly making it a spiritual observance in Sharp's estimation. Paul, of course, exhorted the godly to observe the Lord's supper until Christ returned, but Sharp contended that he had already "come to Judgment" and was present within people. The Lord's supper "was practiced by the apostles and primitive Christians because they (many of them) looked too much at outward things, yet they were under Several Reproofs about it." Christ, then, has returned and is within people, obviating the need to rely on the outward signs of bread and wine. "To Say that outward bread or any outward things of meats, washings, or observing days is a means to heal the leprosie of Sin or open the Blind eyes &c is to preach another Gospel then Paul Preached." Contrary to Whittingham, Sharp contended that the godly do not testify to their status as Christians by partaking of the bread and wine but by fidelity to the Christ within them.[45]

In his remarks to Whittingham on resurrection Sharp covered ground he had already traversed in his dispute with Barry. However, he was more assertive in insisting the raised body would be "glorious and Spiritual."[46]

On the subject of perfection Sharp reiterated his basic position on its attainability by degrees as part of the sanctification process. God, he noted, had commanded Abraham to be perfect and praised Job as an upright, flawless man. To deny the capability to achieve perfection in this life is to reject God's omnipotent power to provide believers with the means to overcome temptation. Taking direct aim at the Book of Common Prayer's teaching on confession, Sharp excoriated Anglicans for their alleged hypocrisy in professing to believe in spiritual rebirth and sanctification even while denying the Spirit's power to accomplish them: "For one or many to be continuing in that Confession or Lesson or rather In that estate and Condition of doing that you ought not to do and leaving undone that which you ought to have done ... but always to continue In Such Rebellion against Gods good Spirit ... deny him [that is, Christ]." The regeneration and sanctification of which Whittingham wrote, Sharp asserted, are imaginary.[47]

Sharp was no less condemnatory of the Anglicans' position on a professional, formally ordained clergy supported by mandatory tithes. Why, he queried, should God be limited to those men "bred up" to the ministry, like apprentices trained to be tradesmen? Christ calls people to be ministers through immediate revelation, without which no one should engage in that work. "The natural man knows not the things of God, for they are to be known or discerned spiritually." This, of course, was tantamount to rejecting the universities as appropriate places to learn spiritual truths. Sharp went on to explain that the Friends had elders, ministers, pastors, and teachers, some of whom had received the spirit of prophecy and others the gift of doctrine. The recipients of such talents are bound to use them to edify the church, not for temporal gain or as "Lords over Gods heritage but as examples to the Flock."[48]

Tithes were objectionable to Sharp because they were part of the first (Hebrew) priesthood, and their continuation amounted in his eyes to a repudiation of the work of Jesus, who terminated that priesthood. Borrowing from Foxe's *Acts and Monuments*, Sharp cited the opposition of John Hus, the Lollard Walter Brute, and King Richard II's Parliament to tithes and the "romish priesthood." He chided Whittingham because the professional clergy monopolized tithes, whereas Hebrew priests had provided substantial relief to orphans, widows, and strangers. "You expect we must take care of your minister" by tithes, he reflected sarcastically, "and he must have the milk of us that is none of his Flock"; Quakers must "take care of your poor . . . that some of you So little regard and relieve."[49]

In the concluding portion of his tract, Sharp explored immediate revelation, the topic that played a major role in his contemporaneous dispute with Adams. Opponents of this doctrine were especially concerned about its impact on Scripture as authoritative, believing that fresh revelation could supplant biblical teachings. Sharp insisted that immediate revelation does not negate "the chief end and authority of the Scriptures," which are themselves inspired; rather, the Spirit's continuing revelatory work enables believers to understand the Bible. Without true faith, Sharp contended, the Bible cannot "make wise to Salvation." Immediate revelation neither diminishes the importance of Scripture nor excludes any external means that God employs to convey truth. Indeed, Sharp considered immediate revelation a crucial element in the cosmic struggle between the forces of good and evil—"the plea," as he phrased it, "of the true church and seed against Antichrist."[50]

To substantiate his point Sharp related his encounter with an Irish priest at Milford, county Cork, as he was preparing to sail for Bristol. Learning that Sharp was a Quaker, the priest offered "to do [him] good on account of his function." Sharp responded with a general reference to God's promise, as recounted in Joel, Daniel, and Acts, to pour his Spirit on humankind, increasing knowledge, teaching everyone of the new covenant, and covering the earth with the knowledge of God as water fills the sea. If the Scripture has already been fulfilled, Sharp asked the priest, where is this reported in the Bible? Sharp was willing to acknowledge only that such a fulfilling had begun during the days of the primitive church before a great "falling away" had occurred. If, then, this bestowal had not happened in the past, how could it occur in the future without immediate revelation? Claiming to be a poor cleric with an income of only £40 *per annum*, the priest admitted he could not answer Sharp's queries. With another dose of sarcasm, Sharp left the questions to Whittingham, "for that I do Suppose he hath a greater Income."[51]

In drawing this substantive work to a close, Sharp stressed two themes, authority and persecution. From Whittingham he requested the biblical commands for a host of traditional practices he deplored: "breed[ing]" boys to be ministers, studying sophistry and vain arts, obtaining commissions to the ministry from a bishop or an ordinary, acquiring academic degrees, collecting mandatory tithes, wearing clerical garb such as surplices and black gowns, issuing writs *de excommunicato capiendo*, sprinkling children, and having godparents. For such practices he found no authority. It pained Sharp that those who upheld such usages enforced them on others. Since the Reformation had proclaimed freedom of conscience, he reflected, much blood had been shed, which he attributed to "the Strange and uncharitable pride of those men who having with Just Cause Vindicated their own reason from the Tyranny of unnecessary ends, endeavour nevertheless to lay them upon others, So that not the use of Such Liberty but the appropriating of it to our Selves only is the true and . . . the sole fountain of the Disorders."[52] It was an eloquent call to those who claimed the right to follow their consciences' dictates not to force their beliefs on others.

Four years after his critique of Whittingham's sermons, Sharp wrote to one Jonathan Dagnal on 19 February 1698. Crabb's calendar indicates only that Dagnal had asked what enabled someone "to Know the holy Scriptures and to qualifie him to Know the blessed truth the Quakers profess, altho the holy Scriptures testifie of those truths." The question had probably been posed polemically rather than as an innocent inquiry, for Sharp responded with what Crabb describes as a lengthy apology vindicating the Quaker belief in the inner light. If Dagnal was related to the General Baptist minister and bookseller Stephen Dagnal, the exchange with Sharp would have been polemic.[53]

This was probably not so with respect to Sharp's letter to Andrew Perry, dated 7 December 1700, though Perry was not a Quaker. He had written to Sharp on 20 November seeking religious counsel, especially on the potential religious significance of dreams, but he also posed a series of questions that reflected suspicion of Quaker tenets: Did they accept Scripture or pervert it? Did they claim to be sinless? Did they deny the resurrection of the dead, baptism by water, and the sacrament of the Lord's supper? Apart from dreams, Sharp had previously dealt with all these subjects, and his replies to Perry reflect his earlier statements. Dreams, Sharp opined, could originate from three sources: good ones from God, evil ones from "the motions of the Flesh or temptations of the Devil," and others—presumably neutral in moral value—from a "Multitude of Thoughts." To discriminate between them, Sharp advised, one had to seek, love, and obey Christ, the true light.[54]

Two of Sharp's disputatious letters were written to lapsed Quakers, the first of whom was Joshua Bows, author of *The White Vizard Pluckt from the Quakers Black Faces by Way of Dialogue Betwixt Dick and*

Thom: Concerning the Hipocriticall Breathren of the Yea and Nea Congregation.[55] As we have seen, Bows had been accused of inappropriate conduct with Grace Newby in 1692, and his public embarrassment may have been a factor in prompting this attack on Quakers. Unlike Sharp's other polemical duels, this one was intensely personal, focusing on aspects of his life rather than the Friends' doctrine, though at the outset Sharp recommended a short list of books to readers interested in Quaker tenets. Sharp devoted more than 5,000 words to his refutation of Bows, whom he deemed "the murtherer of the reputation of honest men."[56] Composed shortly after the time of troubles, when feelings still ran high, Bows' charges dealt primarily with Sharp's alleged amity and complicity with Catholics, the intent of which was material gain. Bows went as far as to assert that if given the opportunity, Sharp and other Quakers would use the inner light to justify their seizure of Protestant estates and the cutting of Protestant throats. To this, Sharp responded that he had enjoyed no more civil or religious freedom than any other Protestant in James' reign, that he was as much a heretic in Catholic eyes as any Protestant and therefore as liable to suffer, and that he was himself a Protestant landowner, with nearly a thousand acres in Ireland as well as dissolved abbey lands in England. He had, he insisted, no prospect of gain had the Catholics triumphed, and he had even sustained losses, having exchanged cloth for James' inflated currency rather than confiscated goods as had other Protestants.[57]

Sharp was quick to deny Bows' accusation that he had loaned £100 to an Irish captain "to make his company look more gracefull" in James' reign, but he was equivocal in responding to the charge that he had employed a Catholic woman while leaving a Protestant to beg. "In the general," he reflected, "I was never of that mind to give work to papists and refuse protestants, although we have great respect to good work." Better to hire a good Catholic, he implied, than an indolent Protestant. He also sought justification by noting that for charitable reasons he had employed more workers than he needed, and in the time of troubles he had assisted Protestants, collected money to aid poor prisoners, and provided clothing for the sick and wounded. Moreover, during James' reign he had publicly opposed Catholics to the mayor of Dublin and others, castigating their belief in "forcing mens faith," transubstantiation, purgatory, prayers for the dead, holy days, the veneration of crosses and relics, rosaries, "mass worship," and other Catholic practices. He also added that the Friends disliked the retention of various Catholic "reliques" by other Protestants.[58]

In a related charge, Bows accused Sharp of receiving a report of a Catholic victory over William's forces in the north from George Gregson and jubilantly passing the news to the Catholic party in Dublin. Acknowledging regular correspondence with Gregson and others about the Irish army's campaign in the north, Sharp admitted having shown Gregson's letter to others, but he insisted he had kept it as private as possible. In any event, he argued, he and Gregson would not have rejoiced at the destruction of any army, especially a Protestant one.[59]

The remainder of Bow's allegations related to distinctive Quaker practices. As master of the weavers' guild, Sharp, he charged, had not taken the prescribed oath on grounds of conscience but he had fined and incarcerated others for refusing to do so. Not true, retorted Sharp. The other accusations applied to Friends in general. Their religion consists of "plain Bands and plain cloaths," charged Bows. Judging from Sharp's reply, Bows had struck a sensitive nerve: "We place not the greatest part of our religion In cloaths, But in our subjecting our wills In all things to Gods Will, both as to our thoughts and desires and conversations, to deny all ungodlyness, and worldly lusts, and to live soberly and righteously in this world." It was easier to dismiss accusations of Quaker swearing, dissembling, cheating, and backbiting because Bows cited no examples, but he brought up the embarrassing case of Jonas Goldby, who had assaulted Bows when the latter accused him of having been cashiered from the army for cowardice. Although Sharp maintained that one man's failing did not undermine the principles of an entire society, he was abashed by another Quaker who had physically punished an errant apprentice.[60]

The personal nature of Bows' attack, his former participation in Quaker meetings, and his recitation of alleged Quaker failings must have pained Sharp. He undoubtedly experienced anger, frustration, and sadness as he replied, yet he concluded on a somber note, expressing hope that Bows would repent and find mercy before it was too late.[61] One could not cite a better example of the Friends' determination to hold out hope that those who had strayed from their fold would eventually respond to the light within and return.

Whereas Sharp's initial response to a lapsed Quaker was to one who had gravitated to a more traditional religious group, his second, composed in February 1695, was to Robert Cook of Cappoquin, county Waterford, who had left the Friends to embark on a more radical, "seeker"-like spiritual quest. Influenced by John Ansloe of Cambridge, Cook believed in the necessity of withdrawing from fellowship with all who in his mind were not guided by the Spirit and were disobeying God's commandments despite their profession of belief in the inner light. The church, he attested, could be known only by those who were truly its members. Strongly committed to religious freedom, he contended that the church had no business seeking to end controversies about conscience, nor was it to attempt to enforce conformity. As Ansloe argued, "the pope and prelates require conformity and force [people] to it, and So do others according to what power they have, but all is from a wrong ground." By extension this principle applied to the Friends, whom Cook therefore repudiated. He found their lives lacking with respect to their obedience to divine precepts, even among leading Quakers. In contrast, Cook believed he had been born of God and no longer sinned. As one who had found "the true Belief," he discovered that "the children of form" no longer accepted him because he did not conform to "the mode and fashion of congregated people." Cook was an extreme spiritualist engaged in solitary communion with God—or so he believed.[62]

In his two letters to Cook, Sharp advised him not to worry about a mote in a brother's eye when he had a beam in his own, an allusion to Matthew 7:3–5 and Luke 6:41–42. Why depart from the Friends, he asked, when Cook agreed with them as to the church's foundation principles?

> If thou hast been long since convinced of Truth and didst profess the Same amongst the people of God called quakers, how come thou to leave them? Did thou Immediately get to a better or was thou under the temptation of the world?

By denying outward congregations in order to worship God in spirit, Cook, averred Sharp, was repudiating the practice of Jesus, the apostles, and the primitive church. His departure from the Friends thus constituted a revolt, an act conducive to disorder and consequently opposed to "the God of order" and the true church. For Sharp, the godly have an indispensable duty "to keep to the power [of the Spirit] and attend on that and the good order of the Spirit and form and government of Christ." Sharp held out hope that Cook would accept these arguments, cease his backsliding, and return to the fold, for his tone in both letters was that of a man saddened to see a colleague delude himself by a quest for spiritual perfection in religious isolation.[63]

Cook apparently persuaded no other Friends to leave the movement, but the writings of John Reeve and his cousin Lodowick Muggleton did.

The first person to embrace Muggletonian views in Ireland was probably the former governor of Cork, Colonel Robert Phaire, who had met
Muggleton in London in 1661. Muggleton wrote to him in 1670, and
Phaire circulated his writings as well as Reeve's. When Edmundson at-
tended the provincial meeting in Cork following his trip to America in
1671, he found that some Quakers had "gone into the loose, foolish
Imaginations of Muggleton, and others, both out of England and of this
Nation, into Looseness, and the Liberty of their Wills and carnal Affec-
tions, from the Cross of Christ, and Self-denial, which caused great
Trouble and Difference among Friends" at Cork, Dublin, and elsewhere. Responding to a letter from the Cork meeting concerning the
Muggletonians, the half-yearly meeting expressed its unanimous detesta-
tion and repudiation of their tenets in May 1673. Sharp, then, would
have been cognizant of Muggletonian concepts no later than the spring
of 1673, and perhaps read Penn's attack on them in *The New Witnesses
Proved Old Hereticks* (1672).[64]

Around 1681 the Muggletonians seem to have gained a few more
converts from the Friends in Cork, but thereafter the movement waned,
particularly after the deaths of Phaire and George Gamble, an ex-
Quaker, in 1682. Of Muggletonians in Dublin very little is known,
which makes the relevant documents among the Sharp manuscripts all
the more valuable. Judging from Sharp's polemical exchanges with John
Turken (or Thacker) and Thomas Gascoigne in the 1690s, concern
among Irish Quakers about the Muggletonian challenge lasted somewhat longer than Kenneth Carroll has surmised.[65]

Two documents survive: an undated copy of Sharp's response to
Turken, to which Crabb assigned a date of 12 February 1694, and a
brief synopsis of another letter to Turken dated 22 February 1698. The
first letter records an exchange with Gascoigne, who refused to tell
Sharp if he believed Muggleton and Reeve were the two witnesses mentioned in Revelation 11; he indicated, however, that he would provide
an answer to those worthy of a full account. Nevertheless Gascoigne did
respond to Sharp's query about whether Muggletonians believe in the
free love of God in Christ to all people. They do not, he explained, because they maintain that God predestined the elect, on whom he be-
stows the ability to know the mysteries of the kingdom. Unbelievers, or
those who are not elect, are "of The divel by generation," are incapable
of trusting in God, and by nature refuse divine mercy. According to
Gascoigne, "God doth not desire the death of Sinners through adams
transgression, but those that became sinners by the original of their own

nature, God hath Decreed their damnation, and [there is] therefore no need to desire their death because decreed of God, being all one as if it were ready done." Christ died only for the elect, who are of the deity's seed and nature. Gascoigne further argued that there are two generations of people, one from the loins of Adam, whose soul is of God's seed and nature, and the other from the loins of Cain, whose soul is of the devil. The Jews who persecuted Jesus, the lord of life, came from Cain's generation.[66]

If Sharp chose to answer Gascoigne directly, the letter is not extant, but he did explain his objections at length to Turken, whom he hoped to dissuade from his embrace of Muggletonian tenets. Asserting that all people are the children of wrath by nature, Sharp maintained that God offers mercy to all and accepts anyone who fears him and lives righteously. Had Cain obeyed God, he would have been embraced like Abel. The atonement, Sharp declared, was not limited, for Jesus died for all, and those who deny him bring destruction on themselves. As in other controversies, Sharp was insistent that God, who is just, does not command anything that men and women cannot fulfil, nor does he desire anyone's destruction.[67]

Sharp took special care to make his case against the Muggletonian doctrine of predestination, insisting that God elected to salvation only those who obey Christ's light and spirit, shun the deeds of the flesh, and live a godly life. Those who fear God know his secrets, having "obeyed the drawings and invitations of christs light and spirit in their own hearts, which is given to all to repentance, to faith and to obedience that they may come to know God." Divine wisdom is thus available to any who choose to believe and is not restricted to a predetermined elite. Sharp rejected the Muggletonian doctrine of the two seeds or generations because, he opined, it has no biblical foundation. Indeed, the devil implants evil thoughts in people, making war against their souls, but his activity extends to believers as well as unbelievers. Through the indwelling Spirit all people have the capacity to resist the devil's advances, obey the Spirit, and thus be divinely chosen. Ultimate damnation is the result, in Sharp's judgment, of human choice. In arguing to the contrary, Muggleton and his disciples were blinded by a "dark Image and Imaginations," and were ignorant of Scripture and divine power. Consequently Muggletonians were not "of God or true witnesses of the Truth or messengers of Christ, but deceivers and deceived, and so growing worse and worse if they repent not." Despite this scathing condemnation, Sharp, as he so often did, held out hope that Muggletonians in general and Turken in particular would repent and embrace the inner light "before the visitation of Gods love to you be over."[68]

Like most leading Friends, Sharp did not shy from polemical debate. Indeed, his unmistakable interest in debating should caution us against assuming that the Friends had lost their commitment to sectarian disputation by the 1670s and 1680s.[69] Sharp was less erudite than Barclay and Penn, less prolific than George and John Whitehead. His readings were largely limited to the Bible, Foxe's *Acts and Monuments*, and leading Quaker authors, but he was also familiar with the Westminster Confession, the Larger Catechism, and the Book of Common Prayer. He did his homework before he entered debate. Not a systematic thinker, he nevertheless demonstrated an adequate degree of organization in his works, perhaps a reflection of his legal background and business acumen. Like most polemicists of his day, he did not hesitate to use *ad hominem* arguments, even when he must have known his charges were of dubious validity, as when he implied that the Muggletonians engaged in drunkenness, fornication, "uncleanness," and foolish conversation.[70] Yet he ultimately manifested no deep-seated hostility toward his opponents, holding out hope that they would denounce their false principles and follow the inner light. For all of his severity, Sharp was a man of compassion.

"To Be Seen and Read Forever"

IN SHARP'S FINAL YEARS the Quakers of Ireland found themselves facing challenges that stemmed from a more tolerant political and social atmosphere. The diminution of persecution and the concomitant decline in the confrontational spirit that had been so prominent in the movement's first four decades tended to blur the distinctions between the Friends and the rest of society. Growing material prosperity further contributed to a creeping accommodation between the Friends and the world. The Quakers' sustained effort in the 1690s and early 1700s to establish more rigorous standards of raiment and home furnishings was a reactionary protest against this drift as well as an attempt to preserve the Friends' pronounced sense of identity as a disjunctive socio-religious entity.

To some extent, of course, the Friends as a sect had always been sensitive to the importance of maintaining tension between themselves and worldly society, but in the 1690s and early 1700s a mounting concern is evident as more of their adherents became increasingly uncomfortable with temporal pursuits and material goals. In May 1690, amid the time of troubles, Ann Sharp and twenty-two other delegates to the national women's meeting expressed concern about declining attendance at meetings on Sundays and weekdays: "A neglect therein causeth much lukewarmness & deadness, so that by degrees the living sense of Truth comes to be lost." They worried as well about the "couldness & carelessnesse" of most people for religious matters.[1] Much of this was undoubtedly a consequence of the contemporaneous upheavals of the war and its attendant dislocations, but growing acceptance, prosperity, and materialism posed no less a threat in the post-revolutionary era. At the national meeting in May 1696, the delegates reflected on the spirit that

was "floating and flowing in the world," enticing people into covetousness and pride, darkening their understanding, and preventing them
from attaining an understanding of God's kingdom. In particular this
meeting concluded that Quakers who could "not bee restrained from
too much Running into the Encumbrances and great concerns of the
World" should not be "put upon Service in the Affaires of Truth." Although Sharp did not go to this meeting, at least in an official capacity,
he was one of the six representatives selected by the Dublin men's
meeting to attend the November session.[2] He was not one of those
whose success in the business world led him to compromise the Quakers' singular lifestyle.

Encroaching secularism sparked renewed interest in prophecies.
Sharp and Amos Strettell received a missive from Benjamin Coale recommending a Durham Friend who had forewarned the people of Bristol
to repent or God would subject their city to great earthquakes that
would cause it to sink into the earth, leaving only a pool of water in its
place. No record of Sharp's and Strettell's response seems to have survived, but Coale's letter may have contributed to the interest in prophecy evident among Irish Quakers by 1697. In November of that year the
six-months meeting asked Friends throughout the island to collect and
report on previous Quaker prophecies, indicating whether they had
been fulfilled. Some of these prognostications, the delegates noted, were
of recent vintage. Leinster Friends subsequently recounted that there
had been little in the way of recent prophecies in their province. Nevertheless, in May 1699 William Edmundson and others, writing on behalf
of the six-months meeting, reported to Irish Friends that many prophecies had lately been delivered, including some at that very gathering
which warned that a day of distress and mortality was imminent. In
light of the "timely warnings" that had preceded the time of troubles,
the delegates took the new round of prognostications seriously.[3]

Against this background, the Leinster provincial meeting issued a
general epistle in September 1698 warning of the great dangers stemming from the pursuit of temporal things and admonishing

> the Church of Christ to beware of the snares of that unwearied Enemy
> which he lays in secret, & baits with the lawful things of this World in this
> time of Ease and great Liberty. . . . He is striving to break in upon the People
> of our Society.

Those who succumb to worldly pursuits lust to be wealthy and influential, acquiring other people's property and causing Friends to be con-

demned for their perceived covetousness. This "Stumbles the minds of some that otherwise might joyn with us," inflicting injury on the church. The delegates unanimously decided they would be bound by the judgment of the provincial meeting or its elders if they were deemed to have exceeded their "Charge, Station, place and service." They were especially concerned by the extent to which some of their members had become engrossed in a quest for great buildings, fine raiment and furniture, and moneyed marriages.[4] In short, Edmundson, Sharp, and the other leaders of the Leinster Friends were gravely concerned about the extent to which some of their compeers were embracing bourgeois values.

The abatement of persecution and the growing accommodation with the rest of society made it more difficult to sustain the zeal and élan of the Lamb's War. So relaxed had the atmosphere become that people were falling asleep at meetings in Dublin in 1700. Six years later Thomas Rudd came from England to preach a prophetic message in the streets of Dublin concerning divine wrath on sinners. This was now apparently so unusual that he was incarcerated for three days.[5] Indeed, in April of the same year the Leinster meeting had complained that "a dullness and flatnesse is come over the minds and Spirits of too many, So that they are not so Zealously and rigorously concerned . . . neither for their own Souls good, nor for the promotion of Truth." The delegates went on to urge each monthly meeting to guard against "such a Spirit of Indifferency and Coolnesse."[6]

Encroaching secularism would have saddened Sharp, but so too must have two developments in his family life. The first of these was Isaac's decision in the late summer of 1700 to move to America. Although Anthony and Ann consented, at their ages they must have wondered if they would ever see him again. After the Dublin men's meeting duly granted Isaac's request for a certificate sanctioning his relocation, he sailed in late November on an arduous eighteen-weeks voyage. The master, Isaac later recounted, "proved very bad" and failed to fulfil his obligations; three passengers, five servants, and two crew members perished, and Isaac himself became very ill. But by 6 April he was safely ashore in Maryland, from where he wrote to his parents before traveling to Pennsylvania and ultimately to New Jersey.[7]

Eighteen months after Isaac sailed for America, his parents became ill, probably with influenza. As Anthony lay in one room, Ann called to him from another. He found her "in a Could Sweat," asking that he "petition" God on her behalf. Sensing the gravity of her condition, Anthony was "under a Concern that the Lord would give [him] a Sutable petition & offering," and this, he later recalled, "the Lord was pleased to grant." Spiritually comforted, she gave thanks "for that Renewed vissitation." These were her last words, and the following morning, 8 June 1702, she died, having been ill for approximately a week. She was interred in the Friends' burial ground by St. Stephen's Green.[8]

Sharp subsequently composed a warm, adulatory testimony to Ann, "a good & Carefull wife & one that had a good understanding, & a good help meet She was both in Spirittuall & Temporal things." He reflected on the pain she had suffered when some of their children perished and the trying times she had experienced because of Joseph's "wild" ways and disobedience. Concerned for her children's education, she had understandably wanted each of them to embrace the Friends' principles and lifestyle. He praised Ann for her unqualified support of his ministerial work, including his travels to England, Scotland, and the Netherlands as well as throughout Ireland. The closeness of their relationship is reflected by the "Sympathy & Sence" she manifested when he felt called to undertake these "labour[s] of Love." Although her physical constitution, in Anthony's judgment, was not strong, she assumed the responsibilities of a *pater familias* in addition to her own while Quaker business occupied him. The Dublin meeting's testimony to Ann echoed Anthony's assessment, praising her for "her carefull and prudent mannagment of their Family [which] made it the more easy for him to leave his Outward Concerns," for her "sober and Orderly Conversation," and for her service as "a true help mate to her husband."[9] Theirs was manifestly a solid marriage, firmly grounded in their common religious convictions, their abundant service to the Quaker movement, and the joys and sorrows they shared in raising their children.

Calling Ann his coworker, Anthony lauded her activities in the Quaker movement: "As She was Somtimes drawn forth in verball testimony in publike in meeting[s], Soe She was tender towards any that in Faith & tenderness was Soe Concerned, & yet She had a great Care not to Incouridge Imaginations & Impostures, or Such as would Impose them Selves Contreary to Christ, freinds Approbation, or unity." Although Ann was one of the most active women among Irish Friends, her work was undertaken without fanfare or ostentation. She never challenged the Puritans of Boston, as did Mary Fisher and Ann Austin, or sought to convert foreign potentates, as did Anne Gargill in Portugal or Fisher and Beatrice Beckly in the Ottoman Empire. Nor did she ever "go naked for a sign," as did Elizabeth Leavens at Kendal around 1654,

Elizabeth Fletcher at Oxford about the same time, Deborah Buffum at Salem in 1662, and the newly married Lydia Wardell at a Quaker meeting at Newbury in the early 1660s. Regrettably, Ann Sharp did not keep a journal, as did Joan Vokins, Elizabeth Stirredge, Alice Hayes, and Deborah Bell.[10] Nevertheless, she was regularly a signatory of documents issued by the national women's meeting as well as an active member of the Dublin women's group, and especially in her later years her voice was heard as these bodies conducted Quaker business. According to the Dublin meeting's testimony to her, "towards the Latter part of her time shee was concerned to bear a publick Testimony in meetings, in which tho' shee was not very large, yet what shee delivered was weighty and to the purpose, appearing to have a deep sence and a good understanding of what shee Expressed." In dealing with other women she used her own spiritual experience to good effect, garnering recognition for her ability to blend sensitivity and firmness in counseling others. In the apt words of the meeting's testimony, "shee had a large Capacity and was of a good understanding, being very serviceable in helping to mannage Truths Affaires in Womens meetings, for shee was tender over that which was good, and not for Encouraging the wrong part in any, haveing gon under Exercises her selfe, so shee did simpathize with those who were Exercised, especially such as were concerned in a publick Testimony, tho shee was against Intruders, and any that would be too forward in that weighty concern."[11]

Anne was, then, a woman who experienced substantive spiritual struggles—her "Exercises"—and who was sympathetic with the doubts and concerns that other tender souls underwent. Simultaneously, she was protective of the Quaker movement, particularly her own meeting, reacting negatively to those who thrust themselves into its affairs without undergoing an appropriate spiritual experience. Like her husband, she seems to have had a flair for administrative tasks, hence the praise she received for helping to manage the group's affairs. In effect, she was a committeewoman, not a leader, nor is there any evidence that she was either charismatic or an eloquent speaker. To have survived the deaths of so many of her children she must have had considerable emotional strength, as indeed she must have been physically strong to undergo sixteen pregnancies. Unquestionably committed to her faith, her husband, and her family, she manifested substantial strength of character.

As the news of Ann's death spread, Thomas Trafford wrote movingly to Anthony of the "great loss." Trafford had shared a spiritual bond with Ann—further evidence of the close ties that linked the Sharps with the Quaker community in the Wicklow area. "She was one with whose spirit I had dear unity and fellowship in the truth because of her soundness of wisdom and understanding in it," Trafford reflected. Although his own health was not good, he expressed regret that he had known nothing of the Sharps' illness and had therefore been deprived of the opportunity to travel from Wicklow to Dublin to comfort them. Now, he said, "my Spirit . . . truly tenders my heart which draws tears of Sorrow from my eyes for the want of her here."[12]

Advancing age had already begun to reduce Sharp's activities on the movement's behalf in the decade preceding Ann's death, but her demise and possibly a lingering weakness from his own illness further curtailed his work. As we have seen, he was still traveling fairly widely as a public Friend in the late 1690s: to the Netherlands in 1695, to Ulster, Scotland, and northern England in 1696, probably to England in 1699, and to Ulster in 1700. In the same period he was characteristically active in numerous endeavors: editing testimonies to deceased Friends, helping to draft reports on Irish Quakers for submission to the yearly meeting in England, making provisions for the new burial ground near Dolphin's Barn, participating in the protests of Irish Friends against the affirmation, and joining with Penn, Story, and Rooke to refute John Plimpton's Ten Charges. He was the principal keeper of the Leinster provincial meeting's accounts through November 1695, and he assisted again in January 1697. He was still distributing Quaker books in the late 1690s, and in 1700 he advised the lord mayor-elect of Dublin on the city's governance. As the new century dawned, he contributed to an account of the Quakers' rise and progress in Dublin and continued his efforts to persuade the authorities to repress the traditional violence against Friends during the Christmas season. On the eve of Ann's death he and Amos Strettell assisted Elizabeth Jerry of London in her quest to recover an Irish estate, searching legal documents, dispersing financial aid, and preparing a written account of their efforts.[13] Such service was typical of the way in which he had so often employed his expertise on behalf of fellow Friends.

Although Sharp's activities abated following Ann's death, he was still involved in the affairs of the Quaker school in Dublin as late as 1704 as well as the activities of the Dublin meeting, including the vetting of potential new members and the maintenance of records. In the summer of 1705 he even volunteered to travel to Drogheda as part of a visitation team.[14] He also remained active in the affairs of the weavers' guild virtually to the end of his life.

Sharp's health began to fail in the fall of 1706. In October the Dublin men's meeting asked him and William Allen to speak to Robert Davis regarding allegations that the latter had impregnated a woman, but in early November someone else was assigned this responsibility. By this point Sharp was physically unable to attend meetings, and he was not part of the Quaker delegation that conferred with magistrates on 17 December. During his final illness "hee seemed very much Resigned to the Will of the Lord, and would severall times say that if hee had any desire that his life might bee prolonged, it was that hee might be serviceable to Truth and friends, and that hee might see his Children Settled, for whom hee had a great concern, and often took Occasion tenderly to express his mind, to those of them who were with him."[15] Of his death on 13 January 1707 Thomas Wight recorded only that "at length, having been very serviceable among friends for many years, and finished his course, he laid down his head in peace."[16] He was interred in the Quaker burial ground adjacent to St. Stephen's Green, "being accompanied by friends of this Citty, some out of the Country, and a great Concourse of other people." The scene must have been reminiscent in many ways of the London funerals of noted nonconformist leaders attended by sizable numbers of people of differing religious views. Clearly Sharp continued to command widespread respect beyond the bounds of the Quaker community. On 26 April the Leinster meeting tersely reported to the national assembly: "One Publick friend deceased. Anthony Sharp."[17] In his journal William Edmundson made no specific reference to Sharp's demise, though he noted his sadness in 1707 at the deaths of Quaker leaders: "My Spirit was deeply affected with Sorrow, in that most of our Elders were taken away from us, who used to attend the Service of such Meetings."[18] Sharp died as he had lived, in simplicity and without fanfare, his substantial wealth, social standing, and prominence notwithstanding.

He had signed his last will on 4 October 1706, though he appended codicils on 11 and 28 October, and on 3 and 8 January 1707. The principal beneficiary was his son Isaac. After revoking Wiltshire lands previously given to Isaac, Anthony bequeathed to him more than 2,000 plantation-acres at Killinure, Lackagh, and Lea in the barony of Upper Ossory, Queen's County, and at Boyle, Clarahill, Upper Coolnamony, "Ballintyne," and "Coolysane" in the barony of Tinnahinch, also in Queen's County.[19] The actual acreage appears to have been much greater than the will indicates, for in 1725 the Clarahill and Upper Coolnamony lands alone comprised nearly 610 acres of profitable land, almost 785 acres of wasteland, and a "town." A deed of 1731 indicates that Killinure, which Anthony Sharp had purchased from Thomas Starkey (Sharkey) of Abbeyliex, comprised 1,700 acres, of which approximately 1,000 were adjudged profitable. The property at Killinure, informally called Friends Town, included houses and other buildings as well as mills. When Isaac leased the property that year to John Duffield, gentleman, he agreed to roof the main house with slate, glaze the windows, and repair the chimney, stable, "Cowhouse," barn, oat kiln, and mills.[20] Anthony also bequeathed to Isaac his lands in West New Jersey, half his property in East Jersey, the largest item of plate, and £200 from outstanding debts, and he granted Isaac's wife a jointure of £40 *per annum* or the moiety of designated farms. Altogether, Crabb estimated that Isaac had inherited estates worth at least £10,000, though he had acquired some of them while his father was alive.[21]

To his son Joseph, a widower,[22] Sharp bequeathed his property at The Lea and Cleverton, Wiltshire, and a quarter of his lands in East New Jersey. Joseph also received the second largest piece of plate and money from outstanding debts.[23]

Anthony gave his son Daniel, who was unmarried, approximately 350 acres at Clonaheen (near Mountmellick) in the barony of Tinnahinch, Queen's County, a quarter of his lands in East Jersey, his houses at Ormond's Gate, and approximately twenty-three houses in Meath Street, Cole's Alley, Elbow Lane, and Marrowbone Lane in Dublin. The Clonaheen grant, as described in 1712, included a village with barns, stables, gardens, orchards, and a meadow; in addition to 350 acres of profitable land, the grant encompassed contiguous bog. Daniel leased Clonaheen to a Dublin gentleman in 1720 for £78 15s. *per annum*.[24] The houses that Daniel inherited in Dublin ranged from substantial to modest, but none appear to have been dwellings inhabited by the poor. The merchant Edmund French, for example, leased a "large Dwelling Ballcony house," with backhouses and garden, in Meath Street adjoining the Quaker meetinghouse, and the merchant Samuel Brogdon rented "the Mansion House, Backside & Ware House" in Cook Street formerly occupied by a brewer. Among the other leasees in the 1710s were merchants, a worsted comber, a surgeon, cordwainers, a feltmaker, a hotpresser, and a slater. At least some houses had access to city water.[25] To Daniel, Anthony also gave half the remaining plate, money from outstanding debts, a green bed and its furnishings, and most of his other goods.[26]

Sharp's only surviving daughter, Rachel, who was also unwed, in-

herited Aghameelick, Clonbrock, and "Faumor" in the barony of
Coolestown, King's County,[27] as well as six houses in Pimlico Street,
Dublin; the remaining plate; £20 in cash and £100 from outstanding
debts; a blue bed and its furnishings, chairs, half the damask linen, and
all the furniture in a new chamber with wainscoting. Rachel and Daniel
would not receive possession of their landed estates until they married
or attained the age of twenty-one, whichever came first. In the event
that Rachel died before her husband and without surviving children, her
spouse would inherit the estate only if she had wed with the consent of
Sharp's executors and overseers.[28]

Others inherited little. Anthony's brother William received permission to live rent-free in his house as long as he lived, and his daughters
Mary (Hodges) and Elizabeth each received £10.[29] So too did Sharp's in-
laws, Rachel and Jane Crabb. In the final codicil, Sharp bequeathed £20
for his daughter Rachel to raise Ann Crabb, who was still a child. His
servant Ruth, who was first remembered in the third codicil, received a
mere £2. Sharp's reluctance to make large donations to the indigent
during his life was reflected in his will, which provided only £10 to poor
Friends in Dublin; the men's meeting distributed this money in October
1707, giving 10s. 10d. apiece to six men and the remainder to fourteen
women, nine of whom were widows.[30] He left another £5 to needy
Quakers in Tetbury.[31]

As late as July 1708 no testimony about Sharp's life had been recorded; hence the Dublin men's meeting appointed Roger Roberts, John
Chambers, George Rooke, and Amos Strettell to peruse the material
submitted by Thomas Ashton and Samuel Baker and draft one. The
meeting heard the testimony on 7 September, after which Thomas
Banks duly recorded it. Bearing the signatures of thirty-eight men, including such stalwarts as the Strettell brothers, Rooke, Roberts, Thomas
Bell, and Joseph Thomas, it summarized his service to Quakers, notably
his hospitality, his assistance to those who suffered for their refusal to
pay tithes, his provision of relief to the needy, and his travels as a public
Friend to England, Wales, Scotland, Schleswig, and parts of Germany.
On those sojourns, the testimony noted, "he was very carefull not to
make the Gospel chargeable, but being truely content with his Lords
Allowance to Eat what was sett before him, not shewing in the least any
uneasiness when his Entertainment hapned to bee otherwise then what
hee was accustomed to." His religious convictions clearly governed his
demeanor. The official testimony described his conversation as honest,
sober, and clean.

> There was no just Cause to reproach Truth on his behalfe, [he] being very carefull to avoid needlesse Company keeping, or to be Leavened into the Spirits of those hee conversed with by too much Familiarity with them. But on the contrary [he] would take occasion to discourse of the Principles of Truth, or some Religious subject, whereby they might be diverted from those vain discourses that are too frequent in many Companies.

Zealous in his desire to convince others of Quaker tenets, he impressed his colleagues as a man with a good mind and plain speaking.[32]

For the most part, Sharp was a generous man, not only with his money, as reflected in his substantial donations to the Friends over the years (especially for buildings), but also with his time and energy, as manifested by his keeping of meeting accounts, his involvement with the Quaker school in Dublin, and the myriad documents he drafted for the Friends. Included in these documents were numerous petitions, some of which survive only as undated summaries in Crabb's calendar. They range from petitions on behalf of all Irish Friends, such as one to Ormond and the Council seeking a respite from persecution for refusal to pay tithes and thanking them for "the great Kindnesses they had often received from them in releiveing them from Several troubles," to pleas for individual Quakers, such as John Harrison's pregnant wife, who had been incarcerated for refusing to pay tithes before she was married.[33] When necessary Sharp not only wrote appeals but also appeared in court on behalf of imprisoned Friends. He directed petitions to a variety of officials, including the lord lieutenant, the lord chancellor, the barons of the Exchequer, the primate of Ireland, and the archbishop of Dublin.[34] Among some officials he enjoyed considerable respect. Crabb refers to a petition by Sharp to the lord chancellor on behalf of Joseph Boardman, who had been excommunicated under the wrong name, which thus became the basis of an appeal. Sharp persuaded the chancellor to refer the case to the bishop of Kildare, who in turn forwarded it to several justices of the peace in the Edenderry area, where the petitioner resided, "soe redy was the Government to Serve Anthony in those dayes in order to releive his distressed Breathren." Respect came as well from his fellow Friends, who acknowledged his ability to proffer substantive advice to suffering Quakers more effectively than many others.[35]

Sharp's efforts to assist his fellow Friends are reflected as well in several vignettes recorded by Crabb. In 1672, for instance, Sharp tried (unsuccessfully) to reconcile a father and a son after the latter had been banished from the family home for becoming a Quaker. On another occasion Sharp tried to locate several parcels of goods removed from the house of one of his comrades following the latter's death. When the Quaker Joseph Webb drowned in 1696 with 95½ guineas in his shoes, his companions sought Sharp's help. After a "Narrow Search and Enquiry" among the fishermen who found Webb's body, Sharp recovered 65½ guineas.[36]

Apart from the grief sustained when members of his family died, especially his son Jonathan and his second wife Ann, and the pain and frustration stemming from the rebellious ways of his son Joseph, clues about Sharp's emotional state are rare. A letter from an unidentified Quaker at Wicklow, which Crabb dated 1701, refers to an especially trying time for Sharp:

> Thy exercises hath been very great, the Lord hath given thee much pacyence, but he hath suffered thee to be tryed acordingly. . . . O who but thee could have gon through what thou hast don. . . . Be not discouraged. . . . The Lord will plead thy cause to the confounding of thy Enimies in his own time.[37]

These difficulties stemmed from Joseph's defiance of his parents, but even greater trials lay immediately ahead for Sharp owing to the deaths of Jonathan and Ann.

Through all his trials a faith firmly rooted in biblical principles sustained Sharp. A lengthy letter to George Fox composed around January 1678 is replete with Old Testament imagery, some of it militant in tone. He envisioned the church as emerging from the wilderness, "the Lords Camp numberless, . . . reach[ing] from Cannaon, Wherein Many are entered, to Egypt Where many are Marching Out." Abundant, he asserted, were the enemies who opposed the church's march. Faithful Moses was afflicted with troubles and opposed by some of his brethren, but General Joshua would lead the Hebrews to victory in their battles and take them into the promised land. Sharp visualized Fox in a similar light, calling him "a pillor in the house of God." This vivid sense of religion as a war in which the godly would ultimately triumph was fortified by Sharp's readings in Foxe's *Acts and Monuments*. Yet Sharp's sense of Christianity as spiritual combat was less pronounced than that of Edward Burrough, who referred to his preaching tours as "campaigns" and "warfare," and whose biographer depicted him as "a soldier in arms, fighting the Lord's battles." Nor was Sharp, his trips as a public Friend notwithstanding, a skilled evangelizer like Burrough, who, with Francis Howgill, for example, led a meeting of some 5,000 at Bristol in May 1656.[38]

At root, Sharp was also different in important respects from Fox. Larry Ingle has painted the latter's portrait as a man of charisma and determination as well as "a prig who took himself . . . very seriously."[39] Perhaps Ingle would also depict Sharp as priggish, for he too believed in the rightness of his ways and pursued a lifestyle characterized by rigid behavioral constraints. Like Fox, Sharp was resolute, but he was in no sense charismatic. Moreover, whereas Fox took himself very seriously, Sharp focused on the movement of which he was a part, never apparently seeing himself as the leader even of the Dublin Quakers, let alone those throughout Ireland. There was substantially less egoism in Sharp than in Fox, and partly for that reason it has been easier to overlook the former's role in the growth and shaping of Irish Quakerism. Equally important in this respect was Sharp's decision not to write a journal, a decision that itself underscores his suppressed egoism and his submersion in the movement's activities. In contrast, Fox utilized his journals to depict himself as the originator and moving force of Quakerism, virtually marginalizing the roles of other early leaders.[40] Nor is there evidence that Sharp, unlike Fox,[41] altered his letters with a view to posterity. Sharp wrote no narrative detailing the growth and organization of the Quaker movement in Ireland, though he helped to collect material for such a history as well as accounts of the Friends' suffering. By not composing a history he eschewed an opportunity to document his own contribution and place it in historical context. That he failed to do so is neither the result of a lackadaisical attitude toward Quaker affairs nor a reluctance to write in defense of Quaker principles. Sharp also differed from Fox in his willingness to participate in civic government and in his extensive involvement in guild affairs, establishing relationships in both areas that contributed to the Quakers' gradual acceptance by those outside the movement. He was part of the new wave of Quaker leaders—commercial and professional men such as Penn, Claypoole, George Whitehead, and Ellis Hookes—who were slowly supplanting "the more rough-hewn rustics from the north and west."[42] Edmundson, though he outlived Sharp, belonged to this first generation of rustic Quaker leaders.

Remarkably energetic, Sharp was both a tireless worker on behalf of the Friends' business and an eager polemicist, though hardly a gifted writer, an intellectual, or a theologian. He was a good committee man, organizer, secretary, and financial officer, not an outspoken, egocentric, and brilliant leader such as Fox or a charismatic oracle such as Nayler. Unlike the latter, Sharp had no unusual attraction for women, nor did he envision himself as a sufferer to the degree Nayler did. One detects hints of vanity in Sharp, as in his preference to donate heavily to building funds rather than indigent relief. Like most Quaker leaders, he was not afraid of controversy, as witnessed by his exchanges with John Plimpton and James Barry, ex-Quakers and Muggletonians, and Roman Catholics, Anglicans, and Presbyterians. His disputes involved other prominent Friends as well, among them William Edmundson, Samuel Clarridge, Abraham Fuller, Thomas Winslow, and James Fade. Such quarrels notwithstanding, for the most part he was a mediating force, both within the Quaker movement and between Friends and the authorities of church and state. Over time he enjoyed access to many in the circles of power, both state and municipal, and it was only fitting that those who mourned him at his death included many outside the Quaker movement. Had more city and guild records survived, his biography undoubtedly would have more effectively reflected his involvement in commercial and civic affairs. His extant letters are overwhelmingly religious, but is this because Crabb opted not to save or calendar business correspondence?

The trials to which the godly were subjected came from within the Quaker movement as well as without, and in this context Sharp enunciated a resolute conviction of the necessity of subordinating the individual to the group. The community was preeminent. In January 1680, we recall, John Edwards had sought Sharp's advice after various Quakers rejected his testimony and refused to engage in religious fellowship with him. Noting that he had no power to compel the parties to settle their differences, Sharp counseled Edwards to assume a more humble posture and to yield to the group's wisdom. In Sharp's estimation, both sides were at fault, and Edwards must consequently accept his duty to submit to the provincial and national meetings in accord with apostolic doctrine. When Crabb calendared this letter, he reflected that Sharp himself had experienced similar opposition, and that he had applied this counsel to his own circumstances.[43] Indeed, Sharp's role in the Quaker movement is distinguished in this regard from that of Samuel Clarridge, who more than once resisted conformity to the church. Sharp's periodic disaffection with Clarridge stemmed primarily from the latter's reluctance to accept communal authority. Like Fox, Sharp embraced such authority at the expense of individualism.[44]

Sharp offered spiritual guidance of a more general nature, as in a letter to an unidentified Friend. He encouraged this person not to forget God's love, but simultaneously warned him, "in the Fear and dread of the Lord," that the time of death and reckoning was imminent.[45] Most of his letters, however, dealt with specific issues or problems, normally at the behest of a meeting.[46] His spiritual counsel is effectively encapsulated in his advice to his nephew Thomas to "be . . . concerned in differances as Litle as posable, but be as much as may be At peace with all & in Cleanness & Rightiousness, Truth, Justice, Mercy & humileity."[47]

Sharp's primary contribution to the Quaker movement in Ireland involved its transformation from a sect into a protodenominational church. I have argued the case for such an evolution in more general terms elsewhere.[48] The early Quakers embodied characteristics of two of the fundamental sectarian types identified by Bryan Wilson, namely the revolutionary, because they opposed the contemporary social order and espoused rapid conversion, and the thaumaturgical, because they stressed the experiential operations of the indwelling Spirit.[49] As a sect, they were a voluntary organization that accepted members according to clearly stated criteria, preserved a marked sense of self-identity, claimed to defend and propagate supernatural truths, and insisted on allegiance to their movement rather than competing groups. In the decades after 1660 the Friends made the transition to a protodenomination, slowly restraining their revolutionary ardor though preserving their thaumaturgical emphasis.

According to Wilson, denominationalism entails less rigor, a decreased sense of dissent, a closer relationship to other Christians, and a softening of claims that the sect's teachings are indispensable for salvation. The transition from sect to denomination is hindered if the group believes in imminent divine intervention or that withdrawal into a sanctified community is necessary to avoid evil. On the other hand, evolution into a denomination is spurred by the acquisition of a professional ministry or, in the case of the Quakers, public Friends and administrators. The process of the Quakers' evolution from sect to denominational church was one of rationalization through the development of institutional means to promulgate their message, nourish their converts, uphold their veteran members, and preserve their traditions. A denomination embodies both an institutionalized religious authority, which controls access to the perceived good (acceptance by and fellowship with the divine), and an agency structure, which comprises organizational units that typically provide education, collect and disburse funds, and publish material. Moreover, in contrast to a sect, a denominational church has a greater awareness of and determination to preserve its traditions, and it is therefore less likely to respond positively to the "revelations" of charismatic leaders. It also has a multiregional network of ministers or leaders (public Friends), whose activities foster a strong sense of common ideals. Denominational churches typically establish their own schools, disciplinary systems, and means to train and vet their leaders. All these characteristics developed among Irish Friends in the late seventeenth century. In one area, however, the Quakers made less progress. The stronger the organization, the more it can embrace within itself disparate theological, ethical, and behavioral strains, but Irish Quakers, like their colleagues in England, were unable to accommodate the Story-Wilkinson tradition, the mediatory efforts of Sharp notwithstanding.[50] In every other characteristic, the Quakers in Ireland evolved into a protodenominational church during the years of Edmundson and Sharp's leadership. More than any other Irish Friend, they were responsible for this development, particularly the process of institutional rationalization. Without this development the Friends might have been hopelessly fragmented by what Barry Reay has aptly termed "the anarchical implications of the doctrine of the light within."[51]

Indeed, Sharp was at the core of the Quaker movement in Ireland. Isabel Grubb appropriately regarded him as "perhaps the most influential member of the Society who has ever lived in Dublin." Among his correspondents were many influential figures in late seventeenth- and early eighteenth-century Quaker history: Fox, Edmundson, Penn, Burnyeat, Sansom, Turner, Gregson, Katherine Evans, James Parke, Thomas Curtis, and William Bingley. For the most part, the letters discuss the spiritual estate, though some deal with business concerns, such as £140 that Edmundson wanted to loan at 8 percent interest for the benefit of his children with Sharp's help. Other missives are concerned with the experiences of traveling Friends, such as Robert Stepney, who reported on the debauchery of Hamburg's residents.[52]

The Sharps generously provided hospitality to visiting Friends. While Ann was in England in the spring of 1676, Anthony was host to twenty Quakers at dinner, at least some of whom were preparing to sail, probably to England or America. Following their visits to Dublin, Friends such as Evans, Sansom, Parke, John Kilburn, Edward Edwards, Mary Worrell, Christopher Bacon, Mary Young, and Thomas Wynne wrote to the Sharps expressing gratitude.[53] Katherine Norton (née McLaughlin) reflected warmly on Sharp's "tenderness and Godly Simplicity," while Sansom expressed hope that they would never forget one another, "but that we may be epistles of Love in one anothers hearts, not written with Ink and paper but with the spirit of the Lord to be seen and read for ever."[54]

Those who visited the Sharps and the Quaker community in Dublin were most impressed with the strong sense of spiritual communion—"the refreshments I have felt in you," as Wynne phrased it, or the Sharps' "tender love and Large respects" in Evans' words.[55] Sharp's social prominence and wealth, his business and legal acumen, his enormous capacity for work, and his financial contributions were crucial factors in his role as a leader of the Dublin Friends, but perhaps none of this would have mattered had he not also been a profoundly spiritual man who led by example.

Reference Matter

Abbreviations

ASD	"An Account or Schedule of the Deeds, Leases and Writings Belonging to the Friends of Dublin, & Some Other Parts of This Kingdom . . ."
BAD	Book of Accounts of the Corporation of the City of Dublin, 1650–1717
Banks	John Banks, *A Journal of the Life, Labours, Travels, and Sufferings* (London, 1712)
Besse	Joseph Besse, *A Collection of the Sufferings of the People Called Quakers*, 2 vols. (London, 1753)
BFW	"A Booke for Freinds That Meet About Wills & Inventoryes"
Braithwaite	William C. Braithwaite, *The Second Period of Quakerism*, 2nd ed., rev. by Henry J. Cadbury (Cambridge: Cambridge University Press, 1961)
Burnyeat	John Burnyeat, *The Truth Exalted in the Writings of That Eminent and Faithful Servant of Christ John Burnyeat* (London, 1691)
CARD	*Calendar of the Ancient Records of Dublin, in the Possession of the Municipal Corporation of That City*, ed. John T. Gilbert, vols. 4–5 (Dublin: Joseph Dollard; London: Bernard Quaritch, 1894–1895)
CSPD	*Calendar of State Papers, Domestic*
DCA	Dublin City Archives
DF	Historical Library of the Society of Friends in Ireland, Dublin
DMM	Minutes of the Dublin Men's Meeting

Edmundson, *Journal*	William Edmundson, *A Journal of the Life, Travels, Sufferings and Labour of Love in the Work of the Ministry*, 2nd ed. (London, 1774)
Fuller and Holme, *Compendious View*	S[amuel] Fuller and T[homas] Holme, *A Compenious View of Some Extraordinary Sufferings of the People Call'd Quakers, Both in Person and Substance, in the Kingdom of Ireland* (Dublin, 1731)
GBS	Great Book of Sufferings, Friends' Library, London
Gilbert, *History*	John T. Gilbert, *A History of the City of Dublin*, 3 vols. (Dublin, 1854–59; repr. Shannon: Irish University Press, 1972)
GLD	Gilbert Library, Dublin
Goodbody, "Sharp"	Olive M. Goodbody, "Anthony Sharp: A Quaker Merchant of the Liberties," *Dublin Historical Record* 14 (1955): 12–19
Greaves, *God's Other Children*	Richard L. Greaves, *God's Other Children: Protestant Nonconformists and the Emergence of Denominational Churches in Ireland, 1660–1700* (Stanford, Calif.: Stanford University Press, 1997)
Grubb, *Quakers*	Isabel Grubb, *Quakers in Ireland, 1654–1900* (London: Swarthmore Press, 1927)
Hatton	Helen E. Hatton, *The Largest Amount of Good: Quaker Relief in Ireland, 1654–1921* (Kingston and Montreal: McGill-Queen's University Press, 1993)
Holme and Fuller, *Brief Relation*	T[homas] H[olme] and A[braham] F[uller], *A Brief Relation of Some Part of the Sufferings of the True Christians, the People of God (in Scorn Called Quakers) in Ireland* (1672)
HYNM	Minutes of the Half-yearly National Meeting, Ireland
Ingle, *First Among Friends*	H. Larry Ingle, *First Among Friends: George Fox and the Creation of Quakerism* (New York: Oxford University Press, 1994)
JFHS	*Journal of the Friends Historical Society*
Kilroy	Phil Kilroy, *Protestant Dissent and Controversy in Ireland, 1660–1714* (Cork: Cork University Press, 1994)
LF	Library of the Religious Society of Friends, London
LurMM	Minutes of the Lurgan Men's Meeting
LPM	Minutes of the Leinster Provincial Meeting
LYM	Minutes of the London Yearly Meeting

MBP	*The Minutes of the Board of Proprietors of the Eastern Division of New Jersey*, 3 vols., ed. George J. Miller (Perth Amboy, N.J.: Board of Proprietors of the Eastern Division of New Jersey, 1949, 1960)
MDA	Minutes of the Dublin Aldermen ("Monday Booke")
MMM	Minutes of the Moate Men's Meeting
NAD	National Archives, Dublin
NLI	National Library of Ireland, Dublin
NWM	Minutes of the National Women's Meeting, Ireland
PA	Poor Accounts, Dublin Monthly Meeting, 1700–1720
PCM	Parliamentary Committee Minutes, Half-Yearly National Meeting, 1698–1731
Penn, *Irish Journal*	William Penn, *My Irish Journal, 1669–1670*, ed. Isabel Grubb (London: Longmans, Green, 1952)
Penn, *Papers*	*The Papers of William Penn*, ed. Mary Maples Dunn, Richard S. Dunn, et al., 5 vols. (Philadelphia: University of Pennsylvania Press, 1981–87)
Pike	Joseph Pike, *Some Account of the Life of Joseph Pike of Cork, in Ireland, Who Died in the Year 1729, Written by Himself*, ed. John Barclay (London: Darton and Harvey, 1837)
PMHB	*Pennsylvania Magazine of History and Biography*
PRONI	Public Record Office of Northern Ireland, Belfast
QH	*Quaker History*
RDD	Registry of Deeds, Dublin
RDDAW	*Registry of Deeds, Dublin, Abstracts of Wills*, vol. 1 (1708–1745), ed. P. Beryl Eustace (Dublin: Stationery Office, 1956)
RSAI	Royal Society of Antiquaries in Ireland
SDMM	Sufferings, Dublin Monthly Meeting, 1660–1780
Sharp MSS	Anthony Sharp Manuscripts, Library of the Religious Society of Friends in Ireland, Dublin
SLPM	Sufferings, Leinster Provincial Meeting, 1656–1701
Stockdale	William Stockdale, *The Great Cry of Oppression* (n.p., 1683)
Swarthmore MSS	Swarthmore Manuscripts, Library of the Religious Society of Friends, London

TDM	Testimonies [to Deceased Ministers] from 1661
TestCD	Testimonies of Condemnation and Denial, Dublin Monthly Meeting
Underwood	Ted L. Underwood, *Primitivism, Radicalism, and the Lamb's War: The Baptist-Quaker Conflict in Seventeenth-Century England* (New York: Oxford University Press, 1997)
UPM	Minutes of the Ulster Provincial Meeting
Vann and Eversley	Richard T. Vann and David Eversley, *Friends in Life and Death: The British and Irish Quakers in the Demographic Transition, 1650–1900* (Cambridge: Cambridge University Press, 1992)
Wight	Thomas Wight, *A History of the Rise and Progress of the People Called Quakers, in Ireland, from the Year 1653 to 1700*, rev. by John Rutty, 4th ed. (London, 1811)
WWP	Richard S. Dunn and Mary Maples Dunn, eds., *The World of William Penn* (Philadelphia: University of Pennsylvania Press, 1986)

Notes

Chapter 1

1. Sharp MSS, S1, fols. 1–2; H. P. R. Finberg, *Gloucestershire Studies* (Leicester: Leicester University Press, 1957), p. 66; N. M. Herbert, ed., *A History of the County of Gloucester*, vol. 11 (Oxford: Oxford University Press for the Institute of Historical Research, 1976), pp. 154, 261, 273, 279–80.

2. Herbert, *Gloucester*, 11: 258–59, 261–62, 269, 271, 273, 277.

3. Sharp MSS, S1, fols. 2 (quoted), 4–5 (quoted); Herbert, *Gloucester*, 11: 278–79, 281; William Page, ed., *A History of the County of Gloucester*, vol. 2 (London: Constable, 1907), pp. 438–39.

4. Sharp MSS, S1, fols. 5–6.

5. Sharp MSS, S1, fol. 6; S3, fols. 36–37; NLI, Records of Births, Marriages, and Deaths (Carlow, Cork, and Dublin), Microfilm POS 1021.

6. Sharp MSS, S1, fols. 6–7 (quoted), 198 (quoted); Herbert, *Gloucester*, 11: 280; Public Record Office, State Papers 29/178/55, 57, 115, 115.1. Dewsbury was in prison for refusing to take the oath of allegiance.

7. Sharp MSS, S1, fols. 2–3 (quoted), 8; S9, fol. 26v (quoted). For the importance of silence in Quaker worship see Richard Bauman, *Let Your Words Be Few: Symbolism of Speaking and Silence Among Seventeenth-Century Quakers* (Cambridge: Cambridge University Press, 1983).

8. Ingle, *First Among Friends*, pp. 24–25, 41–43; Hugh Barbour, "The 'Openings' of Fox and Bunyan," in *New Light on George Fox (1624 to 1691)*, ed. Michael Mullett (York: William Sessions, n.d.), pp. 129–43.

9. Sharp MSS, S1, fol. 9; S4, fol. 8r (quoted).

10. Sharp MSS, S6, fol. 38r–v.

11. Peter Somerville-Large, *Dublin* (London: Hamish Hamilton, 1979), p. 117; *CARD*, 5: 479–80, 574.

12. Sharp MSS, S4, fol. 8r; Goodbody, "Sharp," p. 14; Gilbert, *History*, 1: 183–84; Maurice Craig, *Dublin, 1660–1860*, rev. ed. (London: Penguin, 1992), p. 7. A sense of Clarridge's wealth can be gained from debts owed to him in 1677 in the amount of £300 and £700 by James Attkinson, a gentleman of

county Louth, and Walter Motley, a Dublin merchant, respectively. DCA, Registers of Statute Staple, 1664–1678, fols. 181v, 182v.

13. Anthony Sheehan, "Irish Towns in a Period of Change, 1558–1625," in *Natives and Newcomers: Essays on the Making of Irish Colonial Society, 1534–1641* (Dublin: Irish Academic Press, 1986), p. 97; William Petty, *Further Observation upon the Dublin-Bills*, 2nd ed. (London, 1686), pp. 1–2; David Dickson, "The Place of Dublin in the Eighteenth-Century Irish Economy," in *Ireland and Scotland, 1600–1850: Parallels and Contrasts in Economic and Social Development*, ed. Dickson and T. M. Devine (Edinburgh: John Donald, 1983), p. 179; L. M. Cullen, *An Economic History of Ireland Since 1660* (London: B. T. Batsford, 1972), p. 19; Cullen, *The Emergence of Modern Ireland, 1600–1900* (London: Batsford, 1981), p. 29; Gilbert, *History*, 2: 165; Desmond Clarke, *Dublin* (London: Batsford, 1977), p. 32; Patrick Fagan, *The Second City: Portrait of Dublin, 1700–1760* (Dublin: Branar, 1986), p. 15; S. J. Connolly, *Religion, Law, and Power: The Making of Protestant Ireland, 1660–1760* (Oxford: Clarendon Press, 1992), pp. 146–47, 160. Petty calculated that only 974 dissenters, including Catholics, lived in Dublin in 1682. *Further Observation*, pp. 5–6.

14. BAD, fols. 404r, 577v, 590v; Grubb, *Quakers*, p. 44; Gilbert, *History*, 1: 330–44; *The Flying Post* (2 October 1704).

15. Gilbert, *History*, 1: 165–67; Somerville-Large, *Dublin*, pp. 127, 132, 136, 146–47; Craig, *Dublin*, pp. 4, 47; MDA, fols. 102v, 106v, 108v; BAD, fols. 324v–325r, 529r; RSAI, Book Generall, fol. 114v; CARD, 5: 452 (quoted), 457; J. Warburton, J. Whitelaw, and Robert Walsh, *History of the City of Dublin from the Earliest Accounts to the Present Time*, 2 vols. (London: T. Cadell and W. Davies, 1818), 1: 225. The city hosted a major feast for Ormond, the nobility, and the gentry to celebrate the completion of the Tholsel's reconstruction. BAD, fols. 451r–452r.

16. CARD, 4: 468; BAD, fols. 304r, 324v, 326r, 337r, 504r, 518r, 542r, 557r, 565r, 604v; *Narrative, and an Accompt, Concerning the Hospital on Oxmontown Green, Dublin* (Dublin, 1673), sig. b2r, pp. 7, 18, 54 (quoted); Gilbert, *History*, 1: 326; 2: 66–68, 71; Craig, *Dublin*, pp. 10–11, 14–15, 19–20, 22–24; Clarke, *Dublin*, pp. 27–28, 30. For a contemporary depiction of Dublin see Rolf Loeber, "An Unpublished View of Dublin in 1698 by Francis Place," *Quarterly Bulletin of the Irish Georgian Society* 21 (January–June 1978): 7–15.

17. Somerville-Large, *Dublin*, pp. 137–38; CARD, 5: 114, 212; Fagan, *Second City*, pp. 59, 74–83, 87–88; David Cressy, *Bonfires and Bells: National Memory and the Protestant Calendar in Elizabethan and Stuart England* (Berkeley: University of California Press, 1989), pp. 171–87; BAD, fols. 302r–v, 324r, 329r, 349r, 368r, 37?r, 392v, 410r, 459r, 460r.

18. MDA, fols. 55r, 30r.

19. Vann and Eversley, pp. 47–48; HYNM, 2: 305; Kilroy, p. 90; Hatton, p. 34. In 1680, 780 Irish Quaker householders recorded their names in the Great Book of Tithes. Of these, forty-nine, including ten women, were from

Dublin. John M. Douglas, "Early Quakerism in Ireland," *JFHS* 48 (Spring 1956): 31.

20. LF, Swarthmore MSS 4/238; Edmundson, *Journal*, pp. 58–59 (quoted). Cf. Isabel Grubb, "The Settlement of Church Discipline Among Irish Friends," *JFHS* 45 (Autumn 1953): 75–77; Douglas, "Early Quakerism in Ireland," p. 30; Wight, pp. 115–16, 118.

21. George Fox, *The Journal of George Fox*, ed. Norman Penney, 2 vols. (Cambridge: Cambridge University Press, 1911), 2: 136–39; *Narrative Papers of George Fox*, ed. Henry J. Cadbury (Richmond, Ind.: Friends United Press, 1972), pp. 144–45, 181 (quoted); Ingle, *First Among Friends*, pp. 224–25; Wight, pp. 117–19; Sharp MSS, S4, fol. 8v; "Record of Friends Travelling in Ireland, 1656–1765," *JFHS* 10 (July 1913): 162. A member of the Richmond meeting in Yorkshire, Lodge had preached in Ireland with Burnyeat in 1659–60. Burnyeat, pp. 27–29; Braithwaite, pp. 260, 302; Fox, *Journal*, ed. Penney, 2: 412–13; Kenneth L. Carroll, "Quakerism in Connaught, 1656–1978," *JFHS* 54 (1979): 188. For Stubbs' testimony see LF, Portfolio 16, no. 58. For Briggs see LF, Portfolio 17, no. 1. Lancaster accompanied John Banks on a preaching tour of Ireland in 1694. Banks, p. 135.

22. "Record of Friends Travelling in Ireland," pp. 158–59; Wight, pp. 119–20; GBS, vol. 2, Connaught Province, Galway, 1669; Besse, 2: 476; Carroll, "Quakerism in Connaught," p. 189; Fuller and Holme, *Compendious View*, p. 126.

23. Penn, *Irish Journal*, pp. 21, 26–27, 66; Penn, *Papers*, 1: 106, 109. Penn stayed at Gay's house in Dublin, and Gay served as Penn's agent in London in 1669–70. Penn's colleague was probably the John Gay to whom substantial sums of money were owed in the 1670s, specifically £500 by the gentleman Thomas Nowell of county Kilkenny, £500 by Philip Savage and Richard Ryves of Dublin, and £800 by Daniel Abbott of the same city. Penn, *Irish Journal*, p. 68; DCA, Registers of Statute Staple, 1664–1678, fols. 137r–v, 161v, 171v.

24. TestCD, fols. 6–7 (quoted). See Carroll, "Thomas Loe, Friend of William Penn and Apostle to Ireland," in *Seeking the Light: Essays in Quaker History in Honor of Edwin B. Bronner*, ed. J. William Frost and John M. Moore (Wallingford and Haverford, Penn.: Pendle Hill Publications and Friends Historical Association, 1986), pp. 66, 70.

25. See Carroll, "Sackcloth and Ashes and Other Signs and Wonders," *JFHS* 52 (1975): 314–25. At Brough, near Carlisle, Robert Huntington wore a white sheet in a parish church to prophesy that the surplice would be reintroduced (p. 323). See also Carroll, "Quaker Attitudes Towards Signs and Wonders," *JFHS* 54 (1977): 70–84.

26. Cf. Hugh Barbour, "Quaker Prophetesses and Mothers in Israel," in *Seeking the Light*, ed. Frost and Moore, pp. 41, 44–47.

27. Sharp MSS, S1, fols. 39–45.

28. Sharp MSS, S1, fols. 48–52.

29. MDA, fol. 96r (quoted); BAD, fol. 334v; CARD, 5: 12. Maine had been imprisoned for five weeks in 1669 for attending a conventicle in the Bride Street

meetinghouse. GBS, vol. 2, Leinster Province, Dublin, 1669. A William Main, carpenter, pledged £1 for the construction of the hospital at Oxmantown; he may have been the Quaker of the same name. *Narrative, and an Accompt*, p. 12.

30. Cullen, *Economic History*, pp. 13, 23–24; Raymond Gillespie, *The Transformation of the Irish Economy, 1550–1700*, Studies in Irish Economic and Social History 6 (1991): 28, 41, 46; David Dickson, *New Foundations: Ireland, 1660–1800* (Dublin: Helicon, 1987), p. 46; J. G. Simms, *Jacobite Ireland, 1685–91* (London: Routledge and Kegan Paul; Toronto: University of Toronto Press, 1969), p. 14.

31. Grubb, *Quakers*, pp. 46–47; Simms, *Jacobite Ireland*, p. 14; Goodbody, "Sharp," pp. 16–17; Sharp MSS, S1, fols. 9–10; R. S. Mortimer, "Early Irish Friends in the Records of Bristol Meeting," *JFHS* 48 (Autumn 1956): 70; *Minute Book of the Men's Meeting of the Society of Friends in Bristol, 1667–1686*, ed. Russell Mortimer, Publications of the Bristol Record Society, vol. 26 (1971), p. 201.

32. Cullen, *Economic History*, p. 14; Sharp MSS, S1, fol. 76 (quoted); S3, fol. 44 (numbered 6).

33. Sharp MSS, S1, fols. 28 (quoted), 32–33, 37–39 (quoted), 43, 46–47 (quoted).

34. E. Margaret Crawford, "Subsistence Crises and Famines in Ireland: A Nutritionist's Views," in *Famine: The Irish Experience, 900–1900, Subsistence Crises and Famines in Ireland*, ed. Crawford (Edinburgh: John Donald, 1989), pp. 198–99; L. A. Clarkson, "Conclusion: Famine and Irish History," in *Famine*, ed. Crawford, p. 227; John Walter and Roger Schofield, "Famine, Disease and Crisis Mortality in Early Modern Society," in *Famine, Disease and the Social Order in Early Modern Society*, ed. Walter and Schofield (Cambridge: Cambridge University Press, 1989), p. 33; Cullen, *Economic History*, pp. 14–15, 21–22; Cullen, "Economic Development, 1691–1750," in *A New History of Ireland*, vol. 4: *Eighteenth-Century Ireland, 1691–1800*, ed. T. W. Moody and W. E. Vaughan (Oxford: Clarendon Press, 1986), pp. 132–35. The nineteenth-century statistician William Wilde did not record any famines between 1651–52 and 1690. "William Wilde's Table of Irish Famines 900–1850," ed. Crawford, in *Famine*, ed. Crawford, p. 11.

35. Sharp MSS, S1, fol. 49 (marked 37).

36. Sharp MSS, S1, fol. 49 (marked 37).

Chapter 2

1. Sharp MSS, S3, fol. 32 (quoted); S1, fols. 55–56 (quoted); Grubb, *Quakers*, p. 44.

2. Sharp MSS, S1, fol. 57.

3. Sharp MSS, S1, fol. 58.

4. Robert Barclay, in *Diary of Alexander Jaffray*, ed. John Barclay, 2nd ed. (London: Darton and Harvey, 1834), p. 295; Danial Abraham, quoted in Isabel Ross, *Margaret Fell: Mother of Quakerism*, 2nd ed. (York: William Sessions Book Trust, 1984), p. 315; Sharp MSS, S1, fols. 59–60; Barry Levy, *Quakers*

and the American Family: British Settlement in the Delaware Valley (New York: Oxford University Press, 1988), p. 72 (quoted).

5. Sharp MSS, S1, fols. 61-65 (quoted); S8, fols. 23r-v, 27r-v.

6. Sharp MSS, S1, fols. 66-70 (quoted at 67-68 and 70); S8, fols. 28r-v, 30r-31v.

7. Sharp MSS, S1, fol. 67; S8, fol. 24v.

8. Sharp MSS, S1, fols. 71-73; S8, fols. 25r-26v. The steps leading to the marriage conformed to the procedures approved by the half-yearly meeting in Ireland on 5 November 1672. HYNM, 1: 12-13.

9. Sharp MSS, S1, fol. 74.

10. Sharp MSS, S8, fols. 22r-v, 29r-v (quoted); S1, fols. 74-75 (quoted).

11. Sharp MSS, S3, fols. 36-37; Vann and Eversley, pp. 134, 136, 158-61, 240, 243, 246. Among a sampling of Friends in the middle colonies during the eighteenth and early nineteenth centuries, the average family included 5.69 children, and the average interval between first and second births was 21.38 months. J. William Frost, *The Quaker Family in Colonial America: A Portrait of the Society of Friends* (New York: St. Martin's Press, 1973), p. 70.

12. Sharp MSS, S3, fols. 36-37; S5, fol. 68v; S6, fol. 26r; S7, fol. 36r; NLI, Records of Births, Marriages, and Deaths (Carlow, Cork, and Dublin), Microfilm POS 1021.

13. NWM, fols. 54, 98.

14. Sharp MSS, S2, fols. 49-50 (quoted); S8, fol. 38r; LPM, fols. 280, 465, 471, 551/251, 565/265; HYNM, 2: 33, 349-50; NWM, fol. 99; LF, Swarthmore MSS 5/115, fol. 13 (quoted); DMM, 3: 68v (quoted). Gunson was heavily in debt, necessitating intervention in his financial affairs by the Dublin men's meeting. DMM, 3: 69v.

15. LPM, fols. 372, 486/186 (quoted); HYNM, 2: 39 (quoted), 314; LF, Swarthmore MSS 5/115, fol. 15.

16. LPM, fols. 283, 510/210; Sharp MSS, S2, fols. 47-48 (quoted); S3, fol. 3; S8, fol. 46r-v.

17. Sharp MSS, S2, fols. 49, 51, 53 (quoted), 54; S8, fols. 39v, 40r-v (quoted), 41r, 43r-v, 45v, 54v; Braithwaite, pp. 525-32.

18. Sharp MSS, S2, fols. 45-46, 48, 53, 54-55 (quoted); S8, fols. 36r-v, 37r-v (quoted), 40r-41r, 43r, 45r-v, 51r.

19. Sharp MSS, S2, fols. 68-69; S3, fols. 3-5 (quoted). For the traveling ministry of Quaker women see Catherine M. Wilcox, *Theology and Women's Ministry in Seventeenth-Century English Quakerism* (Lewiston, N.Y.: Edward Mellen Press, 1995), pp. 240-44. In the eighteenth century Quaker women journeyed to England from the American colonies to minister. Margaret Hope Bacon, "Quaker Women in Overseas Ministry," QH 77 (Fall 1988): 93-109. Bacon's reference to gender equality was not true of Irish Friends during Sharp's lifetime except in a strictly spiritual sense; the women's meetings were clearly subordinate to the men's.

20. Sharp MSS, S2, fols. 69-70; S3, fols. 4, 7-9 (quoted).

21. Sharp MSS, S2, fols. 45-48, 54-55; S8, fols. 36r-37v, 43r-v, 45r, 46r-v.

22. Sharp MSS, S3, fols. 11–13 (quoted at fol. 12). For other testimonies see Sharp MSS, S3, fols. 13–29; S13, fols. 8v–18v.

23. Sharp MSS, S8, fols. 33r, 36r, 37v, 40r–v (quoted), 44r–46v, 53v, 54v; S2, fols. 48, 52, 55, 75–76. See the Epilogue for Sharp's will.

24. Sharp MSS, S8, fols. 33r, 34r (quoted), 37v (quoted).

25. Sharp MSS, S8, fols. 34r (quoted), 54r (quoted).

26. DMM, 3: 270v–272r (quoted); Sharp MSS, S8, fol. 45r (quoted); cf. S8, fol. 40v. For Abel Strettell see CARD, 5: 534. Inman was an executor of the will of Thomas Wilson, a member of the Edenderry meeting, a farmer of Lenamarran, King's County (Offaly), and the owner of more than 1,000 acres in Pennsylvania. RDDAW, 1: 141–42. For Ashton see NAD, MS D18500. For Inman see RSAI, Book Generall, fol. 216r.

27. Sharp MSS, S3, fols. 36–37; S8, fols. 33r, 36r–37v, 54r–v (quoted).

28. Lawrence Stone, The Family, Sex and Marriage in England, 1500–1800, abridged ed. (New York: Harper Colophon Books, 1979), Chap. 9.

29. LPM, fols. 33, 54, 56; HYNM, 1: 63–64, 78; DMM, 1: 43–45, 199–201, 217; 3: 85v–86r, 91v–92r; 4: 230.

30. Sharp MSS, S1, fols. 79–80 (quoted); Grubb, Quakers, pp. 46–47.

31. Sharp MSS, S1, fols. 81–82. In 1682–83 Crabb temporarily strayed from the Quaker fold. DMM, 1: 170–71, 207.

32. S. J. Connolly, "Family, Love and Marriage: Some Evidence from the Early Eighteenth Century," in Women in Early Modern Ireland, ed. Margaret MacCurtain and Mary O'Dowd (Edinburgh: Edinburgh University Press, 1991), pp. 278–88. Penn similarly espoused a companionate view of marriage and thought wives should be treated as partners. Some Fruits of Solitude in Reflections and Maxims Relating to the Conduct of Human Life (London, 1693), pp. 27, 32–33, 36. Margaret Fell had companionate marriages with both of her husbands, as did Joseph Pike with his wife, Elizabeth née Rogers. Bonnelyn Young Kunze, Margaret Fell and the Rise of Quakerism (Stanford, Calif.: Stanford University Press, 1994), pp. 7–8, 31–32, 54, 57; Pike, p. 7.

Chapter 3

1. Greaves, God's Other Children, pp. 358–62. Fuller himself was jailed for four weeks in Dublin in 1660 and again at Cork in 1661. Besse, 4: 466; LF, Swarthmore MSS 5/91. See also "Record of Friends Travelling in Ireland, 1656–1765," JFHS 10 (July 1913): 161. Holme subsequently emigrated and became surveyor-general of Pennsylvania. Fuller was later described as a farmer of Lehinch, King's County (Offaly). NAD, MS D18500.

2. Sharp MSS, S4, fols. 17–18.

3. Banks, pp. 34–35, 37–44; "Record of Friends Travelling in Ireland," p. 162. For Tiffin see Braithwaite, p. 302 n. 1.

4. Banks, pp. 45–46.

5. Fuller and Holme, Compendious View, p. 88; "Record of Friends Travelling in Ireland," p. 161. In 1684 or 1685 Trafford accompanied James Dickinson on a preaching tour in Munster. Dickinson, "A Journal of the Life, Travels,

and Labours of Love, in the Work of the Ministry, of . . . James Dickinson," *The Friends' Library*, vol. 12 (Philadelphia: Joseph Rakestraw, 1848), pp. 373–74. See also Wight, p. 117.

6. Sharp MSS, S1, fols. 22–25.

7. Sharp MSS, S4, fols. 15 (quoted), 92; Stockdale, p. 21.

8. HYNM, 1: 8; Sharp MSS, S2, fol. 97. Clarridge, Savage, and others had been jailed for five weeks in 1669 for attending a conventicle in the Bride Street meetinghouse. GBS, vol. 2, Leinster Province, Dublin, 1669. For efforts in England similar to Sharp's see Craig W. Horle, *The Quakers and the English Legal System, 1660–1688* (Philadelphia: University of Pennsylvania Press, 1988), chap. 5.

9. LPM, fols. 42–43, 46; HYNM, 1: 34–35.

10. Sharp MSS, S1, fols. 112–15.

11. LPM, fols. 47–48, 50, 60; Sharp MSS, S4, fol. 91; HYNM, 1: 43; UPM, fol. 22. Cf. HYNM, 1: 29 for Sharp's involvement on Elizabeth Lancaster's behalf in 1674.

12. Greaves, *God's Other Children*, pp. 113–30.

13. HYNM, 1: 57, 71–72, 74–76, 79–80; Sharp MSS, S2, fols. 6, 86, 95–96; LPM, fols. 105, 108, 123–24; Sharp MSS, S8, fols. 14r–15r; Fuller and Holme, *Compendious View*, pp. 85–86. Rogers had been imprisoned at Cork in 1661. LF, Swarthmore MSS 5/91. John Watson traveled in Ireland as a Quaker minister. Norman Penney, ed., *'The First Publishers of Truth': Being Early Records (Now First Printed) of the Introduction of Quakerism into the Counties of England and Wales*, JFHS, Supplements 1–5 (1907), p. 53; "Record of Friends Travelling in Ireland," p. 161. Samuel Watson was still boldly testifying in 1700 against "Greedy shepherds" who preached for money and demanded tithes. LF, Crosfield MSS 1: 16.

14. LPM, fol. 127 (quoted); Sharp MSS, S2, fol. 8 (mismarked 9).

15. Edmundson, *Journal*, pp. 122–24 (quoted); Wight, p. 135; *Statutes of the Realm*, 3: 751 (quoted); Sharp MSS, S2, fol. 8 (mismarked 9).

16. Sharp MSS, S2, fols. 119–20; LPM, fols. 112, 118. Cf. Sharp MSS, S2, fol. 8 (mismarked 9). For Wasly see MMM, fols. 33v, 34v, 56r; Wight, p. 108. In 1685 Wasly's son William behaved inappropriately with a Gaelic Irish woman and beat a young man in the marketplace at Moate. MMM, fol. 27v. England had been arrested three times in 1661 and imprisoned for attending illegal meetings at Mullingar, county Westmeath. Holme and Fuller, *Brief Relation*, pp. 14–15.

17. Sharp MSS, S2, fol. 6; LPM, fols. 119, 132, 148; HYNM, 1: 81, 83, 85–86, 89. In 1662 Taylor had been imprisoned at Wexford for approximately twelve weeks for recusancy. Holme and Fuller, *Brief Relation*, p. 43.

18. HYNM, 1: 85–86.

19. Sharp MSS, S2, fol. 152; S4, fols. 99–100; S5, fols. 1–2, 17–18; Richard T. Vann, *The Social Development of English Quakerism, 1655–1755* (Cambridge, Mass.: Harvard University Press, 1969), pp. 98–101; Banks, pp. 33–35, 62–64; Edmundson, *Journal*, pp. 59–60. The importance of certificates was un-

derscored in 1683 when a man named Foster fraudulently claimed in county Meath that the Dublin Quakers had given him £30 to preach among them and an additional £50 to send him overseas to preach. This fell through, Foster averred, after Sharp saw him leave "a Mass house." The Dublin meeting denied any knowledge of Foster, and Sharp claimed he did not know the man. TestCD, fols. 85–86.

20. Sharp MSS, S4, fols. 23–24, 54. At least 355 public Friends reportedly visited Ireland between 1695 and 1720. Richard S. Harrison, "Spiritual Perception and the Evolution of the Irish Quakers," in *The Religion of Irish Dissent, 1650–1800*, ed. Kevin Herlihy (Dublin: Four Courts Press, 1996), p. 73.

21. Sharp MSS, S5, fols. 4–5, 71r–v (quoted); S8, fol. 13r–v.

22. Wight, p. 192. For a sketch of Wight's life see ibid., pp. 279–81.

23. LPM, fols. 80, 132; DMM, 1: 50; Sharp MSS, S6, fol. 16r.

24. Sharp MSS, S2, fols. 102(2)–104 (quoted); S1, fols. 180(1)–181 (quoted).

25. Sharp MSS, S1, fols. 175–78.

26. Sharp MSS, S1, fols. 182–84. Cf. S4, fol. 98.

27. Sharp MSS, S1, fols. 185–86.

28. Sharp MSS, S1, fol. 187 (numbered 162; quoted); S5, fols. 9–10 (quoted).

29. Sharp MSS, S5, fols. 7r–8r (quoted); DMM, 1: 13–14 (quoted); HYNM, 1: 52–53. Cf. Sharp MSS, S5, fol. 1; S2, fols. 143–44.

30. Sharp MSS, S2, fol. 105.

31. HYNM, 1: 36–38, 44; Sharp MSS, S1, fols. 188–89. For Marshall see Minutes of the Lisburn Monthly Meeting, entry for 27 October 1692.

32. Greaves, *God's Other Children*, pp. 281–82.

33. Sharp MSS, S1, fols. 106–11; S4, fols. 3–7.

34. Sharp MSS, S5, fols. 19–20, 21–24 (quoted).

35. Sharp MSS, S5, fols. 26–27 (quoted); HYNM, 1: 57.

36. Sharp MSS, S8, fols. 20r–21v.

37. Sharp MSS, S8, fols. 18r–19v (quoted); S2, fol. 5.

38. Sharp MSS, S5, fols. 48 (quoted), 64 (quoted); cf. fol. 56.

39. Sharp MSS, S6, fols. 6r–7r (quoted); S7, fols. 24r–26v.

40. Geoffrey F. Nuttall, *The Holy Spirit in Puritan Faith and Experience* (Oxford: Basil Blackwell, 1946), pp. 16–18; Nigel Smith, *Perfection Proclaimed: Language and Literature in English Radical Religion, 1640–1660* (Oxford: Clarendon Press, 1989), pp. 192–205.

41. Smith, *Perfection Proclaimed*, pp. 109, 217 (quoted). In the 1650s Solomon Eccles, William Bayly, and other early Friends had endorsed Boehme's teachings, but in 1678 the morning meeting thought Behmenists had mixed "Light and Darkness." Luella M. Wright, *The Literary Life of the Early Friends, 1650–1725* (New York: Columbia University Press, 1932), p. 104. Boehme was popular among Quakers or their spiritual kin in the Netherlands in the 1670s. *The Short Journal and Itinerary Journals of George Fox*, ed. Norman Penney (Cambridge: Cambridge University Press; New York: Macmillan, 1925), p. 325.

42. DMM, 1: 137–40 (quoted); TestCD, fol. 89. In 1692 the Friends returned Marshall's monetary donation to the Dublin meeting because he had attended a "steeplehouse" service in Chester and taken an oath. DMM, 3: 37v–38r, 47v–48r.

43. DMM, 1: 152 (quoted), 155–58, 162, 164; TestCD, fols. 87–91 (quoted).

44. Sharp MSS, S2, fol. 1.

45. HYNM, 1: 83. The scribe did not record the substance of the allegations.

46. Sharp MSS, S9, fols. 23r–v. Reader, who had been mayor in 1670, was a justice of the peace in 1674, and he served in the same capacity a decade later. He was also appointed coroner in January 1684. Around 1680 he was one of the visitors of the free school at Drogheda, and before his death in 1690 he served as city treasurer. MDA, fols. 76r, 107v, 118r; *Council Book of the Corporation of Drogheda*, vol. 1, ed. T. Gogarty (Dundalk: County Louth Archaeological and Historical Society, 1988), p. 195; Mary Clark, "List of Principal Inhabitants of the City of Dublin, 1684," *Irish Genealogist* 8 (1990): 49.

47. Sharp MSS, S9, fols. 23v–25v.

48. LYM, 1: 98, 121, 133; Burnyeat, pp. 75–77 (quoted).

49. Greaves, *God's Other Children*, pp. 120–22.

50. CARD, 5: 233; LPM, fol. 124.

51. Sharp MSS, S8, fol. 2v (quoted); Greaves, *God's Other Children*, pp. 125–31; Burnyeat, p. 78 (quoted).

52. Bodleian Library, Carte MSS 168, fol. 155 (quoted); Burnyeat, pp. 78–79 (quoted); Wight, pp. 136–37; SDMM, fols. 24r–25r (quoted); Carte MSS 218, fol. 490r (quoted).

53. Burnyeat, p. 81; SDMM, fol. 25r.

54. HYNM, 1: 87; LYM, 1: 154; Burnyeat, p. 82.

55. HYNM, 1: 88. Cf. LPM, fol. 150; Fuller and Holme, *Compendious View*, pp. 58, 85–86.

56. Sharp MSS, S2, fols. 83–84.

57. David Cressy, *Bonfires and Bells: National Memory and the Protestant Calendar in Elizabethan and Stuart England* (Berkeley: University of California Press, 1989), pp. 46–49; Huntington Library, MSS HA 14,499; Sharp MSS, S5, fol. 74v; DMM, 2: 17–20.

Chapter 4

1. Greaves, *God's Other Children*, pp. 133–41; CSPD, 1685, p. 29; J. G. Simms, *Jacobite Ireland, 1685–91* (London: Routledge and Kegan Paul; Toronto: University of Toronto Press, 1969), p. 43; HMC 36, Ormonde, n.s., 8: 343.

2. Sharp MSS, S8, fols. 2v–3r (quoted); Edmundson, *Journal*, p. 129; Burnyeat, pp. 86–87 (quoted), 90. From Marlborough, Wiltshire, Sharp wrote to his wife in April 1685 about the persecution of Friends in England. Sharp MSS, S2, fol. 9 (mismarked 10).

3. "George Fox to Friends in Ireland, 1685," *JFHS* 7 (December 1910): 181.

4. LPM, fol. 155 (quoted); HYNM, 1: 92.

5. LPM, fols. 169, 176; Sharp MSS, S6, fols. 17r–v, 22r–23v; S2, fol. 10; "Record of Friends Travelling in Ireland, 1656–1765," *JFHS* 10 (July 1913): 162. See also UPM, fol. 81. Boate was affiliated with the Mountmellick meeting. Vann and Eversley, p. 49. In 1662 Randall was excommunicated for more than two years at Wexford for recusancy and failure to have his children christened. Holme and Fuller, *Brief Relation*, p. 33. For Brownlow see PRONI, MS D/2224/1; UPM, fol. 23; Wight, p. 81. Sharp was still assisting an unidentified Friend—possibly Brownlow—on behalf of the Ulster provincial meeting in February 1687. UPM, fol. 84. Hull had been imprisoned in 1669 for visiting incarcerated Quakers. Holme and Fuller, *Brief Relation*, p. 22.

6. "Sir Paul Rycaut's Memoranda and Letters from Ireland, 1686–1687," ed. Patrick Melvin, *Analecta Hibernica* 27 (1972): 155, 157, 175; HMC 36, *Ormonde*, n.s., 8: 346–47, 350; Sharp MSS, S2, fol. 9 (misnumbered 10); Simms, *Jacobite Ireland*, p. 43. For the agrarian crime associated with the Houghers see S. J. Connolly, "Law, Order and Popular Protest in Early Eighteenth-Century Ireland: The Case of the Houghers," in *Radicals, Rebels and Establishments*, ed. Patrick J. Corish (Belfast: Appletree Press, 1985), pp. 51–68; Connolly, "The Houghers: Agrarian Protest in Early Eighteenth Century Connacht," in *Nationalism and Popular Protest in Ireland*, ed. Charles H. E. Philpin (Cambridge: Cambridge University Press, 1987), pp. 139–62; Donald E. Jordan, Jr., *Land and Popular Politics in Ireland: County Mayo from the Plantation to the Land War* (Cambridge: Cambridge University Press, 1994), pp. 39–40.

7. Sharp MSS, S6, fols. 28r–29r.

8. HMC 36, *Ormonde*, n.s., 8: 350; DMM, 2: 115, 117–18; Sharp MSS, S2, fols. 82–83 (quoted); LF, Portfolio 16, #25. John Edmundson, who was affiliated with the Mountmellick meeting, had been excommunicated and imprisoned in 1663 for refusing to pay tithes. Besse, 2: 466; Holme and Fuller, *Brief Relation*, p. 31.

9. Besse, 2: 483 (quoted); HYNM, 1: 100.

10. Sharp MSS, S9, fol. 10r–v. In 1662 Tottenham had been fined £5 and jailed "a long time" for refusing to take an oath as high constable at the Wexford sessions. Holme and Fuller, *Brief Relation*, p. 47.

11. LF, Portfolio 16, #25 (quoted); HYNM, 1: 100, 102–4. For Hillary see LPM, fol. 276. In 1694 Cuppage (or Cuppaige) represented Wexford as a trustee for the Meath Street meetinghouse. LPM, fol. 291. In his will, signed on 5 December 1708, Cuppage is identified as a gentleman of Lambstown, county Wexford. His executors were Henry Hillary and Amos and Abel Strettell, and his overseers included John Watson, John Barcroft, and Thomas Wilson. RDDAW, 1: 2–3. For Calvert, from whom the Irish seized goods worth more than £95 during the time of troubles, see UPM, fol. 104; PRONI, MS D/2224/1. For Amos Strettell see CARD, 5: 534.

12. HYNM, 1: 102.

13. Sharp MSS, S2, fols. 12, 13, 95, 110–11; Wight, p. 275.

14. DMM, 2: 76, 78.

15. DMM, 2: 58–59, 64–66, 81–83.

16. CARD, 5: 426; CSPD, 1687–89, pp. 48, 49, 75; DMM, 2: 131, 134.

17. CARD, 5: 449; HMC 36, Ormonde, n.s., 8: 351; Simms, Jacobite Ireland, p. 35; LYM, 1: 201; LF, Barclay MSS 1/103; [William King], The State of the Protestants of Ireland Under the Late King James's Government, 4th ed. (London, 1692), p. 230 (quoted). The government appointed some Friends as justices of the peace. Robert H. Murray, Revolutionary Ireland and Its Settlement (London: Macmillan, 1911), p. 65.

18. Besse, 2: 483; LF, Barclay MSS 1/103 (quoted). Cf. Grubb, Quakers, p. 49. Grubb suggests that Sharp may have loaned money to James II. Isabell Grubb, "Irish Friends' Experiences of War, 1689–92," Friends' Quarterly Examiner (1916): 172.

19. HYNM, fols. 1: 103 (quoted), 105 (quoted).

20. Sharp MSS, S6, fols. 30r–31r. On 12 November Edmundson had written to Fox, expressing concern that the new Quaker magistrates were "like to meet with tryels." LF, Barclay MSS 1/103.

21. Sharp MSS, S6, fols. 32r–34v.

22. LPM, fol. 199; HYNM, 1: 107.

23. CARD, 5: 452 (quoted), 457, 459, 465–66, 486.

24. CARD, 5: 479–80, 487–88.

25. CARD, 5: 459, 461–62; MDA, fol. 115r–v. Clarridge's signature does not appear in the minutes.

26. BAD, fols. 248r, 431r, 439r, 444r, 454r–455v, 468r, 469r, 479v, 484v, 493v, 499v, 512r, 520r, 526r, 532v–533r, 541v, 548v–549r, 555v–556r, 563r–v, 569r, 575v–576r, 587v–588r.

27. BAD, fols. 457v–465r passim.

28. BAD, fols. 457r–466r passim, [567A]r. An additional 40s. was spent to arrest other malefactors whose offenses were unspecified. Ibid., fol. 457v.

29. BAD, fols. 457r, 459r, 460r–v, 462v, 465v–466r.

30. BAD, fol. 463r.

31. L. M. Cullen, An Economic History of Ireland Since 1660 (London: B. T. Batsford, 1972), pp. 22–23; CARD, 4: 459; David Dickson, "In Search of the Old Irish Poor Law," in Economy and Society in Scotland and Ireland, 1500–1939, ed. Rosalind Mitchison and Peter Roebuck (Edinburgh: John Donald, 1988), p. 150.

32. MDA, fols. 104v, 108v–109r; CARD, 5: 457–58, 477. The municipal government also provided relief to a small number of indigent people, including widows, a mentally ill woman in Bridewell, and poor prisoners. Sometimes this aid included grants to bury the indigent, and in 1701–1702 funds were dispensed to relieve seamen who had been captured, presumably by the French. BAD, fols. 457r, 458v, 465r, 466r, 489r–v, 490v, 524v, 559v.

33. CARD, 5: 485–86.

34. Sharp MSS, S2, fol. 117.

35. CARD, 6: 90, 179, 218; Dickson, "In Search of the Old Irish Poor

Law," pp. 150–51; BAD, fol. [567A]v; J. Warburton, J. Whitelaw, and Robert Walsh, *History of the City of Dublin from the Earliest Accounts to the Present Time*, 2 vols. (London: T. Cadell and W. Davies, 1818), 1: 226.

36. *CARD*, 5: 472–73; DCA, Roll of Freemen, 1: 194; 4: 79.

37. Sharp probably served as an alderman until the spring or early summer of 1690. On 7 July of that year Sir Humphrey Jervis and ten other men informed William III that they had been removed as aldermen when James revoked the traditional charter. They had now resumed the exercise of their responsibilities and sought the king's approval. MDA, fol. 117r.

38. *HMC 36, Ormonde*, n.s., 8: 356–57, 359; G. H. Jones, "The Irish Fright of 1688: Real Violence and Imagined Massacre," *Bulletin of the Institute of Historical Research* 55 (November 1982): 148–53; Burnyeat, p. 17; *The Journal of John Stevens: Containing a Brief Account of the War in Ireland, 1689–1691*, ed. Robert H. Murray (Oxford: Clarendon Press, 1912), pp. 11–12; Raymond Gillespie, "The Irish Protestants and James II, 1688–90," *Irish Historical Studies* 28 (November 1992): 128–33.

39. LYM, 1: 195; NWM, fol. 81; LPM, fol. 209; Burnyeat, pp. 17 (quoted), 93; Pike, p. 50.

40. Sharp MSS, S8, fol. 4v; *Tudor and Stuart Proclamations, 1485–1714*, vol. 2: *Scotland and Ireland*, ed. Robert Steele (Oxford: Clarendon Press, 1910), p. 128 (#1009); *HMC 36, Ormonde*, n.s., 8: 359–60; Simms, *Jacobite Ireland*, pp. 54–55. As the fortunes of war turned, Catholics in Dublin were ordered to surrender their weapons in 1690, but the response was poor. Not far from the Sharps' house, prisoners of war were interned in the Catholic chapel near St. Audoen's arch beginning in September 1690. MDA, fol. 119r–v.

41. Sharp MSS, S6, fols. 40r–42v, 45r–v; S8, fol. 4v (quoted).

42. *HMC 36, Ormonde*, n.s., 8: 358; *Tudor and Stuart Proclamations*, 2: 129–30 (#s 1020, 1029); HYNM, 2: 3–4.

43. Stevens, *Journal*, pp. 70–72, 120–30; Sharp MSS, S8, fols. 5r, 7r–v (quoted); Hatton, p. 38; Goodbody, "Sharp," p. 17. In fact, the French had proposed to burn Dublin and make a stand at the Shannon rather than the Boyne. John Childs, "The Williamite War, 1689–1691," in *A Military History of Ireland*, ed. Thomas Bartlett and Keith Jeffery (Cambridge: Cambridge University Press, 1996), p. 201. Following the collapse of James' control in Dublin, the lord mayor, aldermen, and sheriffs saluted William for delivering the people from "Arbitrary Power, Popery and Slavery," and exaggeratedly expressed their gratitude for release from "our frequent causeless Imprisonments, the plundering our Goods, the confiscation of our Estates, the innumerable Oppressions, the illegal Exactions, [and] the tyrannous hatred of our Persons." *To the King's Most Excellent Majesty* (Dublin, 1690).

44. Sharp MSS, S8, fols. 1r–8v (quoted at fols. 1r–v, 8v); Grubb, "Irish Friends' Experiences of War," p. 181.

45. Trinity College, Dublin, MSS 2203; Sharp MSS, S8, fols. 56r–57v.

46. Burnyeat, pp. 17–19, 93–95 (quoted at p. 93); Besse, 2: 484–85.

47. Sharp MSS, S9, fol. 20r–v.

48. Edmundson, *Journal*, pp. 138–39; Sharp MSS, S6, fols. 52r–53r; S2, fol. 111; HYNM, 2: 1. For other accounts of Quakers in the time of troubles see Edmundson, *Journal*, pp. 130–57; Wight, pp. 143–51.

49. HYNM, 2: 2 (quoted), 4–5; LPM, fols. 211, 213 (cf. fol. 224).

50. DMM, 2: 221–25, 255; HYNM, 2: 10–11, 12–13 (quoted); Sharp MSS, S7, fol. 38r–v. Reports to London about Quaker affairs in Ireland, sometimes prepared by Sharp, had been submitted long before the time of troubles. See, e.g., HYNM, 1: 91, 108; 2: 2.

51. Stevens, *Journal*, p. 62 (quoted); Sharp MSS, S6, fols. 47r, 48r–50v, 55r–56r, 57r–59v; S7, fols. 6r–11r, 13v, 34r–35r, 38r–v; S8, fol. 1r; LPM, fols. 227–28, 231–32; PRONI, MS D/2224/1. Cf. Pike, pp. 48–49.

52. LPM, fols. 215, 218; Sharp MSS, S7, fols. 9v–11r, 15r–v.

53. HYNM, 2: 13; DMM, 2: 239, 241; LYM, 1: 212; Sharp MSS, S7, fols. 13r (quoted), 14r–v.

54. LPM, fols. 237, 245, 248–49, 257, 260; HYNM, 2: 11–12, 19–20, 23, 30; UPM, fol. 141.

55. CARD, 5: 622, 627; HMC 36, *Ormonde*, n.s., 8: 373–74; Sharp MSS, S8, fols. 7v–8v; MDA, fol. 116r–v (quoted); "The Letter-Book of Richard Talbot," ed. Lilian Tate, *Analecta Hibernica* 4 (October 1932): 109–10 (cf. p. 112).

56. CARD, 5: 623–24; Stevens, *Journal*, p. 103 (quoted); *An Impartial Relation of the Surrender and Delivery of the Famous City of Dublin* (London, 1690), p. 1; Grubb, *Quakers*, p. 53; DMM, 2: 229, 231, 233.

57. DMM, 2: 189 (quoted), 243–44 (quoted); 3: 7. For John Hutchinson see CARD, 5: 534; RDDAW, 1: 22–23.

58. DMM, 2: 247; Hatton, p. 38; Sharp, quoted in Grubb, "Irish Friends' Experiences of War," p. 181; PMHB 28 (1904): 114; D. W. Jones, "Defending the Revolution: The Economics, Logistics, and Finance of England's War Effort, 1688–1712," in *The World of William and Mary: Anglo-Dutch Perspectives on the Revolution of 1688–89*, ed. Dale Hoak and Mordechai Feingold (Stanford, Calif.: Stanford University Press, 1996), p. 67. For the difficulties in assessing the number of Protestants who fled Ireland between 1688 and 1690, see Gillespie, "The Irish Protestants and James II," pp. 129–30.

59. Sharp MSS, S7, fol. 1r (quoted); S6, fol. 51r (quoted); George Fox, *The Short Journal and Itinerary Journals of George Fox*, ed. Norman Penney (Cambridge: Cambridge University Press, 1925), pp. 222, 353.

Chapter 5

1. Joseph P. Ward, *Metropolitan Communities: Trade Guilds, Identity, and Change in Early Modern London* (Stanford, Calif.: Stanford University Press, 1997), p. 3.

2. RSAI, Book Generall, fols. 26r–27r, 140r; Sharp MSS, S12, fol. 9v (quoted). Grubb repeats Sharp's erroneous dating; *Quakers*, p. 49.

3. CSPD, *1687–89*, p. 143; Sharp MSS, S12, fol. 10v (quoted).

4. RSAI, Book Generall, fols. 158v, 166v, 170r–171r, 172r, 173r, 194r.

5. RSAI, Book Generall, fol. 175r; NAD, MS M740.
6. RSAI, Book Generall, fols. 176r–v, 177v (quoted); Sharp MSS, S12, fol. 11r. The charter also named honorary members, including the bishop of Clogher, the earl of Limerick, Viscount Galway, Lord Mayor Sir Michael Creagh, Dr. James Molyneux (Sharp's neighbor), and the lord chief baron of the Exchequer.
7. Sharp MSS, S12, fols. 9r, 11r–12v.
8. RSAI, Book Generall, fols. 186v, 189r–v.
9. Mary Clark and Raymond Refaussé, eds., *Directory of Historic Dublin Guilds* (Dublin: Dublin Public Libraries, 1993), pp. 14–31. For the number of London livery companies see Valerie Pearl, "Change and Stability in Seventeenth-Century London," *London Journal* 5 (1979): 12–13; Ward, *Metropolitan Communities*, p. 154, n. 9.
10. RSAI, Book Generall, fols. 29r, 56r, 161v; RSAI, Masters' Accounts, fol. 6r–v; NLI, MS 12,123(b), fols. 9, 20; BAD, fols. 393r, 416r, 453r, 473v; NAD, MS TA1431; Clark and Refaussé, eds., *Directory*, pp. 15, 17, 20–21, 27–28. (Folio citations to the Masters' Accounts refer to all of a particular master's disbursements or receipts.) For the tailors' hall see "The Tailors' Hall," *Georgian Society Records of Eighteenth-Century Domestic Architecture and Decoration in Dublin* 4 (1912): 114–20.
11. RSAI, Book Generall, fols. 71r, 75v, 88v; GLD, MS 78, 1: 167r–169r; NLI, MS 680, 1: 22, 30; Clark and Refaussé, eds., *Directory*, pp. 15, 21, 26, 28.
12. GLD, MS 78, 1: 109v; Charles Gross, *The Gild Merchant: A Contribution to British Municipal History*, 2 vols. (Oxford: Clarendon Press, 1890), 1: 135; NLI, MS 12,123(a), fols. 15, 23; 12,123(b), fols. 83, 99; NLI, MS 12,121, fols. 33 (quoted), 35; cf. GLD, MS 81, fol. 5. The property of the weavers' guild included a velvet pall acquired in 1686; it was sometimes rented, typically for 5s. The Trinity Guild permitted its members to use its pall without charge. The cutlers, painters, and stationers paid £8 5s. 10d. for their pall in 1700. Among the other property of the weavers for which Sharp and his fellow masters were responsible were the charters, guild records, standard, seal, and plate. The magnificent chest in which guild records are still kept dates from 1706; its predecessor, which required repair in 1698–99, did not survive. RSAI, Book Generall, fols. 135r, 168v; RSAI, Masters' Accounts, fols. 8r–9r, 18r–v, 43r–v, 46r–47r, 48r–v; RSAI, Quarter Brothers, fols. 3v–4r; RSAI, Old Book of Brothers, fol. 2r; GLD, MS 78, 1: 171r; NLI, MS 12,123(b), fols. 33, 38.
13. RSAI, Old Book of Brothers, fols. 3r–8r; NLI, MS 12,123(a), fol. 12; 12,123(b), fol. 8; NLI, MS 12,121, fol. 6; NAD, MS M6118a; GLD, MS 81, fols. 2, 12; RSAI, Book Generall, fol. 123r. London livery companies normally had between two and four wardens. Ward, *Metropolitan Communities*, p. 83.
14. RSAI, Book Generall, fols. 3r, 10r, 21r, 33v, 47r, 60r–61r, 75r–76r, 121r, 123r, 136r, 154v, 166v, 186v, 189r, 199r, 223r, 236r, 247r, 249r–251v; RSAI, Masters' Accounts, fols. 1v–3r, 21r, 32r; RSAI, Book of Elections, fols. 8r, 10v, 11v. As in 1698, a second election had to be held in 1680 and 1702

when the winners of the first refused to serve. The Quaker Patrick Grumley un-successfully ran for warden in 1706; the winning candidates had forty-one and thirty votes respectively compared to his six. Book of Elections, fol. 15v.

15. GLD, MS 81, fols. 3–4; NAD, MS M6118a; NLI, MS 12,121, fol. 3; NLI, MS 12,123(b), fols. 1, 4, 9, 17, 30, 42, 50, 105r, 109r.

16. Ward, *Metropolitan Communities*, pp. 85–86; Mary Clark, ed., "List of Principal Inhabitants of the City of Dublin, 1684," *Irish Genealogist* 8 (1990): 49; GLD, MS 78, 1: 170r–171r; NLI, MS 12,121, fols. 6–7, 10, 15–16, 29; NLI, MS 12,123(b), fols. 33, 35, 83; NAD, MS M6118a.

17. RSAI, Book Generall, fols. 10r, 33v, 87r, 222r, 249v.

18. NLI, MS 12,123(a), fols. 16–17, 19; 12,123(b), fol. 50; GLD, MS 81, fols. 4, 118; NAD, MS M6118a.

19. RSAI, Book Generall, front cover, verso; GLD, MS 78, 1: 174r. Al-though the cutlers, painters, and stationers initially experienced no difficulties because of the oath, in 1702 the lord mayor exempted two wardens from tak-ing it, sparking debate, and the following year the guild itself excused its mas-ter-elect, Eliphal Dobson. NLI, MS 12,123(b), fols. 20, 69, 71, 78, 80. The Quakers Henry Flower and Patrick Grumley were exempted from the oaths in 1689 and 1695 respectively. Book Generall, fol. 159r.

20. RSAI, Book Generall, fols. 31r, 43r, 71r, 72r, 88r, 99r, 116r, 128r, 143r, 163r, 172r, 189v, 194r, 204r, 230r, 240r; RSAI, Masters' Accounts, fols. 3v, 55r; RSAI, Old Book of Brothers, fols. 8v, 11v, 14v, 17v, 20v, 23v.

21. NLI, MS 12,121, fol. 5; NLI, MS 12,123(b), fols. 5, 11, 20, 80.

22. NLI, MS 12,123(b), fol. 93; GLD, MS 78, 1: 135r–137r.

23. RSAI, Masters' Accounts, fol. 49r.

24. Ward, *Metropolitan Communities*, pp. 74, 91–92; RSAI, Book Generall, fols. 57v, 70r, 135r, 162v; RSAI, Quarter Brothers, fol. 2r; RSAI, Masters' Ac-counts, fols. 1v–3r, 18r–v, 21r, 43r–v, 48r–v. The much more affluent mer-chants' guild had two clerks, one for each master, and paid each a yearly salary of £10. GLD, MS 78, 1: 144r. For clerks of the cutlers, painters, and stationers see NLI, MS 12,123(b), fols. 1, 95.

25. GLD, MS 81, fol. 12; NAD, MS M6118a; RSAI, Book Generall, fols. 17r, 20v, 48r, 122r, 128v, 142r, 161v–162r, 168v, 171r, 203r, 208v, 216r, 223r, 237r; RSAI, Old Book of Brothers, fols. 1r–14v (quoted at 3r), 17v, 20v, 23v, 32v, 35v; RSAI, Masters' Accounts, fols. 1v–3r, 15r–16r, 18r–v, 21r, 23r–v, 30r–v, 37r–39r, 43r–v, 48r–v; RSAI, Quarter Brothers, fol. 2r; Ward, *Metro-politan Communities*, pp. 68–69, 86. For beadles in other Dublin guilds see NAD, MS M6118a; NLI, MS 12,123(b), fol. 2; NLI, MS 12,121, fol. 6; GLD, MS 78, 1: 135r, 143r, 177r.

26. RSAI, Book Generall, fols. 2r–v, 7r–v, 11r–15r, 23r–27r, 49r–52v, 79r–83r, 94r–95v, 107r–111r, 125r–126r, 139r–140r, 157r–158r, 170r–171r, 179r–v, 200r–201r, 211r–212v, 227r–228r, 241r–242r. The London weavers' company for a time allowed only women who were widows of former members to practice the craft of weaving and prohibited its members from teaching it to women, but late in the seventeenth century it began to accept female appren-

tices, and in time some of them became free and took their own apprentices. Steve Rappaport, *Worlds within Worlds: Structures of Life in Sixteenth-Century London* (Cambridge: Cambridge University Press, 1989), pp. 261–73; Ward, *Metropolitan Communities*, pp. 76, 128, 136. In September 1675 the Dublin assembly enacted that henceforth no one could be admitted to a guild as a full or quarter brother unless he or she had first obtained the freedom of the city. GLD, MS 78, 1: 159r. The latter freedom could be acquired through apprenticeship (as in the case of the Quaker skinner Jonathan Bell in 1701), birth (as when children of Sharp and Clarridge were admitted in 1688), fine (as with Sharp and Clarridge), or grant of freedom (grace especial, as when the miller Ezra Thackery was admitted in 1697 in return for pledging to oversee the city's water-course at Dolphin's Barn). Mary Clark, "The Dublin City 'Roll of Quakers' Reconstructed," *Irish Genealogist* 7 (1989): 543–50.

27. GLD, MS 78, 1: 151r (quoted), 172r.

28. GLD, MS 78, 1: 135r, 141r, 143r; NLI, MS 12,121, fol. 32; NLI, MS 12,123(a), fol. 11; 12,123(b), fols. 1, 8, 18, 62; RSAI, Book Generall, fol. 173r; RSAI, Old Book of Brothers, receipts for 1695 and 1696. Both as a quarter and a full brother, Sharp was sometimes late in paying his quarterly fees. Cf. RSAI, Book Generall, fols. 69v, 101r; RSAI, Masters' Accounts, fol. 25r–v.

29. GLD, MS 78, 1: 135r, 165r (quoted); NLI, MS 12,123(b), fols. 23, 59, 70; RSAI, Masters' Accounts, fols. 15r–16r, 18r–v, 37r–39r; RSAI, Old Book of Brothers, fols. 44r–47r; *The Statutes at Large, Passed in the Parliaments Held in Ireland*, 8 vols. (Dublin, 1765), 3: 339–43.

30. GLD, MS 81, fols. 10–11; NLI, MS 12,121, fol. 7 (quoted); NLI, MS 12,123(b), fols. 21, 81, 84, 88, 91; RSAI, Book Generall, fol. 223v; RSAI, Quarter Brothers, fols. 3v, 5r; *The Journal of the House of Commons, of the Kingdom of Ireland*, 8 vols. (Dublin, 1753), 3: 200. The feltmakers' guild limited its members to two apprentices each, fining those who exceeded this number a hefty £20 per offense; in 1698 it tightened its restrictions, allowing a journeyman to take only one apprentice within his first three years of being made free of the corporation. NAD, MS M6118a. A master in the merchants' guild paid £5 to enrol an apprentice. GLD, MS 78, 1: 135r. The cutlers, painters, and stationers required their members to pay 1s. per quarter for each journeyman enrolled. NLI, MS 12,121, fols. 18–19.

31. NLI, MS 12,121, fols. 8, 19; NAD, MS M6118a.

32. RSAI, Book Generall, fols. 196v, 222v (quoted), 229v (quoted), 235v.

33. RSAI, Book Generall, fols. 103r, 147r, 210r, 225r, 248r; RSAI, Masters' Accounts, fols. 37r–39r. During the 1690s the cutlers, painters, and stationers fined interlopers 20s., but allowed at least some of them to show proofpieces displaying their talents and, if acceptable, become guild members. NLI, MS 12,123(b), fols. 6–8, 10, 14, 25–27, 29, 33.

34. GLD, MS 78, 1: 173 (quoted); GLD, MS 81, fol. 13; NAD, MS M6118a; RSAI, Book Generall, fols. 171r, 217v–219r, 231v, 239v; RSAI, Masters' Accounts, fols. 1v–3r, 15r–16r, 18r–v. Few Huguenot weavers were in-

volved in the silk industry. Breandan Breathnach, "The Huguenots and the Silk Weaving Industry in Ireland," *Éire-Ireland* 2 (Winter 1967): 16.

35. RSAI, Book Generall, fols. 132r, 178v; RSAI, Masters' Accounts, fols. 1v–3r. Cf. NLI, MS 12,121, fol. 28; NLI, MS 12,123(b), fols. 36, 90; NAD, MS M6118a. The authority of Dublin guilds extended beyond the city limits in varying distances: three miles for the bricklayers and plasterers, four for the feltmakers, six for the weavers, and seven for the coopers. GLD, MS 81, fol. 9; NAD, MS M6118a; NLI, MS 680, 2: 124.

36. RSAI, Book Generall, fols. 20r, 21r, 34r, 153v (quoted), 198v, 238v; RSAI, Quarter Brothers, fols. 2r, 5r; RSAI, Masters' Accounts, fols. 6r–v, 8r–9r; Rappaport, *Worlds*, pp. 208–9. In 1679 the fine for not bringing cloth for inspection was 5s. Book Generall, fol. 34r. Weavers could also be mulcted for treating spinners unfairly. Ibid., fol. 62r.

37. RSAI, Book Generall, fols. 190v–191r, 222v, 235r; RSAI, Quarter Brothers, fol. 3v. One of the first offenders against the new standards was Mary Bloomer, who made serge thirty-four yards long, for which she was threatened with a fine of 10s. if she committed that offense again. Book Generall, fol. 252v. The guild spent 9s. 6d. in 1694 for a new perch. RSAI, Masters' Accounts, fols. 1v–3r. Notwithstanding Sharp's efforts, the Irish House of Commons found it necessary to specify detailed regulations in March 1704 aimed at preventing the fraudulent manufacture of old and new draperies. *Journal of the House of Commons, of the Kingdom of Ireland*, 3: 199–200.

38. RSAI, Book Generall, fols. 56r, 114v, 122v–123r, 161r–v, 167v, 239v; RSAI, Masters' Accounts, fols. 1v–3r, 9v–11v, 23r–v, 37r–39r, 43r–v, 48r–v.

39. RSAI, Book Generall, fols. 19r–v, 55v–56v, 69v, 75v, 85v, 90r, 99r, 105v, 115v, 117r, 132v, 161v, 163r.

40. For the development of standards of quality in other guilds see NAD, MS M6118a; NLI, MS 12,121, fols. 21, 24.

41. RSAI, Book Generall, fols. 73r, 75v, 89v; RSAI, Old Book of Brothers, fols. 9r–47r *passim*; George Unwin, *The Gilds and Companies of London*, 4th ed. (New York: Barnes and Noble, 1963), p. 123; NLI, MS 12,123(b), fols. 3–35 *passim*; Ward, *Metropolitan Communities*, p. 95. Beginning in 1686 the feltmakers required members to attend meetings every June and December at which the guild's regulations were read; the fine for absenteeism was 1s., with all proceeds donated to the indigent. NAD, MS M6118a.

42. RSAI, Book Generall, fols. 147v, 171r, 177v, 189v, 203v, 225r; RSAI, Old Book of Brothers, fols. 3r–44r *passim*. For courts of assistants in London guilds see Rappaport, *Worlds*, pp. 83, 91; Ward, *Metropolitan Communities*, p. 83.

43. RSAI, Book Generall, fol. 190r (quoted); RSAI, Old Book of Brothers, fols. 9r–29r *passim*.

44. Councils were important institutions in the governance of other Dublin guilds as well. See NLI, MS 12,121, fols. 11, 15, 17; GLD, MS 78, 1: 128r, 132r–133r, 138r–140r, 156r, 164r–165r, 177r. Dublin councils were similar in

size to the courts of assistants in London livery companies (normally twelve to twenty members). Ward, *Metropolitan Communities*, p. 83.

45. RSAI, Book Generall, fols. 129r, 235r (quoted).

46. RSAI, Book Generall, fols. 56r, 114r, 115r–v, 162r, 168v, 238v–239v; RSAI, Masters' Accounts, fols. 1v–3r, 37r–39r, 43r–v.

47. RSAI, Book Generall, fols. 234v, 236v.

48. *Statutes*, 3: 167–74; RSAI, Book Generall, fols. 30r, 154r, 158r, 167r, 204v, 205v, 207v; RSAI, Masters' Accounts, fols. 8r–9r.

49. GLD, MS 81, fol. 7; NAD, MS M6118a; NLI, MS 12,123(a), fol. 27; 12,123(b), fols. 5, 28, 72, 106r, 107v; NLI, MS 12,121, fols. 9, 19, 26–27.

50. GLD, MS 78, 1: 163r.

51. RSAI, Book Generall, fols. 57v, 161v–162r, 167v–168r, 239r; RSAI, Masters' Accounts, fols. 9v–11v, 13r, 15r–16r, 18r–v; Ward, *Metropolitan Communities*, p. 78.

52. RSAI, Book Generall, fols. 161v–162v.

53. RSAI, Book Generall, fols. 168r–v, 239r; RSAI, Masters' Accounts, fols. 9v–11v, 18r–v.

54. RSAI, Book Generall, fols. 115r, 167v–168r; RSAI, Masters' Accounts, fols. 1v–3r, 9v–11v, 37r–39r, 43r–v.

55. RSAI, Book Generall, fol. 239v; GLD, MS 78, 1: 140r–180r *passim* (quoted at 140r and 166r); GLD, MS 80, fols. 71r–75r; NLI, MS 12,123(a), fols. 10, 20, 34.

56. John J. Webb, *The Guilds of Dublin* (Port Washington, N.Y.: Kennikat Press, 1970), pp. 180–81; GLD, MS 78, 1: 150r, 152r–158r, 166r; RSAI, Book Generall, fol. 273v. In time the merchants dropped to thirty-one representatives and the weavers to three; the cutlers, painters, and stationers increased from two to three by 1702. NLI, MS 12,123(b), fols. 34, 70; Clark and Refaussé, eds., *Directory*, p. 43.

57. GLD, MS 81, fols. 9–10; GLD, MS 78, 1: 128r, 167r; NLI, MS 680, 2: 124; RSAI, Book Generall, fols. 184v, 187v, 194v; Sharp MSS, S12, fol. 12v. Among the cutlers, painters, and stationers this offense triggered a fine of 10s. for reviling a master and 5s. for a warden, or incarceration. NLI, MS 12,121, fol. 5; NLI, MS 12,123(b), fol. 44. The guilds sometimes bailed members who were incarcerated, but presumably only in cases involving debts or other civil disputes. RSAI, Book Generall, fols. 123r, 167v–168r; GLD, MS 78, 1: 173r–174r; NLI, MS 12,123(a), fol. 29 (referring to bail for the cutler's clerk).

58. GLD, MS 78, 1: 146r, 158r–159r, 161r, 175r, 178r; NLI, MS 12,123(b), fol. 72.

59. RSAI, Book Generall, fols. 29r, 122v–123r, 162r, 174r, 196r, 203r, 206r, 215r, 232r, 239v; RSAI, Masters' Accounts, fols. 1v–3r, 7r–v, 48r–v. For charitable giving in other Dublin guilds see NLI, MS 12,123(b), fols. 6, 31, 67, 99, 106v, 107v; GLD, MS 78, 1: 143r–144r, 177r, 180r. Occasional almsgiving was also the prevailing pattern of poor relief among London guilds. Rappaport, *Worlds*, p. 197.

60. GLD, MS 78, 1: 129r, 178r; NAD, MS M6118a.

61. RSAI, Book Generall, fols. 56r, 57v, 161r, 162r–v, 168r; RSAI, Masters' Accounts, fols. 1v–3r, 21r, 37r–39r, 43r–v, 48r–v.

62. RSAI, Book Generall, fols. 122v, 215v; RSAI, Masters' Accounts, fols. 37r–39r, 43r–v; GLD, MS 78, 1: 171r–172r; NLI, MS 12,123(b), fols. 76 (quoted), 91; *Dublin Intelligence* (14 August 1703) (quoted).

63. Patrick Collinson, "Elizabethan and Jacobean Puritanism as Forms of Popular Religious Culture," in *The Culture of English Puritanism, 1560–1700*, ed. Christopher Durston and Jacqueline Eales (New York: St. Martin's Press, 1996), p. 44; David Cressy, *Bonfires and Bells: National Memory and the Protestant Calendar in Elizabethan and Stuart England* (Berkeley: University of California Press, 1989), p. xii.

64. GLD, MS 78, 1: 127r–128r, 131r–135r, 137r, 139r–141r, 147r, 149r, 158r–163r, 172r, 177r; GLD, MS 80, fols. 72r–75r; NLI, MS 12,123(a), fols. 11, 24; 12,123(b), fol. 58; RSAI, Book Generall, fol. 247v; RSAI, Masters' Accounts, fols. 4v–5r, 21r, 30r–v. By 1694 the weavers were summoning members in writing to attend the May Day celebrations. Book Generall, fol. 247v.

65. Cressy, *Bonfires and Bells*, pp. 23–24; Ronald Hutton, *The Rise and Fall of Merry England: The Ritual Year, 1400–1700* (New York: Oxford University Press, 1996), pp. 52, 85, 175–76, 217–18, 247.

66. NLI, MS 12,123(a), fol. 48; 12,123(b), fol. 108r; GLD, MS 78, 1: 175r–176r (quoted); RSAI, Book Generall, fols. 56r–v, 114r, 161v, 232r, 239r; RSAI, Masters' Accounts, fols. 9v–11v; BAD, fols. 462v–463r.

67. NLI, MSS 680, 1: 8–11; Sir James Ware, *The Antiquities and History of Ireland* (London, 1705), sig. CCCv.

68. GLD, MS 78, 1: 163r, 166r–167r, 173r, 175r (quoted); BAD, fols. 460r, 462v–463r (the city government laid out £11 10s. in 1686 for the observances); GLD, MS 80, fols. 73r, 75r; NLI, MS 12,123(a), fols. 13, 48; 12,123(b), fols. 16–17, 49, 87; RSAI, Book Generall, fols. 16r, 53r, 57v, 100r, 114r, 147r, 150v, 161v, 215r, 232r, 233r, 238r, 239r–v; RSAI, Masters' Accounts, fols. 9v–11v, 18r–v, 25r–v, 37r–39r, 43r–v; RSAI, Book of Elections, fols. 14r, 40v–42r.

69. RSAI, Masters' Accounts, fols. 25r–v, 41r–42r, 46r–47r (cf. 8r–9r); NLI, MS 12,121, fol. 24; NLI, MS 12,123(a), fol. 11; 12,123(b), fols. 16, 108v.

70. GLD, MS 78, 1: 130r, [139A]r, 141r, 165r–166r (quoted), 179r; NLI, MS 12,121, fol. 30; NLI, MS 12,123(a), fol. 28; 12,123(b), fols. 12, 32; RSAI, Book Generall, fol. 114v; RSAI, Masters' Accounts, fols. 30r–v, 43r–v. For the downplaying of religion in London livery companies, see Ward, *Metropolitan Communities*, p. 115.

71. RSAI, Book Generall, fols. 36r, 115r, 139r, 201r, 228r, 242r; RSAI, Masters' Accounts, fols. 12r–13v; Greaves, *God's Other Children*, pp. 264–65; Kevin Herlihy, "'A Gay and Flattering World': Irish Baptist Piety and Perspective, 1650–1780," in *The Religion of Irish Dissent*, ed. Herlihy (Dublin: Four Courts Press, 1996), pp. 55–58.

72. Mark A. Peterson, *The Price of Redemption: The Spiritual Economy of Puritan New England* (Stanford, Calif.: Stanford University Press, 1997), *passim*.

73. Rappaport, *Worlds*, p. 387.

74. John E. Pomfret, *Colonial New Jersey: A History* (New York: Charles Scribner's Sons, 1973), pp. 4–7, 22–26; Pomfret, *The Province of West New Jersey, 1609–1702: A History of the Origins of an American Colony* (New York: Octagon, 1976), pp. 57–58.

75. Pomfret, *Colonial New Jersey*, pp. 31, 36–37, 40; Pomfret, *West New Jersey*, pp. 86–87; Richard S. Dunn, "Penny Wise and Pound Foolish: Penn as a Businessman," in *WWP*, p. 42; Audrey Lockhart, "The Quakers and Emigration from Ireland to the North American Colonies," *QH* 77 (Fall 1988): 69; *Documents Relating to the Colonial History of the State of New Jersey*, vol. 21, ed. William Nelson (Paterson, N.J.: Press Printing and Publishing, 1899), p. 559.

76. Pomfret, *Colonial New Jersey*, pp. 38, 40–41; Pomfret, "Thomas Budd's 'True and Perfect Account' of Byllynge's Proprieties in West New Jersey, 1685," *PMHB* 61 (July 1937): 328–29; Pomfret, "The Proprietors of the Province of West New Jersey, 1674–1702," *PMHB* 75 (April 1951): 133; Pomfret, *West New Jersey*, pp. 92–98; Julian Parks Boyd, ed., *Fundamental Laws and Constitutions of New Jersey, 1664–1964* (Princeton, N.J.: Van Nostrand, 1964), pp. 71–104.

77. Lockhart, "Quakers and Emigration," pp. 69–71; Pomfret, *West New Jersey*, p. 123; *Documents Relating to New Jersey*, 21: 400–401. Newby (or Newbie) was a member of the Dublin meeting. Sharp MSS, S4, fol. 10.

78. Sharp MSS, S4, fol. 60.

79. Sharp MSS, S4, fols. 60–61.

80. Sharp MSS, S4, fols. 68–69.

81. Sharp MSS, S5, fols. 46–47.

82. Penn, *Papers*, 2: 88–89. See also R. Dunn, "Penny Wise and Pound Foolish," p. 43.

83. Lockhart, "Quakers and Emigration," pp. 74–75; Samuel Hazard, *Annals of Pennsylvania, from the Discovery of the Delaware, 1609–1682* (1850; repr. Port Washington, N.Y.: Kennikat Press, 1970), pp. 641–42; Pomfret, "The First Purchasers of Pennsylvania, 1681–1700," *PMHB* 80 (April 1956): 151. See also Gary B. Nash, *Quakers and Politics: Pennsylvania, 1681–1726*, 2nd ed. (Boston: Northeastern University Press, 1993), pp. 11–17. Sharp's name does not appear in the list of 589 first purchasers and reputed first purchasers in the definitive edition of Penn's papers, though the list is incomplete. Penn, *Papers*, 2: 630, 636–64.

84. Lockhart, "Quakers and Emigration," pp. 72–73; Grubb, *Quakers*, p. 47; Pomfret, *West New Jersey*, pp. 123–24, 236; *Documents Relating to New Jersey*, 21: 664; Peter O. Wacker, *Land and People: A Cultural Geography of Preindustrial New Jersey: Origins and Settlement Patterns* (New Brunswick, N.J.: Rutgers University Press, 1975), pp. 289, 296–98.

85. Pomfret, *West New Jersey*, pp. 127–28, 131–32.

86. Sharp MSS, S2, fols. 6–7 (misnumbered 8); S8, fol. 11r.

87. Sharp MSS, S8, fols. 11r–12v (quoted); Pomfret, *West New Jersey*, p.

132. Sharp accused Jennings and the commissioners of intent to defraud in a letter to Lawrie, Robert Barclay, and others dated 14 July 1683. Sharp MSS, S2, fol. 7 (misnumbered 8).

88. *Documents Relating to New Jersey*, 21: 56; LF, Minute Book of the Lords Proprietors of New Jersey, 1664–1683, entries for 6 June, 26 June, 27 June, 1 July, 4 July, 12 July, 16 September 1682; Pomfret, *The Province of East New Jersey, 1609–1702: The Rebellious Proprietory* (Princeton, N.J.: Princeton University Press, 1962), pp. 130, 134–35; Pomfret, *The New Jersey Proprietors and Their Lands, 1664–1776* (Princeton, N.J.: D. van Nostrand, 1964), pp. 36–37. West last attended on 1 June 1683, two weeks before the Rye House conspirators correctly suspected that Josiah Keeling had betrayed them to the government. For the conspiratorial activities of West, Ayloffe, Wade, Freke, Gerard, and Ingoldsby see Richard L. Greaves, *Secrets of the Kingdom: British Radicals from the Popish Plot to the Revolution of 1688–1689* (Stanford, Calif.: Stanford University Press, 1992), *passim*. The involvement of Barclay and other Scots is usefully analyzed by Ned Landsman, "William Penn's Scottish Counterparts: The Quakers of 'North Britain' and the Colonization of East New Jersey," in *WWP*, pp. 241–57.

89. *James Claypoole's Letter Book: London and Philadelphia, 1681–1684*, ed. Marion Balderston (San Marino, Calif.: Huntington Library, 1967), pp. 143, 149–50; *MBP*, 1: 227, 229; 2: 82, 86; Pomfret, *East New Jersey*, pp. 145, 250–51. Each of the twenty-four proprietors initially received 10,000 acres; an additional 5,000 were granted in 1698, followed by 2,500 more in 1702. Pomfret, *East New Jersey*, p. 230. Sharp had to pay an additional £6 18s. 11d. for title to the land. Sharp MSS, S5, fol. 76r–v.

90. Pomfret, *East New Jersey*, pp. 253–55, 259–63; Sharp MSS, S6, fols. 13r–14v (quoted); S2, fol. 9 (mismarked 10); Lockhart, "Quakers and Emigration," p. 74. In November 1681 Anthony deeded 1/30 of a share of West Jersey to his nephew Thomas, who was described at this time as a "woolstead comber" of Dublin. *Documents Relating to New Jersey*, 21: 664.

91. Sharp MSS, S7, fol. 12r–v; Penn, *Papers*, 3: 291–92 (quoted). The government of William and Mary rejected Coxe's request for the grant, and Penn dropped plans for his Susquehanna settlement until 1696. Sharp received letters from Pennsylvania, including several from Turner and Philip England in the early 1690s concerning his nephew Thomas. Sharp MSS, S6, fols. 39r–v, 46r; S7, fols. 22r–23v, 27r–28r, 40r–v.

92. *Correspondence Between William Penn and James Logan, Secretary of the Province of Pennsylvania, and Others, 1700–1750*, ed. Edward Armstrong, vol. 1 (Philadelphia: J. B. Lippincott, 1870), pp. 97–98 (quoted), 123; Penn, *Papers*, 4: 168, 170, 212 (quoted), 216; Charles P. Keith, *Chronicles of Pennsylvania from the English Revolution to the Peace of Aix-la-Chapelle, 1688–1748*, 3 vols. (Port Washington, N.Y.: Ira J. Friedman, 1969), 1: 48. See the map in Penn, *Papers*, 2: 257.

93. *PMHB* 28 (1904): 113–14.

94. DMM, 3: 251v–252v; *MBP*, 2: 82; 3: 446; Grubb, *Quakers*, p. 56.

Among the Sharps who emigrated to America from Ireland were James and Mary Sharp of Dublin, who settled in Philadelphia in 1738; the tanner Joseph Sharp, who joined the Quaker meeting at Newark (Kennett) in 1711 and purchased 400 acres at New Garden three years later; and John Sharp, possibly this Joseph's brother, who married Ann Bryan of New Garden in 1726. Kerby A. Miller, *Emigrants and Exiles: Ireland and the Irish Exodus to North America* (New York: Oxford University Press, 1985), p. 151; Albert Cook Myers, *Immigration of the Irish Quakers into Pennsylvania, 1682-1750, with Their Early History in Ireland* (Swarthmore, Penn.: The Author, 1902), pp. 131, 134, 136, 142, 229, 296, 329, 333-34, 385.

95. Thomas M. Truxes, *Irish-American Trade, 1660-1783* (Cambridge: Cambridge University Press, 1988), pp. 77, 121. When the proprietors, including Bingley (on Sharp's behalf), petitioned the crown in March 1699 for the right of ships to use the port at Perth Amboy for the exporting of goods (with duties identical to those imposed in the port of New York), they were concerned not only with transatlantic commerce but also with the colonists' ability to survive. Had the port of Perth Amboy failed, the value of New Jersey land would have plummeted. *Calendar of State Papers, America and West Indies, 1699*, pp. 94-95.

96. Sharp MSS, S8, fol. 12v.

Chapter 6

1. HYNM, 2: 15; DMM, 3: 23-24.
2. HYNM, 2: 17; Sharp MSS, S7, fols. 32r-33r. The physical hardships were compounded in February 1692 by "very violent storms." *Dublin Intelligence* 71 (2-9 February 1692).
3. LPM, fol. 285; British Library, Additional MSS 47, fol. 144; HYNM, 2: 33 (quoted). Friends who had been forced to flee their homes during the war were returning to Leinster as late as 1699. HYNM, 2: 204.
4. Sharp MSS, S9, fols. 35r (quoted), 37r-38r (quoted); "Record of Friends Travelling in Ireland, 1656-1765," *JFHS* 10 (July 1913): 161. A native of Cumberland, Rooke had been convinced of Quaker principles by John Greaves and subsequently settled in Limerick. He fled Ireland in the time of troubles but returned to live in Dublin in 1693. Wight, pp. 313-16.
5. HYNM, 2: 17; LPM, fols. 276, 336, 573/273.
6. LPM, fols. 285, 287 (quoted), 299, 305-6; HYNM, 2: 37-38.
7. HYNM, 2: 37-38, 52-53, 81; PCM, fol. 16v. Cf. LPM, fol. 371.
8. HYNM, 2: 97, 259, 298; *RDDAW*, 1: 55, 187-88.
9. HYNM, 2: 64 (quoted), 83, 88-89, 112, 121-23, 157, 304.
10. HYNM, 2: 309, 411, 504.
11. DMM, 3: 66v-67r, 89v-90r, 114v-115r (quoted), 141v-142r, 174v-175r, 262v-263r; SDMM, fol. 37r-v (quoted). For Smallman see *CARD*, 5: 534. For Seaton see John Barclay, "Memoirs of the Rise, Progress, and Persecutions of the People Called Quakers, in the North of Scotland," *ad cal. Diary of*

Alexander Jaffray, ed. Barclay, 2nd ed. (London: Darton and Harvey, 1834), pp. 490–95.

12. DMM, 4: 24–25, 90–91, 98 (quoted), 100, 158(1)–159(1), 160, 234, 236–37, 337–38, 342–43; SDMM, fol. 48v (quoted). For Pettigrew see *CARD*, 5: 534.

13. HYNM, 1: 7, 14–15, 51.

14. LurMM, fols. 10, 17, 22, 31; MMM, fol. 72v; UPM, fols. 107, 151; LPM, fols. 224, 349; Richard L. Greaves, "Shattered Expectations? George Fox, the Quakers, and the Restoration State, 1660–1685," *Albion* 24 (Summer 1992): 247–48. In September 1696 the Leinster meeting blamed the "backwardness of the Harvest" for the failure of many monthly meetings to submit reports. LPM, fol. 349.

15. HYNM, 2: 57 (quoted), 111. Williamson was very active in the Ulster provincial meeting. UPM, *passim*. See also Besse, 2: 484; Sharp MSS, S7, fol. 7r.

16. HYNM, 2: 125 (quoted), 147, 182, 255–56.

17. LF, Swarthmore MSS 5/115, fol. 12; LPM, fol. 255.

18. LPM, fol. 298.

19. HYNM, 2: 39 (quoted), 97–98 (quoted), 146. See pp. 216–21 below.

20. LPM, fol. 256 (quoted); HYNM, 2: 35–36 (quoted).

21. LPM, fols. 412 (quoted), 485/185.

22. HYNM, 2: 144; Banks, p. 137; DMM, 3: 113v (quoted).

23. DMM, 3: 26v, 247v, 253v.

24. DMM, 3: 200v, 202v, 247v, 272v; LPM, fol. 366.

25. DMM, 3: 101v–102r (quoted); Sharp MSS, S2, fol. 20.

26. Sharp MSS, S2, fols. 20–23 (quoted); *CSPD, 1694–95*, p. 490; TDM, fol. 31v. For Baker see Banks, p. 137; *CARD*, 6: 97.

27. Sharp MSS, S2, fol. 26; "Record of Friends Travelling in Ireland," pp. 161, 163.

28. Sharp MSS, S2, fols. 36–37; "Record of Friends Travelling in Ireland," p. 164.

29. DMM, 3: 207v–208r; Sharp MSS, S8, fol. 35r; LPM, fol. 489/189 (quoted).

30. HYNM, 1: 16, 69 (quoted); DMM, 2: 109 (quoted). Hall also performed scribal tasks for the Ulster provincial meeting. UPM, fol. 25.

31. HYNM, 2: 58–59, 70, 81.

32. DMM, 3: 129v–137v; LPM, fol. 519/219.

33. Burnyeat, pp. 15–20 (quoted at p. 16); Sharp MSS, S7, fol. 37r–v; S2, fols. 120–21.

34. DMM, 3: 302v–303r; 4: 360–61, 374; DF, Testimonies [to Deceased Ministers] from 1661, fols. 19r–21r. For Fletcher see also *CARD*, 6: 60.

35. Sharp MSS, S7, fol. 37r; DMM, 3: 163v, 170v, 172v–173r, 182v; Minutes of the Lisburn Men's Meeting, entry for 26 August 1697; HYNM, 2: 126.

36. HYNM, 2: 146, 166; DMM, 3: 191v, 192v, 196r.

37. HYNM, 2: 147 (quoted); DMM, 3: 226v, 227v.

38. HYNM, 2: 288, 254–55, 283–87; LPM, fols. 457 (quoted), 461; DMM, 3: 243v–244r, 260v, 267v–268r.

39. Sharp MSS, S2, fols. 12 (quoted), 23–24 (quoted).

40. Edmundson, *Journal*, pp. 359–61. Cf. his earlier epistle (24 February 1672) written to Friends from Jamaica, ibid., pp. 313–15. At root the tension between the acquisition of wealth and condemnation of the acquisitive spirit is characteristic of the Quaker movement. See the exploration of this tension by Frederick B. Tolles, *Meeting House and Counting House: The Quaker Merchants of Colonial Philadelphia, 1682–1763* (Chapel Hill: University of North Carolina Press, 1948), Chaps. 3–4. Notwithstanding the tension, in the late seventeenth and eighteenth centuries numerous Quakers achieved economic success, especially in the business world. Frequent meetings and traveling public Friends facilitated business contacts, and the Quakers' generally frugal lifestyle enabled them to reinvest much of their profits. See M. W. Kirby, *Men of Business and Politics: The Rise and Fall of the Quaker Pease Dynasty of North-East England, 1700–1943* (London: George Allen and Unwin, 1984), pp. 4–6; David Harris Sacks, *The Widening Gate: Bristol and the Atlantic Economy, 1450–1700* (Berkeley: University of California Press, 1991), pp. 316–20.

41. Sharp MSS, S2, fol. 36 (quoted).

42. Sharp MSS, S2, fols. 28–30.

43. Sharp MSS, S2, fols. 30–32.

44. Sharp MSS, S2, fols. 33–34.

45. Sharp MSS, S2, fol. 28.

46. HYNM, 2: 161; John Dunton, Gilbert MSS (Gilbert Library) 189, fols. 127–28; Wight, pp. 166–68.

47. Penn, *Papers*, 5: 451–52; Thomas Story, *A Journal of the Life of Thomas Story* (Newcastle upon Tyne: Isaac Thompson, 1747), p. 128; Kilroy, pp. 208, 223. The broadsheet is reprinted in Penn's *Defence* (see the next note), pp. 1–5, but with the date of 4 May 1698. For the Quaker critique of the doctrine of the Trinity see Braithwaite, pp. 665–66; Hugh Barbour, *The Quakers in Puritan England* (New Haven, Conn.: Yale University Press, 1964), p. 145; and Underwood, pp. 46–47, 49.

48. Joseph Smith, *A Descriptive Catalogue of Friends' Books*, 2 vols. (London: Joseph Smith, 1867), 2: 565; Penn, *Truth Further Clear'd from Mistakes* (Dublin, 1698), p. 33 (quoted); Penn, *Papers*, 5: 453–54. An anonymous Anglican attacked Plimpton in *A Vindication of the Quakers Innocency Occasioned by John Plimpton's Late Paper Crying About the City, A Quaker and No Christian* (1698). E. R. McC. Dix, *Catalogue of Early Dublin-Printed Books, 1601 to 1700*, 2 vols. (New York: Burt Franklin, 1971), 2: 306.

49. Penn, *A Defence of a Paper, Entituled, Gospel-Truths, Against the Exceptions of the Bishop of Cork's Testimony* (London, 1698), pp. 6–18 (Wetenhall's critique), 19–119 (Penn's reply); Sharp MSS, S2, fols. 106(2)–107; Kilroy, pp. 208–10, 223.

50. DMM, 3: 264v–265r. In January 1703 the Dublin meeting refused to

accept Beck's donation of 15s. 4d. toward the building of a wall around the Dolphin's Barn graveyard or to permit him to be buried there because "he hath left friends & appeared as an open enemy against truth." He therefore requested and obtained the return of the 18s. he had contributed to the Sycamore Alley meetinghouse. DMM, 4: 96, 100, 103.

51. Sharp MSS, S2, fols. 39r, 56–63; S8, fol. 44r. O'Regan was commissioned as a major in Colonel Theodore Russell's regiment of foot on 1 March 1686. A native of Ballynecloghy, county Cork, O'Regan led the unsuccessful Jacobite attempt to defend Charlemont in 1690, but was knighted by James II and given command of Sligo. CSPD, 1686–87, p. 50; J. G. Simms, War and Politics in Ireland, 1649–1730, ed. D. W. Hayton and Gerard O'Brien (London: Hambledon Press, 1986), pp. 145–46, 174–78. At least three lieutenants with the surname of Bourke were active in the late 1680s: Edmund, Ulick, and Walter. CSPD, 1685, p. 283; CSPD, 1686–87, pp. 22, 52, 339; The Journal of John Stevens: Containing a Brief Account of the War in Ireland, 1689–1691, ed. Robert H. Murray (Oxford: Clarendon Press, 1912), p. 203n.

52. Holme and Fuller, Brief Relation, p. 75 (quoted); LYM, 1: 201.

53. BAD, fols. 473v, 480r, 494r, 513r, 521r, 526v, 534v; CARD, 5: 534; 6: 29, 38, 60, 97, 120; BAD, fols. 480v, 485v, 494v, 502v, 514v; DCA, Roll of Freemen, 1: 96; 2: 29, 103–5, 203–5; 3: 2, 12, 39, 172; 4: 27, 80, 140, 142–43, 207–9; Mary Clark, "The Dublin City 'Roll of Quakers' Reconstructed," Irish Genealogist 7 (1989): 545–50. For Quaker fines see BAD, fols. 480v, 485v, 494v, 502v, 514v.

54. 3 William and Mary, c. 2; DMM, 3: 11.

55. Braithwaite, p. 183; DMM, 3: 32v–33r; HYNM, 2: 22, 24.

56. Sharp MSS, S2, fols. 98–102. For Archer see Sharp MSS, S6, fol. 54r.

57. Sharp MSS, S2, fols. 86–88.

58. HYNM, 2: 25; DMM, 3: 37v; LPM, fol. 254.

59. DMM, 3: 116v–117r.

60. Braithwaite, pp. 183–84; Stephen B. Baxter, William III and the Defense of European Liberty, 1650–1702 (New York: Harcourt, Brace and World, 1966), pp. 336–37; MDA, fol. 135r; CARD, 6: 139–40.

61. HYNM, 2: 81, 83, 88–89; J. William Frost, "The Affirmation Controversy and Religious Liberty," WWP, p. 314.

62. Sharp MSS, S2, fols. 26–27; HYNM, 2: 96, 103–5 (quoted). Sharp, Hoope, Wight, Trafford, and John Pimm (or Pym) signed the letter. For Hoope see LurMM, fol. 31. For Pike, whose father had come to Ireland with the English army by 1648 and had been cashiered when he espoused the peace principle, see Pike, passim. A native of Skelton, Yorkshire, Hoope was active in the Ulster provincial meeting. UPM, fols. 104, 113, 149; Wight, pp. 262–63. Pimm, a member of the Mountmellick meeting, was excommunicated and incarcerated in 1663 for refusing to pay tithes. LPM, fol. 275; Holme and Fuller, Brief Relation, p. 31; see also Wight, p. 99; RDDAW, 1: 122.

63. LPM, fols. 380–81.

64. LPM, fol. 395 (quoted); DMM, 3: 179v–180r (quoted); HYNM, 2: 146.

65. HYNM, 2: 146; LPM, fols. 404, 408. Sharp was a guest in Hutchinson's home in October 1697. A farmer, Hutchinson had been imprisoned in 1672 for refusing to remit tithes. Sharp MSS, S2, fol. 37; Stockdale, p. 22; *RDDAW*, 1: 76.

66. HYNM, 2: 166, 434–35 (quoted).

67. HYNM, 2: 435–36.

68. LPM, fol. 419; HYNM, 2: 200, 202; Fuller and Holme, *Compendious View*, p. 131.

69. HYNM, 2: 259–60.

70. HYNM, 2: 325–27.

71. HYNM, 2: 327–29.

72. Braithwaite, pp. 188–89; HYNM, 2: 362 (quoted). In July 1703 the Leinster provincial meeting ordered the printing of 200 copies of the voting record on the Affirmation Act. LPM, fol. 528/228.

73. LPM, fol. 543/243; Wight, pp. 161–64.

74. HYNM, 1: 24, 27.

75. LPM, fols. 250, 381 (quoted), 530/230, 534/234, 537/237, 539/239, 556/256, 558/258; UPM, fols. 133, 153; HYNM, 2: 124, 126, 128, 443. For the 1692 Parliament see James I. McGuire, "The Irish Parliament of 1692," in *Penal Era and Golden Age: Essays in Irish History, 1690–1800*, ed. Thomas Bartlett and D. W. Dayton (Belfast: Ulster Historical Foundation, 1979), pp. 1–31.

76. PCM, fols. 4r–5r.

77. PCM, fols. 4r–v, 5v, 9v–10v, 13r–v. The Friends were understandably careful not to abuse their contacts with political leaders. In a statement signed by Sharp, Boate, Amos Strettell, and three others in November 1692, the Dublin meeting disowned Luke Dillon for having "troubled the Government with writeing papers and delivering them to the Cheife Rulers." TestCD, fols. 172–73.

78. PCM, fols. 4v–6r, 13r, 17r; *The Statutes at Large, Passed in the Parliament Held in Ireland*, vol. 4 (Dublin, 1765), pp. 12–31; *The Journals of the House of Commons, of the Kingdom of Ireland*, 8 vols. (Dublin, 1753), 3: 30, 235 (recovery of small tithes); 31, 44, 128, 137 (blasphemy and profanity); 34, 157 (abjuration oath); 34, 41, 68, 208, 279 (growth of popery); 68, 105, 106 (church rates); 103 (plantations); 137 (valuation of houses).

79. PCM, fols. 9v, 10v–12r.

80. PCM, fols. 13r–v (quoted), 14v–15v, 17v–19v (quoted at 18v); HYNM, 2: 399–400, 409; Edmundson, *Journal*, p. 266.

81. PCM, fols. 20r, 23r–27r (quoted at 26v–27r).

82. PCM, fols. 27r–28v, 29v–30v, 31v–37v (quoted at 34v).

83. PCM, fols. 28v, 30r–v, 37v–38r; *Statutes at Large*, 4: 132–37 (6 Anne, c. 9); *Journals of the House of Commons*, 3: 35, 41, 85, 101, 103–4, 128, 137, 199, 278, 350–51.

84. PCM, fols. 38v–41v (quoted at 41v).

85. PCM, fols. 42r–43r.

86. LPM, fol. 554/254.

87. Sharp MSS, S2, fols. 40–42; S8, fol. 52r–v. This advice was apparently

given to Samuel Walton, lord mayor in 1701; Sir Mark Rainsford held that office in 1700. Sir James Ware, *The Antiquities and History of Ireland* (London,
1705), p. 172.

88. Sharp MSS, S2, fols. 76–77.

89. Jonathan Scott, "England's Troubles: Exhuming the Popish Plot," in
The Politics of Religion in Restoration England, ed. Tim Harris, Paul Seaward,
and Mark Goldie (Oxford: Basil Blackwell, 1990), pp. 121–22; Scott, *Algernon
Sidney and the Restoration Crisis, 1677–1683* (Cambridge: Cambridge Univer-
sity Press, 1991), pp. 267–68; Richard L. Greaves, *John Bunyan and English
Nonconformity* (London: Hambledon Press, 1992), p. 139; Ingle, *First Among
Friends*, p. 274. Cf., e.g., *The Flying Post* (19 February 1701).

90. Sharp MSS, S2, fol. 77.

91. For this development, see the Epilogue, below, and Greaves, *God's
Other Children*, pp. 2–6 and Chapters 7–8.

Chapter 7

1. LF, Swarthmore MSS 4/238; Sharp MSS, S1, fol. 92 (quoted).

2. DMM, 3: 36v, 224v; 4: 390–91.

3. DMM, 1: 203, 205, 207–8, 241; 3: 121v, 123v, 124v, 161v, 255v; 4:
362–63.

4. DMM, 3: 206v; 4: 132, 134.

5. DMM, 1: 63 (quoted), 65–66 (quoted); 2: 85–87 (quoted).

6. DMM, 3: 46v.

7. DMM, 1: 63–64.

8. DMM, 1: 271–72; 3: 61v–62r, 128v–129r, 159v–160r, 244v–245r
(quoted), 261v–262r, 274v–275r.

9. DMM, 1: 35, 101–2, 125, 127, 137, 145, 147, 149, 151–52, 166–67; 2:
62; 3: 110v, 117v–118r; 4: 46; Sharp MSS, S2, fol. 102.

10. DMM, 1: 1–2, 61–62; 3: 31v, 262v–263r.

11. Stockdale, sig. B4r–v; cf. sig. B3r. A member of the Charlemont meeting, Stockdale himself spent ten months in jail in 1682 for attending a conventicle in county Tyrone. Fuller and Holme, *Compendious View*, p. 58. See also
James Bowden, *The History of the Society of Friends in America*, 2 vols. (New
York: Arno Press, 1972), 2: 117. Stockdale emigrated to North America in
1682. Audrey Lockhart, "The Quakers and Emigration from Ireland to the
North American Colonies," *QH* 77 (Fall 1988): 80.

12. HYNM, 1: 7, 14–16, 51; 2: 182. When Friends in England established
the meeting for sufferings in 1676, Penn, James Claypoole, and Samuel Newton
were responsible for corresponding with Clarridge about persecution in Ireland.
LF, Leek MSS, fol. 93.

13. Sharp MSS, S2, fol. 6; S3, fol. 90 (marked 22); DMM, 1: 9, 213–14; 2:
131–32 (quoted); 3: 184v–185r; 4: 388.

14. DMM, 3: 64v, 79v, 85v, 92v (quoted), 283v; 4: 714. For Webb see
CARD, 5: 534.

15. DMM, 1: 47.

16. DMM, 1: 3, 7, 15, 39–40, 43, 51–52, 57–58, 81, 83, 166, 195, 197, 277; 2: 23, 193, 247, 249.

17. DMM, 1: 164–66, 168, 174, 176, 243–44; 3: 172v.

18. DMM, 2: 197–98; 3: 25, 38v, 72v, 101v–102r.

19. LPM, fols. 31, 35, 267, 273; Sharp MSS, S1, fol. 93 (quoted).

20. LPM, fol. 62.

21. HYNM, 2: 118 (quoted); LPM, fols. 408 (quoted), 440.

22. LPM, fols. 446, 468.

23. LPM, fol. 391.

24. LPM, fols. 499–500/199–200.

25. LPM, fols. 45, 382, 396, 469; DMM, 3: 175v; 4: 14; Sharp MSS, S6, fol. 39r.

26. DMM, 1: 15, 37, 223, 255; 2: 11, 225, 257; 3: 232v, 233v, 234v, 236v, 237v, 238v, 240v.

27. HYNM, 1: 66–67.

28. HYNM, 2: 80 (quoted), 110; DMM, 1: 133.

29. HYNM, 2: 154, 169; DMM, 3: 139v, 169v, 184v, 198v, 239v, 272v; LPM, fols. 526/226, 551/251.

30. HYNM, 2: 80; LPM, fols. 25, 49; MMM, fol. 33v.

31. HYNM, 1: 83–84 (quoted); 2: 42, 80, 110, 210–11; DMM, 3: 238v; LPM, fol. 545/245.

32. Sharp MSS, S1, fol. 94 (quoted); HYNM, 1: 34; Oliver Sansom, "The Life of Oliver Sansom," *The Friends' Library*, ed. William Evans and Thomas Evans, vol. 14 (Philadelphia: Joseph Rakestraw, 1850), pp. 77–78 (quoted).

33. Sansom, "Life," p. 78. For his account of the half-yearly meeting in May 1687, at which Sharp was also present, see p. 18.

34. Banks, p. 62. Cf. his account of the meeting in May 1671; ibid., pp. 34–35.

35. HYNM, 2: 148, 231–32, 276, 335–36.

36. HYNM, 2: 30, 41, 273–74; LYM, 1: 121; DMM, 3: 273v.

37. UPM, fols. 70, 72; Sharp MSS, S5, fol. 82r–v; S6, fol. 5r–v; S2, fol. 106; DMM, 1: 215.

38. HYNM, 2: 13, 19, 32, 97.

39. Gilbert, *History*, 1: 36; Penn, *Irish Journal*, p. 70; HYNM, 1: 24–25, 30. The entry for 8 March 1687 in DMM (2: 104) makes it clear that the Friends had been using houses in both streets. The Quakers leased the garret in the Bride Street meetinghouse to Abraham Fuller until 1685. DMM, 1: 229; 2: 29–30.

40. DMM, 1: 95, 113, 157; 2: 219–20; 3: 11, 13, 17–18, 26v–27r, 32v.

41. DMM, 1: 57, 129, 255–56, 261–62.

42. HYNM, 1: 8, 16; DMM, 1: 15–17, 191, 197–201, 217–18, 277; 2: 27–28, 119. The Burnyeats periodically received reimbursement from the Dublin men's meeting for unexplained damages, presumably because of their property's proximity to the meetinghouse. DMM, 2: 99–100.

43. HYNM, 1: 43–44, 78; DMM, 1: 15–17, 69, 80, 91.

44. DMM, 1: 199, 239–40; HYNM, 1: 81 (quoted), 90.

45. HYNM, 1: 84 (quoted); MMM, fols. 21v–22r. The building stood in what is now Meath Place, just off Meath Street.

46. DMM, 1: 243(1), 259; HYNM, 1: 88. In May 1685 the half-yearly meeting added Roger Roberts to the committee assigned to rent the houses. It seems to have had difficulty finding tenants, for on this occasion the meeting did not stipulate that renters had to be Quakers. HYNM, 1: 91.

47. HYNM, 1: 84; LPM, fol. 141; DMM, 2: preliminary folios (which give the total as £211 14s. 9d.). Of the £65 15s. 8d. donated by 91 members of the Dublin men's meeting to construct a meetinghouse at Castledermot, Sharp contributed £7. DMM, 4: 708–9. For Joseph Thomas see CARD, 6: 29.

48. HYNM, 1: 86, 89, 91–93, 95; DMM, 2: 140, 145; MMM, fol. 38v; LPM, fols. 179, 197.

49. HYNM, 1: 95–96.

50. DMM, 2: 79.

51. LPM, fols. 173–74; DMM, 2: 103; 3: 139v, 143r, 237v–238r, 244v; ASD, fol. 9; DF, Deed Box X, Folder 2: 1, and NAD, MS D18499 (which indicates that the Friends paid Sharp 1d. per annum to have windows looking onto his garden; Sharp rented the property itself to another party).

52. HYNM, 1: 107; DMM, 2: 168, 201; 3: 184v, 189v–190r; 4: 14, 222, 426. Banks described Hanks, Amos Strettell, and Samuel Baker as "Considerable Dealers in outward Affairs." Banks, p. 137.

53. DMM, 3: 53v. Bell's will, signed on 8 February 1711, indicates that he was relatively prosperous. To the Friends he bequeathed £40 and ultimately a field for the grazing of horses (leased at the time to George Rooke). RDDAW, 1: 31–32. He is not to be confused with the merchant Thomas Bell, who served as a Dublin alderman beginning in 1692, and the following year used "indecent words, and scandalous and abusive Expressions" to the lord mayor in the Tholsel. Bell was lord mayor himself from Michaelmas 1702 to Michaelmas 1703, but refused in 1704 to take the sacramental test required by the Act to Prevent the Growth of Popery and lost his post as municipal treasurer. BAD, fol. 473v; MDA, fols. 126r, 129r–v (quoted), 138r, 153v, 158r–v; DCA, Liber Manucaptorum, C1/J/4/2, fol. 9.

54. HYNM, 1: 98–99; LPM, fols. 197, 200; DMM, 2: 145, 177–78.

55. DMM, 2: 164.

56. HYNM, 1: 99; DMM, 2: 104–6.

57. LPM, fols. 197, 204; Sharp MSS, S6, fol. 35r; DMM, 2: 145; 3: 139v, 140v–141r, 142v–143r; Hubert Lidbetter, "Quaker Meeting Houses, 1670–1850," Architectural Review 99 (April 1946): 100.

58. DMM, 2: 187, 189; 3: 88v, 150v–151r; LPM, fols. 227, 242–43, 249–50, 253, 308; HYNM, 2: 385–86, 403–4.

59. DMM, 2: 191–92, 241–42; LPM, fol. 250; HYNM, 2: 24 (quoted).

60. LPM, fols. 288, 291; DMM, 3: 67v, 68v; 4: 713; ASD, fol. 7.

61. DMM, 3: 11, 13, 32v, 41v, 49v, 50v, 51v, 52v, 61v, 104v, 159v; 4: 118; ASD, fol. 13; DF, Deed Box XII, Folder 5: 3 (with a copy at 5: 4); Gilbert,

History, 2: 169. Dated 25 October 1693, the indenture between Abel Strettell and Hutchinson on the one part and the trustees on the other includes the signatures of all parties (except Hutchinson, whose mark is affixed) and their seals.

62. LPM, fol. 528/228; DMM, 4: 176-77 (quoted), 182-83, 192, 224, 276. In November 1697 the six-months meeting had recommended that provincial assemblies ensure that all leases were secure. HYNM, 2: 126.

63. DMM, 4: 228-29.

64. HYNM, 1: 51. The problem at Lurgan involved wet ground. LurMM, fols. 11, 14, 18, 28-29. This may have been the Thomas Cooke who was imprisoned at Cork in 1661 for meeting illegally; again in 1664, when he refused to pay tithes of 6s.; and in 1668 and 1669 for attending conventicles. LF, Swarthmore MSS 5/91; Holme and Fuller, *Brief Relation*, p. 33; GBS, Munster Province, County Cork.

65. DMM, 1: 49-50 (quoted), 51, 53, 87 (quoted). The burial ground adjoining St. Stephen's Green was located on the west side, at the corner of York Street. It had been leased from the city in September 1664 and subsequently purchased. In 1805 the cemetary had a frontage of 100 feet on the green and 250 feet on York Street. That year the Royal College of Surgeons acquired the site from the Society of Friends on condition that it not build on a space 100 feet long by 100 feet wide for a century. The College brazenly violated this agreement in 1825 and 1836 by extending its buildings. Sadly, the site is now completely covered. ASD, fol. 1; Sir Charles A. Cameron, *History of the Royal College of Surgeons in Ireland and of the Schools of Medicine*, 2nd ed. (Dublin: Fannin and Company, 1916), pp. 164-65.

66. DMM, 1: 89, 279; 3: 63v-64r, 72v-73r, 141v, 218v-219r.

67. DMM, 1: 209-10, 221; 2: 81-82; 3: 223v; 4: 108-108(1), 166, 176-77, 210.

68. DMM, 1: 137; 3: 55v, 56v-57r, 61v, 168v, 170v, 172v-173r, 184v-185r, 281v-282r; ASD, fol. 5.

69. LPM, fol. 409.

70. DMM, 4: 34, 108, 110, 118, 166, 258.

71. HYNM, 1: 88; DMM, 2: 15-16, 107-8; 3: 69v (quoted), 180v-181v, 195v; 4: 713.

Chapter 8

1. HYNM, 1: 7, 31-32 (quoted); LPM, fols. 53-54, 75. Routh moved back to England in 1685. Sharp MSS, S6, fol. 10v. The city of Dublin was paying the schoolmaster Matthew Spring £25 *per annum* in the period 1669-71. BAD, fols. 301r, 339v.

2. HYNM, 1: 54; Minutes of the Cork Monthly Meeting, entry for 30 August 1697; cited in Richard S. Harrison, *Cork City Quakers: A Brief History, 1655-1939* (N.p.: The Author, 1991), p. 66.

3. DMM, 1: 69, 71-72, 83, 97-98, 127; Wight, p. 277; HYNM, 1: 64; LPM, fol. 95. In 1690 Logan became the master of the Quaker school in Bris-

tol. Braithwaite, p. 530; *Minute Book of the Men's Meeting of the Society of Friends in Bristol, 1686–1704*, ed Russell Mortimer, Publications of the Bristol Record Society, vol. 30 (1977), pp. 35, 36, 38. For more on Logan see LurMM, fols. 11, 38, 40. In 1660 Rose had been incarcerated several months for attending a conventicle at Carlow. GBS, vol. 2, Leinster Province, County Carlow; Holme and Fuller, *Brief Relation*, pp. 15–16; see also Wight, p. 105.

4. HYNM, 1: 62, 68, 71.

5. LPM, fols. 92, 94, 96; DMM, 1: 89, 93, 95–96; HYNM, 1: 69.

6. DMM, 1: 179; 2: 21, 23.

7. HYNM, 1: 104.

8. DMM, 2: 164, 166, 233–34.

9. DMM, 2: 265; 3: 40v, 48v, 51v; HYNM, 2: 11. In 1699 Seaton relocated from Glasgow to Hillsborough, county Down. Wight, p. 278.

10. The problem of Quaker parents who sent their children to non-Quaker schoolmasters was not confined to Dublin. HYNM, 2: 57; LPM, fol. 321.

11. DMM, 3: 59v (quoted), 62r–v, 75v, 95v–96v, 107v, 109v–110r (quoted), 122v. For Deane see *CARD*, 5: 534.

12. DMM, 3: 119v–120r, 127v–128r, 139v, 142v, 147v. Dobbs (or Dobb) had been appointed in 1688 to record marriages, births, and burials for the Lurgan meeting. He sought his meeting's approval to move to Dublin in 1694. LurMM, fols. 35, 48, 57–58. Henry Molyneux does not appear in the genealogical chart of the Molyneux family found in J. G. Simms, *William Molyneux of Dublin, 1656–1698*, ed. P. H. Kelly (Blackrock, co. Dublin: Irish Academic Press, 1982), p. 16.

13. DMM, 3: 150v–151r, 154v–155r, 157r. Chambers wrote a preface to Barclay's *Apology*. Wight, p. 213.

14. DMM, 3: 168v, 169v, 170v, 171v, 187r, 226v; HYNM, 2: 59.

15. DMM, 3: 155v–156r, 172v, 174v, 246v–247r (quoted).

16. DMM, 4: 123–24, 154, 156–57, 170, 172, 176, 194–95 (quoted), 418; Wight, p. 215; J. William Frost, *The Quaker Family in Colonial America: A Portrait of the Society of Friends* (New York: St. Martin's Press, 1973), p. 93.

17. DMM, 3: 263v (quoted); LPM, fol. 478/178 (quoted), 482/182, 514/214; HYNM, 2: 278. Insufficient means was probably at most a minor factor in the decision of some parents not to send their children to the Dublin school, for the meeting offered to pay the fees of the indigent. See, e.g., DMM, 3: 158v. For the Friends' utilitarian view of education see Richard L. Greaves, "The Early Quakers as Advocates of Educational Reform," *QH* 58 (Spring 1969): 22–30.

18. DMM, 4: 16; LPM, fol. 271; HYNM, 2: 369, 388. The most popular primers were George Fox's *Instructions for Right Spelling* (1673), Stephen Crisp's *A New Book for Children to Learn in* (1681), and Francis Daniel Pastorius' *A New Primmer or Methodical Directions* (1698).

19. HYNM, 2: 448 (quoted), 460–61 (quoted); DMM, 4: 230 (quoted); Stubbs, in George Fox, Benjamin Furly, and John Stubbs, *A Battle-Door for Teachers & Professors to Learn Singular & Plural* (1660), [part 3], pp. 1–28.

Stubbs, whose attack focused on textbooks by John Clark, Charles Hoole, William Walker, and Richard Bernard, thought their works should be consigned to the flames. He particularly singled out quotations from Terence and Ovid.

20. *CARD*, 5: 530; LF, Swarthmore MSS 5/115, fol. 6; HYNM, 2: 279–80, 459 (quoted).

21. LF, Swarthmore MSS 5/115, fol. 7; DMM, 3: 85v–86r, 211v; 4: 230.

22. DMM, 1: 43–45, 199–201, 217; 3: 141v–142v, 144v, 158v–159r; 4: 94 (quoted), 128 (quoted).

23. *Calendar of State Papers, Ireland, 1669–70*, p. 152; HYNM, 1: 29–30, 38, 58. In 1672 the London yearly meeting began sending two copies of every book it issued to each monthly and quarterly assembly, but not until 1690 did the Philadelphia yearly meeting ask its London counterpart to supply six copies of each publication. Frost, *Quaker Family*, p. 223; Edwin B. Bronner, "Quaker Discipline and Order, 1680–1720: Philadelphia Yearly Meeting and London Yearly Meeting," in *WWP*, p. 332.

24. HYNM, 1: 26–27; 2: 29, 34, 40, 167, 185, 213, 257, 313; DMM, 3: 178v–179r, 268r. Moon visited Ireland as a public Friend in 1693. "Record of Friends Travelling in Ireland, 1656–1765," *JFHS* 10 (July 1913): 162.

25. Sharp MSS, S4, fol. 16; DMM, 1: 280; 2: 278; 3: 284v; Frederick B. Tolles, *Meeting House and Counting House: The Quaker Merchants of Colonial Philadelphia, 1682–1763* (Chapel Hill: University of North Carolina Press, 1948), Chaps. 7–8; Carla Gardina Pestana, *Quakers and Baptists in Colonial Massachusetts* (Cambridge: Cambridge University Press, 1991), p. 143. The Salem meeting did not establish a lending library until 1714, but the Philadelphia meeting had one by 1705. Pestana, op. cit., p. 143; Tolles, op. cit., p. 153.

26. DMM, 1: 45, 129, 205–6, 209, 213–14; 3: 232v, 235v, 244v–245r, 267v–268r (quoted); HYNM, 1: 38, 86, 88; 2: 24, 53; LPM, fols. 303–4, 306. When Friends were blamed for the murder of a child at her mother's hands in 1681, the Dublin meeting sent Sharp and Daniel Thackery to obtain statements from her husband and neighbors exonerating the Quakers, and to have these statements printed. DMM, 1: 121–22.

27. HYNM, 1: 74, 76–78, 80, 82–83, 85, 90; 2: 126; DMM, 2: 25.

28. Thomas O'Malley, "'Defying the Powers and Tempering the Spirit,' A Review of Quaker Control over Their Publications 1672–1689," *Journal of Ecclesiastical History* 33 (January 1982): 77–79; HYNM, 1: 91; 2: 24. A Cumberland native, Carleton died in 1684 at Ballycarrig, county Wicklow. Wight, p. 138.

29. DMM, 3: 173v, 178v–179r; HYNM, 2: 387–88 (quoted), 404. In November 1700 the Dublin men's meeting asked Sharp, the Strettell brothers, Ashton, Roberts, Rooke, Edward Webb, and John Chambers to examine a critique of George Keith's *A Serious Call to the Quakers* (1700) and determine if all or part of the former should be reprinted. DMM, 3: 260v.

30. Sharp, in Samuel Fuller, Nathaniel Owens, *et al.*, "Memoranda Against Tithes" (1716), bound with the copy of Thomas Story, *A Journal of the Life of Thomas Story* (Newcastle upon Tyne: Isaac Thompson, 1747) in LF, MS vol. 340, p. 542 (fol. 2r).

31. HYNM, 1: 12–13. The importance Sharp attached to obtaining proper consent prior to marriage is reflected in the provisions in his will for his daughter Rachel. (See the Epilogue.) The care with which Friends treated marriage reflected not only religious concerns but, to a limited degree, practical ones as well, for conformists could deny the legitimacy of Quaker marriages and seek material gain by having the children of such unions declared illegitimate. As in England, however, there is no evidence that this was a major problem. See Greaves, *God's Other Children*, p. 348; Craig W. Horle, *The Quakers and the English Legal System, 1660–1688* (Philadelphia: University of Pennsylvania Press, 1988), pp. 234–38.

32. Sharp MSS, S1, fols. 85–95.

33. Sharp MSS, S1, fols. 98–100 (quoted).

34. Sharp MSS, S1, fols. 96–98 (quoted), 101–2.

35. Sharp MSS, S1, fol. 84 (quoted); LPM, fol. 64; DMM, 1: 9, 20.

36. LPM, fols. 13, 20, 24; DMM, 1: 9, 17, 23–25, 99, 155, 160, 166, 179, 199, 201–2, 211, 215, 231, *et seq.*; 2: 52, 97, 99, 105, 127–28, *et seq.*; 3: 13, 25, 30v, 40v, 49v, 78v, *et seq.*; 4: 16, 98, 102, 158(1)–159, 204, 262, 378. Fox thought certificates for those coming from other countries or counties enabled a meeting to counsel couples "Soe that there may bee an unity and a Concord in the Spirit." LF, Swarthmore MSS 2/108.

37. LPM, fol. 15; DMM, 1: 3–4, 109–10; Sharp MSS, S6, fol. 24r–v (quoted).

38. DMM, 1: 23–25, 29 (quoted), 33, 49; LPM, fols. 69 (quoted), 72 (quoted), 75–76.

39. Sharp MSS, S4, fols. 9–10. Cf. DMM, 3: 3–4.

40. TestCD, fols. 62–63; HYNM, 1: 64–66.

41. DMM, 1: 59; HYNM, 1: 66–67, 72. Cf. Vann and Eversley, p. 123.

42. LPM, fol. 4; Sharp MSS, S1, fols. 83–84.

43. DMM, 1: 113, 117, 121, 158, 160, 162–63, 170–73, 181–84, 191–92, 195–96, 263; 2: 25–26, 43–44, 243, 255; 3: 78v, 116v–117v, 174v–176r; TestCD, fol. 216. Cf. DMM, 1: 176, 187; Sharp MSS, S5, fol. 34.

44. DMM, 1: 117–19; TestCD, fols. 52–55; *Minute Book of the Men's Meeting of the Society of Friends in Bristol, 1667–1686*, ed. Russell Mortimer, Publications of the Bristol Record Society, vol. 26 (1971), p. 167. Among the marital cases with which Sharp dealt was one involving a couple (Edward Dickinson and Rebecca Gotely [or Goatly]) who decided to live together as husband and wife without consulting anyone; this may have been a case of handfasting. The couple acknowledged their offense. TestCD, fols. 35–37.

45. TestCD, fols. 1, 240–41 (quoted); DMM, 4: 28, 30–31, 60–61, 68–74 (quoted at 71), 80. Clarridge was permitted to attend meetings for worship but explicitly prohibited from sitting in the gallery. DMM, 4: 74. Clarridge's first wife was Margery Nugent, whom he married in 1655. NLI, Records of Births, Marriages, and Deaths (Carlow, Cork, and Dublin), Microfilm POS 1021.

46. HYNM, 2: 353 (quoted); LPM, fols. 517/217–519/219.

47. LPM, fols. 28 (quoted), 44 (quoted); DMM, 3: 46v.

48. Sharp MSS, S6, fol. 27r–v (quoted); DMM, 2: 203–4; LPM, fol. 229; TestCD, fol. 155.

49. DMM, 3: 174v–175r, 176v, 179v–180r, 213r–214v (quoted). Cf. DMM, 3: 249v.

50. LPM, fol. 55; DMM, 2: 113 (quoted), 115–16, 119–20, 123–25, 131, 136, 138–39. For Wilson see also DMM, 3: 212v–214v, 215v.

51. DMM, 2: 117 (quoted), 119 (quoted), 123. For other cases see DMM, 3: 34v, 36v, 193v, 200v–201v, 202v, 203v–204r; LPM, fol. 399.

52. HYNM, 2: 82; TestCD, fol. 221 (quoted); LPM, fol. 482/182 (quoted). For cases involving failure to obtain parental consent see DMM, 1: 141–42, 153–54; 3: 95v; 4: 54–55; LPM, fols. 269, 277–78, 322.

53. DMM, 3: 266v–267r.

54. DMM, 1: 187, 189, 192 (quoted).

55. HYNM, 1: 107; LPM, fols. 202–3. The instructions were reiterated in 1693. LPM, fol. 283.

56. Arnold Lloyd, *Quaker Social History, 1669–1738* (London: Longmans, Green, 1950), p. 58; LPM, fols. 426, 581/281; NWM, fols. 108–9; HYNM, 2: 180.

57. HYNM, 2: 97 (quoted); DMM, 1: 245–46; 2: 9, 11–12; 3: 86v, 87v, 88v; 4: 60.

58. DMM, 2: 47, 50, 95, 97–100; 3: 239v, 240v, 264v–265r; 4: 10–11, 16 (quoted).

59. DMM, 2: 199–200; 3: 77v, 88v, 89v.

60. HYNM, 1: 23; LPM, fols. 157–58, 264; DMM, 2: 113–14.

61. DMM, 3: 52v–53r, 88v–89r, 245v; 4: 152–57; HYNM, 2: 90–91.

62. DMM, 1: 275; 2: preliminary folio, 25, 27; 3: 1, 46v–47r, 96v, 99r, 148v, 223v, 224v–225r; 4: 1, 242–43, 264, 292, 304, 316, 326, 336, 338, 342–43, 382; HYNM, 1: 89, 91; LPM, fols. 153, 156. At the time of his death Sharp had in his possession money from several estates he was administering. DMM, 4: 664.

63. BFW, fols. 1r–6v.

64. HYNM, 1: 32–34; 2: 94; Sharp MSS, S2, fol. 44 (quoted).

65. DMM, 1: 105–8, 117, 119–20, 131, 133–34; 2: 5, 9–10, 29, 43–44, 146, 148, 168–69; 3: 40v, 64v, 190v, 191v, 193v, 224v–225r; 4: 32; LPM, fol. 60; Sharp MSS, S2, fol. 97.

66. DMM, 1: 33, 139, 141, 143–44, 176, 178; 3: 11; HYNM, 1: 27–28, 95–96.

67. DMM, 1: 111, 113, 125–26; 3: 99v–101r (quoted); 4: 10, 12–13, 61. In 1697, however, the Dublin men's meeting approved the use of non-Quaker arbitrators in the case of Moses Sykes, which involved a disputed debt. The quarrel had originated in 1669. DMM, 3: 151v–152v, 153v–155r, 156v–157v.

68. DMM, 2: 50–51, 54–55, 58, 60–61, 68, 89–90 (quoted).

69. Sharp MSS, S9, fols. 21r–22v (quoted); LPM, fol. 73; HYNM, 1: 58–60. For preaching at Newtown, county Fermanagh in 1660, Edwards was fined £100 and confined for six months, and in 1669 he was beaten and put in the

stocks for preaching in a parish church. Besse, 2: 464, 476; Holme and Fuller, *Brief Relation*, pp. 41–42. Like John Edmundson, Jackson had been excommunicated and jailed in 1663 for refusing to pay tithes. Holme and Fuller, *Brief Relation*, p. 31. Jackson and the Edmundson brothers had established a Quaker community in county Cavan before founding the Mountmellick meeting. Wight, pp. 99, 107.

70. DMM, 1: 273; 3: 33v (quoted).

71. DMM, 3: 132v–133r, 134v–135r, 157v, 158v, 159v–161r; TestCD, fol. 206. The younger Joseph Deane is described as Abigail's son-in-law, but the intent is more likely stepson.

72. DMM, 3: 99v–100r, 102v–104r.

73. DMM, 3: 172v, 177v, 178v–179v, 180v, 183v, 185v, 190v, 194v–195r.

74. LPM, fol. 23; HYNM, 1: 63, 76–77.

75. DMM, 1: 119, 121, 223–24; 3: 147v, 201v. In his capacity as treasurer Sharp periodically disbursed funds to assist needy Friends with their moving expenses. LPM, fols. 127–28; DMM, 3: 148v–149r, 161v, 219v; 4: 130.

76. DMM, 1: 95–96; 3: 222v (quoted).

77. *Minute Book of the Men's Meeting of the Society of Friends in Bristol*, p. 81.

78. Sharp MSS, S5, fols. 44r–45r.

79. Sharp MSS, S4, fols. 42–44.

80. DMM, 3: 35v (quoted); 1: 205–6, 219–20 (quoted); Audrey Lockhart, "The Quakers and Emigration from Ireland to the North American Colonies," *QH* 77 (Fall 1988): 67, 76–77. After his arrival in Pennsylvania, Turner continued to acquire indentured servants, most of whom worked on his thousand-acre estate outside Philadelphia. In general, 12.2 percent of Pennsylvania's indentured servants came from Ireland and 85.8 percent from England. Sharon V. Salinger, *"To Serve Well and Faithfully": Labor and Indentured Servants in Pennsylvania, 1682–1800* (Cambridge: Cambridge University Press, 1987), pp. 24–25, 28, 42, 45, 118. The pace of emigration to America by Irish Friends quickened in the eighteenth century, particularly as traders were hit by substantial downturns in the business cycle. Richard T. Vann, "Quakerism: Made in America?" in *WWP*, p. 160.

81. HYNM, 2: 39 (quoted); LPM, fol. 291. Cf. LPM, fol. 556/256.

82. PA, fols. 3v–4r, 6r, 8r.

83. PA, fols. 7v–10v, 17v, 24v–28v. In December 1687 Anthony Wilkinson testified against himself for having taken some of the money being collected for the poor on the grounds that he himself was indigent. TestCD, fol. 144.

84. PA, fols. 5r, 9r, 10r, 11r, 13r, 18r.

85. Sharp MSS, S1, fol. 179; S7, fols. 30r–31v.

86. LPM, fols. 46, 69, 120; DMM, 1: 53–54, 113, 176, 221–22, 243, 255; 2: 185, 189, 191, 227, 229, 243; 3: 49v–50r, 70v–71v, 216v, 217v; 4: 82.

87. DMM, 1: 53–54, 65, 99, 223–24, 231, 255, 259–60; 2: 243, 245 (quoted), 247, 265, 267; 3: 206v, 207v–208r.

88. DMM, 2: 273–74; 3: 242v (quoted).

89. Sharp MSS, S5, fols. 58–59.

90. Sharp MSS, S1, fols. 190–92.

91. Sharp MSS, S1, fols. 190, 193–94.

92. Sharp MSS, S1, fols. 195–96.

93. Sharp MSS, S1, fols. 198–200.

94. Hatton, pp. 5–28; DMM, 2: 127–30 (quoted at fol. 127).

95. DMM, 1: 239–40 (quoted); 2: 97–98; 3: 125v, 138v; HYNM, 1: 87–88 (quoted). Scot had been imprisoned in 1661 for attending a conventicle at Mountmellick. GBS, vol. 2, Leinster Province, Queen's County; Holme and Fuller, *Brief Relation*, p. 15.

96. HYNM, 1: 86 (quoted); Sharp MSS, S6, fols. 1v–4v; LPM, fols. 147–50; DMM, 1: 263, 267.

97. HYNM, 1: 90–91; LPM, fols. 159, 161–63; DMM, 2: 35–37.

98. LPM, fols. 216, 218–19; DMM, 2: 229–30.

99. LPM, fols. 225–27; DMM, 2: 241.

100. DMM, 2: 233; LPM, fol. 223; HYNM, 2: 7–9, 11–12.

101. DMM, 3: 9, 11, 13; LPM, fol. 237 (quoted).

102. LPM, fol. 240; DMM, 3: 19. The Dublin men's meeting was still helping poor Quakers in Moate more than a year later. DMM, 3: 54v–55r. For Wilcocks, James Fade's brother-in-law, see *CARD*, 5: 534; 6: 60; *RDDAW*, 1: 59. Cf. MMM, fol. 49v.

103. HYNM, 2: 19–20, 23, 30; LPM, fols. 249, 254, 260; DMM, 3: 29v–30r, 43v, 45v–46r, 53v. Sharp and Amos Strettell received and were accountable for distributing the £600. HYNM, 2: 18–19. According to LPM, fol. 245, Dublin's share of the £810 was £297 15s. 6d.

104. HYNM, 1: 63, 69; LPM, fols. 91–92; DMM, 1: 81, 85; George Fox, *A Collection of Many Select and Christian Epistles, Letters and Testimonies* (London, 1698), epistle 391 (p. 503); MDA, fols. 100v, 103r. Cf. LYM, 1: 88. Wight (p. 132) gives the total as £333.

105. HYNM, 1: 90, 92; Sharp MSS, S6, fol. 12r–v; LPM, fol. 164; DMM, 2: 52, 54. Still a captive, Bealing died in Morocco on 30 September 1693.

106. LPM, fol. 169; DMM, 2: 66; HYNM, 1: 94–95, 98. The best accounts of the captive Friends are Kenneth L. Carroll, "Quaker Slaves in Algiers, 1679–1688," *JFHS* 54 (1982): 301–12; and Carroll, "Quaker Captives in Morocco, 1685–1701," *JFHS* 55 (1985–86): 67–79.

107. TDM, fol. 30v.

Chapter 9

1. DMM, 1: 9, 89–90, 105–6 (quoted); 2: 136–37; 3: 67v (quoted), 123v–124r, 125v–126r; 4: 96–97 (quoted). One of the more unusual cases of scandalous behavior involved James Davenport and his brother, who sought passage on "The Owners' Adventure," captained by Thomas Lurting. Although the Davenports had no funds to pay for their passage, Lurting allowed them to come aboard and fed them, but the young men changed their minds, protested to the mayor, and obtained a warrant permitting them to return to shore on the

grounds that they had not been indentured. A scandal ensued because of the implication that Lurting had intended to take them to America against their wills. James Davenport professed his regret in a letter to the Dublin meeting dated 5 November 1681. TestCD, fols. 60–62.

2. HYNM, 2: 23–24 (quoted), 32–33 (quoted); Sharp MSS, S5, fols. 32–33 (quoted); DMM, 3: 59v, 62v, 118v, 143v–144r, 154v (quoted), 167v, 217v, 237v–238r. Cf. the Dublin meeting's testimony against Patrick Grumley (or Grumby) on 14 February 1692 for "Scandallous Conversation" and for living "loosely and disorderly." TestCD, fols. 176–77.

3. DMM, 2: 103–4 (quoted); 3: 81v (quoted), 82v, 86v, 121v–122r, 252v; LF, Swarthmore MSS 5/115, fol. 13; LPM, fols. 270–71. Cf. Sharp MSS, S4, fols. 45–46. For Ezra Thackery see CARD, 6: 154. Zane and his family had moved to Dublin from Ballinakill, Queen's County (Laois), in 1684, at which time they needed charitable relief. DMM, 1: 255, 259–60.

4. HYNM, 1: 57 (quoted), 58 (quoted), 61 (quoted).

5. HYNM, 1: 36 (quoted); DMM, 2: 111–12. In March 1674 the Leinster provincial meeting had launched a search for Fox's letter to Irish Quakers concerning precedents against swearing. LPM, fol. 23.

6. LPM, fols. 48, 58–59, 61, 63–65, 67–68, 71–72, 74; HYNM, 1: 44; TestCD, fols. 39–40 (quoted); Kenneth L. Carroll, "Quakerism in Connaught, 1656–1978," JFHS 54 (1979): 191–92. For similar cases see DMM, 2: 213; LPM, fol. 43. Symbolic acts were very important to the Friends, as also reflected by their refusal to remove their hats in the presence of social superiors. In 1682 the Dublin men's meeting dispatched Sharp and Starkey to speak with Thomas Cooke, who argued that he could not conduct business without removing his hat. Sharp and Starkey countered that his actions would increase the suffering of Friends who rejected this convention. DMM, 1: 160–62, 164–65.

7. HYNM, 2: 449; LPM, fol. 562/262.

8. Sharp MSS, S7, fol. 29r. For another example of strictness see the paper of Jeremiah Scott, a shoemaker, addressed to the Dublin men's meeting in March 1702 expressing sorrow for not having more zealously condemned his wife when she took an oath. DMM, 4: 42; TestCD, fols. 237–38. In 1699 the same meeting had castigated Patrick Naylan for taking an oath as part of a suit in forma pauperis. DMM, 3: 213v–214r, 215v, 216v. Not even poverty was an excuse.

9. HYNM, 1: 32, 43, 100 (quoted); 2: 441.

10. LPM, fol. 188; DMM, 4: 6. For other legal disputes between Friends see DMM, 3: 23, 132v, 133v, 165v–166r, 167v, 168v–169r, 192v–193r.

11. Holme and Fuller, Brief Relation, passim.

12. LPM, fols. 91 (quoted), 94; DMM, 1: 81, 89; HYNM, 1: 70–71; 2: 274–75.

13. Sharp, in Samuel Fuller, Nathaniel Owens, et al., "Memoranda Against Tithes" (1716), bound with the copy of Thomas Story, A Journal of the Life of Thomas Story (Newcastle upon Tyne: Isaac Thompson, 1747) in LF, MS vol. 340, p. 542 (fol. 2r).

14. DF, Testimonies Against Tithes, fols. 119–20, 125.

15. SLPM, fols. 14–15; SDMM, fols. 3v, 10r–v.

16. SDMM, fols. 3v, 4v, 10r–v, 13r–v, 16v, 19v–20r, 21r, 23r, 27r, 28r, 29r.

17. SDMM, fols. 10r–30r. During Sharp's years in Dublin, the meeting recorded only one distraint for James Fade, namely, 17s. for tithes of 15s. in 1683. Ibid., fol. 23v.

18. SDMM, fols. 32r–69r *passim*.

19. SDMM, fols. 31r–71r *passim*. One of the assessments for Strettell included a joint distraint with his brother Abel (30s. in 1692); if this were apportioned equally, Amos Strettell's average distraint would be 18s. 1d.

20. DMM, 1: 225–26 (quoted); 2: 134–35.

21. LPM, fol. 144; DMM, 3: 142v; 4: 90 (quoted), 93.

22. DMM, 2: 215.

23. HYNM, 1: 100, 102–3; 2: 2 (quoted); DMM, 3: 90v.

24. DMM, 1: 170–73, 176; 2: 121, 123, 125, 127, 129–30.

25. DMM, 2: 56–57; 3: 74v–75r, 76v–77r, 79r, 213v–214r.

26. LPM, fol. 545/245 (quoted); HYNM, 1: 98. Cf. NLI, MS 94, fol. 41.

27. DMM, 3: 98v, 198v–199r. For other loans see DMM, 3: 15r, 110v, 146v–147r. Naylan may be the Patrick Noland who did paving work for the city in 1676. BAD, fol. 374r.

28. LPM, fol. 29; DMM, 3: 128v–129r, 241v–242r, 257v–258r.

29. LPM, fol. 13 (quoted); DMM, 3: 113v–114r; TestCD, fol. 162.

30. DMM, 1: 243–44; 2: 13, 15; 3: 88v–89r, 182v, 194v, 241v–242r.

31. DMM, 3: 118v–119r.

32. DMM, 1: 147, 155, 181, 191, 231–32, 237–38, 247–48, 269–70; 2: 7, 13, 15; 3: 57v, 58v, 60v, 65r, 73v–74r, 75v–76r, 79v, 89v–90r, 115v–116r, 171v–172r, 225v–226r; 4: 230.

33. DMM, 1: 53; 2: 182–84, 186–88; 3: 94v–95r; LPM, fol. 64. If this John Redman is the Quaker who lived in Limerick in the early 1670s and was persecuted for his beliefs, his economic difficulties in 1688 may have stemmed from further suffering.

34. Sharp MSS, S6, fols. 36r–37v.

35. NAD, MSS D18500 and D18501. Page had served as sheriff in 1693–94, and as an alderman beginning in 1695. He was elected receiver general of the city revenue in August 1701. DCA, Liber Manucaptorum, C1/J/4/2; BAD, fols. 134r, 138r, 151v.

36. DMM, 1: 241–42; 3: 197v, 202v–203r; 4: 24–25, 34–35; HYNM, 1: 43.

37. DMM, 1: 131, 143; 2: 247, 249; 3: 181v–182v; TestCD, fol. 64; LPM, fols. 316, 404, 415, 497/197 (quoted); HYNM, 2: 230–31 (cf. 2: 35).

38. HYNM, 2: 368 (quoted); LPM, fol. 545/245; TestCD, fol. 255 (quoted). Sharp was one of sixteen Friends who signed Taylor's condemnation.

39. HYNM, 2: 232–33, 267–70; DMM, 3: 246v.

40. LPM, fols. 341 (quoted), 497/197; LF, Swarthmore MSS 5/115, fol. 18; DMM, 3: 60v, 62r. Sharp was one of a group of Friends who received Alexander Rigg's testimony against himself in July 1681 for having ignored Quaker

advice when he complained to Essex and a justice about his landlord. TestCD, fol. 59.

41. LPM, fol. 182.

42. DMM, 1: 273–74; 2: 7 (quoted), 31–32, 70–73, 79–80.

43. DMM, 4: 138.

44. DMM, 3: 101v, 151v, 269v; 4: 274 (quoted); LPM, fol. 582/282.

45. LPM, fol. 535/235 (quoted); TestCD, fol. 259; DMM, 4: 68–69, 180–82 (quoted).

46. DMM, 3: 145v–147r; HYNM, 1: 39–42 (quoted).

47. HYNM, 1: 44, 197–200 (quoted); DMM, 1: 5, 11, 37–38; LPM, fols. 70, 120, 125, 126–27 (quoted).

48. DMM, 4: 406–8 (quoted), 410, 412–14 (quoted), 416–17.

49. TestCD, fols. 9–10 (quoted); DMM, 3: 17r, 19r; 4: 200–201 (quoted), 208, 212, 215. This may have been the Edward Swan who purchased twenty acres of forfeited land in county Dublin following William's victory. He may have been the only Friend to acquire such property. J. G. Simms, *The Williamite Confiscation in Ireland, 1690–1703* (London: Faber and Faber, 1956), p. 190. As late as August 1706 Sharp was a signatory of a statement condemning James Whitehill for alleged sexual misconduct with a woman of ill repute while in England. TestCD, fol. 269.

50. *Minute Book of the Men's Meeting of the Society of Friends in Bristol, 1667–1686,* ed. Russell Mortimer, Publications of the Bristol Record Society (1971), p. 167; DMM, 1: 183. For the similar case of the Dublin linen-weaver George Mento see DMM, 4: 146.

51. DMM, 3: 247v, 248v, 253v, 255v–256r, 267v–268r.

52. DMM, 1: 221–22, 225, 227; 3: 59v, 62v, 63v, 143v–144r, 167v–168r; 4: 20–21, 122; TestCD, fols. 10–12, 30–31 (quoted), 250. Cf. DMM, 1: 219–22; 3: 29v–30r, 114v–115r, 119v, 149v–151r; 4: 62–63, 116–17, 140–41. In February 1694 the same meeting accused Barnard of "a very bad, unclean Act," and sent Sharp, Ashton, Roberts, and Joseph Thomas to speak to him and his mother. Because he is described here as a "boy," he may have been the son of the heavy imbiber of the same name. DMM, 3: 70v–71r.

53. DMM, 3: 225v, 226v–227r; 4: 140–41.

54. DMM, 1: 107–10; 3: 212v–213r, 214v, 215v.

55. Frederick B. Tolles, *Meeting House and Counting House: The Quaker Merchants of Colonial Philadelphia, 1682–1763* (Chapel Hill: University of North Carolina Press, 1948), p. 86; Raymond Gillespie, "The Transformation of the Irish Economy, 1550–1700," *Studies in Irish Economic and Social History* 6 (1991): 48, 52–53; L. M. Cullen, *An Economic History of Ireland Since 1660* (London: B. T. Batsford, 1972), p. 18; Thomas M. Truxes, *Irish-American Trade, 1660–1783* (Cambridge: Cambridge University Press, 1988), pp. 21, 228–30; Nicholas Canny, "The Irish Background to Penn's Experiment," in *WWP,* pp. 148, 155 n. 46; Pike, pp. 123–24; HYNM, 2: 70; William Edmundson, *An Epistle to Friends Given Forth from Leinster-Province Meeting in Ireland* (1699), p. 27 (quoted); LPM, fols. 490–91/190–91 (quoted), 493/193.

Excessive use of tobacco became a problem among Massachusetts Friends in the 1710s. Carla Gardina Pestana, *Quakers and Baptists in Colonial Massachusetts* (Cambridge: Cambridge University Press, 1991), p. 99. Friends in North Carolina and London were involved in the tobacco trade by the early eighteenth century. Jacob M. Price, *Perry of London: A Family and a Firm on the Seaborne Frontier, 1615–1753* (Cambridge, Mass.: Harvard University Press, 1992), pp. 47–48, 160 n. 83.

56. TestCD, fol. 250; DMM, 4: 116–17, 272, 274; 3: 116v, 120v–121r; LPM, fol. 521/221; HYNM, 2: 406 (quoted).

57. DMM, 2: 19; 4: 132–33 (quoted). Cf. TestCD, fols. 30–31.

58. DMM, 1: 181–82, 187; 3: 54v, 70v–71r, 213v–214r, 248v, 249v, 251v–252r; NWM, fol. 3; HYNM, 2: 207 (quoted), 275 (quoted); LPM, fols. 435 (quoted), 581/281. In Philadelphia only the stricter Friends opposed horse racing. Tolles, *Meeting House*, p. 137.

59. Robert Barclay, *An Apology for the True Christian Divinity* ([Aberdeen], 1678), pp. 387–88 (prop. 15, sect. 9); LPM, fols. 484, 568 (quoted).

60. Mabel Richmond Brailsford, *Quaker Women, 1650–1690* (London: Duckworth, 1915), p. 326; HYNM, 1: 3 (quoted), 5–6 (quoted), 8, 70.

61. Sharp MSS, S4, fols. 45–50.

62. HYNM, 1: 43, 70; LPM, fol. 96; DMM, 1: 99–100, 183–84 (quoted).

63. HYNM, 1: 90, 96–97 (quoted); LPM, fol. 159; DMM, 2: 74, 76, 142. Ambrose Rigge subsequently enunciated comparable views on wigs in a broadside entitled *A Faithful Testimony Against Extravagant and Unnecessary Wiggs* (London, 1698).

64. HYNM, 1: 100–101 (quoted), 102 (quoted).

65. HYNM, 1: 106–7.

66. NWM, fol. 82. Barclay had denounced the plaiting of hair as superfluous, but Irish Friends were more concerned with hairstyles that attracted attention. *Apology*, p. 382 (prop. 15, sect. 7).

67. DMM, 2: 263; 3: 9–10; Pike, pp. 59–61, 63, 65.

68. For a premature claim of the declining role of women in Irish Quakerism see Phil Kilroy, "Women and the Reformation in Seventeenth-Century Ireland," in *Women in Early Modern Ireland*, ed. Margaret MacCurtain and Mary O'Dowd (Edinburgh: Edinburgh University Press, 1991), p. 188.

69. NWM, fols. 89–90. Buckinghamshire Friends had condemned both the manufacture and sale of lace in March 1669. LF, Penington MSS, 4: 116.

70. NWM, fols. 101, 126–28 (quoted). Barclay was not opposed to silk clothing as long as such attire was fairly common in society. *Apology*, p. 382 (prop. 15, sect. 7).

71. LF, Swarthmore MSS, 5/115, fol. 17; DMM, 3: 103v, 273v–274r; HYNM, 2: 166–67 (quoted), 369; LPM, fol. 487/187.

72. HYNM, 2: 70, 351–52, 378–79 (quoted).

73. HYNM, 2: 282–83, 366; NWM, fols. 90, 111, 121.

74. Margaret Fox, quoted in Isabel Ross, *Margaret Fell: Mother of Quak-*

erism, 2nd ed. (York: William Sessions Book Trust, 1984), p. 380; Tolles, *Meeting House,* p. 126.

75. HYNM, 1: 5–6 (quoted), 43.

76. LPM, fol. 179. Cf. DMM, 2: 129, 131. Turkey-work chairs were relatively expensive; those purchased for the Tholsel ranged from 10s. to 23s. apiece. BAD, fols. 348r, 459v, [567A]v.

77. Pike, p. 66 (quoted); NWM, fols. 89–92; HYNM, 2: 40–41.

78. NWM, fols. 94–95 (quoted), 100–101 (quoted), 104–5, 123.

79. HYNM, 2: 41 (quoted), 166–67, 206.

80. HYNM, 2: 181; NAD, MS T6899; Frederick B. Tolles, *Quakers and the Atlantic Culture* (New York: Macmillan, 1960), pp. 84–88. In a letter from Philadelphia dated 25 February 1708, Isaac Norris told Pike about the objections he had confronted when "vindicating the discipline of Ireland." Consequently he concluded that "every man ought soberly and discreetly to set bounds to himself, and avoid extremes." *Correspondence Between William Penn and James Logan, Secretary of the Province of Pennsylvania, and Others, 1700–1750,* ed. Edward Armstrong, vol. 2 (Philadelphia: J. B. Lippincott, 1872), p. 259.

81. DMM, 1: 27–28 (quoted); Burnyeat, p. 82.

82. Sharp MSS, S5, fols. 37r–43r (quoted at fol. 37v).

83. LPM, fols. 105, 287–88; TestCD, fols. 141–42 (quoted); HYNM, 1: 75; 2: 38 (quoted); DMM, 2: 125–28 (quoted at fol. 126). The wedding supper at the Bull Inn was for George Newland and his bride.

84. DMM, 4: 296 (quoted), 366.

85. LPM, fols. 105, 287–88; HYNM, 1: 75.

86. LF, Swarthmore MSS 5/115, fol. 17 (quoted); HYNM, 2: 59; DMM, 3: 238v; NWM, fol. 111; LPM, fol. 487/187; J. William Frost, *The Quaker Family in Colonial America: A Portrait of the Society of Friends* (New York: St. Martin's Press, 1973), pp. 173–74. Yet Carla Pestana notes that wedding receptions did not pose problems for Massachusetts Friends until 1737. There, too, non-Friends attended Quaker weddings. *Quakers and Baptists,* pp. 99, 141.

87. NWM, fols. 53–54, 58, 64.

88. NWM, fols. 100–101, 120 (quoted); LPM, fol. 453 (quoted).

89. DMM, 1: 51; 3: 77v–78r; HYNM, 2: 40–41. For comparable concerns among American Friends see Frost, *Quaker Family,* pp. 43–44.

90. NWM, fol. 111 (quoted); HYNM, 2: 313–14 (quoted); LPM, fol. 487/187 (quoted); DMM, 4: 274. Cf. Frost, *Quaker Family,* p. 44.

91. Sharp MSS, S4, fols. 29–36 (quoted at fols. 29, 31–32).

92. LPM, fol. 63 (quoted); HYNM, 1: 79; 2: 126–27.

93. HYNM, 2: 183 (quoted); LPM, fols. 115, 117. For the rejection of monetary contributions from those not deemed to be in good standing see DMM, 1: 83–84; 2: 209–10; 3: 37v–38r, 41v–42v, 48v, 82v–83r, 109v–110r, 146v–147r, 149v–150r, 187v–188r, 203v–204r, 205v–206r, 219v–220r; 4: 37, 96, 100, 103, 122, 206–7 (a donation from Clarridge). Most of the returned

contributions came from the period after the time of troubles, when the Friends seem to have become more prosperous.

94. DMM, 1: 55-58, 109, 111, 121, 160-61, 166, 227-28, 235, 237, 239; 2: 185, 195; 3: 7-8.

95. LF, Swarthmore MSS 5/115, fol. 12 (quoted); LPM, fol. 270.

96. LPM, fol. 565/265.

97. DMM, 3: 81v, 82v, 83v, 196v, 216v; 4: 196-97, 200, 202, 208 (quoted), 240.

98. HYNM, 1: 70-72; DMM, 1: 105, 111, 183.

99. DMM, 1: 237-38; 2: 113-16; Sharp MSS, S1, fol. 76(1)r-v (quoted).

100. DMM, 2: 138. Carroll's suggestion that Lynch probably died around 1678 is erroneous. "Quakerism in Connaught," p. 191.

101. DMM, 1: 7, 101, 125; NWM, fols. 44-45 (quoted); Frost, *Quaker Family*, p. 53.

102. DMM, 1: 7, 127; 2: 83-84, 97, 123, 158.

103. Pike, p. 85 (quoted); Sharp MSS, S2, fols. 118-19.

104. HYNM, 1: 98, 101; DMM, 2: 97-99 (quoted), 159 (quoted).

105. HYNM, 1: 101; NWM, fol. 62; Sharp MSS, S6, fol. 54r-v.

106. NLI, MS 94, fol. 41; DMM, 2: 275; 3: 3 (quoted), 11-12; HYNM, 2: 15.

107. NWM, fols. 85-86 (quoted); HYNM, 2: 22 (quoted).

108. LPM, fols. 254-55, 262; DMM, 3: 40v, 47v. Cf. DMM, 3: 39v-40r. Although Sharp was not a visitor in early 1693, the Dublin meeting sent him and Atherton to speak with Clarridge about his absence from meetings. See Epilogue, note 42.

109. DMM, 3: 48v, 50v; LPM, fols. 264, 266, 272-73 (quoted); HYNM, 2: 27. Pike reported some dissatisfaction with visitations among "libertines" who opposed church discipline and others who feared that excessive formality would impede the Spirit's teachings. The Quaker community in Dublin seems to have been free of such tensions. Pike, pp. 88-89.

110. LPM, fol. 275; DMM, 3: 62v.

111. LPM, fols. 283-84; DMM, 3: 74r (quoted); HYNM, 2: 42-51; NWM, fols. 92-94 (quoted).

112. HYNM, 2: 31-33, 62, 119, 132-33; LF, Swarthmore MSS 5/115, fols. 16-17; LPM, fol. 392 (quoted); DMM, 3: 102v-103r, 139r, 152r, 160r, 167r.

113. DMM, 3: 204v, 214v-215r; HYNM, 2: 22, 199, 222-23; LPM, fols. 254-55.

114. NWM, fols. 113-14 (quoted); DMM, 3: 262v-263r, 275v-276r.

115. LPM, fols. 472-73 (quoted); DMM, 3: 265v, 267v (quoted), 268v (quoted).

116. DMM, 3: 45v, 50v-51r, 53v (quoted), 101v-102r; 4: 304; HYNM, 2: 55-56 (quoted).

117. Jack D. Marietta, *The Reformation of American Quakerism, 1748-1783* (Philadelphia: University of Pennsylvania Press, 1984), p. 26.

Chapter 10

1. James Nayler, *The Lambes Warre Against the Man of Sinne* (London, 1658), pp. 1–4, 14–15.

2. HYNM, 2: 34, 94–95 (quoted).

3. Sharp MSS, S1, fols. 116–18 (quoted), 120 (quoted). Judging from Joseph Smith's *Bibliotheca Anti-Quakeriana* (London: Joseph Smith, 1873), disputes between Quakers and Catholics, at least in printed form, were infrequent.

4. Sharp MSS, S1, fols. 118–21.

5. Sharp MSS, S1, fols. 121–24.

6. Sharp MSS, S1, fol. 124.

7. Sharp MSS, S1, fols. 125–27.

8. Sharp MSS, S1, fols. 127–28.

9. Sharp MSS, S1, fol. 128.

10. Sharp MSS, S2, fol. 113.

11. Sharp MSS, S2, fols. 89–93 (quoted), 114 (quoted).

12. Sharp MSS, S1, fols. 130–39 (quoted at fols. 132, 137). For earlier debates on this theme see Underwood, pp. 92–93.

13. Sharp MSS, S1, fols. 138 (quoted), 141–44 (quoted). The best analysis of the Nayler episode is Leo Damrosch, *The Sorrows of the Quaker Jesus: James Nayler and the Puritan Crackdown on the Free Spirit* (Cambridge, Mass.: Harvard University Press, 1996).

14. Sharp MSS, S1, fol. 155.

15. Hugh Barbour, *The Quakers in Puritan England* (New Haven, Conn.: Yale University Press, 1964), p. 157; Underwood, pp. 23–24.

16. Sharp MSS, S1, fols. 144–58 (quoted at fols. 145, 153).

17. Sharp MSS, S1, fols. 159–61.

18. Sharp MSS, S1, fols. 162–63.

19. Sharp MSS, S1, fols. 164–65.

20. Sharp MSS, S1, fols. 165–68.

21. Sharp MSS, S1, fols. 169–73.

22. Sharp MSS, S2, fol. 109.

23. Sharp MSS, S2, fol. 11; S9, fols. 3v–4v.

24. Sharp MSS, S2, fol. 10 (quoted); S8, fol. 4v; S9, fol. 3r–v (quoted). Some of those who heard Barry's charges went to Quaker meetings to determine if they were true, listened to Burnyeat and others, and became Friends. Wight, p. 142.

25. Sharp MSS, S8, fol. 16r–v; cf. S9, fol. 1v. For Quaker opposition to a physical resurrection see Underwood, p. 63.

26. Sharp MSS, S8, fol. 7r; S9, fol. 2r.

27. Sharp MSS, S8, fol. 17r–v (quoted); S9, fols. 2v–3r.

28. Sharp MSS, S9, fol. 2v; John Burnyeat and Amos Strettell, *The Innocency of the Christian Quakers Manifested* (Dublin, 20 March 1689), *ad cal.* Burnyeat, *The Truth Exalted in the Writings of That Eminent and Faithful Servant of Christ John Burnyeat* (London, 1691), pp. 189 (quoted), 190–93, 201.

29. DMM, 2: 148, 150, 156; Burnyeat, p. 203; Kilroy, pp. 155-59. Barry's reply was published as *The Doctrine of Particular Unconditionate Election (Before Time) Asserted* (London, 1700).

30. Sharp MSS, S11, fols. 2r, 3v, 18v (quoted), 42r (quoted), 71r.

31. Sharp MSS, S11, fols. 2r (quoted), 32r (quoted), 35r, 36v-37r, 47r, 63r-v. For Quaker teaching on perfection see Underwood, pp. 60-61.

32. Sharp MSS, S11, fols. 2v-3r (quoted), 19v (quoted), 20v (quoted), 43v (quoted), 47v-48v. For Quaker teaching on immediate revelation see Underwood, pp. 26-27.

33. Sharp MSS, S11, fols. 55r-v (quoted), 57v, 59v.

34. Sharp MSS, S11, fols. 37r (quoted), 39v-40r, 59v.

35. Lodowick Muggleton, *The Neck of the Quakers Broken* (Amsterdam, 1663 [London, 1667?]), pp. 14-15 (quoted), 22 (quoted).

36. Sharp MSS, S11, fols. 21r-v (quoted), 41r-v, 43r. For Driver, who got in trouble for comparing Mary Tudor to Jezebel because of Mary's persecution of Protestants, see John Foxe, *The Acts and Monuments of John Foxe*, ed. George Townsend, 8 vols. (New York: AMS Press, 1965), 8: 493-96.

37. Sharp MSS, S11, fols. 52v-53r, 60r-v.

38. Sharp MSS, S11, fols. 4r, 71v-72v (quoted).

39. Sharp MSS, S11, fols. 1r-70v; cf. S2, fols. 16, 19.

40. Sharp MSS, S11, fols. 4r (quoted), 5r, 6v (quoted), 12v, 23r, 23v (quoted), 24r (quoted), 35v, 38r, 70r.

41. Sharp MSS, S10, fols. 1r-59v; DMM, 3: 66v-67r.

42. Sharp MSS, S10, fols. 1r (quoted), 6r-v (quoted), 7r-v, 10v, 11v.

43. Sharp MSS, S10, fols. 14r-16r. For a fine analysis of Quaker teaching on baptism see Underwood, pp. 73-77.

44. Sharp MSS, S10, fols. 17r-23v (quoted at fols. 19r-v, 23v).

45. Sharp MSS, S10, fols. 24r-32r (quoted at fols. 28v, 30r, 32r). For Quaker views of the Lord's supper see Underwood, pp. 78-81.

46. Sharp MSS, S10, fol. 33v.

47. Sharp MSS, S10, fols. 34v-37r (quoted at fol. 36r).

48. Sharp MSS, S10, fols. 38r-43r (quoted at fols. 38v-39r, 43r).

49. Sharp MSS, S10, fols. 43r-47(1)r (quoted at fols. 43r, 46r). In 1391 Brute was accused, *inter alia*, of teaching that tithing was not mandatory because neither Jesus nor the apostles had commanded them. An Oxford graduate and a layman from the diocese of Hereford, Brute denounced the pope as Antichrist, rejected transubstantiation, argued that justification is by faith, and repudiated "corporal" in favor of spiritual war. Foxe, *Acts and Monuments*, 3: 131-88.

50. Sharp MSS, S10, fols. 47(1)v-49r (quoted at fol. 47(1)v), 51r-v (quoted).

51. Sharp MSS, S10, fols. 50r-51r.

52. Sharp MSS, S10, fols. 55v-57v (quoted at 56r). In 1701 an anonymous Anglican attacked Sharp in *Animadversions on a Discourse Delivered by Anthony Sharp, at the Quakers Meeting House in Siccamore Ally, Dublin* (Dublin, 1701). I have been unable to locate a copy.

53. Sharp MSS, S2, fol. 39. For Stephen Dagnal see the entry by T. L. Underwood in Richard L. Greaves and Robert Zaller, eds., *Biographical Dictionary of British Radicals in the Seventeenth Century*, 3 vols. (Brighton, Sussex: Harvester Press, 1982–84), 1: 209–10.

54. Sharp MSS, S8, fols. 47r–50r (quoted at fol. 47r).

55. This title reflects two versions in the Sharp Manuscripts: S2, fol. 14, and S12, fol. 1r.

56. Sharp MSS, S12, fol. 13r. The works Sharp recommended were George Keith's *Immediate Revelation* ([Aberdeen?], 1668), Robert Barclay's *An Apology for the True Christian Divinity* (1678), Francis Howgill's *The Invisible Things of God Brought to Light by the Revelation of the Eternal Spirit* (London, 1659), and Penn's replies to John Faldo, Thomas Hicks, and Thomas Jenner. Sharp MSS, S12, fol. 2v.

57. Sharp MSS, S12, fols. 3r–4r, 16r.

58. Sharp MSS, S12, fols. 6v–7r (quoted), 8v (quoted), 16r.

59. Sharp MSS, S12, fols. 7r–8r.

60. Sharp MSS, S12, fols. 4v–6r (quoted at fol. 4v), 8v–12r.

61. Sharp MSS, S12, fols. 14r, 16v.

62. Sharp MSS, S9, fols. 26r, 30r–34v (quoted at fols. 30r, 32v).

63. Sharp MSS, S9, fols. 5r–8v (quoted at fols. 6v, 7r), 26r–29v (quoted at fol. 28r).

64. Edmundson, *Journal*, p. 78 (quoted); HYNM, 1: 15, 20–22; Kenneth L. Carroll, "Quakers and Muggletonians in Seventeenth-Century Ireland," in *A Quaker Miscellany for Edward H. Milligan*, ed. David Blamires, Jeremy Greenwood, and Alex Kerr (Manchester: David Blamires, 1985), pp. 49–53; Hugh Barbour, "The Young Controversialist," in *WWP*, p. 23.

65. Carroll, "Quakers and Muggletonians," pp. 54–55. Kilroy (p. 89) notes the Muggletonians' later presence. In a letter dated 10 April 1697 to Thomas Tenison, archbishop of Canterbury, Narcissus Marsh, archbishop of Dublin, noted that four (unnamed) Muggletonians had recently come to Ireland from London in search of converts. Lambeth Palace Library, Gibson MSS 942, fol. 133.

66. Sharp MSS, S9, fols. 13r–14r. Cf. Christopher Hill, Barry Reay, and William Lamont, *The World of the Muggletonians* (London: Temple Smith, 1983), pp. 28–29.

67. Sharp MSS, S9, fols. 14r–15v.

68. Sharp MSS, S9, fols. 15v–19r (quoted at fols. 16r, 17v, 18v–19r). Crabb's calendar of Sharp's letter to Turken dated 22 February 1698 indicates that Sharp revisited the same themes. Sharp MSS, S2, fol. 38.

69. As Barry Reay has argued, referring to England. *The Quakers and the English Revolution* (London: Temple Smith, 1985), pp. 111–12.

70. Sharp MSS, S9, fol. 15v.

Epilogue

1. NWM, fols. 83–84.

2. HYNM, 2: 82–83 (quoted); DMM, 3: 139v.

3. Sharp MSS, S9, fol. 9r–v; HYNM, 2: 127, 155, 186–92.

4. William Edmundson, et al., *An Epistle to Friends* (1699) (Gilbert Library, Gilbert MSS, 260/8/23/a).

5. DMM, 3: 254r; Wight, p. 190.

6. LPM, fol. 577/277.

7. DMM, 3: 251v–252v; Sharp MSS, S8, fol. 44r (quoted).

8. Sharp MSS, S3, fols. 32–33 (quoted); TDM, fol. 29v. According to the Dublin meeting's testimony to Ann, she died on 29 June.

9. Sharp MSS, S3, fols. 32–34; TDM, fol. 28v.

10. Sharp MSS, S3, fols. 33–34 (quoted); *Records and Files of the Quarterly Courts of Essex County, Massachusetts*, 8 vols., ed. George Francis Dow (Salem, Mass.: Essex Institute, 1911–21), 3: 17, 64; Kenneth L. Carroll, "Early Quakers and 'Going Naked as a Sign'," *QH* 67 (Autumn 1978): 77, 80, 82; Luella M. Wright, *The Literary Life of the Early Friends, 1650–1725* (New York: Columbia University Press, 1932), pp. 162, 164.

11. TDM, fol. 29r–v.

12. Sharp MSS, S7, fol. 41r–v.

13. DMM, 4: 17, 44, 52.

14. DMM, 4: 304, 436–37.

15. DMM, 4: 406v; TDM, fol. 32r.

16. TDM, fol. 32r (quoted); Wight, p. 192 (quoted).

17. TDM, fol. 32v (quoted); HYNM, 2: 514 (quoted).

18. Edmundson, *Journal*, p. 283.

19. NAD, MS T6899. A plantation-acre (or Irish acre, 7,840 square yards) is approximately 1.62 times larger than an English acre (4,840 square yards). The 1922 fire destroyed Sharp's will, but the National Archives possesses a copy and a transcription. A transcription also is included in the *Prerogative Court Will Book, 1706–08*. The will was probated on 20 January 1707. On 18 September 1707 the Dublin meeting directed Joseph Fade to enter Sharp's will in its book of wills, but he failed to do so. The meeting assigned the task to Thomas Banks on 25 March 1709. BFW, fols. 9r, 12v–13r.

20. RDD, 51-129-33074; 50-160-32424; 100-278-70479. By the late eighteenth century the great house at Killinure, which was largely built by Anthony's grandson, Isaac's son Anthony, was known as Roundwood, its present name. RDD, 353-289-238920. See Baron Brian de Breffny, "Roundwood and the Sharps," *Irish Ancestor* 9 (1977): 59–67. The younger Anthony owned property in Bristol, but this is not mentioned in his grandfather's will and may have been acquired by his father Isaac if, as de Breffny conjectures, Isaac married into the Pocock or Hackett families in Bristol. But de Breffny wrongly asserts that the elder Anthony owned land at "New Creek, Gloucestershire." This is a mistaken reference to the lands held by Thomas Sharp at Newton Creek and Timber Creek in Gloucester County, New Jersey. De Breffny, pp. 60, 65–66; see RDD, 353-289-238920; *RDDAW*, 1: 286–87.

21. Sharp MSS, S2, fol. 52; *MBP*, 2: 82. If we accept Larry Ingle's suggested conversion rate of approximately 1 pound to 100 American dollars, Isaac's in-

heritance was worth roughly $1,000,000 in modern terms. *First Among Friends*, p. ix.

22. Joseph's wife, Catherine (or Katherine) née Savage, had died, leaving one daughter, also named Catherine. RDD, 100-278-70479

23. NAD, MS T6899.

24. NAD, MS T6899; RDD, 7-412-2772; 28-80-16418; 31-283-19073. The lease to Clonaheen was held by the merchant Joshua Beale when Anthony died. After Beale's death Daniel leased the property to Edmund Ryan, a Dublin gentleman, in 1712, and to the Dublin merchant James Wamesley (or Walmsley) in 1712. Ryan also leased lands and houses from Sharp in Meath Street and Elbow Lane in 1725. RDD, 44-364-29801.

25. RDD, 13-149-5453; 18-77-8409; 22-497-12682; 22-502-12690; 23-75-12681; 23-402-13837; 23-508-14233; 24-246-13697; 27-46-15089; 28-118-16812; 30-68-16427; 30-390-18938; 33-62-19664; 32-80-19015; 43-63-27378; 131-491-89971. For additional, later deeds see the bibliography of manuscripts. "A Booke for Friends That Meet About Wills & Inventoryes Beginninge 27 of x^{br} 1704" is bound in a partial copy, on parchment, of Sharp's lease with the earl of Meath for property, including mills, in the liberty of Thomas Court and Donore.

26. NAD, MS T6899. The extent of Sharp's Dublin holdings is reflected to some degree in the pipe-water accounts. The city began piping water to some of the residents south of the Liffey in the thirteenth century, charging an annual fee. The first list of payees dates from 1680 and includes 303 entries, thirty of which were for brewing, distilling, and related activities. The basic rate, charged to individuals and taverns, was 20s., whereas distillers paid 30s. and brewers between 30s. and £6 10s. Sharp tendered 20s. in 1680, but in 1705 and 1706, when the norm was still 20s., he paid double that amount. His fellow Quaker Amos Strettell of Back Lane and his neighbor, Dr. James Molyneux, each remitted 20s. BAD, fols. 404r–408r, 577v–578r, 590v–591r; Mary Clark, "Dublin City Pipe Water Accounts, 1680," *Irish Genealogist* 7 (1987): 201. See also Clark, "Dublin City Pipe Water Accounts, 1704/5," *Irish Genealogist* 9 (1994): 76–88. Strettell leased his property in Back Lane from the city. DCA, Catalogue and Index to Wide Streets, Expired Leases, Deeds to the City, Trust Deeds, and Opinions of Counsel, comp. by John P. McEvoy, p. 219. Hearth tax records for Sharp have not survived, but at the conclusion of fiscal 1700–1701 the Dublin municipal government reduced his land tax 15s.; the total is not given, but nine other people received reductions ranging from 1s. to 10s. BAD, fol. 547r.

27. Some of this land was in the possession of the counselor William Sprigge. This may have been the Cromwellian educational reformer who had been a member of Gray's Inn beginning in 1657, and who had moved to Dublin to practice law around 1664. See Richard L. Greaves, "William Sprigg and the Cromwellian Revolution," *Huntington Library Quarterly* 34 (February 1971): 99–113; Greaves and Robert Zaller, *Biographical Dictionary of British Radicals in the Seventeenth Century*, 3 vols. (Brighton, Sussex: Harvester Press, 1982–84), *s.v.*

28. The executors were Daniel Sharp and the Dublin alderman John Page, and the overseers were Samuel Baker, Thomas Ashton, Joseph Fade, and Amos and Abel Strettell. NAD, MS T6899.

29. A like amount was given to Patrick Henderson.

30. DMM, 4: 514. The Rachel Crabb in Sharp's will was almost certainly the woman of that name who wed the mariner John Lewis and became a widow by February 1736. RDD, 81-431-58234.

31. NAD, MS T6899.

32. DMM, 4: 588–89, 598; TDM, fols. 30v–32r (quoted).

33. Sharp MSS, S2, fols. 96–97.

34. Sharp MSS, S2, fols. 85–86, 89, 94, 96–97, 112.

35. Sharp MSS, S2, fols. 85, 112 (quoted); TDM, fol. 30v.

36. Sharp MSS, S2, fols. 25 (quoted), 106(1), 130(1)–131; S4, fol. 19.

37. Sharp MSS, S2, fols. 66–67.

38. Sharp MSS, S2, fols. 109, 114–16 (quoted); Elisabeth Brockbank, *Edward Burrough: A Wrestler for Truth, 1634–1662* (London: Bannisdale Press, 1949), pp. 77, 93.

39. H. Larry Ingle, "Unravelling George Fox: The Real Person," in *New Light on George Fox (1624 to 1691)*, ed. Michael Mullett (York: William Sessions, n.d.), p. 38. See also Ingle, *First Among Friends*, p. 18.

40. Mullett, in *New Light on George Fox*, pp. 2–3; Ingle, *First Among Friends*, pp. 251–52.

41. Ingle, *First Among Friends*, p. 250.

42. Ingle, *First Among Friends*, p. 255.

43. Sharp MSS, S9, fols. 21r–22v; S2, fol. 3.

44. In 1693, for instance, Clarridge told Sharp and Ashton he had been absent from Quaker meetings because they "were not appointed in places to his mind & likeing." DMM, 3: 48v, 49v, 52r (quoted). He was sufficiently out of fellowship in 1702 and 1704 to prompt the Dublin men's meeting to return his monetary contributions. DMM, 4: 37, 206–7.

45. Sharp MSS, S2, fol. 110. Apparently, only Crabb's synopsis of this letter has survived.

46. Cf., e.g., HYNM, 2: 31; Sharp MSS, S2, fol. 14.

47. *PMHB* 28 (1904): 114.

48. This paragraph and the one that follows are based on Greaves, *God's Other Children*, pp. 2–6.

49. Bryan A. Wilson, *The Social Dimensions of Sectarianism: Sects and New Religious Movements in Contemporary Society* (Oxford: Clarendon Press, 1990), p. 47; Wilson, "A Typology of Sects," in *Religion and Ideology*, ed. Robert Bocock and Kenneth Thompson (Manchester: Manchester University Press, 1985), pp. 299–303; Wilson, *Religious Sects: A Sociological Study* (London: Weidenfeld and Nicolson, 1970), Chaps. 3–9.

50. Wilson, *Social Dimensions*, pp. 109–10, 115–16, 118–19; Wilson, *Religious Sects*, pp. 19–20; Mark Chaves, "Denominations as Dual Structures: An Organizational Analysis," *Sociology of Religion* 54 (Summer 1993): 147–51.

51. Barry Reay, *The Quakers and the English Revolution* (London: Temple Smith, 1985), p. 121.

52. Isabel Grubb, "Irish Friends' Experiences of War, 1689–92," *Friends' Quarterly Examiner* (1916): 172; Sharp MSS, S5, fols. 75r–v, 77r–78r; S2, fol. 144.

53. Sharp MSS, S1, fol. 105; S4, fols. 12–13, 25–26, 41, 56–57, 93, 95–97; S5, fol. 67r–v; S6, fol. 25r–v; S7, fol. 5r.

54. Sharp MSS, S5, fol. 15 (quoted); S2, fol. 146; S4, fol. 56 (quoted).

55. Sharp MSS, S6, fol. 25r (quoted); S4, fols. 12 (quoted), 13; S7, fol. 5r.

Manuscripts

Bodleian Library: Carte MSS 168, 218

British Library: Additional MSS 47 (Epistles)

Dublin City Archives: Book of Accounts of the Corporation of the City of Dublin, 1650–1717 (MSS MR/36); Catalogue and Index to Wide Streets, Expired Leases, Deeds to the City, Trust Deeds, and Opinions of Council, comp. John P. McEvoy; Liber Manucaptorum, 3 vols. (C1/J/4/1-3); Minutes of the Dublin Aldermen, 1658–1712 ("Monday Booke"; MSS MR/18); Registers of Statute Staple, 1664–1678; Roll of Freemen, 1468–1485, 1575–1774, 4 vols., ed. Gertrude Thrift (1919)

Gilbert Library, Dublin: John Dunton, "Tour of Ireland" (Gilbert MS 189); Transcript, Bricklayers' Guild, Charters and Documents, and Cutlers' Guild, Charters and Documents (Gilbert MS 81); Transcript, Merchants' Guild, Charters and Documents, 1438–1824, 2 vols. (Gilbert MS 78); Transcript, Tailors' Guild, Documents, 1296–1753 (Gilbert MS 80)

Henry E. Huntington Library: MS HA 14,499

Historical Library of the Society of Friends in Ireland, Dublin: "An Account or Schedule of the Deeds, Leases and Writings Belonging to the Friends of Dublin, & Some Other Parts of This Kingdom . . ." (Deed Box VI); "A Booke for Freinds That Meet About Wills & Inventoryes Beginninge 27 of x^{br} [December] 1704" (YM L1); Indenture Between Abel Strettle, John Hutchinson, Anthony Sharp, *et al.*, 25 October 1693 (Deed Box XII, Folder 5: 3); Indenture Between Anthony Sharp, Roger Roberts, Samuel Baker, and George Newland, 6 August 1700 (Deed Box X, Folder 2: 1); Minutes of the Dublin Men's Meeting, 1677–84, 1684–91, 1691–1701, 1701–10; Minutes of the Half-Yearly National Meeting, 1671–88, 1689–1706; Minutes of the Leinster Province Meeting, 1670–1706; Minutes of the Moate Men's Meeting, 1680–1731; Parliamentary Committee Minutes, 1698–1731 (YM N1); Poor Accounts, Dublin Monthly Meeting, 1700–1720 (MMII P1); Records of the National Women's Meetings, 1676–1776; Sharp MSS; Sufferings, Dublin Monthly Meeting, 1660–1780 (MMII G1); Sufferings, Leinster Quarterly

Meeting, 1656–1701 (QMI G1); Testimonies Against Tithes (YM G4); Testimonies of Condemnation and Denial, 1662–1756, Dublin Monthly Meeting (MMII F1); Testimonies [to Deceased Ministers] from 1661 (YM F1)

Lambeth Palace Library: Gibson MSS 942

Library of the Society of Friends, London: Barclay MSS; Crosfield MSS; Gibson MSS; Great Book of Sufferings, vol. 2; Leek MSS; Minute Book of the Lords Proprietors of New Jersey, 1664–1683; Minutes of the London Yearly Meeting; MS vol. 340; Penington MSS; Portfolios 16 and 17; Swarthmore MSS

National Archives, Dublin: "The Humble Petition of the Corporation of Clothiers or Weavers of the Citty of Dublin," 27 September 1688 (MS M740); Extracts, Feltmakers' Guild, 1668–1771, ed. John J. Webb (MS M6118a); Indenture Between Anthony Sharp, Roger Roberts, Samuel Baker, and George Newland, 6 August 1700 (MS D18499); Indenture Between James Fade, John Page, Anthony Sharp, *et al.*, 10 January 1701 (MS D18500); James Fade's Settlement, 11 January 1701 (MS D18501); Tailors' Guild, Notes (MS TA1431); Transcription of the Will of Anthony Sharp (MS T6899); Weavers' Guild, Notes (MS TA1441)

National Library of Ireland: Cutlers' Guild, Bye-Laws, 1670–1723 (MS 12,121); Cutlers' Guild, Transactions (MS 12,123); Minutes of the Half-Yearly National Meeting (MS 94); Notes and Extracts, Dublin Guild Records, ed. Henry S. Guinness (MS 680); Records of Births, Marriages, and Deaths, Carlow, Cork, and Dublin (Microfilm POS 1021)

Public Record Office, London: State Papers, Charles II (SP 29)

Public Record Office of Northern Ireland, Belfast: Documents Relating to the Suffering of Quaker Families in Ulster, 1689–91 (D2224/1); Minutes of the Lisburn Monthly Meeting, 1675–1735 (Q/5/LBM 1/1–3); Minutes of the Lurgan Men's Meeting, 1675–1710 (LGM 1/1); Minutes of the Ulster Provincial Meeting (MIC 16/1A)

Registry of Deeds, Dublin: 7-412-2772; 13-149-5453; 18-77-8409; 22-497-12682; 22-502-12690; 23-75-12681; 23-402-13837; 23-508-14233; 24-246-13697; 27-46-15089; 28-80-16418; 28-118-16812; 30-68-16427; 30-390-18938; 31-283-19073; 32-80-19015; 33-62-19664; 40-180-24894; 43-63-27378; 44-364-29801; 45-411-29802; 50-114-32262; 50-160-32424; 51-129-33074; 52-488-35403; 54-189-35380; 56-443-38644; 56-502-38932; 57-374-38933; 58-149-38934; 81-431-58234; 85-27-58893; 100-278-70479; 102-409-71478; 104-45-71895; 108-148-75474; 131-491-89971; 137-430-93940; 141-227-95140; 198-56-131076; 240-347-155727; 353-289-238920

Royal Society of Antiquaries in Ireland, Dublin: "A Book Generall from 1676 to 1702 for the Corporation of Weavers"; Book of Elections, Weavers' Guild, 1704–1760; Masters' Accounts, Weavers' Guild, 1694–1714; the Old Book of Brothers, Weavers' Guild; Quarter Brethren Book, Weavers' Guild, 1707–1729

Trinity College, Dublin: Proclamation, 2 August 1689 (MS 2203)

Index

In this index an "f" after a number indicates a separate reference on the next page, and an "ff" indicates separate references on the next two pages. A continuous discussion over two or more pages is indicated by a span of page numbers, e.g., "57–59." *Passim* is used for a cluster of references in close but not consecutive sequence.

Library of Congress Cataloging-in-Publication Data

Greaves, Richard L.
    Dublin's Merchant Quaker : Anthony Sharp and the Society
of Friends, 1643–1707 / Richard L. Greaves.
        p. cm.
    Includes bibliographical references and index.
    ISBN 0-8047-3452-6 (cloth)
        1. Quakers—Ireland—Dublin—History—17th Century.
2. Sharp, Anthony, 1643–1707—Homes and haunts—
Ireland—Dublin.   3. Merchants—Ireland—Dublin—
Biography.   4. Quakers—Ireland—Dublin—Biography.
I. Title.

DA995.D75G74   1998
941.8'.350088286—dc21   98-3683
                                                            CIP

This book is printed on acid-free, recycled paper.

Original printing 1998
Last figure below indicates year of this printing:
07   06   05   04   03   02   01   00   99   98